I0886326

British bottom mine blown up in Tannis Bay off Hirtshals, March 2013. The Swedish mine clearance ship *Kullen* rocks in the pressure wave from the mine blast. The picture was taken from the Dutch minesweeper *Makkum*.

Operation Gardening

Bomber Command minelaying in Danish waters 1940–1945

Frank Weber

Helion & Company

Helion & Company Limited
Unit 8 Amherst Business Centre
Budbrooke Road
Warwick
CV34 5WE
England
Tel. 01926 499619
Email: info@helion.co.uk
Website: www.helion.co.uk
X (formerly Twitter): @Helionbooks
Facebook: @HelionBooks
Visit our blog at helionbooks.wordpress.com

Published by Helion & Company 2025
with financial support from:
Helen & Ejnar Bjørnow Foundation
Consul George Jorck and wife Emma Jorck's Foundation
Designed and typeset by Mach 3 Solutions (www.mach3solutions.co.uk)
Cover designed by Paul Hewitt, Battlefield Design (www.battlefield-design.co.uk)

ISBN 978-1-804518-95-3

British Library Cataloguing-in-Publication Data.
A catalogue record for this book is available from the British Library.

Contents

Acknowledgements

I have received invaluable help and support in my research and writing work from many quarters. I would therefore like to extend a big thank you to:

Lieutenant Commander Count Christian of Rosenborg, Naval College of Arms.
Søren Flensted, Aviation Consultant, Member of the Denmark Team.
Commander N. Friis, Danish Defence Command.
Commander P. Garde, former head of the Stevns Fort.
Associate Professor Birger U. Hansen, PhD, University of Copenhagen.
Commander Carsten Høgh, former navy weapons inspector.
Commander S.S.v.F.Kieler.
Former museum director Henrik S. Kristensen DPhil.
Professor D.Phil. Henning Poulsen, Department of History, Aarhus University.
Military historian Cand.mag. Niels Klingenberg Vistisen.
Many thanks to the 'Helen and Ejnar Bjørnow Foundation' and 'Consul George Jorck and wife Emma Jorck's Foundation' for making this English publication possible.
Last but not least, my dear wife, vicar Gitte Ishøy, should be thanked for her patience and forbearance with me throughout the many years of research.
Cand.mag. Frank Weber.
Life associate member of the Bomber Command Association.
Former member of the Bomber Command Historical Society.

Debriefing
Members of Bomber Command returning from a minelaying operation on the enemy coastline are interviewed by a WAAF Intelligence Officer at RAF Lakenheath, April 1944.

Introduction

Why This Book?

Against the backdrop of the last 80 years of weapons technology development, with the introduction of nuclear weapons of all kinds, it may seem redundant to retain a conventional weapon like the sea mine. However, the reality, in the light of military history, is different. In an age of nuclear weapons, there is a need for conventional crisis management tools, including the use of the mine weapon. The full utilisation of this weapon requires careful planning, which must necessarily be based on historical experience, both our own and that of our allies. It is therefore very natural to investigate naval mine warfare in Danish waters during World War II. At the same time, the laying of mines has until now only been treated peripherally. This applies to both mainstream works on the air and naval warfare during World War II. Stephen Roskill's *The War at Sea 1939–451 and Denis Richards and Hilary St. George Saunders' The Royal Air Force 1939–1945.*[2] In later monographs on the RAF's activities during the war, the laying of mines is only treated sparingly and sporadically. It seems to have always been the lot of the sea mines.

During World War I, the laying of 792 Danish and 580 German sea mines ensured that Denmark remained neutral from 1914–1918. At the outbreak of World War II, Denmark again tried to emphasise its neutrality by laying 666 sea mines in Danish waters. This time, however, it was not enough, and it was German and British sea mines that came to dominate the Danish waterways from 1940–1945.

Many of these mines are still in Danish waters, and in the last 10–15 years alone, more than 50 British wartime mines have been found and neutralised. In most people's minds, the mine weapon is a defensive weapon, that is, a weapon of defence. Sea mines have also been used in this function for the most part. The original purpose of sea mines was to protect the layer's own harbours and strategically important stretches of water. As such, mines were mainly used at the beginning of World War II. However, the mine as a weapon underwent a revolutionary development during the war years 1939 to 1945, which completely changed the characteristic features of naval mine warfare.

1 Stephen W. Roskill, *The War at Sea 1939–45*, vols 1–3 (London: HMSO, 1954–1962).

2 Denis Richards & Hilary St George Saunders, *Royal Air Force, 1939–1945*, vols 1–3 (London: HMSO, 1953–1954).

This was mainly due to two factors: the use of distance mines, also known as bottom mines,[3] and the involvement of bombers in the role of minelayers. It was now possible to mine areas, such as harbour entrances and distant waters, which had previously been beyond the reach of naval vessels. The mines could be used to a greater extent than before to restrict the operational freedom of movement of enemy naval forces in their home waters. The enemy's navigation along their own and neutral countries' coasts was now threatened. Previously protected training areas in inland waters for surface vessels and submarines were mined from the air, and training and education of naval crews, as well as testing of new naval vessels, became more difficult and in some cases impossible. In particularly urgent situations, mines were laid directly in front of a moving enemy naval force in order to slow down or, at best, sink it. The mine thus became an important strategic as well as tactical weapon in offensive warfare.

During World War II, a lot of work was done to make mines as 'sweep-proof' as possible, i.e. attempts to make it difficult or impossible for the enemy to render the mines harmless, which in turn meant increased demands on the tactical, scientific, manpower and material resources of each country's mine sweeper organisation. For example, by the end of 1941, the British already had around 20,000 men and 1,000 naval vessels on constant standby to clear the mines that 30–40 German minelaying aircraft, a few U-boats and minelayers laid every night.[4]

By the end of the war, when the Germans were laying even fewer mines, especially from aircraft, around 57,000 men and 1,500 minesweepers were on standby.[5] Similarly, in autumn 1944, the German *Befehlshaber West* (BSW) had 31,000 men and 476 naval vessels at its disposal in the minesweeper organisation.[6] By the end of the war, approximately 40 percent of the total German Navy was involved in mine sweeping.[7] Since Denmark's entry into NATO, the Danish Navy has benefited from the existing technological knowledge in the defence alliance regarding sea mines.

The UK and the USA in particular gained a lot of experience in the use of naval mines during World War II and in the subsequent conflicts and wars. In both the Korean and Vietnam wars, the use of sea mines played a major role. In recent years, we have seen this relatively cheap but effective weapon used in Central America and the Middle East. We can therefore conclude that naval mines have been used both before and after the introduction of nuclear weapons and will most likely continue to be used in major and minor military conflicts around the world. The question can then be raised as to how useful the mine weapon is in a Danish naval defence in the twenty-first century? As oil reserves become limited, whether for political or natural reasons, coal and nuclear power will continue to be viable alternative fuels. As ships can utilise these two fuels better than many other modes of transport, shipping will continue to be a dominant mode of transport well into this century.

3 Magnetic, acoustic and pressure mine types were all available in bottom mine, anchor rope and floating mine versions. In Danish waters, the Royal Air Force only dropped bottom mines, which is why this term will be used here.
4 *Historical Overview Of The Sea Mine And Its Utilisation* (without place and year of printing), Marinens Bibliotek, p.2.
5 Hans Forshell, *Minan i Sjökriget* (Karlskrona: Forshell, 1959), p.116.
6 Friedrich Ruge, *Im Küstenvorfeld* (Munich: 1974), p.112.
7 Arthur T. Harris, *The Bomber Offensive* (London: Macmillan, 1947) p.39.

Today, globalisation has increased the need for sea freight, and as long as cargo ships and tankers exist and individual countries maintain their military naval forces, the sea mine will remain a necessary and useful weapon.

As the geography of Danish waters makes them well suited for mine warfare, it is only natural that the mine weapon continues to play a central role both in invasion defence and in connection with control measures in transit waters. However, this geostrategic fact also means that an enemy may use mines in an attempt to cut off the connections between the Danish regions, which is why the navy must always maintain a sufficiently large mine-clearing capacity. It is difficult to assess the military effect a Danish mine defence would have in a conflict or war situation. Experts do not agree on how important the passage from the Baltic Sea to the Atlantic is for Russia's naval forces today. But the mere awareness that such a defence and blockade weapon is present should help deter potential enemies from attempting military advances through Danish waters. At the same time, we can contribute to solving military tasks in conflict-affected areas by utilising our knowledge and experience in this field.

In order to establish a realistic model that can form the basis for an effective and well-functioning mine defence, the historical experience of mine warfare in Danish waters must be clarified. Tactical information such as suitable minefields, degree of mining, frequency of laying, maintenance and other conditions must be analysed. At the same time, strategic experience, the psychological effect of minefields on the enemy, the yield of the military effort in relation to other weapon systems, the use of mines in a 'grey' period of international tension, et cetera must be examined. This information is crucial for mine defence operations, both in peacetime and in times of crisis. For example, mining in a 'grey' period could demonstrate our defence policy commitment to the counterpart, allies and neutral parties.

What are the particular advantages of mine defence? Do sea mines have special characteristics that other weapon systems cannot provide? Yes, in general you could say that:

1. They lie in wait for the enemy without you being threatened.
2. They can win battles by their mere presence. They can influence the enemy to retreat without a fight.
3. They can be used to hold ships where they can be attacked with other weapons.
4. They can force ships to take longer, alternative routes than planned, thereby reducing the number of active enemy ships.
5. They are a constant threat to enemy morale.
6. They can attack targets that are impossible for a human observer to hear or see, such as certain specialised submarines.
7. Not only do they sink and damage ships as other weapon systems can, but their effectiveness is also measured in the delay of enemy operations.
8. They force the enemy to commit large resources in terms of manpower and equipment to countermeasures such as surveillance, mine sweeping and repairs.
9. They are cheaper than most other types of weapons, also in relation to the losses inflicted on the enemy. This fact also means that, from a realpolitik perspective, the mine weapon is a realistic alternative or supplement to the costlier, existing weapon systems that are currently available and can be called 'potentially offensive.'

10. They are useful even if the enemy is able to neutralise them, as the removal of the mines imposes high resource costs on the enemy.
11. They are well suited for 'bluffing', for example laying out mine containers without content, publishing 'mined fields' where there are none, using new mine types without being able to swipe them yourself, et cetera.

Although the sea mines laid by the RAF in Danish waters during the war were used in offensive warfare, the mine weapon itself is defined by being a decidedly non-offensive weapon. Enemy ships sail into minefields of their own volition and under their own power, thereby exposing themselves to the mine hazard. The enemy is free to keep the ships in harbour and avoid casualties. A very important advantage of the mine weapon is that it does not damage or destroy facilities that are important for civilian peacetime functions. Minefields do not hit hospitals, schools and other public institutions. The homes of the civilian population are in no way threatened.

If you examine the use of naval mines in the wars of the last century through statistical summaries, you realise just how important and effective a weapon it is. The actual loss figures in terms of damaged and sunk ships alone are surprisingly high compared to the number of mines laid. The indirect effect is for good reason difficult to determine exactly. But today there is no doubt that the mine weapon is also extremely effective in this field. The success of the mine weapon over the last 100 years is surprising to most military and political decision-makers, but it should not be.

In the usual works on the air war during World War 2, as mentioned, the laying of mines has only been treated peripherally. In several works about the war, authors have emphasised this fact. For example, Ken Delve writes in *Bomber Command, 1936–1968: An Operational & Historical Record* about Operation Gardening:

> It is one of the most oft ignored, yet vital contributions made by Bomber Command … The inevitable conclusion must be that the Gardening carried out by Bomber Command between 1940 and 1945 deserves to be recognised as an important facet of the air power story of the Second World War.[8]

An American naval mining expert, G. K. Hartmann, had already mentioned this 30 years earlier:

> The greater surprise should be that we are surprised; that we have not heard about this before. The public relations organisation of the mine community is rather ineffective, or more accurately, rather nonexistent.[9]

8 Ken Delve, *Bomber Command 1936–1968 An Operational & Historical Record* (Barnsley: Pen and Sword, 2005), pp.128 and p.134

9 G. K. Hartmann: 'Mine Warfare, History and Technology,' speech at Naval Surface Weapons Centre, Silver Springs, 1 July 1975.

Western Allied Air Strikes on Targets in Denmark, 1939–1945

Originally, the idea to investigate the RAF's minelaying in Danish waters 1940–1945 arose in connection with the preparation of my Master's Thesis at the Department of History at Aarhus University in 1984–1985. Together with two fellow students, Claus W. Kofoed and Henrik S. Kristensen, the ambition was to describe the Western Allied air attacks on targets in Denmark during World War II. Aarhus University Press offered to publish the thesis in an edited version. It was therefore published as a two-volume work in 1988 as *Vestallierede luftangreb i Danmark under 2. verdenskrig*. The work placed the air war over Denmark in an overall context, so that many of the dramatic events that were perceived as incomprehensible during the occupation and therefore gave rise to numerous hypotheses and speculations between men could now be explained by the military strategies and tactical operations of the warring superpowers. By combining material studies from British, German and Danish military archives, it had become possible to see the events in new and, if not always logical, then real contexts. It was a pioneering piece of work, not only in a national context, but also in an international context, as no previous systematic study of the Western Allied air raids had been conducted in any country. The work was published in a relatively modest edition for several reasons. Firstly, military historical studies were not part of the paradigm of historical research at the time and were seen as odious and suspect. At the same time, with its extensive registers and large scope, the work had the character of a reference work, which would have libraries as its immediate target audience.

Air raids during World War II. One of the chapters that had been significantly reduced in the new edition was Bomber Command's minelaying operations. Therefore, there is a good reason to publish this part of the story on its own.

Based on a renewed interest in military history after the turn of the millennium, perhaps in light of Denmark's activist security policy with war participation in Europe, the Middle East and Asia, we decided to republish the book at the request of Nyt Nordisk Forlag. The intention was to publish the work in a single and more manageable volume. To this end, a number of chapters were shortened and tightened up. A number of appendices and the English captions, as well as an extensive English summary, were omitted. Corrections and additions were made to the original edition and a little more space was added on the image page. So the two-volume work totalling 861 pages became a book of 864 pages, published in 2012 as *Bomber over Denmark – Vestallierede luftangreb under 2. Verdenskrig.*

Methodological Considerations

Theory of War and Military History

> The military expert can determine whether a particular event was possible or impossible from a tactical or technical point of view; but only the historian can determine whether the possible is also the actual occurrence.[10]

War theory deals with general theoretical questions about war, warfare and conflict, and is therefore the central element of the science of war itself, covering all levels of warfare, including analyses of war and of the initial preparations for war and conflict. It also includes the study of how wars and conflicts can be ended and eventually won. In other words, war theory focuses on describing and explaining the effectiveness and relevance of military force to achieve political goals.

Even though a theory of war is based on empirical evidence, it typically cannot be tested and thus achieve a normative status. Actions based on war theory will therefore always be of an uncertain nature. But through a descriptive theoretical approach, where we account for the factors that determined the outcome of specific battles, wars and conflicts, we can choose an ideographic approach through descriptions of what is unique and singular in the specific historical events. It is then possible, through a nomothetic theoretical approach, to establish a form of general laws for how wars and conflicts should be conducted to achieve the political goal, thus approaching the normative through the establishment of options for action. Carl von Clausewitz's work *Vom Kriege* from 1834 is a well-known example of this.

Military history is empirical and includes many facets beyond the history of war itself, such as military technological development, organisational forms, changing doctrines and actual war memories. While war theory primarily attempts to identify and analyse general military issues that can form the basis of a scientific framework for military thinking, the empirical background is largely provided by military history.

The insight and knowledge of the individual military historian is likely to have a greater or lesser impact on the theory of war developed, and on how empirical data is compiled and applied. Are military and war history studies sufficient or is practical military experience a necessary prerequisite? Can a former conscript in the Civil Defence like me have the same insight and approach as an officer in the armed units? This is just one of the issues that dictate that problem areas and questions must be illuminated from several angles and using different empirical and analytical methods and combinations of these.[11]

---

10 Kr. Erslev, *Nils Kjeldsen on 28 February 1864. En kritisk Undersøgelse* (Historisk Tidsskrift. 7. rk. IV, 1902–04), p.252.

11 Niklas Zetterling, 'Why military theory?' pp.59–65 in *Kung. Krigsvetenskabsakademiens Handlinger och Tidsskrift*, 3rd issue 2002, 206th year

Military History Methodology

Military history, like all history, has many approaches and points of view, and therefore methods from several related disciplines can be used, primarily history and social sciences. This provides a broad palette of methodological possibilities. Both quantitative and qualitative methods can be used, as well as comparative, explanatory and interpretative methods. In fact, the range of methods encompasses everything from actual experiments to hermeneutics.

My view of history stems from historicism, a realist paradigm where reality can to a large extent be recognised directly. This means that knowledge about reality is obtained on the basis of objective data collection – in order to uncover universal laws/causalities – and systematise the observed into theoretical hypotheses that can be tested. Through further development of our logical thinking and additional empirical observations, I believe that we can explain 'what really happened'[12] more and more thoroughly and adequately, as Leopold von Ranke put it in 1824. I am aware that I have been influenced in this view of history by my thesis and PhD supervisor Professor Henning Poulsen at the Department of History at Aarhus University. He believed that historians' descriptions of their source observations should be objective in the sense that others can declare them to be true or false by observing them again. No more and no less. Concretised perspective on a source-argued basis was what Henning Poulsen demanded of his own and others' presentations. People act, and it is the patterns that emerge that must be presented in a concretised perspective.

This is of course reflected in my choice of method. For me, the document is a source material that neutrally reflects certain conditions and events. The document proves conditions that lie outside the text itself. It is a communication tool that provides direct access to reality. Ideally, the document is an unambiguous entity that should be systematically purged of traces of uncertainty, ambiguity and subjectivity. An 'authorless' text that provides factual information and whose statements can be taken at face value. The reading is content-focussed and source-critical in terms of credibility, neutrality and representativeness. However, the document does not have an inherent meaning, but only becomes meaningful to the extent that it is interpreted and related to subjective analyses.

Written documents have a diverse character:

a) Primary documents, produced for circulation in a limited/closed forum, e.g. minutes of meetings, personal letters, negotiation papers, internal memos, orders, briefings and confidential documents.
b) Secondary documents are in principle available to anyone who wishes to access them at a time in the immediate vicinity of the event or situation to which the document refers, e.g. legislative texts, government reports, newspaper articles, news reports, statements of intent from parts of the administration.
c) Tertiary documents are publicly available and are an analytical treatment of events and situations created some time after they have taken place, such as

12 '... Man hat der Historie das Amt zu richten die Vergangenheit, die Mitwelt zum Nutzen zukünftiger Jahre zu belehren, beigemessen; so hohe Ämter unterwindet sich gegenwärtiger Versuch nicht: er will bloß sagen wie es eigentlich gewesen ... ' appendix to Leopold von Ranke's first printed work *Geschichten der romanischen und germanischen Völker von 1494 bis 1514* (Reimer 1824) p.57 (online edition on Google Books).

> published memoirs, historical accounts, background articles and scientific publications.[13]

In the 80 years since Denmark was liberated, countless books have been written about the occupation and Denmark during World War II. Until today, and for a few years yet, historians have had a unique opportunity to confront and include various participants' memories, interpretations and perceptions of what happened with available primary source material. This has been both an enrichment for research and a source of endless debate about who knew best: the participants, who experienced the events with their own senses and on their own bodies, or the historians, who created a historical overview using scientific methods through research in the written sources.

The first wave of presentations about the occupation was for some prepared before the liberation and came immediately after 5 May 1945. They were characterised by a very black and white view of what it was all about. The collaborators, the Germans and the political collaborators were the villains on one side, while the resistance fighters and the Allies were the heroes on the other, and whom all real Danes had actually supported from the start. This was followed by slightly larger, well-researched works by authors who had been heavily involved in either resistance or political work, all of which were characterised by strong opinions but also contributed to a slightly more nuanced and diverse picture of the time. The historian Jørgen Hæstrup was the first to treat the occupation from a historically scientific method. His significant work in collecting large amounts of memoirs, reports and accounts during his research work formed the basis for the research of subsequent historians. Hæstrup reflected the fundamental view of the occupation in his dissertation 'Contact with England' from 1954 and his other books and articles: The Danish people stood together, and everyone offered whatever resistance they could muster, from the common man to civil servants and politicians, while a few traitors, opportunistic companies and Danish Nazis stood outside the national community. The Allies' recognition was proof that the Danish people as a whole had been on the right side from start to finish. Hæstrup reflected the general popular consensus, known as the 'basic narrative of the occupation.' He was praised by both veterans of the resistance as well as the Director of the Ministry of Foreign Affairs, Nils Svenningsen, who headed the department after August 1943.

Hæstrup was an excellent historian, and in addition to his groundbreaking works, he also helped to organise and systematise further research, including the formation of the Publishing Society for Recent Danish History (DNH) in 1960–1961. This society consisted largely of Hæstrup's former students and formed an institutional framework for much of the subsequent 25 years of collecting source material and research. In the 1970s and 1980s, this second generation of occupation researchers did away with the above-mentioned basic narrative by focusing on crucial areas of conflict and fracture during the occupation. One consensual myth after another was refuted and debunked. The talk was no longer of delay, concession or negotiation, but of collaboration and cooperation. Today, I find the term 'adaptation policy' to be a more appropriate term.

13 Betina W. Rennison: 'Theory of Science, Theory and Method', Master's project, AAU 2015.

The historians around DNH were thus also influenced by their time, a period of rebellion against authority and a critical attitude towards both those in power and more generally the power structures in society. The focus was now on class antagonisms and the conditions and role of individual social groups in political and social development. At the same time, there was a renewed interest in a more internationalised perspective, where developments in Denmark between 1940 and 1945 were more closely compared with developments in other German-occupied countries.

The last 40 years have been characterised by 3rd generation historians, who were typically students of the second generation. Again, there is a common denominator in the topics addressed by the newest generation: the multi-faceted analysis, involving different academic approaches and in many cases a moral petition about guilt and responsibility. In the media, and by some politicians, this has been skewed towards a sometimes strident ethical and moral approach, which may sometimes distort the picture. There are two trends, one of which highlights the 'history of the forgotten': the rejected refugees, Eastern Front volunteers, socalled germanfriendly girls, German workers, informers, Nazis and their children, et cetera The other trend focuses on the economic and business aspects of the cooperation policy, including Danish companies' involvement in the German war economy, and generally the connections and interdependence that were established between the Danish and German economies.

In a strange way, we have today arrived at a view of the occupation that has certain commonalities with Hæstrup's consensus narrative. Kirchhoff, who over the years has gained a more nuanced view of cooperation policy,[14] calls it a neo-consensual line, with a demonstration of both how far-reaching the cooperation was in the military, economic, industrial and trade policy areas, and how broad this cooperation was in reality rooted in Danish society. There was a pragmatic approach to an external situation and an internal survival instinct that together did not allow for many other alternatives.[15]

As a student of Professor Dr Phil Henning Poulsen at Aarhus University, and thus a 3rd generation occupation researcher, I see the Danish Navy's participation in mine sweeping and water surveillance as a pragmatic arrangement, beneficial to both the occupying power and Danish society, and thus of crucial importance for the adaptation policy.

Topic Delimitation

Of the Royal Air Force's total minelaying effort 1940–1945, I have chosen to concentrate on Bomber Command's minelaying efforts, as Coastal Command did not have long-range aircraft types that could operate in Danish waters. Geographically, I have chosen to describe the mine war in Danish waters as they were and are defined today. For the most part, both the British and German military leadership considered the Danish waters and the western part of the Baltic Sea to be one coherent area of operations, and for that reason it might have been logical to let it be decisive. However, as the Danish participation in the 1940–1943

14 Joachim Lund: 'Today, I certainly have a greater understanding of the politics of cooperation.' Interview with historian Dr Phil Hans Kirchhoff, Information, 10 May 2014

15 Bo Lidegaard, *Kampen om Danmark, 1933–1945* (Gyldendal, 2006, 2nd ed.), pp.578–590.

mine sweeping took place exclusively in Danish waters, called 'The Baltic Approaches' or simply 'Danish Waters' by the British, and I want to look at the consequences for shipping traffic here, I have limited the study to the 19 British minefields that correspond to this. As a result, four of the large British minefields on the German Baltic coast have been omitted from the inventory: 'Forget-Me-Not' and 'Lettuces' on the Kiel Canal and Bay, as well as 'Geranium' at Swinemünde and 'Jasmin' at Travemünde.

Unfortunately, there is not enough space for topics that could have been dealt with in more detail, such as the development of German air defence in Denmark, technological developments in both German and British means of navigation and radar, and a more detailed description of both parties' air forces and aircraft types. I have tried to compensate for this by referring to the respective chapters in *Bomber over Denmark* and adding a few appendices.

While British minelayers laid conventional minefields in the North Sea and a relatively few bottom mines were laid by British submarines in the Skagerrak and Kattegat, German minelayers laid mine barrages in Danish waters to replace the Danish fields that were taken up shortly after the occupation. The largest German field was in the Skagerrak, between Kristiansand and Hanstholm. The Germans called the mine barrage *Skagerrak-Sperre* or *Skagerrak Warngebiet*. In the first few years there were relatively few mines, but from 1942 the number increased considerably and further again in 1944 and the end of the war. When the war ended, a total of 8,810 German sea mines and 4,298 explosive buoys had been laid in the Skagerrak. I have chosen not to describe these minefields, even though the majority of the German and Danish mine sweepers' work in the period 1940–1944 consisted of sweeping detached anchor rope mines and explosive buoys.

Early in the planning of the research project, I considered including a cost-benefit analysis of the British minelaying effort, and also trying to derive the total cost to Britain and Germany of the 'mine war' in Danish waters. I was inspired by Christina J. M. Goultier's interesting work *A Forgotten Offensive* from 1995,[16] which had several new and exciting angles of analysis. However, her book makes it clear that the task is almost impossible, and my PhD supervisor at the time, Professor Henning Poulsen, advised me not to go in that direction, which advice I followed.

In the course of my search for sources, I have found many interesting memories from those involved in the 'mine war'. They provide a more vivid and personal perspective on the daily events during the war. I have used a few along the way, but due to space constraints I have not had the opportunity to include all the relevant memoirs I would have liked.

16 Christina J. M. Goultier, *A Forgotten Offensive: Royal Air Force Coastal Command's Anti-Shipping Campaign 1940–1945* (London: Routledge, 1995).

Chapter 1

1.1 Naval warfare in International Law before World War I

The use of sea mines is so different from other types of naval warfare that it is a special kind of 'mine warfare' with its own strategy and tactics. The great importance of mines lies in the fact that they are relatively quick and cheap to produce and have a great effect on enemy morale, not least because it is difficult to secure against them. Smaller naval powers in particular can benefit from the mine weapon.

Today, sea mines can be divided into 2 main groups; contact mines and distance mines. Contact mines require physical contact with a vessel – including a submerged submarine – whereas distance mines can be detonated solely by magnetic field, propeller noise or pressure change in the water by passing vessels. These three things can often be combined in various combinations. In addition, distance mines can act as cable mines, whereby the individual mines in an entire minefield can be connected to each other and armed or disarmed from land as required.

The first precursor to the sea mine is mentioned from as early as the early Ming Dynasty by Chinese artillery officer Jiao Yu, known as Huolongjing in his fourteenth century military treatise.[1] Chinese records also tell of naval explosives in the sixteenth century that were used to fight Japanese pirates. These mines consisted of gunpowder that was placed in a wooden box, sealed with putty, and then sent drifting towards the enemy Japanese pirate ships.[2]

Naval mine warfare, as we usually define it, is however a new phenomenon. It was used during the American War of Independence of 1775–1783, when American David Bushnell invented the first practical mine for use against British ships. It was a watertight barrel filled with gunpowder that floated with the current against enemy naval vessels. A spark mechanism ignited the powder if the mine struck a ship. The mine was used on the Delaware River as a floating mine and was considered an insidious and unethical weapon. [3]

As can be seen, the mines were quite primitive and it was not until the middle of the nineteenth century that truly effective mines were constructed. During the Crimean War of 1853–1856, the Russians used mines in both the Black Sea and the Baltic Sea, but not until

1 Joseph Needham: *Science and Civilisation in China*, volume 5, part 7 (Taipei: Caves Books Ltd,1986), pp.203–205.

2 Asiapac Editorial, *Origins of Chinese Science and Technology* (Asiapac Books, 2007, 3rd ed.), p.18.

3 National Research Council (US). *Oceanography and Mine Warfare* (National Academies Press, 2000), p.12.

the American Civil War of 1861–1865 did the mine weapon gain some real importance. It was mainly the south, lacking ships, that secured their estuaries and harbours with minefields. Rear Admiral of the Union Navy, David Farragut's, famous order, "*Damn the torpedoes, full speed ahead*!" refers to a naval minefield off Mobile, Alabama, but which would not prevent Farragut from securing victory.[4] The Danish Navy used sea mines for the first time during the 1864 war.

Between 1880 and 1890, passive mine warfare was developed in all countries with naval capacity, as naval forts and naval stations were now protected by 'non-self-acting', i.e. controlled, mine barrages. The main purpose of passive mine barrages was to block the entrance of enemy ships without preventing the passage of friendly ships, or at best to delay enemy forcing operations during an attack. They could also make it difficult to effectively bombard naval stations or other military installations behind them from the sea, as well as making it difficult to fire at close range on forward sea fortifications. A passive mine barrage therefore had to be guarded and defended.

Etching showing the effect of Bushnell's mine on a small ship near the British frigate HMS *Cerberus* in 1777. Published 1852.

In the Russo-Japanese War of 1904–1905, mines began to be used for offensive purposes. Offensive mines, laid without the opponent's knowledge of their position, greatly disrupt and impede his movements. In this war, over 5,000 mines were laid along the coast of Siberia and at Port Arthur. Both Russia and Japan laid offensive fields. A total of 6 Russian and 11 Japanese ships totalling 60,000 GRT were sunk by mines.[5] In addition, a large number of neutral ships were sunk due to mine blasts after

4 The exact wording of the order was, 'Damn the torpedoes! Four Bells! Captain Drayton, go ahead! Jouett, full speed!' <http://www.civilwar.org/education/history/biographies/david-farragut.html>.

5 GRT, Gross Register Tonnage, is a measurement of a ship's internal volume capacity for stores, fuel, passengers, et cetera. GRT is expressed in 'register tons' with each register ton equal to 100 cubic feet. GRT is also used to determine a ship's manning regulations, safety rules, registration fees, and port dues. (Ed.)

The 1907 conference in The Hague.

the end of the war, as mine technology was not yet so advanced that the mines could be neutralised automatically. This situation caused so much frustration and anger in the public press of the leading superpowers that special conventions were formulated and adopted at the 1907 Hague Peace Conference to ensure freedom of navigation against the danger of mines.[6]

Held in The Hague in 1899 and 1907 on the initiative of Tsar Nicholas II of Russia, The Hague Peace Conferences aimed to limit the armament of individual states, to regulate the conduct of war and to create mechanisms for the settlement of disputes between states by peaceful means. The conferences therefore resulted in the adoption of a number of conventions and declarations on warfare on land and sea, on the rights and duties of neutral powers and persons during war, and on the establishment of the Permanent Court of Arbitration in The Hague. Unfortunately, the 26 participating states in 1899, and the 44 countries in 1907, did not succeed in reaching agreement on general limitations on armament, but the conferences did manage to adopt a number of conventions to regulate relations between the warring parties. Technical developments have made some of these conventions redundant, such as Convention 14 on the release of explosives from balloons, which has not been used for a long time, but perhaps it should be replaced by a convention on the use of drones? Other Hague Conventions have been superseded by the Geneva Conventions, while the rest remain in force.

6 Rotem Kowner, *Historical Dictionary of the Russo-Japanese War* (Lanham: The Scarecrow Press, 2006), p.238

The 2nd International Peace Conference in The Hague concluded on 18 October 1907 with a Convention on the laying of underwater self-activating mines (contact mines), with the following wording:

> [A convention] proceeding from the principle that the seaways are free and open to all nations; considering that, while in the present state of things it is not possible to prohibit the use of underwater self-activating mines, it is important to limit and regulate their use in order to reduce the severity of war and, as far as possible, to give peaceful navigation the security to which it is entitled despite the presence of war; Awaiting a time when it will be possible to arrange matters in such a manner as to give every desirable guarantee to the interests concerned; have resolved to conclude a convention to this end, and have accordingly appointed as their plenipotentiaries: [Indication of the representatives of the signatory countries].[7]

Just one month later, the Danish Parliament ratified the convention with the signature of King Frederik VIII. The following rules were agreed upon:

> Article 1.
> It is prohibited:
>
> 1) to lay unanchored self-activating contact mines, unless they are so designed that they become harmless at most one hour after the person laying them has lost control of them;
> 2) to lay anchored self-acting contact mines, which do not become harmless as soon as they break free from their moorings;
> 3) to use torpedoes which do not become harmless when they have failed in their purpose.
>
> Article 2.
> It is forbidden to lay self-acting contact mines off the coasts and harbours of the Adversary for the sole purpose of interrupting merchant shipping.
>
> Article 3.
> In the use of anchored self-acting contact mines, all possible precautions shall be taken for the safety of peaceful navigation. The belligerents undertake, as far as possible, to ensure that these mines are rendered harmless after a limited period of time has elapsed, and in the event of their control ceasing, to draw attention to the dangerous areas, as soon as military requirements permit, by means of an announcement to seafarers, which shall also be communicated to governments through diplomatic channels.

7 <https://www.retsinformation.dk/Forms/R0710.aspx?id=70143>: 'Announcement concerning the Convention on the Laying of Underwater Self-acting Anti-personnel Mines concluded at the 2nd International Peace Conference in The Hague on 18 October 1907.' (and still in force!)

Article 4.
When a neutral power lays self-acting contact mines off its coasts, it must observe the same rules and take the same precautions as are prescribed for belligerents.

The neutral power shall, by prior announcement, inform seafarers of the areas where self-activating contact mines would be anchored. This announcement shall be communicated without delay to the governments through diplomatic channels.

Article 5.
The contracting Powers undertake, at the end of the war, to do what they can, each on their own side, to remove the mines which they have laid.

In the case of anchored self-acting contact mines laid by one of the belligerents along the coasts of the other, their location shall be notified to the other party by the power which has laid them, and each of the Powers shall proceed with the least possible delay to remove the mines found in its waters.

Article 6.
The contracting powers which do not yet possess such improved mines as are the object of the present Convention, and which consequently cannot at present comply with the rules laid down in Articles 1 and 3, undertake to convert their mines as soon as possible and bring them into conformity with the aforesaid regulations.

Article 7.
The provisions of this Convention shall apply only in relations between the Contracting Parties and only when all the belligerents are Parties to the Convention.

Articles 8–10.
[The practical arrangements for the ratifications]

Article 11.
This Convention shall remain in force for seven years from the sixtieth day after the date of the first deposit of ratifications.

If it is not cancelled, it shall remain in force even after the expiry of this period.

The termination must be notified in writing to the Dutch Government, which will immediately send a certified copy of the notification to all Powers, stating the date of its receipt … [here follow the practical arrangements regarding terminations].

Article 12.
The contracting powers undertake to reopen the question of the use of self-propelled anti-personnel mines six months before the expiry of the period mentioned in the first paragraph of the preceding Article, if it has not previously been reopened and settled by the Third Peace Conference.

If the contracting powers conclude a new Convention on the Use of Mines, this Convention shall cease to apply immediately upon its entry into force.

> Article 13.
> A Register maintained by the Dutch Ministry of Foreign Affairs must indicate the Date of Deposit of Ratifications ... [here are the practical arrangements for the deposit and storage of the ratifications].

At the end of the document is a list of the delegates who signed the convention. For some, certain reservations were noted. For example, Germany and France made reservations regarding Article 2, the prohibition of laying self-activating contact mines off the coasts and harbours of the adversary for the sole purpose of interrupting merchant shipping! Britain noted that:

> In signing this Convention, the British Plenipotentiaries declare that the mere fact that this Convention does not prohibit any act or practice shall not be deemed to deprive His Britannic Majesty's Government of the right to dispute the legality of the act or practice in question.[8]

Article 2 of the Convention is particularly relevant when it comes to the British laying of mines in Danish waters 1940–1945. The Colombian delegate at the Conference, General Jorge Holguin, actually proposed a total ban on laying mines of any kind outside their own territorial waters. 16 states voted in favour, 15 against, 6 abstained and 7 were absent. As there was no absolute majority in favour of the Colombian proposal, it failed. Therefore, the wording was watered down as much as it was.

Germany referred to the noted reservation to Article 2 when it informed the neutral states on 7 August 1914 that it intended to close all trade routes to the United Kingdom by means of mines in both international and territorial waters. At the same time, it was pointed out that the article said nothing about the distance from enemy coasts and harbours where mines were to be laid. Germany followed exactly the same procedure at the outbreak of war in 1939.

Britain failed to mine the trade routes to Germany, but only until Germany had sent the above-mentioned message on 7 August 1914. Despite Germany's reservation in 1907, it was, in Britain's opinion, a breach of the purpose of the Convention, and therefore illegal, and could therefore justify a British blockade of Germany using sea mines.[9]

Considering the great efforts expended by the warring parties during World War I to develop their own naval mines and combat the enemy's naval mines, the question of the framework and regulation of naval mine warfare received virtually no attention in the interwar years. In the Treaty of Versailles, the issue of mines is mentioned only sporadically. Although numerous international naval conferences were held between 1918 and 1939, naval mines were not on the programme, neither formally nor informally.[10]

---

8 A third Hague Peace Conference was planned to take place in 1914–1915, but could not be realised due to World War I. The themes of the Hague Peace Conferences were later continued under the League of Nations and the United Nations. <https://www.retsinformation.dk/Forms/R0710.aspx?id=70143>.

9 J. S. Cowie, *Mines, Minelayers and Minelaying* (Oxford: OUP, 1949), pp.172–174.

10 Howard S. Levie, *Mine Warfare at Sea* (Leiden: Brill, 1992), p.75.

Shortly after the declaration of war in September 1939, Britain announced that minefields were being laid by the Royal Navy in specified areas off the British coast, as well as off the harbours and coasts of Germany. Neutral countries were made aware of the danger, and at the same time it was emphasised that the mines were aimed at German warships and U-boats, and therefore did not violate Article 2 of the Convention, which of course would be respected. It is interesting to note that Denmark's neutrality was apparently not taken into account by the British in the attempt to close off the German fleet's access to the North Sea.

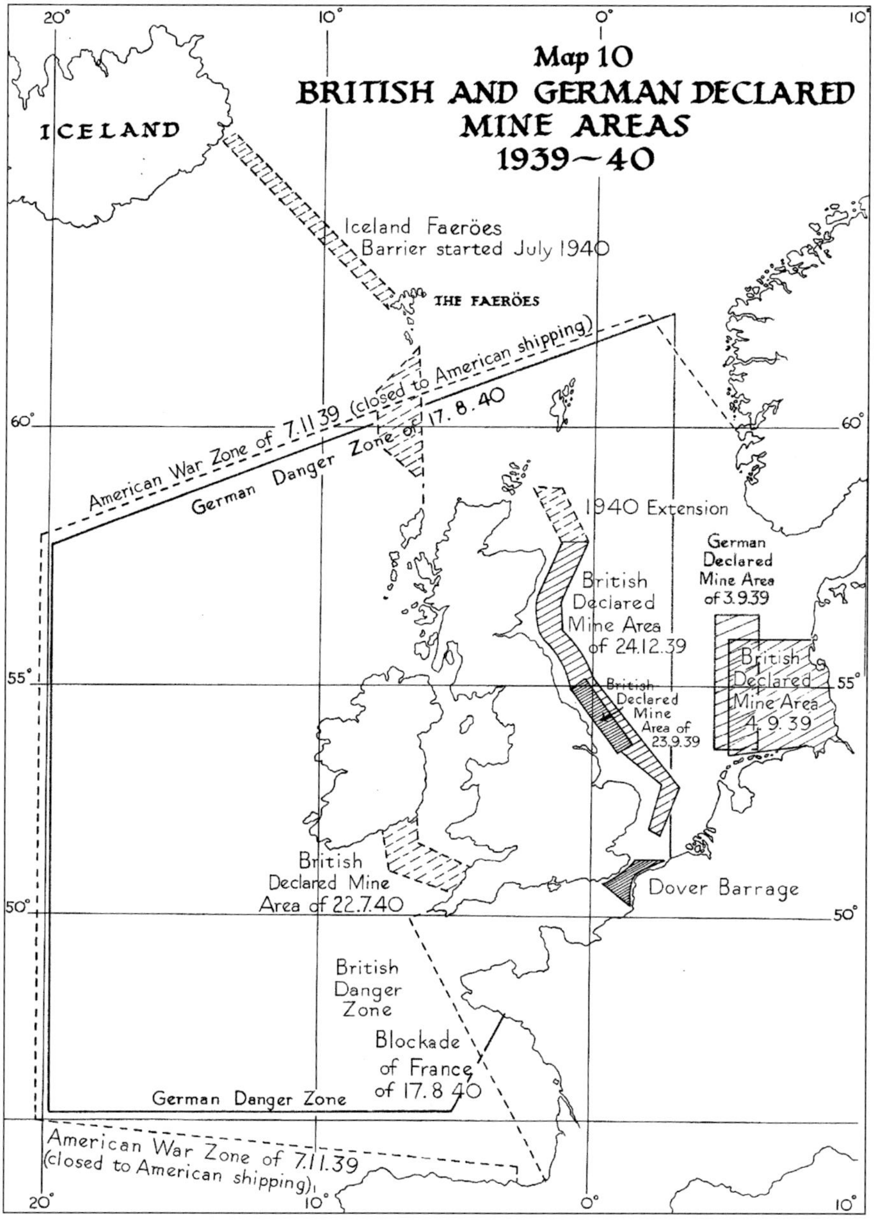

On 18 January 1940, Germany similarly announced that, as in World War I, there was a war zone in the waters around the British Isles and that this zone would be intensively mined. By making this announcement, the minefields were legal under the Convention. During 1940, Britain expanded its Dover Barrage of the English Channel, the East Coast Barrage and the North Sea Barrage, which after the German invasion of Denmark and Norway in April-June was changed to a mine barrage from the Orkney Islands to Greenland via the Faroe Islands and Iceland. This prompted Germany to protest this illegal blockade and violation of the Mining Convention. Given Germany's own use of minefields, the protest was apparently only for propaganda purposes.[11]

Nevertheless, this led Britain to accuse Germany of violating two articles of the convention: a) the prohibition of laying mines off the enemy coast and b) not publicising the presence of specific minefields. To the first, Germany replied that as long as Britain used convoy navigation, where merchant ships were protected by warships, these were legitimate targets. Secondly, according to the convention, minefields were to be specified when the military situation required it. As British warships were constantly in the waters around England, the entire area was a constant military target for the duration of the war. The first answer could be justified, while the second answer showed that the influence of the Convention, with the German interpretation of it, was more than questionable.[12]

As World War II progressed, most waters were included in the war zones, and thus exposed to mines. As a final note, when the German occupying power declared martial law in Denmark on 29 August 1943, the German side was fully aware that this could not be done with direct reference to The Hague Land Warfare Regulations, because Denmark and Germany were not formally at war with each other. Therefore, the German version of *General* von Hanneken's order stated that the state of emergency had been introduced 'in the spirit of the Hague Land War Regulations.' However, the Danish translation stated that the state of emergency had been introduced in accordance with articles 4 –56 of the Hague Regulations of War, which was formally and legally incorrect![13]

11 Howard S. Levie, *Mine Warfare at Sea* (Leiden: Brill, 1992), pp.78–79.
12 Howard S. Levie, *Mine Warfare at Sea* (Leiden: Brill, 1992), p.80.
13 Source: <https://da.wikipedia.org/wiki/Haager_Landkrigsreglementet>.

Chapter 2

2.1 Denmark – Harbourmaster of the Baltic Sea, 1857–1939

Denmark's geographical position as the 'harbour master' of the Baltic Sea[1] has, both in the current situation and in historical perspective, been crucial to the country's strategic importance. Control of the connection routes between the Baltic Sea and the open sea has often been the cause of conflicts where great power interests have been involved. Whether it was to ensure the unhindered passage of their own ships, prevent the other party from utilising this passage opportunity, or preferably both!

Baltic Sea powers with the ability to exert dominance in the area have generally tried to turn the Baltic Sea into a *mare clausum*, i.e. a 'closed sea', by blocking the Danish straits themselves, or by using military and political pressure to force Denmark to make a blockade. Conversely, Western naval powers, especially England, endeavoured to turn the Baltic Sea into *a mare liberum*, a free sea, and therefore tried to prevent the Danish straits from being closed.

The national interests in maintaining the integrity of our country and asserting sovereignty have therefore historically always been closely linked to the great power interests that may be present around the Baltic Sea and access to it. The Danish territory has thus been of strategic importance in any conflict of interest between a major maritime power among the Baltic coastal states and one or more major maritime powers outside the Baltic Sea. Denmark's strategic importance has been greatest in cases where the Baltic Sea power involved has not had direct or indirect control over the Danish territory.

In the twentieth century, Denmark has had limited resources, economically, technologically and therefore also militarily, so it has not been able to utilise this strategically important position itself. Instead, Denmark has found itself in a vulnerable position, as the great powers considered it necessary to take action themselves. Against this background, the following is a brief account of the importance of Danish waters as a strategic passage in the first half of the twentieth century.

However, we have to go back to the Øresund Treaty of 14 March 1857 to find the basis for the freedom of passage that has existed to this day. In the Treaty, Denmark relinquished the Sound and Belt customs duties and assumed certain obligations regarding the maintenance of waterway markings and lighthouses. In return, the other treaty countries: Sweden,

1 In *The Soviet Naval Threat to Europe* (Bruce W. Watson & Susan M. Watson (eds) London: Routledge, 1989) Hans Garde calls Denmark 'The Harbormaster of the Baltic'. This Chapter is essentially identical to my article: 'Denmark's naval strategic position in the great power game 1900–1939' in *Tidsskrift for Søvæsen*, no.2, 162. Årg, 1991.

Norway, Belgium, France, The Netherlands, Prussia and 6 other German states, Russia, Great Britain and Austria, paid a lump sum 30,476,000 Reichsdaler. The United States, Spain, Portugal, Turkey, Venezuela, Sardinia, Sicily and Tuscany also joined the treaty, paying a total of 1,682,000 Reichsdaler. Although the treaty, which is still in force, only refers to trade relations and therefore does not include warships, the following passage has been found to apply to all ships in practice:

> ... No ship shall in future, under any pretext whatsoever, dare to be arrested or subjected to any stoppage while travelling through the Straits and Belts, ...

and

> ... in future, as hitherto, to have the pilotage service supervised, the use of which in the Kattegat, the Sound and the Belts is at all times left to the discretion of the captains and masters.[2]

This freedom of passage was to apply not only in peacetime, but also in times of tension and war, when Denmark was neutral. In the first half of the twentieth century, when Denmark was trying to maintain freedom of alliance in peacetime and neutrality in times of crisis and war, the question of a possible blockade of the Danish straits gave rise to many considerations, both among the European powers and in Denmark.

2.2 Russian Crossing 1904

Neutrality was first threatened in 1904 when Denmark feared a naval clash in Danish waters during the Russo-Japanese War. On 11 October 1904, the Russian Baltic Sea Squadron, under the command of Admiral Rozestvensky, sailed from Libau (today Liepaja in Latvia) and headed for Danish waters. It was to attempt to break the Japanese naval supremacy in the East Asian theatre of war. In the name of neutrality, the Copenhagen sea defence was manned while the passage through the straits was kept clear. Danish pilots had already boarded the Russian ships while they were in Libau, and when the Russian fleet reached Danish territorial waters, Danish warships were ready and marked the most dangerous points on the route. There were no incidents of any kind, and the Danish naval leadership in particular could breathe a sigh of relief when the Russian naval force had left Danish waters.

Japan protested Denmark's favourable pilotage of the Russian fleet. England, which since 1902 had a defence agreement with Japan to enter a war if more than one other superpower attacked the country, asked Denmark if the British Fleet would receive the same service.

That Admiral Rozestvensky was not entirely comfortable with the situation became apparent 10 days later. On the night of 22 October, while the Russian warships were in the North Sea, heading south towards the English Channel, parts of the Russian fleet fired on some English fishing vessels that were peacefully fishing as usual on Dogger Bank. The

2 *Denmark's Strategic Importance*, Defence Command (Copenhagen: 1984), p.13.

Russian naval command had assumed them to be Japanese destroyers. Nerves had played a trick on the Russians, but this episode obviously worsened Russian-English relations, which at this point were not too good. This should be seen in the light of the aforementioned Japanese-English agreement on mutual military aid, which was established because the British feared that increased Russian expansion in East Asia would threaten India.

Although the Russian Baltic Fleet was reinforced with a small squadron from the Black Sea Fleet en route to Japan, it suffered a crushing defeat from the Japanese fleet in the Tushima Strait on 27 May 1905.[3]

At first glance, it may seem strange that Germany let the Russian fleet out of the Baltic Sea without a second thought. An alliance-like relationship had existed between Russia and France since 1891, based on their common interest in keeping Germany in check. But on the other hand, Germany was only interested in getting the Russian naval power out of the way, and since 1900, Kaiser Wilhelm had tried to pursue a policy of rapprochement with Russia. The intention was to take the air out of the Russo-French relationship. By encouraging the Tsar Nicholas of Russia to pursue an active policy in East Asia, the Russian 'pressure' on Germany's eastern border was greatly reduced. Moreover, the United Kingdom was further isolated in this way.

With the Russian Baltic Fleet out of sight by October 1904, the Germans had suddenly become the dominant naval power in the Baltic Sea. This prompted sections of the British press to suggest in November that the British Navy should attack and defeat the German fleet before it became too strong and dominant in European waters. A similar action had worked when the Danish Navy was put out of action in 1807 after the bombardment of Copenhagen, so why not do something similar in the current situation? Such statements put a serious scare into the German naval leadership, a reaction that has been dubbed 'The Copenhagen Complex' by an English historian.[4] But much to the relief of the Germans, these plans were not followed up by the British naval leadership. The uncertainty about which naval power would be the strongest in Europe in the future set the two navies' arms race in motion.

The thought that the ideas in the British press might one day be realised prompted the German Emperor to approach the German Foreign Minister Bülow to investigate the possibilities of establishing a German-Danish alliance. As early as 1903, the Emperor had been working on plans for a joint German-Russian guarantee of Danish neutrality, which would enable the two superpowers to exert more influence over Denmark. However, Bülow was concerned that a German-Danish alliance would only be perceived abroad as an unequal agreement where a small country gave up its independence in favour of a great power. On the contrary, such a proposal could be the very thing that could bring about an alliance between France, Russia and England, which was the last thing Germany wanted.[5] The alternative to an alliance or other form of agreement with Denmark to secure the passage to and from the Baltic Sea was, of course, German military action.

---

3 Salmonsens Leksikon, 'Russian-Japanese War 1904–05' and 'Dogger Bank'. Lorenz Rerup, *Danmarks historie*, Gyldendal, vol. 6, *1864–1914* (Copenhagen: 1989), p.303.

4 Jonathan Steinberg, 'The Copenhagen Complex' in *Journal of Contemporary History*, vol. I, 3rd series, vol. I (1966), pp.23–46.

5 Troels Fink, *Spillet om dansk neutralitet, 1905–09* (Aarhus: 1970), p .22f.

In 1895, the Kiel Canal was opened, allowing the German Navy to move units from the Baltic to the North Sea for the first time without having to cross the belts. At the same time, Danish waters, like the strongpoints in the German Bight, could be used for a quick strike against enemy naval forces. On the other hand, the enemy could not pursue German ships without great risk if the Germans controlled the coasts. A German attack on Denmark might even lure parts of the British Fleet to the area where it could be more easily attacked and defeated. The German Army opposed such plans, as they needed the troops for a possible two-front war against France and Russia. There were no resources for a third front in the north. In 1905, the Admiral Staff was therefore told that troops could not be made available for an occupation of Danish territory. The presumed plans for a British landing at Esbjerg and in North Jutland did not worry the German General Staff either. They were only interested in Denmark continuing to pursue a German-orientated policy that could accommodate the demands of the German Navy.

After 1905, the German naval leadership drew up another plan, which was heavily influenced by the experience of the Russian Baltic Fleet's defeat in the war against Japan. According to the new plan, the German Navy's main effort was to be concentrated in the North Sea. Within five years, Wilhelmshaven had become the navy's main base, while the Bay of Kiel became a training area. The reason it took so long to move the naval centre of gravity from Kiel to Wilhelmshaven was because the relocation of the new large battleships required extensions to the Kiel Canal. The final extensions to the canal and the necessary harbour facilities were not completed until 1914. The change in German naval strategic planning also meant a reduced interest in Denmark in offensive plans, but not as a bastion of defence against a British attack. It was therefore necessary to pretend that the previous plans for the German Navy still stood.

Therefore, plans to occupy strategic points in Denmark, or the entire country, apparently continued to play a major role in leading military circles in Germany in the years from 1905 to 1910. However, they were still convinced that, in the event of war, the British were planning a landing in Southern Jutland and a naval action in the Baltic Sea.[6]

However, the British perception of Denmark's neutrality and ability to defend it was different. If Britain and Germany went to war, it was certain that Denmark would remain 'benevolently neutral' in relation to the nearest major power, Germany. Denmark would not be able to prevent the German fleet's passage to and from the Baltic Sea and the German laying of minefields. Consequently, Britain did not hope to prevent a German occupation of Denmark, or parts of the country.[7] However, an agreement between Russia and the United Kingdom on 31 August 1907, regarding the settlement of their differences in Asia, increased the British Navy's ability, in a war situation, to take action through Danish waters into the Baltic Sea.

With the Anglo-Russian agreement, the alliance between the later allies was taking shape, as France already had alliance relations with the two countries separately.

---

6 Troels Fink, *Spillet om dansk neutralitet, 1905–09* (Aarhus: 1970), p.28; Lorenz Rerup, *Danmarks historie*, Gyldendal, vol. 6, *1864–1914* (Copenhagen: 1989), p.295.

7 Troels Fink, *Spillet om dansk neutralitet, 1905–09* (Aarhus: 1970), p.79.

2.3 North Sea and Baltic Sea Declarations, 1908

However, the new relationship between the United Kingdom and Russia was not directed against Germany, but rather a consequence of their common understanding of the situation in Asia. Russia wanted to be on good terms with Germany and in early August 1907, the German Emperor and the Russian Tsar held a meeting in Swinemünde. The meeting was initiated by Russia and negotiations were held regarding the formation of a Baltic Sea alliance. The starting point was the common desire of the two countries to maintain the *status quo* in the Baltic Sea region to the exclusion of any foreign influence. Denmark and Sweden could join the alliance if they so wished.

But, the negotiations between the two great Baltic Sea powers did not lead to an alliance agreement. Perhaps inspired by talks and discussions at the International Peace Conference in The Hague, which ended on 18 October 1907, representatives of Germany and Russia signed a secret protocol on 29 October in which the two countries mutually recognised each other's Baltic Sea possessions. For the sake of the aforementioned Anglo-Russian agreement, the challenging words about keeping foreign influence out of the Baltic had been omitted. It had quickly become clear to Germany that a common policy among the Baltic Sea powers towards Britain could not be established. An actual Baltic Sea alliance was therefore not possible.

The German-Russian negotiations had been conducted in the utmost secrecy, but in November England, through its intelligence sources, nevertheless received information about the plans of the two Baltic powers.

The Germans, not wanting to challenge Britain any more than necessary, hastened to assure the British that there was of course no attempt to close the Baltic Sea. To get out of the somewhat embarrassing situation, Germany suggested, to the great annoyance of the Russians, that the North Sea powers, to which Russia did not belong, should also conclude a similar agreement with the aim of mutually recognising each other's possessions. The United Kingdom was in favour of this proposal, but demanded that France should be included in such an agreement. At the same time, the British suggested that the two agreements could be linked. Germany, on the other hand, would not agree to this, as it would achieve the direct opposite of what was originally intended by the agreement. The Western powers would gain increased influence in the Baltic Sea, while the reverse would not apply, as Russia would have nothing to do with a North Sea agreement.

The original proposal had gradually lost its deeper political perspective. Negotiations became more and more formal and positions became more symbolic than real. However, as both a Baltic Sea power and a North Sea power, located at the junction of the two seas, the situation was very exciting for Denmark. In Danish statements, consideration for the United Kingdom played a major role. Denmark would not agree to any precautions that could be interpreted as excluding the United Kingdom from the entrance to the Baltic Sea. This strong stance in England's favour is somewhat surprising in relation to the German-orientated foreign policy Denmark had pursued in 1905–1907. Perhaps they finally saw a chance to escape dependence on Germany's almost exclusive military dominance in the Baltic Sea?

In December 1907, the Danish Foreign Minister, Count Raben-Levetzau, was informed of the plans for a Baltic Sea Treaty. He therefore approached the Russian Foreign Minister

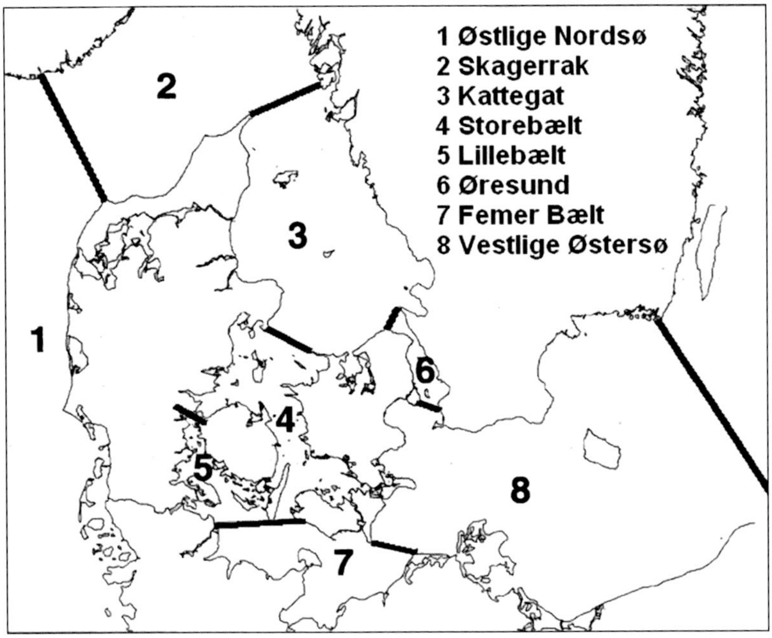

The Danish waters as they are defined today.

Isvolsky to ask whether it would be a good idea to include the United Kingdom in such an agreement. Isvolsky did not think so. Later, when the United Kingdom put forward the idea of linking the two agreements, the Danish Foreign Minister gave the proposal his full support. But this came up against the opposition of Germany and especially Russia. It was then agreed to conclude the two agreements separately. So far so good.

But now a curious problem arose. Where was the border between the North Sea and the Baltic Sea? Germany and the United Kingdom had agreed that the border should be drawn so that there would be no waters between the two seas and that all access to the seas would fall under one or the other agreement. But that was the end of the agreement. Germany wanted the border as far north-west as possible, while the United Kingdom wanted it as far south as possible. The two proposals were therefore far apart: either the Skagerrak and Kattegat should be part of the Baltic Sea or the North Sea should go south of the Danish belts!

During February 1908, this issue was discussed and Sweden and Denmark were now involved in the polemic. Sweden insisted on joining a North Sea agreement, which in turn meant that Germany had to agree that the Baltic Sea could only start from the Kattegat. There was also friction between Russia and Sweden, as no agreement could be reached on the status of the Åland Islands. Therefore, for a while it seemed that it would only be a question of concluding a North Sea agreement. With this in mind, the Danish Foreign Minister proposed that the border between the North and Baltic Seas should be a line drawn between Falsterbo and Åbenrå! The ulterior motive was obvious and both Germany and Russia opposed this proposal, which would give the United Kingdom almost free rein in the Danish straits. As the negotiations progressed, the border issue was becoming such an insurmountable problem that the agreements were finally finalised.

A Franco-British proposal to leave the question of the border between the two seas to a third agreement was rejected by both Germany and Russia. A Danish compromise proposal to include the Danish straits in both agreements was not even considered. In the end, all that was agreed upon was to approve the principle that the North Sea ended where the Baltic Sea began, and vice versa! No geographical definition of this point was therefore included in the Baltic Sea Agreement, and in the North Sea agreement it was worded as: ' … that the North Sea for the purposes of this declaration shall be deemed to extend eastwards until it joins the waters of the Baltic Sea.'

On 23 April 1908, the two declarations were signed. Along the way, they had become so watered down that none of the great powers attached much importance to them. However, there was good reason for the smaller powers to emphasise their value. At the same time, the agreements had to be seen as a sign of a much-needed Anglo-German détente, even though they did not feel particularly bound by the declarations.

From the British side, this view was expressed in a letter from the Foreign Office in London to the British ambassador in St Petersburg on 5 February 1908, a letter that could just as easily have been written in 1938:

> If, in the event of war, the straits remain open, that's all we want. If Germany tried to close them, we should consider ourselves absolutely free to do as we please, even ignoring the integrity of Norway if we need a naval base on the Norwegian coast. For these reasons the agreements are hardly worth the paper they are written on, since we know that Germany has made preparations to invade Denmark in case of war with us.[8]

The German position was determined by political rather than military considerations, as the declarations created useful political relations between The Netherlands, Denmark and Sweden on the one hand and Germany on the other. The German naval leadership considered the agreements to be particularly favourable to England, which in times of war had less interest in violating the neutrality of the small North Sea states than Germany did. However, the Admiral Staff was reassured by the politicians that in a critical situation, both the Germans and the others would disregard the agreements.

Within two months, the foundations of the Baltic Sea Agreement began to crumble. Russia, which had not achieved its wishes regarding the Åland Islands, was far from satisfied with the outcome. Moreover, with unrest in the Balkans, where Austria-Hungary and Russia were competing to dominate the region, with Germany supporting Austria-Hungary, Russia became increasingly interested in deepening its good relations with the Western powers at the expense of its relationship with Germany. In June, the British King Edward VII met with the Russian Tsar Nicholas II in the Estonian Capital of Reval (now Tallinn). The Tsar and his military advisers emphasised that the two countries had to be united in a policy of keeping the Belts and the Baltic Sea open. The British promised to support the Russians if the issue of closing the straits should arise again.

---

8 Einar Maseng, *1905 og 1940, en leksion i maktpolitikk* (Oslo: 1953), p.175

Russia's position on this issue had thus once again taken a new course. In 1903 it was in favour of closing the straits, in 1904 it was interested in free passage, in 1905 Germany and Russia negotiated how to keep the United Kingdom out, which was again the topic in 1907, when Russia opposed a Dutch proposal to prohibit the closing of straits connecting two free seas. But now in 1908, after first attempting to make an exclusive agreement with Germany, they were still interested in allowing the British Fleet to enter the Baltic Sea.

Once again, the question of Denmark's position was in the spotlight. Danish politicians sent out feelers to investigate England's attitude to the war issue in general and Denmark's position in particular if it came to war. The answers that emerged were discouraging from the point of view of the British-orientated. Britain would not be able to prevent a possible German occupation of Denmark, nor would it be possible to send reinforcements, at least not in the first phase of the war. But if Denmark defended its neutrality as well as possible, Britain would, in the event of victory, consider Denmark an ally after a possible peace settlement. The United Kingdom would then take guarantees against a future offensive against Denmark.[9]

All in all, the discussion and signing of the two declarations showed how the neighbouring great powers viewed the importance of Denmark and the Danish waters. The individual countries' views did not change radically in the following two decades. Denmark was slightly more relaxed in its neutrality, now that a balance had been established between England, Russia and Germany to a greater extent than before. The aforementioned British attitude meant that Denmark had to remain in Germany's military shadow, with no hope of a British rescue in the event of war. Denmark therefore had to maintain a 'benevolent neutral' attitude towards Germany right up to and including the First World War.

2.4 The 'Neutral' Denmark

In the Danish population and among Danish politicians, there was a distinctly pro-British attitude. Despite the real military power relations in the Baltic Sea, Danish politicians opted for a defence policy that almost unilaterally focussed on the land fortification of Copenhagen. The plans for the Danish neutrality defence were aimed at both Russia and England, but especially against Germany through an expansion of the Copenhagen land fortifications. Kofoed-Hansen, Director of the Ministry of the Navy, was not easily influenced by the general pro-British attitude in Denmark. Based on a sober military and power-political assessment of the situation in Europe in general, and in Denmark's neighbourhood in particular, he became increasingly dissatisfied with the politicians', in his eyes, unrealistic ideas of what Denmark's position would be in the event of a war between two or more superpowers. Consequently, he chose to resign his position after the Defence Commission submitted its report in the summer of 1908.[10]

To express his opinion on the existing defence policy considerations, he wrote a pamphlet entitled: *Udenrigspolitik og Forsvar. En sammentrængt Fremstilling af Forsvarssagens*

9 Troels Fink, *Spillet om dansk neutralitet, 1905–09* (Aarhus: 1970), p.104ff 'The North Sea and Baltic Sea declarations in 1908'

10 Tage Kaarsted, *Flåden under Første Verdenskrig* (Odense: 1976), p.XIIf.

Udvikling og dens stilling i Øjeblikket, Maj 1909 (*Foreign Policy and Defence. A Condensed Presentation of the Development of the Defence Cause and its Position at the Moment, May 1909*). Kofoed-Hansen made it clear that in a future war, power over the Baltic Sea would, as always, be of central strategic importance, but that Germany would have to be prepared to dominate this sea, whether they liked it or not. Should British naval vessels cross the Belt and Sound, Danish territories would automatically be drawn into the war, as modern navies could not operate without bases on land. Kofoed-Hansen outlined the following scenarios for the military dispositions in such a war, where the main opponents were the United Kingdom and Germany:

1. If the United Kingdom is alone in the fight against Germany, the British Navy cannot take action in the Baltic Sea until the German North Sea fleet is defeated. Only when the British Fleet can divide its strength without risk will such an action be possible. It follows that in the first phase of a war Germany will retain control of the Baltic Sea and its straits.
2. If the UK is allied with France and possibly Russia, a naval action into the Baltic Sea will be faster, but still not fast enough to prevent a German action *against* Denmark, as the exit from the Elbe Estuary must first be cut off.
3. In order for the UK to make a major push into the Baltic Sea, it is strategically necessary to establish bases in Denmark.
4. Germany's interest in the Danish territory is partly determined by its importance to the Western powers and partly by Denmark's ability to defend itself against enemy attacks.

In the autumn of 1909, a new defence system was adopted, which clearly reflected Kofoed-Hansen's views. His pamphlet had made an impression. Five years later, when the World War broke out, he was ready to steer Denmark through the dangerous glare of the Great Powers in his capacity as Admiral and Navy Commander.[11]

In fact, during the same period, the British naval leadership had reassessed their naval strategy. Drawing on the lessons learnt from the Russo-Japanese War, a new blockade and battle strategy had been drawn up in 1905. The need of steamships for fuel and the development of torpedo boats and submarines made the traditional close blockade close to the enemy coast too risky for large warships. Technological developments had given the ships greater speed and the guns a longer range, enabling a more open blockade of, for example, the entire North Sea, the English Channel and the waters between Scotland and the Norwegian coast. Similarly, the battle strategy was moved away from enemy coastal defences, home bases and minefields and far out into the open sea.

However, these overall changes in the British naval dispositions were made over a longer period, from 1907 to 1912. Along the way, the British Navy worked on plans for direct actions such as a landing on Funen, an Anglo-Russian landing in Pomerania and attacks aimed at strategic points on the German North Sea coast. But the British Army also rejected the navy's plans. In the army's opinion, an English expeditionary force would be most useful

11 Tage Kaarsted, *Flåden under Første Verdenskrig* (Odense: 1976), pp.XIII-XV.

in Belgium or France. The reorganisation of the naval strategy made the Baltic Sea area even less interesting in the eyes of the British. Although Germany had the opportunity to occupy Denmark, and the area would thus have some importance for the British blockade, the British had no illusions about England's ability to come to the Danes' aid. Germany's position of power in the Baltic Sea was unassailable. When the war broke out in August 1914, the British Navy had therefore written off the Baltic Sea as an area of operations, at least in the first phase of the conflict.[12]

Based on a joint Scandinavian declaration in 1912, a Royal Decree of 20 December laid down certain provisions regarding Denmark's neutrality in the event of war between foreign powers. Among other things, it was established that ships of belligerent powers had free access and the right to pass through Danish territorial waters, except for certain internal waters.[13] What had been the practice since the Danish pilotage of the Russian Baltic Sea fleet in 1904 was now enshrined in print.

In 1912–1913, the major European powers rearmed in a race, confident that at some point there would be a confrontation. As arsenals grew and mobilisation exercises became more frequent in Europe, unrest in the Balkans continued to simmer. As mentioned, in 1905 Germany had begun to shift its naval strategy from the Baltic to the North Sea, in line with the widening of the Kiel Canal and the expansion of Wilhelmshaven. Whereas before 1905 it had been hoped that in the event of war it would be possible to persuade the United Kingdom to divide its naval forces in order to launch a British naval action in the Baltic Sea, possibly provoked by a German occupation of Danish territories, in the period 1905–1914 it was hoped to avoid such a situation. Around 1910–1912, the German Baltic Sea Fleet was reduced to a minimum. In the event of a superpower war, Denmark was expected to adopt a favourable neutral stance, i.e. cordoning off and controlling Danish waters. However, the danger of British action in the Baltic Sea had also been significantly reduced after plans had been made in the United Kingdom for a more open blockade of Germany, i.e. a closure of the English Channel in the south and the waters between Scotland and Norway in the north. In 1914, neither the British Army nor navy had any plans for a Baltic Sea offensive and Denmark therefore only occupied a marginal place in the British strategy.[14]

In the period 1912–1914, there was still some uncertainty in the German naval leadership. The Russian fleet had recovered from its defeat by Japan in 1905, while the German force in the Baltic Sea was reduced to training vessels and a very weak army force along the coast. Perhaps there would be a British naval action through Danish waters after all, now that a joint Russian-English operation was a theoretical possibility? Despite a sometimes heated exchange of arguments between the German Army and Navy, as well as within the naval leadership, the overall naval strategy could not be changed. The only possible defence against a possible British attempt to reach the Baltic Sea was to cultivate German-Danish relations, encouraging Denmark to strengthen its neutrality defence combined with its own minelaying.[15]

12 Lorenz Rerup, *Danmarks historie*, Gyldendal, vol. 6, *1864–1914* (Copenhagen: 1989), p.296.

13 Poul Garde, *Forudsætninger for Dansk søminekrigsførelse* (Copenhagen: Søe-Lieutenant-Selskabet, 1976), pp.190–191.

14 Hans Branner, *Småstat mellem stormagter* (Copenhagen: 1972), pp.108–109 .

15 Hans Branner, *Småstat mellem stormagter* (Copenhagen: 1972), p.96ff.

During the summer of 1914, the German naval leadership became increasingly convinced that in the event of war with Germany, an English naval force would still penetrate the Danish straits in an attempt to attack the weak German northern flank. Plans to blockade the access routes to the Baltic Sea with mines were therefore taken up at the highest level of the German naval leadership. Until 3 August 1914, however, the navy did not receive any support for these plans from the army command, which was still hoping that Britain would stay out of the war. A provocation, in the form of a minelaying operation near, and perhaps in, Danish waters, could be the straw that broke the camel's back.

It was not until 4 August, when a British declaration of war was considered inevitable following the German attack on Belgium, that the German Navy received the full support of the top military leadership. The only condition for the laying of a mine barrage was that Danish neutrality had to be respected, meaning that the mines had to be laid outside Danish territorial waters.[16] A rumour that British warships had already been at sea the day before prompted the German commander of the Baltic Sea area, Prinz Heinrich of Prussia, to take immediate action. Without asking or informing the German military leadership, he ordered the laying of mines in the waters between the southern tip of Langeland and the westernmost point of Lolland, Albuen, at 19.00. The order was issued 45 minutes before the state of war between Germany and the United Kingdom had formally begun! On the night of 5 August, two German ships laid mines partly in Danish territorial waters. Early in the morning of 5 August, the Danish Foreign Ministry received a German note asking whether Denmark was prepared to immediately implement an effective mine blockade of the Great Belt against both warring parties?[17]

2.5 Danish Waters During the World War

As soon as war was declared, the Danish response would be crucial to the fate of Denmark. Although the German note was in the form of a question, Denmark realised that it contained a strong invitation to lay mines. The enquiry meant that if Denmark answered in the affirmative, the declared neutrality would be broken, as it presupposed that there was free navigation through the belts. If they answered in the negative, there was a risk that Germany would take action itself, which meant a great risk that parts of Denmark would be occupied.

The German minelaying and the German enquiry therefore put the Danish Government in a serious dilemma. Throughout the day, the situation was discussed between the government, the other political parties and the military leadership. Despite great disagreement between these parties, the dispute centred on the question of whether neutrality could be respected by bowing to the German demand, or whether to stand firm instead. Only when the King stated his position on the issue, namely that there was no other way out than for Denmark to mine the belts itself, could they agree to follow the German request. Late in the

16 Hans Branner, *Småstat mellem stormagter* (Copenhagen: 1972), p.154ff.
17 Hans Branner, *Småstat mellem stormagter* (Copenhagen: 1972), p.166ff.

day, the government sent a message to Germany that Denmark would lay mine barriers in the belts and in the Danish part of the Øresund.[18]

The King's commitment, which ultimately proved decisive, was based on his knowledge of how Denmark's situation was perceived by the British Government. They were fully aware that Denmark was part of the German sphere of influence, and therefore the British also accepted that Denmark did not follow a strict policy of neutrality on certain points. In comparison, on 4 August, the United Kingdom addressed Sweden, promising to respect the country's neutrality as long as Sweden would defend it. In a communication to Norway, the British went even further, offering military support if Germany threatened the country. The importance of the three Nordic countries to the United Kingdom was thus clearly marked in order of priority: Norway, Sweden and Denmark. [19]

Immediately after the Council of State had made the decision to lay the mine barriers in the Danish straits, King Christian X sent a reassuring telegram to the British King at the request of the government:

> Dear George.
> Under the extraordinary and unfortunate circumstances, I and my Government, in order to maintain Denmark's neutrality and, as far as possible, keep war operations away from Danish regions, have decided to block the Great Belt, and the Danish channels in the Sound and in the Little Belt. This is moved by circumstances which you, who know my affection for you, will be able to understand.
> Christian.[20]

When the United Kingdom was officially informed of Denmark's decision in this way, the British made it clear that they fully understood the Danes' behaviour and that they still considered the country to be neutral.

From 6 to 9 August, Danish ships laid 492 contact mines in the Great Belt. On 10 August, 6 mines were laid in the Little Belt and on 13 and 14 August, 50 were laid in Agerøsund and Omøsund. In addition, mines were laid north of Copenhagen and in the cordoned-off area around the capital, including a bombardment barrage in the northern part of Køge Bay.[21]

The Danish minefields proved to be a major nuisance to German U-boat traffic, and after a few months the Germans asked for the mines to be removed again. However, they had to bow to the Danish Foreign Minister's reference to the fact that the roadblocks could not be removed as part of the Danish defence of neutrality without creating distrust in the Danish neutrality policy. [22]

---

18 Karl Chr. Lammers, *Danmarks historie*, Gyldendal, vol. 7 *Udenrigspol. 1918-33* (Aarhus: 1988), pp.85–86

19 Hans Branner, *Småstat mellem stormagter* (Copenhagen: 1972), pp.186–188.

20 Johnny E. Balsved: 'Mine Laying in World War 1' <http://navalhistory.dk/Danish/Historien/1914_1918/Mineudlaegningen.htm>.

21 Tage Kaarsted, *Storbritannien og Danmark, 1914–1920* (Odense: 1974), pp.8 & 193.

22 Erik Rasmussen, 'Velfærdsstaten på vej, 1913–1939' in *Danmarks Historie* vol. 13, (Copenhagen: Politikens forlag, 1965), p.53.

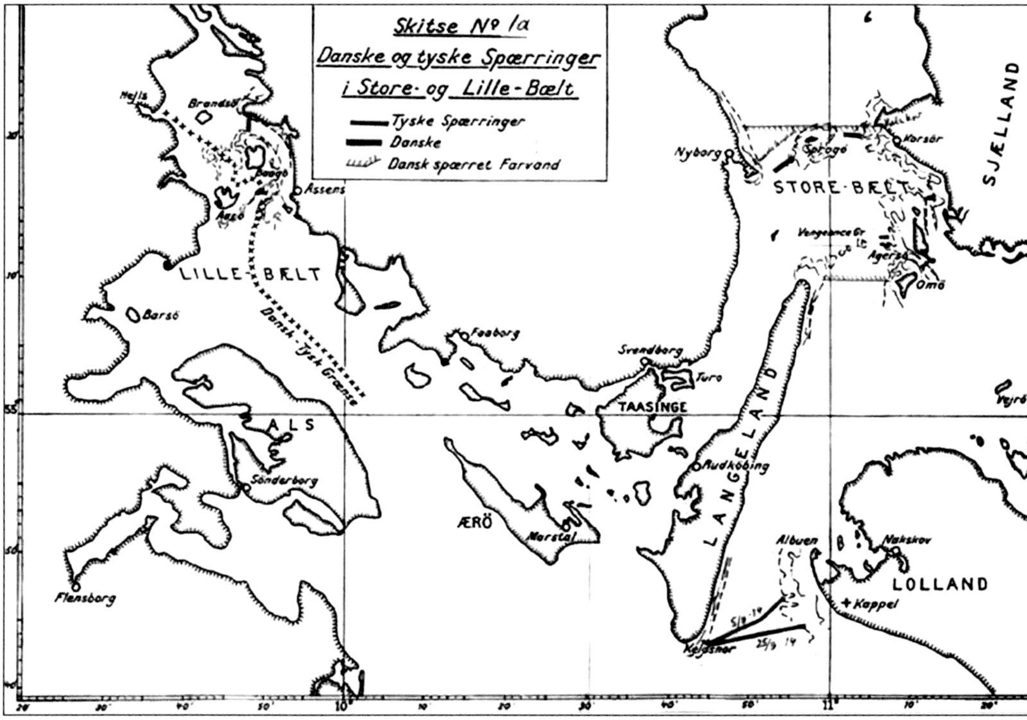

Minefields in the Great Belt and Little Belt during World War I.

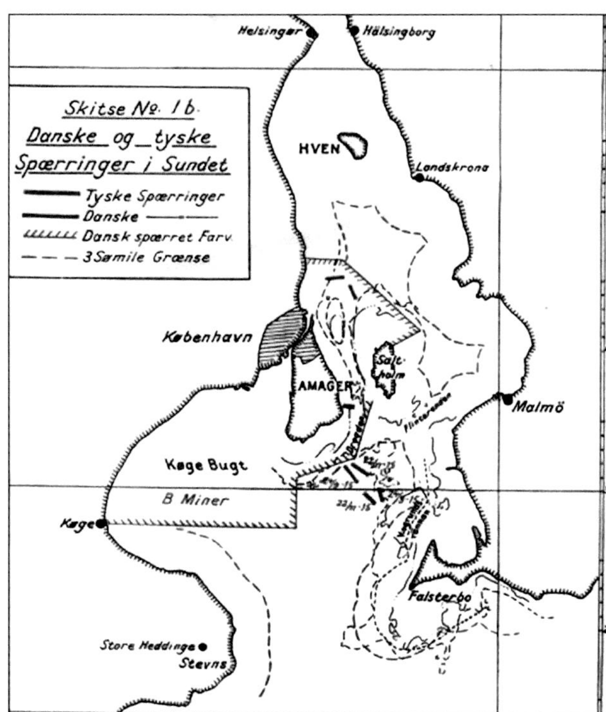

Minefields in Øresund and Køge Bugt during World War I.

Both German and British vessels laid contact mines close to Danish waters during the war, and shortly after the outbreak of the war, the danger of mines really began to make itself felt. As can be seen from the mine maps, the German mines, in particular, were located alongside and in the transit waters. An effective search of the busiest waters was therefore quickly established with the Danish Navy's inspection ships, torpedo boats, patrol boats and rented equipment, and mine clearance teams were also stationed on the west coast of Jutland, at Albuen on West Lolland and on Bornholm. The search for mines in the North Sea was carried out as a Nordic cooperation, as agreed at a mining conference in 1915.

Germany insisted that no mines had been laid on Danish territory since the first mine barriers were laid on 5 August. By November, however, the Germans were forced to admit that several mines had drifted into Danish territory near Langeland, and promised to remove them immediately. While attempting to remove them, one of the German trawlers struck a German mine and sank. After several days of easterly storms, several mines were found drifting in the Great Belt, 5 of which were found by Danish ships and destroyed.

Defusing drifting mines was quite a daunting task. From August 1914 to March 1919, the Danish Navy defused a total of 5,803 mines during the *Sikringsstyrken* period,[23] which equates to an average of around 3 mines per day. It was not a job without risk, and during the war 9 Danish marines were killed and 7 wounded. In total, almost 10,000 mines were found and neutralised during and after the end of the First World War. The majority of these mines were British, but it was still the German mines that posed the greatest danger. According to the 1907 Hague Convention, a mine had to defuse itself if it broke free from its mooring. However, it turned out that 75 percent of German mines were still armed when they were found![24]

As mentioned, Britain had no intention of undertaking a major operation into the Baltic Sea. Everyone in the British military leadership agreed on this, except for the two most prominent figures in the British Navy, the First Sea Lord, Baron John Fisher, and the Secretary of the Navy, Winston Churchill. The two had grand plans for a naval action into the Baltic Sea, but their ideas met with strong opposition. When they both left their posts in May 1915, the plans were shelved.[25]

The few British naval operations that were actually carried out in the Baltic Sea were purely symbolic – they wanted to 'show the flag'. On 10 October 1914, three submarines were ordered into the Baltic Sea under strict orders not to violate Danish neutrality. Two of the boats, *E.1* and *E.9*, followed each other and both escaped unhindered through the Danish and German blockades. The third boat, *E.11* left a little later and was unluckier. On 19 October, when the crew spotted a foreign submarine at Nakkehoved Lighthouse (near Gilleleje), they fired two torpedoes. Fortunately, they missed, as one just scraped

23 The *Sikringsstyrken* (Security Force) was Denmark's neutrality defence during World War I, 1914–1918. The call-up of the *Sikringsstyrken* was not a mobilisation of the Army or Navy, which might be seen by England and/or Germany as an offensive policy, but it was a political demonstration of Denmark's will to defend the country – primarily the state institutions of the Government and not least the Royal Family.

24 Johnny E. Balsved: 'Mine Laying in World War 1' <http://navalhistory.dk/Danish/Historien/1914_1918/Mineudlaegningen.htm>.

25 Tage Kaarsted, *Storbritannien og Danmark, 1914–1920* (Odense: 1974), pp.43–46.

The grounded British submarine *E.13* is fired upon by German warships in Danish waters, August 1915. The most serious violation of neutrality on Danish territory during the war.

the underside of the submarine – the Danish *Havmanden*, which was on exercise! The commander of *E.11* was convinced that he had fired on a German U-boat, and therefore he believed that the breakthrough attempt had now been discovered. He thus abandoned further attempts to pass the Danish barriers in the Sound and returned home. The incident gave rise to a lot of correspondence between the two countries, but ended with an English apology for what had happened.

The two submarines that got through conducted several successful operations in the Baltic Sea, based in Russian harbours. Therefore, in the summer of 1915, two more submarines were sent to the Baltic Sea. This time, again one of them got into trouble; *E.13* ran aground on 19 August 1915 in Flinterenden southeast of Saltholm. Although Danish torpedo boats were ordered to protect the grounded vessel and Danish guards were quickly established,

German warships were still allowed to fire on the U-boat. Half of the crew drowned as a result of the shelling and the rest were picked up by Danish naval vessels and interned. Denmark sent a sharp note of protest to Germany over this, the most serious violation of neutrality in the war.[26]

On 31 May 1916, the Battle of Jutland was fought between the German High Seas Fleet and the British Grand Fleet. The British Fleet suffered the greatest losses but remained in the area, while the German fleet chose to leave the battle. Therefore, the outcome was interpreted by the British as a victory for the United Kingdom. In Denmark, this led to renewed fears of a British attempt to penetrate into the Baltic Sea. This fear was reinforced by the British Foreign Office spreading false rumours that the United Kingdom would soon land in Southern Jutland and Schleswig. The intention was to entice the Germans to tie up as many troops as possible on the northern flank before a planned offensive on the Western Front was launched. However, there was a danger that Germany would ultimately decide to occupy Denmark. During 1916, the Danish General Staff and government were repeatedly assured that Britain would not under any circumstances carry out the operations, which were merely intended to distract Germany.[27]

In April 1917, the US entered the war on the side of the Triple Entente and the blockade of Germany was further tightened. At the same time, things were beginning to go wrong with another ally, Russia. In March 1917, revolution broke out and the Tsar abdicated. Germany immediately seized the opportunity and moved eastwards. The new Russian Government asked the British Government for urgent assistance and a British naval force was sent to Horns Rev to keep the German Fleet in the North Sea while the Russians laid minefields in new defence lines. Nevertheless, the Germans began to threaten both the Russian base in Reval (now Tallinn) and Petrograd itself (now St Petersburg). Like a troll out of a box, Admiral Fisher, former First Sea Lord, approached the British Prime Minister as early as 28 March and proposed an attack into the Baltic Sea. During his time as Second Sea Lord, October 1914 to May 1915, Fisher had commissioned an armada of 622 ships, all with a shallow draught, specifically for a British naval action in the Baltic. Although Fisher was no longer commander of the navy after his departure in 1915, he held a significant position and influence in both government and the Admiralty. His ideas were therefore once again the subject of discussion. But there was still strong opposition in the military and political leadership. The costs of such an action would be too high. The plan was therefore again taken off the table. In October, the Russian Government pushed hard and once again the British Government had to weigh the military and political consequences of a Baltic Sea operation. It was agreed to send a small naval force into the Kattegat, and between 31 October and 2 November 1917, a British naval force of 20 ships, including 9 destroyers, managed to sink a German auxiliary cruiser and 10 armoured trawlers. This action had more symbolic than military significance and therefore had no consequences for Denmark's position or the balance of power in the Baltic Sea. But it was close![28]

---

26 Tage Kaarsted, *Storbritannien og Danmark, 1914–1920* (Odense: 1974), pp.47–48.

27 Christian Paulin,'Paths to strategic control of Denmark – German plans for a pre-emptive attack 1916 –1918' <http://www.historisktidsskrift.dk/pdf_histtid/109_2/418.pdf>.

28 Tage Kaarsted, *Storbritannien og Danmark, 1914–1920* (Odense: 1974), p.54.

The Bolshevik Revolution on 7 November 1917 led to Russia withdrawing from the war, and on 3 March 1918, the new Soviet Government made peace with the central powers – Germany and Austria-Hungary. This development shifted the balance of power in the Baltic and North Sea again, as the Soviet Navy could now unite with the German Navy, while the latter could sail Danish waters without danger. The British Navy therefore tried to stop a possible German breakout into the North Sea via the Danish straits by sending a naval force into the Kattegat on 19 March. Due to fog, the force was unable to accomplish anything and had to return. But on 16 April they tried again, this time with greater success. A total of 12 German trawlers were sunk and 111 Germans were captured in Kattegat. During the summer and autumn, the British Navy carried out further raids into Danish waters. On 2 November, a German auxiliary cruiser was sunk near Kullen in Sweden. A week later, the war was over.[29]

Throughout the war, the British Government took the position that it was not interested in violating Denmark's neutrality. Individuals like Fisher and Churchill could propose naval actions that might have threatened this neutrality, but as a result of overall military planning and policy, these plans were always cancelled in time. The cost to Britain would be far too great:

1. The long lines of communication would cost disproportionately high losses in equipment and manpower.
2. Psychologically and strategically, it would be disastrous to lose the attempt to reach the Baltic Sea.
3. Morally, such an operation would probably be easily equated with Germany's violation of Belgium, the act that formally brought Britain into the war.
4. An attempted attack would likely trigger a German occupation of Denmark, which in turn could affect Britain's relationship with both Norway and Sweden.
5. The above uncertainties surrounding military action could affect Denmark's food supplies to the UK, which, from the perspective of British politicians, were extremely valuable.

Germany's real military supremacy in the Baltic Sea and strong pressure on Denmark, combined with the importance of Danish agricultural production, prudent British politicians, and a Danish Government that knew how to utilise the opportunities for balance, were in other words the prerequisites for Denmark to remain 'benevolently neutral.'[30]

2.6 Denmark, the League of Nations and the Neutrality Issue

Although the Soviet Union withdrew from the war, the internal power struggle between the Bolsheviks and the Belarusian forces continued. The Western powers intervened in this conflict by sending military supplies and troops to aid the 'Belarusian' generals in 1919. The

29 Tage Kaarsted, *Storbritannien og Danmark, 1914–1920* (Odense: 1974), pp.65–67.
30 Tage Kaarsted, *Storbritannien og Danmark, 1914–1920* (Odense: 1974), pp.68–69.

British ships that brought the military reinforcements to the Russian Baltic Sea ports were given free passage through Danish waters.[31]

To support their forces, the British anchored depot ships in Copenhagen's outer harbour, well protected by the Danish coastal forts.[32] Denmark's previous neutrality, which ensured free passage for foreign ships, had conveniently been reinstated. But allowing this British traffic had consequences for Denmark on the economic front. Before the Russian Revolution of 1912, Denmark had had extensive trade with Russia and was one of the first countries in the world to recognise the new Bolshevik regime in 1917. But from the turn of the year 1918–1919, Denmark followed the Western powers' attempt to isolate the Soviet Union in order to nip the new regime in the bud. All diplomatic and trade relations were severed. Denmark did not officially participate in military support for the Belarusian Army, but a corps of Danish volunteers took part in the fight against the Bolsheviks. Now many Danish possessions were in danger of falling victim to nationalisation and the interruption of trade relations had cost Denmark dearly. Danish holdings and investments in the Soviet Union alone were roughly equivalent to the Danish state's annual income of DKK 400,000,000. The Soviet Union had supplied raw materials to Denmark, which in turn had supplied finished industrial products.

In 1920, the Western powers realised that the Bolsheviks' power was here to stay, so began economic and trade negotiations with the new regime and Denmark followed suit. In 1921, a trade agreement was signed between the United Kingdom and the Soviet Union, but it was not until 1923 that Denmark signed an agreement. The following year, the regime again received full recognition from Denmark.[33] The Soviet Union, which had been allied with the Western powers for most of World War I and therefore opposed the Danish closure of the straits, was now more than interested in the same Danish waters being closed to all but the countries around the Baltic Sea. This became apparent in 1923, when the Soviet Union protested Denmark's minor deepening of the shipping channel in Drogden (Øresund), as the Soviets suspected the UK of being behind it. This gave Britain improved opportunities to send larger naval units into the Baltic Sea. In 1924, a maritime disarmament conference was held in Rome, where the Soviet Union, as a condition for reducing its navy, demanded the introduction of a ban on access to the Baltic Sea for naval vessels from countries other than Baltic Sea countries.[34]

As a result of the war, the victorious powers agreed to create a body for the preservation of peace, that is, the peace of the victors. The Treaty of Versailles included the creation of a new forum to fulfil this ambition: the League of Nations. When the treaty came into force on 10 January 1920, the neutral countries, including Denmark, were invited to join. The countries' respective governments were given two months to consider!

The invitation put Denmark in a difficult position. On the one hand, membership required Denmark to participate in the diplomatic and economic sanctions of the League of Nations against a country that broke the peace, and on the other hand, Denmark had to allow troops from the League of Nations to pass through its land and sea territory. However, the neutral

31 Halfdan Barfod, *Sømagt og dens indflydelse på Danmarks historie* (Copenhagen: 1936), p.87.

32 Halfdan Barfod, *Sømagt og dens indflydelse på Danmarks historie* (Copenhagen: 1936), p.91.

33 Karl Chr. Lammers, *Danmarks historie*, Gyldendal, vol. 7 *Udenrigspol. 1918-33* (Aarhus: 1988), pp.235–236.

34 'Prerequisites for Danish naval mine warfare', Copenhagen 1978, chap. V, part 4, section C2; Poul Garde, *Forudsætninger for Dansk søminekrigsførelse* (Copenhagen: Søe-Lieutenant-Selskabet, 1976).

countries avoided a demand for automatic participation in military sanctions against a peace breaker. This could only happen after negotiation. But in any case, Denmark's neutrality would be questionable under membership. Of course, the League of Nations sanctions were primarily aimed at Germany, which was not a member.

The other major power that was considered a potential peace breaker was the Soviet Union, which was also not invited to join the League of Nations. This was partly because of the separate peace with Germany and partly because of the subsequent regime change in the country, which the Western powers now realised was here to stay. Naturally, these facts had to be a cause for concern for the Danish Government. Membership could lead to Denmark suddenly having to impose sanctions on the two geographically closest superpowers. Conversely, by declining the invitation, Denmark would easily be lumped in with the aforementioned great powers, which had so far not been considered worthy of membership. The Danish Government therefore decided in February to accept the invitation. In 1920 Austria and in 1922 Hungary became members of the League of Nations, with Germany joining in 1926. By 1928, there were a total of 55 member states, but two great powers, the US and the Soviet Union, did not join. The US did not ratify the Treaty of Versailles because of the Monroe Doctrine and therefore never joined, while the Soviets only joined in 1934.

Denmark and the other neutral countries tried to introduce various special rules for what were termed 'particularly vulnerable countries' immediately after accession. For example, the following year, the so-called '1921 directives' were adopted, according to which a particularly vulnerable country, such as Denmark, could postpone the implementation of sanctions or avoid them altogether if the sanctions from the League of Nations were directed against Germany. While the Danish Government thus tried to be released as much as possible from the collective obligations of the League of Nations, an early footnote policy, it wholeheartedly supported another of its main goals: general disarmament across the world.

For Denmark, the World War resulted in Southern Jutland becoming Danish again on 15 June 1920, as a consequence of the Versailles Treaty's wording on the right of peoples to self-determination. The member states of the League of Nations ratified the new border demarcation agreement with Denmark, while Germany did not sign the agreement. This created some uncertainty in Denmark in the following years, which became particularly pronounced when the German Nazis began to raise the border issue again 10 years later.

Immediately after the reclaimed territory was incorporated into Denmark, Danish troops were stationed in Southern Jutland. For the first 10 years after the defeat, Germany no longer posed a potential threat to Denmark's security. This meant that in 1922 Denmark felt able to cut its defence budget in half. Whereas an average of around DKK 100,000,000 had been spent in each of the war years, the annual budget in 1922 was set at DKK 48,000,000. The worst hit was the army, which had to cut the number of battalions from 51 to 35. The navy's budget was reduced from around DKK 24,000,000 to around DKK 16,000,000. Nevertheless, the size of the fleet remained more or less unchanged.[35] The coastal artillery, which was part of the Danish Army, was reduced from 3 battalions to 1, and 5 of the 17 coastal batteries, whose task it was to secure laid-out minefields, were disbanded.[36]

35 Johs. Lomholt-Thomsen, *Problemer i dansk politik 1901–1946* (Copenhagen: 1948), p.191.

36 Palle Bolten Jagd, *Danske forsvarsanlæg i 5.000 år*, Part III: *Efter 1932* (Rødovre: 1984), p.42.

At the same time, for the first time since the defeat in 1864, the centre of gravity of the Danish defence was moved from the land fortifications of Copenhagen to Jutland. Now it was safe to show its teeth to its militarily, and economically, weak neighbour to the south.[37]

Denmark thus demonstrated its good will for peace by halving its defence spending in the Defence Act of 1922. However, the disarmament of the great powers was slower and later stalled due to mutual distrust of each other's real intentions and actual results. There was also the unresolved paradox of whether peace was secured through disarmament or real peace was the condition for disarmament? France, in particular, was against too much disarmament for fear that Germany would gain military parity.

As the international climate deteriorated around 1930, the League of Nations proved to be of little consequence when it came to reining in an aggressive superpower. When Japan invaded Manchuria in 1931, the League of Nations condemned this action, but could not agree on sanctions against Japan. Nevertheless, Japan felt offended and angrily left the League in 1932. In 1933, the disarmament efforts of the great powers collapsed completely. Nazi Germany withdrew from the League of Nations and began an armament programme that clearly violated the Treaty of Versailles. The League of Nations was again unable to establish effective sanctions. [38]

However, Denmark continued to cut back on military defence. The Defence Act of 1932 further reduced the defence budget from DKK 48,000,000 to DKK 35,000,000, of which DKK 11,500,000 was allocated to the navy and coastal defence. This meant a drastic weakening of the navy, which now consisted of only 3 artillery ships, 9 torpedo boats, 7 submarines, 1 minesweeper, 18 naval aircraft and various specialised vessels.[39] The coastal artillery was now placed under the navy, under the name Coastal Defence, and another 3 coastal batteries were disbanded. Eventually, only 9 coastal fortifications remained, none of which were located at the Great Belt.[40] The army was also reduced further, from 35 battalions to 24, although there was a qualitative improvement in technical and organisational terms.[41]

When Hitler came to power in Germany in 1933, new winds began to blow in the European arena. In October, Germany left the disarmament negotiations and, as mentioned, withdrew from the League of Nations. Although Denmark eagerly supported the idea behind the League of Nations and the European disarmament efforts, Germany's position clashed with Danish security interests. Denmark's dilemma really became apparent when Germany in 1935 considered itself released from the Treaty of Versailles and began an overt rearmament programme, including the introduction of conscription and the formation of an air force. Denmark abstained from voting in favour of a League of Nations resolution condemning the German steps. But no actual sanctions were imposed on Germany.[42] For Denmark, the consequences were clear. A smaller state's membership of the League of Nations could not

---

37 Johs. Lomholt-Thomsen, *Problemer i dansk politik 1901–1946* (Copenhagen: 1948), p.176.

38 Karl Chr. Lammers, *Danmarks historie*, Gyldendal, vol. 7 *Udenrigspol. 1918-33* (Aarhus: 1988), p.226ff.

39 Johs. Lomholt-Thomsen, *Problemer i dansk politik 1901–1946* (Copenhagen: 1948), p.196.

40 Jagd, Palle Bolten, *Danske forsvarsanlæg i 5.000 år*, Part III: *Efter 1932* (Rødovre: 1984), p.42. The 9 coastal fortifications consisted of: 6 batteries near Copenhagen, as well as Lynæsfort, Masnedøfort and Borgsted Battery (at Lillebælt).

41 Johs. Lomholt-Thomsen: 'Problemer i dansk politik 1901–1946', Copenhagen 1948, p.196.

42 Henrik S. Nissen, *Danmarks historie*, Gyldendal, vol. 7, *1914–45* (Aarhus: 1988), p.340.

be expected to provide any kind of security against a great power like Germany. When Britain and Germany surprisingly signed a naval agreement the same year, in which Britain renounced its maritime interests in the Baltic Sea, there was nothing for Denmark to do but gradually try to return to the benevolent policy of neutrality towards Germany that had been pursued before the World War.

All attempts to establish an alternative in the form of Nordic defence cooperation failed. When Swedish newspapers in March 1937 attacked the Danish Defence Arrangement of 1932 for posing a direct threat to the security of the other Nordic countries by weakening Danish defence, it was too much for Prime Minister Stauning. He made it clear in no uncertain terms that Denmark was not a 'lapdog' in relation to Germany on behalf of the Nordic countries. The fact that Denmark once more had to take great consideration of the military superpower in the south was again emphasised when, a month later, Stauning had a conversation with the British Foreign Secretary, Anthony Eden, who made it clear that in the event of a German demand for a border revision, Britain would only provide Denmark with diplomatic support.[43] At the same time, the Danish Parliament was negotiating the adoption of a new defence system. For the first time since 1909, the defence budget was not reduced further, but rather increased to DKK 45,000,000 compared to the previous DKK 35,000,000. Taking into account inflation in the intervening 5 years, however, this was a modest increase. While the Army remained more or less unchanged in size, the navy was reduced to 1 artillery ship, 8 torpedo boats 4 submarines, 3 minesweepers, 1 *mineskib*, 1 minelayer ship, 1 workshop ship, 20–24 aircraft (2 squadrons) and some survey and inspection ships.[44] *Peder Skram*, a decommissioned artillery ship from 1908, and some older submarines were to be kept in reserve.[45] At the same time, it was decided that another coastal fort, Tårbæk Fort, would be closed down in 1938.[46]

In March 1938, Austria was incorporated into the German Reich and in September it was the turn of Sudetenland (a part of Czechoslovakia). In the meantime, during the spring, work began on a joint Nordic declaration of neutrality, which resulted in the Stockholm Declaration of 22 May 1938. It set out the conditions that the Nordic countries, Denmark, Finland, Iceland, Norway and Sweden considered necessary to maintain classic neutrality. There was free passage for ships of foreign powers in international waters, while there were restrictions on the use of territorial waters and harbours. For Denmark, the 1912 declaration thus lapsed. As a new addition, any belligerent countries were now also warned against violating national airspace. In addition to this joint Nordic declaration, work began on plans for a regular Nordic defence cooperation. However, no consensus could be reached on this point. The strategic starting points of the individual countries were far too different. Meanwhile, the threat of war grew closer month by month.

The remainder of Czechoslovakia was occupied by Germany in March 1939. Memel was forced from Lithuania and the question of Danzig and the Polish corridor was raised. The other countries of the League of Nations protested each time to a greater or lesser degree.

43 Henrik S. Nissen, *Danmarks historie*, Gyldendal, vol. 7, *1914–45* (Aarhus: 1988), pp.347–48.

44 The artillery ship was a coastal service battleship armed with heavy artillery. The *mineskib* was an unusual combined minelayer and minesweeper

45 Johs. Lomholt-Thomsen, *Problemer i dansk politik 1901–1946* (Copenhagen: 1948), pp.199–200.

46 Jagd, Palle Bolten, *Danske forsvarsanlæg i 5.000 år*, Part III: *Efter 1932* (Rødovre: 1984), p.42.

In April, US President Roosevelt informed Hitler and Mussolini that Germany's behaviour over the past year was a threat to world peace and called on them to make declarations that they would not attack their neighbours, including the Nordic countries. Germany responded by offering the Nordic countries non-aggression pacts, among other things! Only Denmark was in favour of negotiating such an agreement, while the other countries refused. Sweden considered it a breach of neutrality if such an agreement was reached. However, when Denmark and Germany signed the agreement in Berlin on 31 May 1939, the other Nordic countries had indicated that they considered the agreement to be a contribution to Nordic stability.

Denmark added a clause stating that normal trade with third powers would not be in violation of the agreement. Denmark could therefore continue its trade with the United Kingdom during a new war.[47] They were well aware of how flimsy the signed agreement was, but this particular clause was important in the first phase of the war, when the German Foreign Ministry actually endeavoured to get the German Navy to refrain from attacks on Danish merchant ships.[48] During 1939, everyone realised that a great power conflict and probably war was brewing, therefore, most countries vigorously rearmed. In Denmark additional funds were also allocated to the military to speed up the procurement of equipment and supplies. Stockpiling of essential goods and measures to protect the civilian population against air raids were also rapidly implemented.[49]

As the situation became increasingly tense during the summer of 1939, Denmark kept a very low profile. Both the Danish press and the Danish military exercised a high degree of self-censorship. The question of whether the Danish straits should be kept open or sealed off depended entirely on which naval strategy Germany chose. A German offensive strategy would require free passage and possibly German support points on Danish territory. Denmark considered this situation to be the most dangerous for the country's neutrality, as the preconditions for this, as laid down in the Stockholm Declaration, would no longer apply. A German defensive strategy, on the other hand, would require the laying of guarded mine barrage rings in Danish waters and would probably lead to a situation similar to that during World War I. An attack by the western powers was considered out of the question, but their overflights of Denmark were a problem that could only be prevented to a limited extent.

When the Soviet Union also signed a non-aggression pact with Germany in August, everyone realised that war was imminent. A few days later, that war broke out when German troops entered Poland on 1 September.[50] Denmark immediately mobilised a contingency force of 36,000 men, and mine barrages were laid near Copenhagen. At the same time, minesweepers were activated in Øresund and Køge Bay. In organisational terms, the guard, watch and pilot service was placed under the Coastal Defence as an extraordinary

47 Erik Rasmussen, 'Velfærdsstaten på vej, 1913–1939' in *Danmarks Historie* vol. 13, (Copenhagen: Politikens forlag, 1965), p.470.

48 Henrik S. Nissen, *Danmarks historie*, Gyldendal, vol. 7, *1914–45* (Aarhus: 1988), p.350.

49 Erik Rasmussen, 'Velfærdsstaten på vej, 1913–1939' in *Danmarks Historie* vol. 13, (Copenhagen: Politikens forlag, 1965), p.471.

50 Henrik S. Nissen, *Danmarks historie*, Gyldendal, vol. 7, *1914–45* (Aarhus: 1988), p.352

military measure.[51] When the United Kingdom and France became involved in the war on 3 September, the Danish Government hoped that it would be able to conduct the same kind of neutrality policy as during World War I. But in Germany, conditions were not the same as in 1914.

51 Jagd, Palle Bolten, *Danske forsvarsanlæg i 5.000 år*, Part III: *Efter 1932* (Rødovre: 1984), p.43.

Chapter 3

3.1 Germany's Naval Rearmament and British Countermeasures, 1918–1939

When the armistice was signed on 11 November 1918, Germany agreed to surrender most of its fleet to the victors. The United Kingdom took over the German ships and took them to the Royal Navy's main base at Scapa Flow in the Orkney Islands north of Scotland, where they would await their fate. However, on 21 June 1919, a few days before the peace treaty was signed, most German naval vessels were sunk by their crews, and the Imperial German Navy no longer existed.[1] The Treaty of Versailles did not allow Germany to possess a 'great power' fleet again. The treaty stated that Germany's navy in the future could consist of no more than:

6 *Deutschland* class liners[2]
6 Light cruisers
12 Destroyers
12 Torpedo boats or other vessels of similar size
400 (approx.) smaller support vessels including 300 minesweepers
0 Submarines
0 Aircraft for naval use

The navy's strength could not exceed 15,000 men, including a maximum of 1,500 officers. In comparison, there were approximately 83,000 men in the German Navy in 1914. The personnel was to consist of volunteers who committed to 12 years of service. As there were far more people who volunteered than could be enlisted, the navy was able to handpick the most suitable, which would later prove to be an advantage for the rebuilding of the navy. Germany was ordered to clear all mined areas in the North and Baltic Seas, a task that required the full efforts of 300 minesweepers for the following 3 years. In Danish waters alone, almost 10,000 mines were found and neutralised during and after the end of World War I. The crews from the minesweepers thus formed the backbone of the new German

1 J. Østrup (ed.), *Illustreret Verdenshistorie*, Vol. 6, Our time (Copenhagen: 1927), p.308.

2 These ships were built around 1900 and were 13,600 tons while the ships that would later replace them could not exceed 10,000 tons. The victorious powers set their own battleships to a maximum size of 35,000 tons.

Navy.[3] Despite a major mine sweeping effort, both German and Danish, loose, drifting mines in the Baltic Sea remained an ever-present danger until 1924.[4]

The victorious powers held a disarmament conference in Washington in January 1922 and determined the future limits for the size of their respective fleets. At that time, Germany had not yet reached the upper limit, as the fleet still only consisted of 2 older ships of the line, 2 light cruisers, 20 torpedo boats and the aforementioned 300 minesweepers, of which the cruisers, torpedo boats and about half of the minesweepers should have been replaced by newbuilds long ago.[5] Although Germany did not yet need to increase the upper limit on the size of its navy, the government still demanded that it be put on an equal footing with the other superpowers. Whether this was to be achieved through German rearmament or the disarmament of the other great powers was, in principle, secondary. This could not yet be agreed upon at the conference. However, one of the agreements reached in Washington had a major impact on German naval construction, as it was decided to calculate the displacement of ships based on the amount of water displaced by an empty ship. German designers had previously used the displacement calculation method, which calculated the weight of water displaced by a fully equipped ship, including fuel, ammunition, water in the boilers and so on. The introduction of the new so-called 'Washington displacement' thus meant a real increase of about 25 percent of the previously determined tonnage.[6]

When arguing for the justification of a relatively strong navy, the Germans referred to the need to secure the sea link between Germany and East Prussia, which, by the Treaty of Versailles, had been separated by 'the Polish corridor'. This was seen as the primary task of the navy. In the longer term, greater emphasis would be placed on mine warfare, which had proved to be of great importance in naval warfare during World War I. As it was France and Poland that Germany considered to be its main potential enemies in the early interwar years, the navy needed to secure the sea routes to and from the North and Baltic Seas, while also keeping the French Fleet at bay in the Atlantic, as there was an alliance agreement between these two countries.[7]

In order to check whether Germany was complying with the conditions, the victorious powers had decided that warships could only be built in two specific shipyards with limited capacity. But throughout the 1920s, and even more so in the 1930s, the German military leadership circumvented these restrictions. Almost before the ink was dry on the Treaty of Versailles, Germany was already working to secure vast knowledge and expertise in building U-boats for future use. In 1922, under the guise of an apparent Dutch shipping company, a 'Submarine Development Bureau' was set up to employ the best German submarine designers. Submarines were allegedly built for Spain, Turkey and Finland, and German sailors were in charge of the 'sea trials'. When the Anglo-German Naval Treaty of 1935 again allowed Germany to build U-boats up to parity

3 Rolf Bensel, *Die Deutsche Flottenpolitik von 1933 bis 1939* (Berlin: 1958), p.6; Kurt Assmann, *Deutsche Seestrategie in zwei Weltkriegen* (Heidelberg: 1957), p.102.

4 J. Østrup (ed.), *Illustreret Verdenshistorie*, vol. 6, Our time (Copenhagen: 1927), p.316.

5 Rolf Bensel, *Die Deutsche Flottenpolitik von 1933 bis 1939* (Berlin: 1958), p.7.

6 Kurt Assmann, *Deutsche Seestrategie in zwei Weltkriegen* (Heidelberg: 1957), p.107.

7 Rolf Bensel, *Die Deutsche Flottenpolitik von 1933 bis 1939* (Berlin: 1958), pp.8–9; Kurt Assmann, *Deutsche Seestrategie in zwei Weltkriegen* (Heidelberg: 1957), p.104.

with Britain, plans for the German Navy's new U-boat organisation were already well advanced. Parts to assemble several U-boats were secretly stored in various warehouses, ready to be assembled when needed. The first small coastal submarine (*U1*) was actually launched on the day before the naval agreement was signed. Together with the Swedish and Spanish navies, a new type of torpedo was developed in 1927. In order to train future U-boat crews, in 1932 the German Navy set up a training centre under the guise of an anti-submarine warfare school![8]

In recent years, a lot of new information has emerged about how Germany circumvented the provisions of the Treaty of Versailles in this way. It may seem strange that the controlling powers did not devote more resources to keeping an eye on the German armaments industry. Mainly due to a conservative and professionally ineffective intelligence service, they did not realise that they had been deceived until it was too late. Part of the explanation for the poor British intelligence seems to be the internal rivalry between the Royal Navy and the Royal Air Force over the allocation of military resources throughout the 1930s. At the same time, all reports of the superiority of new German weapons over British ones were arrogantly dismissed as myths with no basis in reality.[9]

Germany still wanted a revision of the treaty provisions in order to equalise the naval forces of the great powers. As a last resort, it threatened to revise its own naval expansion plans and refuse to participate in future disarmament treaties. At a disarmament conference in December 1932, Britain, France, the USA and Italy therefore recognised Germany's demand for equality in order to keep the country in the ongoing efforts to establish a joint disarmament programme.[10]

In 1933, Hitler came to power and from this point on, the rearmament of Germany gained momentum. One of the Nazis' programme points was a total rejection of what they called the 'Versailles Diktat' and before long, Germany withdrew from the League of Nations. The existing disarmament agreements then became more or less worthless, as there no longer seemed to be any sanctions against Germany.

As Poland and France, and later the Soviet Union, were considered to be Germany's potential main adversaries, the greatest emphasis in the period 1933–1938 was placed on the development of surface ships. The strategy in a war situation was still to keep the French Fleet in the Atlantic and, above all, secure the passage routes to and from the North and Baltic Seas. The larger warships were therefore built with a relatively shallow draught, which made them especially useful for operations in the Western Baltic Sea, Kattegat and Skagerrak. While both the Polish and French Armies posed the greatest threat to Germany on land, it was the French navy that was the main adversary at sea. Both the Polish and Soviet Navies were relatively weak, the latter not least because it was spread across three seas: the Black Sea, the Baltic Sea and the Pacific Ocean.[11]

8 Rolf Bensel, *Die Deutsche Flottenpolitik von 1933 bis 1939* (Berlin: 1958), pp.11–12. John Barratt: 'Rebirth of the U-boat' 2002 <http://www.militaryhistoryonline.com/wwii/atlantic/uboat.aspx>.

9 F. H. Hinsley, *British Intelligence in The Second World War* (Cambridge: Cambridge University Press, 1979), vol. 2, p.77.

10 Ole Helmer Jensen, *Anden Verdenskrig. Hvornår-skete-det* (Copenhagen: 1968), p.15.

11 Rolf Bensel, *Die Deutsche Flottenpolitik von 1933 bis 1939* (Berlin: 1958), pp.32–33.

In June 1935, the German fleet consisted of: 3 armoured ships,[12] 3 heavy cruisers, 6 light cruisers, 12 torpedo boats, 3 minelayers, 16 minesweepers, 5 troop transport ships and 20 smaller training and special vessels. In addition, 14 submarines were completed before the end of the year. Precisely because the naval strategy was aimed at control of access and confronting the French Fleet, the building of U-boats was prioritised lower than surface vessels. In the period from 1935 to the outbreak of war in September 1939, only a total of 57 U-boats were produced, in comparison to the following 5-year period, when approximately 1,100 U-boats were produced.[13]

For Hitler, a war with Britain at this time was unthinkable. On the contrary, 1935 saw a rapprochement between the two countries, which came as a surprise to many. In March, Hitler proclaimed that Germany once again had an air force and that conscription had been reintroduced, a clear break with the Treaty of Versailles. In response to this German move, delegates from England, France and Italy met in the northern Italian town of Stresa, later called the 'Stresa Front', to discuss what to do about this German treaty violation. It was agreed to condemn the German action under the auspices of the League of Nations. This in itself was a rather toothless reaction that only confirmed Hitler in his belief that he could safely and without risk proceed with his plans. With the formation of the Berlin-Rome Axis the following year, any value of the condemnation lapsed.

Influenced by developments in Germany, France and the Soviet Union signed a pact on mutual military aid in the spring, which was one of the reasons why Britain accepted a German proposal for an Anglo-German naval negotiation. For centuries, one of the cornerstones of Britain's foreign policy was to secure a military balance of power in Europe. Germany offered to limit its navy size to 35 percent of Britain's to end the ever-escalating arms race between the two countries. Britain looked favourably on this proposal, not least because ending the arms race could save a lot of money on the strained state budget. The agreement was therefore signed on 18 June 1935. Germany was to have a fleet tonnage of 35 percent of that of the British Fleet, and the ratio between the number of German and British ships in each ship class/type was to be 35:100, except for submarines, where the United Kingdom had a ratio of 45:100. Germany had demanded parity, and the possibility was opened for Germany to raise this ratio at a later date, but only after new negotiations between the two countries.

For Britain, the agreement provided a welcome opportunity for a temporary slowdown in rearmament and a sense of having re-established some form of control over the build-up of the German fleet. For Germany, the agreement meant an increase in tonnage to four times the previous limits. This was effectively removing any limitation, as it would take Germany at least 10 years to reach this goal.[14]

---

12 *Panzerschiffe*, D-class heavy cruisers. Classified as *panzerschiffe* by the Reichsmarine and built in the early 1930s while Germany was still paying lip service to the limitations placed on their armed forces by the Treaty of Versailles. The *panzerschiffe* were initially built as replacements for the elderly pre-Dreadnoughts battleships that Germany had been permitted to retain. Limited to 10,000 tons displacement, it was assumed that the ships would be built as coastal defence ships, similar to those that some of the Scandinavian navies possessed, such as the Danish Artillery ship.

13 Rolf Bensel, *Die Deutsche Flottenpolitik von 1933 bis 1939* (Berlin: 1958), pp.33 and p.38; Kurt Assmann, *Deutsche Seestrategie in zwei Weltkriegen* (Heidelberg: 1957), p.171–172.

14 Rolf Bensel, *Die Deutsche Flottenpolitik von 1933 bis 1939* (Berlin: 1958), pp.30–31; Kurt Assmann, *Deutsche Seestrategie in zwei Weltkriegen* (Heidelberg: 1957), pp.117–118.

Germany reoccupied the Rhineland on 7 March 1936, again breaking the existing treaties. France immediately considered sending troops into Germany, but hesitated, partly due to domestic political unrest and partly due to a lack of support from Britain. However, Hitler's repeated breaches of the treaties encouraged France and Britain to form a real military alliance.

On 25 March 1936, Britain, the US and France held a naval conference in London. Under the fact of the German invasion of the Rhineland, it was agreed to stop disarmament by removing the restrictions adopted at the Washington Conference in 1922 and freeing the individual powers from them. The only requirements were to comply with the stipulated maximum tonnage sizes for the individual ship types, for example battleships could not exceed 35,000 GRT, and to inform the other great powers each year of the increase in their respective fleets.[15] For Germany, the authorised tonnage sizes were still smaller than for the other great powers. However, as the London Agreement led to a sharp increase in naval construction in the United Kingdom, Germany, by virtue of the 35:100 principle, also increased its authorised tonnage.[16]

Germany and the United Kingdom negotiated another naval agreement in 1937, and the British explained the agreements made the year before. It was announced that the United Kingdom would nevertheless expand its fleet further, and that this was therefore of importance for a possible German expansion. It was agreed that Germany would continue to provide the other great powers with an annual report on additions to the fleet.[17]

Hitler was still convinced that Germany would not go to war with Britain. Despite the growing tension in Europe, as Germany broke one agreement after another and all the great powers prepared for a test of strength, until the summer of 1938 there were no German plans for a possible war with Britain. On the contrary, the German Navy had until then been strictly forbidden to launch any exercises or war games that operated with the British Navy as an opponent. The United Kingdom's weak reaction to the latest German proposals convinced Hitler that the she would continue to stay in the background.[18]

Germany's invasion of Austria in March 1938 and the escalation of the Sudetenland question during the summer prompted Hitler to begin drawing up plans for a naval war with Britain. Although the outcome of the Munich Agreement in September that year was a total political and military victory for Hitler, as German troops occupied the Sudetenland without a fight in early October and Germany signed a friendship treaty with France in December, there were still new, more threatening murmurs coming from Britain. During the autumn of 1938, the German naval leadership conducted the first war games, based on a confrontation between Germany-Italy and England-France, with the naval forces that the respective countries would have at their disposal in 1943.[19] It was expected, and hoped, that war would not break out sooner.

15 Rolf Bensel, *Die Deutsche Flottenpolitik von 1933 bis 1939* (Berlin: 1958), p.39.
16 Kurt Assmann, *Deutsche Seestrategie in zwei Weltkriegen* (Heidelberg: 1957), p.119
17 Rolf Bensel, *Die Deutsche Flottenpolitik von 1933 bis 1939* (Berlin: 1958), p.41.
18 Rolf Bensel, *Die Deutsche Flottenpolitik von 1933 bis 1939* (Berlin: 1958), pp.42 and 49; Kurt Assmann, *Deutsche Seestrategie in zwei Weltkriegen* (Heidelberg: 1957), p.120.
19 Rolf Bensel, *Die Deutsche Flottenpolitik von 1933 bis 1939* (Berlin: 1958), p.52.

Hitler's realisation that Britain might still be a potential adversary led him to order a total change in naval planning. Firstly, a far greater number of U-boats were to be built and, in general, the rearmament of the navy was to be prioritised over both the army and air force. This was laid down in an order from Hitler in January 1939, when the so-called 'Z(iel) Plan' – the rearmament programme of the German Navy, was launched. According to this 6-year plan, firstly, battleships of 50,000–54,000 tons were to be built, while the number of naval vessels would rise to around 800 with a personnel strength of 200,000 men. Secondly, a completely new strategy had to be developed. Three tasks were identified that needed to be solved:

1. British naval and especially commercial traffic in coastal waters was to be attacked with mines and submarines.
2. On the open oceans, powerful forces consisting of surface ships and U-boat groups would attack Britain's sea trade routes. This would force Britain to reinforce the defence of the convoys and simultaneously defeat them with special super battleships, aircraft carriers and their escort of cruisers and destroyers.
3. In the North Sea, only a contingency and training fleet was to be kept that could force Britain to commit a significant force in and around these waters.[20]

By occupying Czechoslovakia in March 1939, Germany broke the Munich Agreement and in late April Hitler declared the 1937 Anglo-German Naval Agreement cancelled. Both France and Britain now realised that more force had to be put behind any future negotiations. Britain introduced conscription and both countries increased rearmament. They tried to make a deal with the Soviet Union, which failed. Surprisingly, it was Germany instead that signed a non-aggression pact with the Soviet Union in August.

As early as spring 1939, everyone realised that German political pressure on Poland would ultimately become the next opportunity for confrontation between the two alliance blocs. During the summer, the armament reached its preliminary peak and the tension grew during August. Despite a strong diplomatic effort by the British to negotiate a solution to the problem of the German demand for possession of Danzig and a traffic connection through the 'Polish corridor', it still ended with a German invasion of Poland on 1 September. Two days later, the War was a reality.

Hitler did not understand why Britain entered the war and hoped until the last days of August that it would not happen, and at the outbreak of war, Germany was not yet ready to fight a war against Britain. There were no finalised plans for such a war and the military build-up had not been completed, especially not for the navy. The Commander-in-Chief of the German Navy, *Grossadmiral* Raeder, expressed his opinion on this to Hitler:

> In this war, which broke out about eight years before we could have built the 35 percent according to the fleet treaty of 18 June 1935 –the little that is ready, or ready for war, can only go down fighting gallantly.[21]

20 Rolf Bensel, *Die Deutsche Flottenpolitik von 1933 bis 1939* (Berlin: 1958), pp.56–57.
21 Rolf Bensel, *Die Deutsche Flottenpolitik von 1933 bis 1939* (Berlin: 1958), pp.67–68.

3.2 Britain's Naval Policy Towards Germany, 1933–1939

After 1918, Britain embarked on a general disarmament programme in full accordance with one of the main objectives of the League of Nations. In 1919, the British armed forces were instructed to plan ahead on the assumption that the British Empire would not be involved in a major war within the next 10 years.[22] For the Royal Air Force (RAF), for example, this meant that by 1920 the number of aircraft had been reduced to a tenth of the 1918 strength. British foreign policy in the 1920s was primarily concerned with limiting Britain's commitments to countries in Continental Europe and East Asia. At the disarmament conference in Washington in 1922, the British accepted the United States as an equal naval power and, as a consequence, the British position of power in relation to Japan was downgraded, with the US now occupying a similar position of power to the UK in the Far East.[23]

Despite the cutbacks, the Royal Navy was still an important instrument of Britain's military power in interwar Europe. But in the long run, the 10-year rule meant that the naval force that had existed during the Great War could not easily be replaced. The trend of the time was against allocations for military purposes and at the same time, disarmament conferences put a cap on the size of the navy. Around 1930, the age of the ships began to show in the form of increased repairs and weaker performance in terms of speed and manoeuvrability. Most ships were pre-1914 and in need of replacement. The shipbuilding industry was shrinking and a well-trained workforce of shipyard labourers was disappearing into other trades. The Admiralty searched high and low for a way to release the fleet from the 10-year rule.

This way out came when Japanese troops moved into Manchuria in 1932. The British Defence Staff immediately warned the British Government that if Japan directed its aggression against British possessions in the Far East, the navy could not, on the present basis, do anything to prevent this. The Defence Staff was released from the 10-year rule – but no alternative defence policy was outlined, nor were increased funds allocated for military purposes.[24] The British Government contacted the US Government and referred to the Washington Agreements of 1922, in which the US committed itself to ensuring the integrity and security of China in the future. The US referred to the issue as a League of Nations decision. In the end, neither side felt obliged to take any military sanction against Japan, a position that convinced the Japanese military leadership that further expansion would likely bring the same weak response from the major powers.[25]

Hitler's rise to power in Germany in 1933 was, for the British Admiralty, the wrong crisis at the wrong time. Over the next 18 months, Britain's foreign policy strategy was completely reorganised and Germany replaced Japan as the biggest potential danger to Britain. Although the navy had traditionally been the 'Shield of the Empire', it was now the

22 Dr Adrian Preston, *General Staffs and Diplomacy before the Second World War* (London: Routledge, 1978), pp.103–104.

23 Sven Henningsen, *Det tyvende århundrede*, vol. 2 *1930–1945* (Odense: 1972), p.156; Chaz Bowyer, *Royal Air Force Handbook, 1939–1945* (Worthing: Littlehampton Book Services, 1984), p.4.

24 Wesley K. Wark, *The Ultimate Enemy. British Intelligence and Nazi Germany 1933–1939* (Oxford: OUP, 1985), pp.126–127.

25 Sven Henningsen, *Det tyvende århundrede*, vol. 2 *1930–1945* (Odense: 1972), p.171.

RAF that the public and politicians relied on as the cornerstone of British defence.[26] This reprioritisation naturally had an impact on the defence budget, with the RAF leadership having to increase activity beyond the already budgeted expansion plan, while the army and navy had to bear further cuts.[27]

The Admiralty, in view of the navy's responsibility for the defence of the Empire's possessions, was soberly correct in maintaining that Japan still posed the greatest threat to Britain. In the early 1930s, Germany could not be considered a potential military threat. By 1933, Germany had not even brought its navy up to the strength that had been authorised by the Treaty of Versailles. The only modern naval vessels were 5 light cruisers and 12 torpedo boats. The secret German rearmament was apparently still unknown to the British. It may seem strange, for example, that Britain was unaware of the German arms purchases in Russia, as France, through the military agreement with Russia, was aware of them and even complained about them at the disarmament conference of December 1932.[28] Thus, until 1935, the weak German Navy only posed a threat to the British naval budget. The powerful First Sea Lord, Admiral Chatfield, who also held the important post of Chairman of the Defence Staff from 1933 to 1938, struggled to convince politicians that Japan, not Germany, was the main enemy. Chatfield could not see what interest Britain could have in getting involved in a European conflict. The Admiralty took German assurances that the German naval building programme was not aimed at Britain at face value and tried to convince the government of the same.[29]

After Germany's withdrawal from the League of Nations and the unsuccessful conference in Geneva in 1934, disarmament was over. Britain's naval power was at its lowest in 1934–1935: the main fleet was greatly reduced and age-weakened, so rapid manoeuvres were impossible. The naval air force had been greatly reduced and naval bases were not of sufficient size.[30] In the spring of 1934, the British Prime Minister, Neville Chamberlain, proposed further drastic cuts to the army and navy budgets and increased the RAF's expansion programme. Bombers were to become the main defence against any German military threat.

The Chancellor of the Exchequer supported the Prime Minister, justifying the cuts to the naval budget on the grounds that Britain simply could not afford to confront two enemy powers at once and that Germany should be prioritised as the potential main enemy over Japan. There was no point in investing in the defence of the Empire's possessions in the Far East if the mother country itself was threatened. Admiral Chatfield responded by accusing the Prime Minister of both single-handedly creating a new and weaker basis for the Empire's defence, and at the same time gambling on the cheapest way to maintain it without losing face to the rest of the world. This was one of the reasons why the navy ultimately avoided the announced cuts, as it wanted to await the outcome of the International Naval Conference that was scheduled to be held in London in 1936.[31]

26 National Archives, CAB 16/110, Cipher 205(34), 31 July 1934.

27 Wesley K. Wark, *The Ultimate Enemy. British Intelligence and Nazi Germany 1933–1939* (Oxford: OUP, 1985), p.127.

28 Sven Henningsen, *Det tyvende århundrede*, vol. 2 *1930–1945* (Odense: 1972), p.175.

29 Wesley K. Wark, *The Ultimate Enemy. British Intelligence and Nazi Germany 1933–1939* (Oxford: OUP, 1985), p.128.

30 Max Werner, *The Military Strength of The Powers* (London: Victor Gollancz, 1939), p.235

31 Wesley K. Wark, *The Ultimate Enemy. British Intelligence and Nazi Germany 1933–1939* (Oxford: OUP, 1985), p.129.

In 1935 came a decisive and unexpected turning point for the British Navy: the conclusion of the Anglo-German Naval Treaty and Italy's demand that Britain recognise the Mediterranean as an Italian possession. From the end of 1934, Germany had begun sending feelers to the United Kingdom in an attempt to reach a naval agreement. The German arguments, put forward by *Admiral* Raeder and Hitler, centred on the advantage Britain would gain by allowing a small but strong German fleet, whose main purpose was to achieve dominance in the Baltic. At the same time, through a peaceful agreement with Germany, Britain would be able to concentrate its strength in the East and regain its place as the leading naval power there. German assurances that a German naval build-up would never be directed against the United Kingdom were also used as an argument, assurances that would be repeated many times over the following five years.[32]

In the spring of 1935, as previously mentioned, Germany proclaimed the introduction of universal conscription and the creation of an air force. Both actions were against the terms of Versailles. However, the Stresa Front's disagreements over sanctions and the Franco-Soviet agreements contributed to the British Admiralty taking an interest in the German offer. Two Admiralty departments, the Plans Division and the Naval Intelligence Division (NID), were independently assigned to analyse the German proposal. Of the two, the Plans Division's judgement was given the most weight, as the NID had suffered from repeated cutbacks since World War I and had therefore been reduced to a minimum. The modest resources still available to NID were mainly directed towards Japan. The consequence of this was clear – they were completely unaware of how far the German naval armament had progressed. The main source in Germany was the British naval attaché in Berlin, and he received only the most necessary and mostly essential information from the German naval leadership. One of the British motives was therefore to obtain more accurate information. The Plans Division estimated that in 1939 Germany would have 5 large ships and 10 U-boats. It therefore came as something of a shock when *Admiral* Raeder announced in April 1935 that Germany was already building 12 U-boats. However, there was no doubt that Hitler and Raeder meant it when they emphasised to the British that the German Navy would never be directed against the United Kingdom and that the main purpose of the naval build-up was to achieve dominance in the Baltic Sea. Plans Division also convinced the Admiralty that it was not physically possible for Germany to fulfil the 35 percent quota of the British Fleet until sometime in 1943. The German demand for a naval force in the ratio 100:35 should thus be seen as a question of Germany's right to possess a fleet of a reasonable size rather than a real goal for the German naval armament. The British arguments in favour of the agreement were thus mainly based on:

1. A desire to gain better insight into the structure of the German Navy.
2. The conviction that the German fleet would not be directed against England.
3. A hope that they could once again concentrate on keeping Japan at bay.
4. A desire to reach an arms agreement with Germany that could pave the way for a similar agreement regarding the air force, which was considered crucial by politicians and large sections of the military.

32 Wesley K. Wark, *The Ultimate Enemy. British Intelligence and Nazi Germany 1933–1939* (Oxford: OUP, 1985), pp.130–131.

5. The desire to bring Germany back into the League of Nations.
6. The desire to limit the cost of rearmament.
7. The desire to re-establish the balance of power in mainland Europe in light of the Franco-Soviet military agreement.

However, what was not considered when the naval agreement was signed on 18 June 1935 was that it would weaken the Stresa Front, as France and Italy would probably resent the Anglo-German agreement. Moreover, no thought had been given to the strategic situation that would arise if a third potential enemy naval power, Italy, appeared. In the naval agreement with Germany, Britain's ship tonnage was locked at the 1935 level, which was in accordance with the Washington Agreement, and could not be changed until negotiations were resumed at the naval conference in London in 1936. This could mean that by then the Royal Navy had been overtaken in strength by the potential adversaries, Japan and Italy. Finally, it had not occurred to the British negotiators that they had so far not succeeded in creating a correct picture of German naval construction and that, despite the naval agreement, they would not necessarily get the correct information from Germany. No actual control system had been agreed. Germany had simply committed to submitting an annual report on the number of newly built ships, including information on ship type, size and armouring.[33]

The German invasion and reoccupation of the Rhineland on 7 March 1936 naturally influenced the outcome of the naval conference in London 18 days later. The participants, England, the United States and France, agreed to lift the previously set limit on the three countries' naval tonnage. However, in order to limit qualitative armament, the limits on the size and armament of individual ship types were retained. The agreement, which was to last until the end of 1942, was weakened by a new addendum that made a reservation in case other countries exceeded these limits or built new types. For example, the United Kingdom suspended the maximum limit of 35,000 tons for battleships when it learnt of the latest Japanese building plans in 1938. The contracting countries were to inform each other about tonnage additions in an annual report.[34]

The fact that the German occupation of the Rhineland, which was a clear breach of the Locarno Agreement, did not have consequences for Germany in the form of military or other sanctions, was because the contracting powers were divided. Immediately after the invasion, Hitler had offered the Locarno powers a new security system based on non-aggression treaties, air force agreements and Germany's re-entry into the League of Nations. Britain was convinced that this was a serious offer. France, seeing a chance to remove some of the threat of a future strong German Air Force, was not dismissive either, especially after Britain had expressed a positive attitude towards Hitler's proposal. However, when Britain sent out feelers in May to press the German offer, they were rebuffed. Hitler had achieved his objective: to take the sting out of any joint sanctions by the Locarno powers.[35]

33 Dr Adrian Preston, *General Staffs and Diplomacy before the Second World War* (London: Routledge, 1978), p.111; Wesley K. Wark, *The Ultimate Enemy. British Intelligence and Nazi Germany 1933–1939* (Oxford: OUP, 1985), pp.132–133 & 138–139.

34 Sven Henningsen, *Det tyvende århundrede*, vol. 2 *1930–1945* (Odense: 1972), p.219; Kurt Assmann, *Deutsche Seestrategie in zwei Weltkriegen* (Heidelberg: 1957), p.119.

35 Sven Henningsen, *Det tyvende århundrede*, vol. 2 *1930–1945* (Odense: 1972), pp.220 & 222.

What really set the British naval construction in motion was not the German breach of the treaty, but the proclamation of the Rome-Berlin Axis on 1 November 1936. At the same time, Mussolini demanded that the United Kingdom recognise the Mediterranean as an Italian sea, as, according to the Italian dictator, it was only a passage for England. As the Italian Fleet posed a much greater threat to British naval supremacy than the German, this was a serious statement in the eyes of the British Admiralty. Italy was putting pressure on the 'lifeline of Empire' as it was called in England, a route now secured by naval bases in Gibraltar, Malta, Cyprus and Alexandria. Britain might need to send a larger naval force to the Mediterranean to emphasise its interests in freedom of navigation and thereby reduce the force that it might have to face Germany. A building programme for the fleet was hastily organised. While 139,000 tons of ships were built in 1934 and 376,000 tons in 1936, a total of 547,000 tons were built in 1937.[36]

Large parts of the British Fleet were gradually replaced. The increase in total tonnage resulted in an increase in the German maximum, following the 100:35 strength ratio of the Anglo-German Naval Agreement. However, as the British Admiralty did not doubt that Germany would honour its part of the agreement in the period 1935–1939, they did not see a problem with this.

When they trusted the German information, they did not put much effort into the NID maritime intelligence service. The fact that wishful thinking should not have prevailed to such an extent was only realised at the outbreak of war, and for some ships even later. For example, in July 1936, Germany announced that it had started building a battleship of 35,000 tons that would be equipped with 15-inch guns. In reality, it was a battleship of 41,000 tons which was only discovered when the Royal Navy sank the ship in May 1941, now under the name *Bismarck* and equipped with eight 15-inch guns! The British had been informed of the correct deck width, which was somewhat larger than usual, and the relatively shallow draught of just under 9.5 metres, but this had only convinced them that the battleship was destined to operate in the Baltic Sea.

The interpretation of German naval strategy as a desire for dominance in the Baltic dominated the British Admiralty's thinking until the end of 1938. It was understood that it was important for Germany to:

1. Secure trade routes to the Nordic countries.
2. Maintain the communication link with East Prussia.
3. Prevent a military connection between France and Poland or France and the Soviet Union.
4. Be able to provide naval support for military operations in the Polish corridor or the three Baltic states.

They emphasised the German *Drang nach Osten* (Expansion to the East) and had not done any further studies into the role the German Navy should play according to Hitler and his naval commanders. Such studies of the 1930s German publications on naval strategy would have revealed a different picture.[37]

36 Max Werner, *The Military Strength of The Powers* (London: Victor Gollancz, 1939), pp.236–237; Sven Henningsen, *Det tyvende århundrede*, vol. 2 *1930–1945* (Odense: 1972), p.337.

37 Wesley K. Wark, *The Ultimate Enemy. British Intelligence and Nazi Germany 1933–1939* (Oxford: OUP, 1985), pp.141–142.

Even when Germany annexed Austria in March 1938, and six months later occupied Sudetenland, the British Admiralty maintained the belief that the Anglo-German Naval Agreement was a guarantee of European security. What they failed to realise was that Hitler's expansionist urge was primarily directed against Germany's immediate neighbours, where the army and air force were the most important weapons and Germany therefore did not need a strong navy.

However, there were signs in the United Kingdom that the faith in German intentions was beginning to waver. After the German invasion of Austria, Hermann Göring, the man in charge of Germany's economy and *Oberbefehlshaber der Luftwaffe* (Supreme Commander of the Air Force), warned the British Ambassador that if Britain took a hostile stance as a result of the events, Germany would build a navy the size of the British one. At first this threat was dismissed by the British Admiralty as a bluff – Germany did not have the shipyard capacity for such a project! Therefore, it was something of a shock, especially for the British naval leadership, when Germany informed the United Kingdom in December that it intended to take advantage of the opportunity to expand the U-boat tonnage to 100 percent of that of the United Kingdom, which was part of the naval agreement. At the same time, they would increase the armament of the German cruisers beyond the maximum stipulated in the agreement. The fact that this could not happen without prior negotiations between the two countries, as stipulated in the agreement, was completely ignored by the Germans.[38] The British Admiralty's faith in Germany's intentions of a dominion limited to the Baltic Sea began to crumble.

During the spring of 1939, events gathered momentum. Germany occupied Czechoslovakia in March, breaking the Munich Agreement. When Hitler cancelled the Anglo-German Naval Agreement at the end of April, the British naval leadership had to come to the same conclusion that the RAF and the army had reached three years earlier – that a conflict between the two countries was no longer unthinkable. The erroneous assumption about Hitler's intentions had been based solely on the size of the *Kriegsmarine*. The Royal Navy had failed to build a sufficiently effective intelligence service that might have detected German intentions at an earlier stage, and had failed to recognise the *Kriegsmarine*'s efforts to build up tonnage in an overall picture of German rearmament. The German Navy, like the British, had to compete with the other two services for resources in the form of raw materials, trained labour and financial means. Hitler's primary objectives, all of which were of a land-military nature, led to a de-prioritisation of the navy. It was little consolation that the German naval commander, *Admiral* Raeder, did not consider his navy even remotely suitable for a war against Britain.[39]

Within six months, the British Admiralty had to reassess the entire naval situation. They finally got around to studying the articles and books of German naval commanders from 1918–1939. One of the works studied with great interest was *Admiral* Wolfgang Wegener's *Die Seestrategie des Weltkriegs*,[40] as the book had been referred to as Hitler's 'naval bible' from several quarters. It was left to the British naval attaché in Berlin to prepare an annotated

38 Sven Henningsen, *Det tyvende århundrede*, vol. 2 *1930–1945* (Odense: 1972), p.280

39 Wesley K. Wark, *The Ultimate Enemy. British Intelligence and Nazi Germany 1933–1939* (Oxford: OUP, 1985), pp.152–153.

40 Admiral Wolfgang Wegener, *Die Seestrategie des Weltkriegs* (Berlin: E. S. Mittler & Sohn, 1929).

summary of the book. The result was a very precise account of Germany's path towards a strategic use of the fleet. According to Wegener, the German Navy during World War I should have launched a more intensive effort against the western powers' commercial traffic from the outbreak of the war, including occupying Denmark to gain a better starting position for the battle for supremacy in the North Sea. The British naval attaché pointed out, with reference to Wegener's book, that the larger German warships, including the cruisers, had a sufficient radius of action to operate in the Kattegat and along the Norwegian coast. In the final report, dated 15 May 1939, the attaché wrote about a possible German naval offensive:

> The capture of Bergen and Trondheim would not prove of insuperable difficulty and would make our task harder. The possibility of such operations to improve the 'geographic position' should not be overlooked.[41]

The statement prompted the Chief of Naval Intelligence, Admiral Godfrey, to add:

> Reports of German intentions to seize Skagen and Læsøo and the Norwegian fears concerning Stavanger aerodrome give colour to the views expressed.[42]

The realisation of German intentions regarding the strategic use of the fleet in the event of an Anglo-German conflict came very late – only three months before the outbreak of war!

3.3 'The Phoney War' and the Nordic Waters

Early in the morning of 1 September 1939, large German forces entered Poland. With the German attack, the Franco-British guarantee declaration came into effect. On the same afternoon, Britain sent a warning to Germany expressing its willingness to help Poland if German forces were not immediately withdrawn from Polish territory. The French position was somewhat weaker, proposing a symbolic German escape the following day, which was clearly rejected by the British, who demanded an immediate withdrawal. On 3 September at 09:00, an English ultimatum was delivered to Hitler, ordering German troops to withdraw from Polish territory within two hours, otherwise, Britain would consider itself at war with Germany.

Hitler, who until 30 August had hoped to keep Britain out of the conflict, realised that it was no longer possible to avoid a military confrontation with the Western Allied powers. The French ultimatum arrived at 12.00 and demanded a response by 17.00. At this point, Germany was at war with Poland, with the United Kingdom and with France. Apart from some regrouping and increased reconnaissance, the Anglo-French Army and Air Forces were not engaged in any significant warfare against Germany. The subsequent period of just over seven months is therefore called 'the Phoney War.'[43] It was only on the naval front that real fighting took place. The RAF's first action was an attack on the German

41 National Archives, ADM 1/9956 Naval Attaché Berlin to DNI, 15/5–1939

42 National Archives, ADM 1/9956 DNI Minute, 30/5–1939

43 The period has also been labelled as, 'The Strange War', '*Drôle de guerre*', 'The Lost War' and '*Sitzkrieg*', the latter as a parody of '*blitzkrieg*'.

naval base in Wilhelmshaven, but only minimal success was achieved with a loss of eight bombers. Thereafter, air operations were limited to dropping leaflets over Germany, attacks on U-boats and naval surface ships, but also without much success.

When the RAF only attacked naval targets during this period, it was mainly to avoid the risk of German retaliation against British cities, but also because they wanted to leave it to Germany to be the country that started the actual fighting. Many of these Western Allied directives may seem absurd today, and the fact that they deliberately left the initiative to Hitler may seem downright self-destructive in hindsight, as German victories depended on the blitzkrieg and the element of surprise. But for the governments of the two Western Allies, it was extremely important to gain time to build up the necessary war resources, including adapting industry to war production, and to remove any doubt in the minds of world opinion, especially in neutral countries, as to who was the aggressor.

The consequence of this restrained policy was that the war was largely fought at sea for the first six months, and here the Western Allies seemingly held the best cards. The navy was the weakest link in Germany's military structure, although during 1939 it was built up at an accelerated pace. The expansion of the German Navy had been hampered not only by the provisions of the Treaty of Versailles and later the Anglo-German Naval Agreement, but even more by the industrial and raw material requirements of the other two German services (see Chapter 2). Another significant brake on naval construction was Hitler's political and military strategy, which assumed that the war would be short and that the Western Allies, especially Britain, would keep out of the conflict. The naval programme had targeted Poland, the Soviet Union and France as potential adversaries and only during the last year before the actual outbreak of war was Britain included. By September 1939, Germany had not even reached the authorised tonnage under the Anglo-German Naval Agreement. On 3 September 1939, the total German naval strength, compared to the Anglo-French fleet, thus consisted of: [44]

Class	German Navy	Anglo-French Fleets
Battleships / Pocket Battleships / Battlecruisers[45]	5	25
Aircraft Carriers	0	8
Heavy Cruisers	2	33
Light Cruisers	6	81
Destroyers	22	212
Coastal Patrol / Escort Ships	0	38
Corvettes	8	8
Torpedo Boats	30	12
Motor Torpedo Boats	17	30
Minelayers[46]	0	11

44 Winston S Churchill, *Den Anden Verdenskrig*, (Copenhagen: 1948), vol. 1, p.526, Appendix 'A'

45 The term 'pocket battleship' refers to the three German capital ships of the *Deutschland* class: *Deutschland, Admiral Scheer* and *Admiral Graf Spee*. The designation is due to the ships' relatively small size compared to their relatively powerful armament.

46 Until the naval agreement in 1935, the German Navy did not have an actual minelaying vessel. In the event of war, mine laying was to be carried out by destroyers and torpedo boats. Most German warships could easily be fitted with mine laying equipment if necessary. This also applied to U-boats and other ships. In 1938, as part of the Z-plan, a total of four offensive minelayers with a capacity of 400 mines each were planned. Because of the outbreak of war the following year, they were never built.

Minesweepers	32	68
Submarines	57	135
Monitor ships	0	2
Gunboats, Submarine Chasers, other smaller warships	0	123

The so-called Z-plan for the expansion of the German Navy, which foresaw a war starting in 1944–1945, was cancelled and the German Navy concentrated on completing two large battleships and a heavy cruiser. In addition, the emphasis was placed on building U-boats. By 1939, capacity had been increased to construction of two U-boats per month.[47]

Despite this naval superiority, it was still not possible for the Western Allies to send naval forces to help Poland. Firstly, they had to cover several areas: the North Sea and the Atlantic in case of a German breakout attempt, the Mediterranean to counter a possible Italian threat, and finally, Britain could not afford to weaken its forces in the Far East because of the Japanese threat. Secondly, such a rescue operation would require a crossing of the Danish Straits and Belts, and it was considered too risky a venture, which, as during World War I, was rejected by the top military leadership.

However, this did not mean that all plans for a British naval campaign through Danish waters were cancelled. The newly appointed First Lord of the Admiralty (in effect, the British naval minister) had a plan.

3.4 Churchill and 'Operation Katarina'

On 17 September, Soviet troops moved into eastern Poland in accordance with the secret agreement with Germany. With this action, the Soviet Union was, to put it mildly, close to breaking its declared neutrality and the Western Allies were in great doubt as to what stance they should take towards the Soviet Union. The Prime Minister of the United Kingdom, Neville Chamberlain, argued in favour of a strong condemnation, but was opposed by the newly appointed First Lord of the Admiralty, Winston Churchill. He had been Secretary of State for the Navy from 1911–1915 and had played a key role in the development of Britain's naval strategy and naval rearmament in the run-up to World War I. When he urged the Western Allies to keep a low profile towards the Soviet Union, it was not out of love for the communist regime. On the contrary, during his time as Secretary of State for War 1919–1921, he had contributed greatly to British support for the White Russian armies fighting against the Bolsheviks. Like Chamberlain, he was anti-communist, but he was also a realist – and he had a plan.

During World War I, the Navy Secretary, Churchill, and First Sea Lord, Fisher, were two of the strongest advocates of British naval action into the Baltic Sea. Fisher's 'Baltic Project', which had appeared in various forms as early as 1905, was scrapped in January 1915 in favour of the Dardanelles offensive, but which ended in disaster. Then, in 1916–1917, Fisher's

Instead, ships such as the artillery training ships *Brummer* and *Bremse* and several merchant ships were equipped as minelayers. It was these minelayers, along with destroyers and light cruisers, that laid the first large fields of contact mines. Until 9 April, 1,000 magnetic mines were also laid, 68 of them from aircraft.

47 Sven Henningsen, *Det tyvende århundrede*, vol. 2 *1930–1945* (Odense: 1972), pp.322–323.

plans were reconsidered again at the highest level, but by this time Fisher was no longer First Sea Lord and the army's strong opposition to the project prevented its realisation.[48]

Similarly, in 1913 Churchill had several plans to open new fronts on the northern and southern flanks. The Dardanelles offensive was one of his many proposals for the latter. With a view to an offensive on the northern flank, he had commissioned the Admiralty to draw up plans to establish a naval base on the Danish coast. Initially, however, they did not dare to aim for more than Esbjerg and Læsø. Further incursions into Danish waters were considered too risky by the naval leadership. In 1914, however, Churchill proposed that plans be drawn up to send a regular naval force through Danish waters, combined with a landing operation in Schleswig-Holstein. Churchill's proposal also met strong opposition from the army and when both he and Fisher left their posts in May 1915, their proposals were effectively off the table.[49]

Now Britain was once again at war with Germany and Churchill had once again been appointed First Lord of the Admiralty. As in the last war, the Royal Navy's main tasks were blockade and convoy. This meant containing the German Fleet in the North Sea by blocking passage to the Atlantic and securing Britain's vital sea trade routes. However, this meant that the fleet was given a number of distinctly defensive tasks. Churchill believed this could pose a danger that Britain would slowly be forced to pursue a purely defensive naval strategy. He could not accept such a development and therefore looked for opportunities for more offensive tasks for the fleet, tasks that could counteract this trend and push Germany into the defensive role. If the German naval leadership were to speculate on where the British Fleet would strike next, it would tie up more German naval units in German harbours and thereby greatly relieve the large British naval forces assigned to protect the important supply convoys.[50] The 25-year-old plans were therefore taken out of the drawer and dusted off.

As early as 7 September, Churchill requested that a plan be drawn up for a British forcing of the passage to the Baltic Sea. The naval command's operations department immediately replied that such an action required Italy and Japan to remain neutral and that the threat from the *Luftwaffe* was considered a crucial obstacle to such an endeavour. However, more detailed planning of a naval action was begun with a view to its possible realisation by March 1940. Churchill had some ideas of his own and presented them to the Chief of Naval Construction, Sir Stanley Goodall, who immediately set about exploring their possibilities.

As early as 12 September, Churchill was able to issue a preliminary memorandum to the authorities concerned. He codenamed the operation 'plan Katarina' after Catherine the Great of Russia. This in itself revealed one of his intentions behind the plan. Non-aggression pact or not, no one, not even in the Soviet Union, was in any doubt that at some point a German-Soviet confrontation was bound to happen, the only question was when. By sending a large naval force into the Baltic Sea, sweeping away German dominance there and

48 Hans Branner, 'Østersøen og de danske stræder i engelsk krigsplanlægning 1904–14' in *Historie, Jyske Samlinger*, ny rk. IX, 1972, nr. 4, pp.510–512.

49 Tage Kaarsted, *Storbritannien og Danmark, 1914–1920* (Odense: 1974), pp.43–46; Shawn T. Grimes, *Strategy and War Planning in the British Navy, 1887–1918* (Martlesham: Boydell & Brewer, 2012), Chapter 6, pp.159–189.

50 Winston S Churchill, *Den Anden Verdenskrig*, (Copenhagen: 1948), vol. 1, p.365.

threatening Germany's northern flank, the Soviet Union could perhaps be 'lured' into the Western Allied camp at an early stage.[51]

The plan was to send 2 or 3 battleships of the *Royal Sovereign* class through the Skagerrak, Kattegat and Øresund to the Baltic Sea. The German minefields at the southern end of the strait were to be breached by a dozen 'minebreakers' – merchant ships with a reinforced bow that could withstand the pressure of a detonating mine.[52] In addition, the force, which was to pass down through the Sound in wake order, would also consist of a total of five cruisers, two flotillas of the strongest destroyers, a flotilla of submarines and a significant number of support ships, including armoured-deck tankers with fuel for the entire force for three months, depot ships and a workshop ship.

As neither Swedish nor Danish coastal batteries would pose any danger en route, only two major problems remained: the danger of German air attacks and the passage of the relatively shallow strait itself. By reinforcing the deck armour on the large battleships and providing a large number of anti-aircraft batteries on all ships, the German bombers could be kept at bay.

With a depth of around 8 metres in the Sound and a draught of around 9 metres for the battleships, more unconventional means had to be used to solve this problem. Churchill and Goodall had jointly come up with an ingeniously simple idea of providing the sides of the battleships with two layers of pontoons. These 'ballast tanks', which would increase the ships' width from 31 to 43 metres, could, when filled with air, raise the large battleships 3 metres above their normal waterline during the passage of the strait. The pontoons could then be filled with water, bringing the ships' waterline, and thus the side armour, down to normal level. At the same time, the pontoons would also act as an extra defence against German torpedoes. According to Churchill's preliminary calculations, 'Operation Katarina' could be launched as soon as the ice disappeared from Danish waters during March 1940.[53]

After reading Churchill's memoranda, the First Sea Lord, Admiral Pound, replied on 20 September that it was a clear precondition for the implementation of 'Operation Katarina' that the participating force would be dispensable regardless of the combination of opponents Britain might risk going to war with. He doubted that such a large expeditionary force would be available if Italy and Japan joined the war on Germany's side. A successful outcome of the action would also depend on the Soviet Union's continued neutral stance and the willingness of Norway and especially Sweden to cooperate with the UK. Access to Swedish harbours was considered vital for the maintenance of a British naval force in the Baltic. However, he was of the opinion that the possibilities of the plan should still be investigated further, and the next day a working group was set up for this purpose. After about a week's work, it concluded that the installation of the necessary pontoons on the battleships could

51 Winston S Churchill, *Den Anden Verdenskrig*, (Copenhagen: 1948), vol. 1, p.368.

52 The type of 'mine breakers' Churchill had in mind was very similar to the philosophy behind the German *Sperrbrechere*, namely extra-strength ships that could withstand destroying mines by detonating them without significantly damaging the ships. While Churhill's 'minebreakers' were intended to be used against anchor rope mines, contact mines, the German *Sperrbrecherne* were intended for bottom mines, distance mines.

53 Winston S Churchill, *Den Anden Verdenskrig*, (Copenhagen: 1948), vol. 1, pp.529–530, Appendix 'B' ('Plan Katarina').

not be completed until late spring 1940. The working group also considered it a minimum requirement that the planned expeditionary force should be further reinforced so that it had a superiority in strength of about 30 percent compared to the German Baltic Fleet, in order to avoid possible British losses during the passage to the Baltic Sea. After this message, the plan began to look less realistic.[54]

When the Soviet Union effectively seized control of the three Baltic states between 28 September and 10 October 1939, and attacked Finland on 30 November 1939, one of the main prerequisites for the implementation of 'Operation Katarina' was no longer present. From being 'unfriendly neutral', the Soviet Union was now close to direct war with the Western Allies, who immediately gave Finland their full support. Initially, however, only diplomatically and morally. It could not be expected that Sweden, whose harbours they had gambled on being able to use, would expose themselves to a German or even Soviet attack by helping the United Kingdom in this situation. Without British dominance in the Baltic Sea, a Swedish harbour could not be counted on as a base, and without one, there was no risk of naval action to achieve dominance. This strategic 'Gordian Knot' helped force Churchill to abandon his 'Operation Katarina.'[55] One of the purposes of sending a naval force into the Baltic Sea had been to stop German iron ore shipments from northern Sweden to Germany. The British naval leadership was now busy investigating how to stop this traffic by other means.

54 Winston S Churchill, *Den Anden Verdenskrig*, (Copenhagen: 1948), vol. 1, pp.368–369.
55 Winston S Churchill, *Den Anden Verdenskrig*, (Copenhagen: 1948), vol. 1, p.366.

Chapter 4

4.1 Magnetic Mines, 1918–1936

At some point around the outbreak of World War I, the idea arose that a magnetic or compass needle might be used in a naval mine detonation mechanism. Metals such as iron and steel are affected by the Earth's magnetic field. This 'soft' influence is always present and the strength of the field depends on the geographical position of the ship in relation to the poles, in other words, what latitude it is at.

When a ship made of iron or steel is built, the Earth's magnetism also causes a magnetic field to be 'knocked' into the hull, so to speak, during the machining of bolts and plates. In other words, the ship becomes a floating magnet in itself. The strength of each ship's own magnetic field depends on how the hull is positioned geographically in relation to the poles during construction.

The Earth's magnetic field acts in both the horizontal and vertical planes. The vertical effect is independent of where the ship is travelling, while the horizontal effect changes depending on the ship's course. The angle between the magnetic field lines and the horizontal plane is called the inclination, while the angle between the ship's course and one of the poles is called the declination.

At the end of the First World War, the Royal Navy (RN) succeeded in developing and manufacturing a bottom mine that was detonated by magnetic action. However, the mine was not the result of targeted research, but rather a 'side benefit' from a search for a type of mine that was independent of the changing tides. The trigger was based on the compass needle principle and was not very effective. The first mines were used in warfare in the summer of 1918 at the mouth of the River Scheldt off the Dutch coast and in Belgian waters off Zeebrugge and Ostend.[1] The mines were laid by surface ships in relatively small numbers and therefore resulted in only a few German casualties.[2] The *Kriegsmarine* had been working on the same idea, although they had not got very far. Only after it was discovered that the Royal Navy was using magnetic bottom mines was a mine testing commission set up in the autumn of 1918 to develop a German mine of the same type. Despite the diligent efforts of the highly qualified research team, a magnetic ignition system was not developed before the end of the war.

1 Gerhard Frhr. v. Ledebur, *Die Seemine* (Munich: 1977), p.86.
2 Friedrich Ruge, *Im Küstenvorfeld* (Munich: 1974), p.17

Graphical explanation of the principle of using magnetic bottom mines:

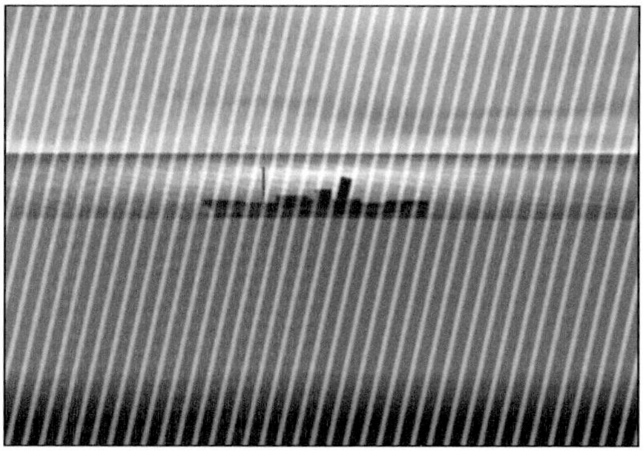

The Earth's magnetic field can be measured locally.

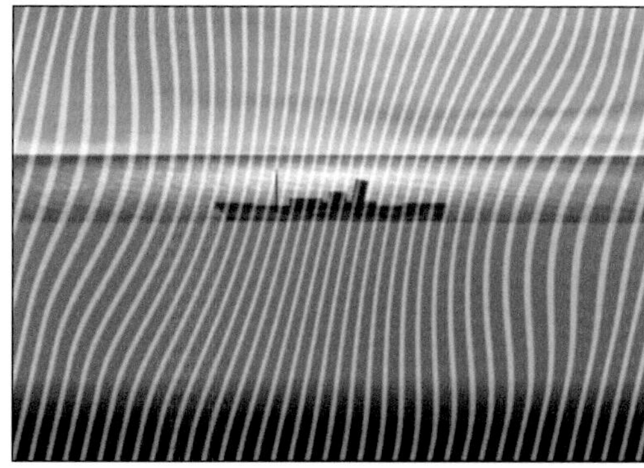

The ship's magnetic field briefly changes strength locally during the passage.

Magnetic fields are measured in milligauss – mg.

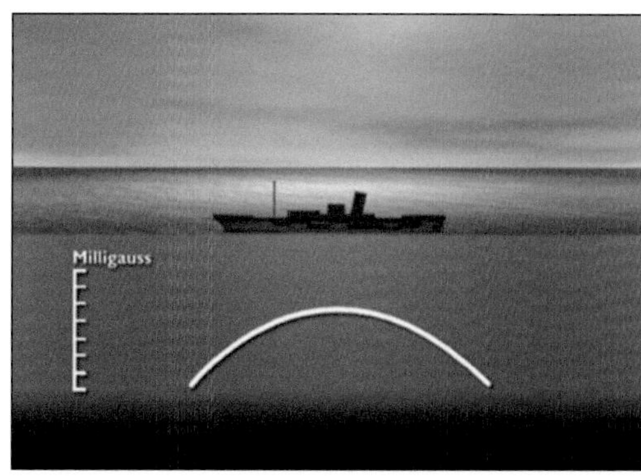

The magnetic effect of the passage can be read on a curve.

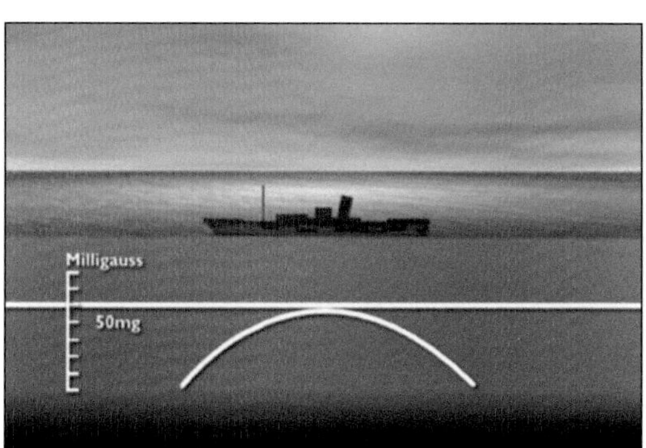

The mine detonates at the highest impact above a set value, for example 50mg.

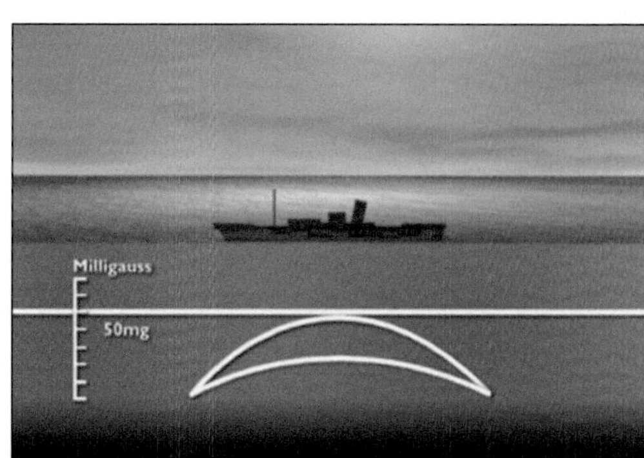

The ship's magnetic field should therefore be reduced to below this value, here 20mg.

As one of the Versailles peace terms, Germany had to accept a future naval mine capacity of no more than 35,000 mines.[3] In comparison, Germany had laid a total of 43,000 mines during the First World War.[4] With the already large stockpiles of naval mines Germany had at its disposal at the end of the war, the ceiling of 35,000 naval mines was reached in a relatively short time. As a result, all German development work in the field of mine warfare came to a virtual standstill. Only when a huge explosion in 1922 destroyed a large number of mines in *Minelager Groden* did the development of a magnetic sea mine pick up again.

The highly sensitive magnetic needles that both the British and Germans used in the mines were difficult to handle. On the one hand, they had to be able to detect even the slightest change in the surrounding magnetic field, and on the other hand, the mine had to be able to withstand quite rough treatment when being laid. This and several other problems were not solved until 1929, when the Germans' first magnetic mine was finally developed and tested.

The mine's cover name was *Reguläre Mine A* (RMA), while the magnetic ignition system itself was given the code name BIK. The word was not chosen at random, as the letters stood for *Balloninklinatorium*. This referred to the aluminium ball inside which the magnetic needle was placed and the fact that the mine was sensitive to changes in the vertical magnetic field, the inclination.[5]

Although Germany also had a number of magnetic bottom mines in the 1930s, there was a crucial difference between the British and German ignition mechanism at the time. In short, the German type of mine still worked on the compass needle principle, which was a further development of the first British type of mine, while the British had meanwhile switched to the induction coil principle.

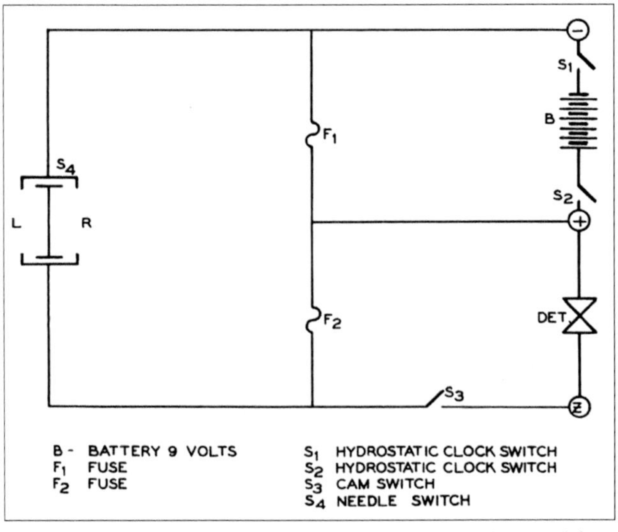

Diagram of the mechanism of the German M Mark IV Mine dropped from aircraft.[6]

3 Gerhard Frhr. v. Ledebur, *Die Seemine* (Munich: 1977), cf p.88.
4 Per Wessel Tolvig. Unpublished lecture to the Artillery Officers Association on 14 February 1955.
5 Friedrich Ruge, *Im Küstenvorfeld* (Munich: 1974), p.22
6 *Mine Disposal Handbook*, 1945 , was created by the US Navy Bomb Disposal School near the end of WW II. It covers all forms of underwater ordnance, not just mines. <https://maritime.org/doc/minedisposal/index.php#part3> (01.03.2025).

4.2 The German Bottom Mine Type RMA

German magnetic bottom mine type RMA. On display in the Muzeum Wojska Polskiego, Warsaw.

In the German RMA mine, a magnetic needle, approx. 4cm wide, 18cm long and 1mm thick, was suspended on a horizontal axis and placed in an aluminium ball. This 'light metal balloon' was designed to protect the magnetic needle from moisture and shock and to dampen the needle's movements. Around it was a detonator and an explosive charge of 800kg. The mine container itself was also made of aluminium. The entire mine weighed approximately 1,000kg.

When a ship passed near the mine and thereby affected the magnetic field around it, the needle would strike and hit a contact point, completing a circuit that activated the detonator. To prevent the needle from swinging round prematurely and triggering the detonation, a small spring was attached to the needle to slow down the impact. The needle could only reach the contact point when a sufficiently large magnetic force was applied. This first ignition system was labelled *Rotes BIK*. Although the needle was held back by the spring, it was conceivable that a ship could occasionally have such a strong magnetic field that the mine detonated prematurely. This is why a *Blaue BIK* was created, where the needle only hit the contact point on its way back to the starting position after the magnetic field had reached its maximum strength and weakened again. This detonated the mine as close to the ship as possible.

One of the weaknesses of the early BIK types was that you had to be very careful to set the mines according to the 'natural' inclination value of the target area. In the event of a misalignment, the mine could either detonate prematurely, sometimes during emplacement, or not at all. During 1940, the Germans solved this problem by developing a self-setting BIK (SE-BIK) that was equipped with a so-called latitude-degree corrector. Although a number of improvements were eventually introduced, such as a multi-needle version (M-BIK), the Germans maintained this basic magnetic needle principle in many of their mines throughout the war.[7]

4.3 The British Mine Type

The magnetic bottom mines laid by the British in the summer and autumn of 1918 were of the compass needle type. The Germans had more or less copied the basic principle of these mines, with the difference that the magnetic needle in the British mines was suspended

7 Gerhard Frhr. v. Ledebur, *Die Seemine* (Munich: 1977), pp.90–91.

on a horizontal axis, like a compass. However, in the interwar years, British weapons scientists moved on to develop a different and in many ways better system: the induction principle. The new trigger system was developed in 1936, when the Admiralty initiated a further development of the existing type.

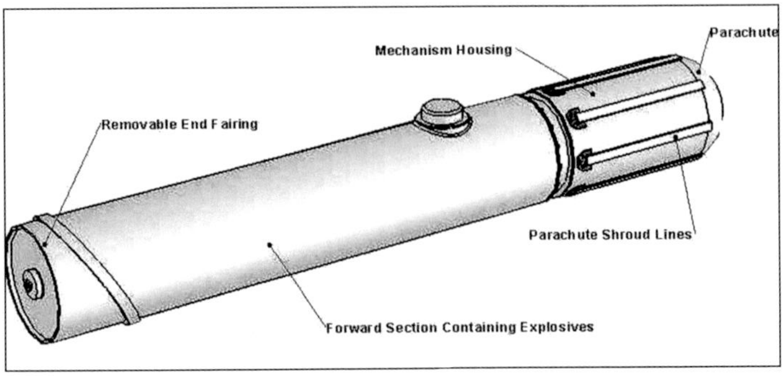

Mk I Air Deployable Anti-Ship Mine.

The mine itself was a closed cylinder, 3 metres long and 45cm in diameter, with an explosive charge of approximately 340kg trotyl. In the centre of the container was an induction coil consisting of a 1.9m Permalloy rod[8] with a diameter of approximately 2.5mm around which a 0.8mm insulated copper wire was wound. When a ship passed close enough to the mine, the ship's magnetic field induced a voltage in the copper coil which, via a trigger relay, caused the mine to detonate. This ignition system had several advantages over the original compass needle system. As the induced voltage was created by a change in the magnetic field around the mine, the cheaper and more robust iron containers could easily be used instead of the aluminium containers used by the Germans. The induction coil was also more robust against shock and impact than the 'delicate' compass needle. The coil could easily measure both increasing and decreasing magnetic influence. Since the mine, and thus the induction coil, was intended to lie horizontally on the seabed, it was the horizontal earth magnetism that was utilised. Because of the many advantages of the system, the induction coil mine was favoured during, as well as after, World War II. The Admiralty ordered 30 mines for testing in July 1939, of which the Air Ministry received a few. When war broke out a few months later, the Admiralty calculated that the first magnetic mines would be ready for use in the summer of 1940.[9]

4.4 The Effectiveness of Landmines As a Weapon

The first types of mines, the contact mines, detonated when the ship sailed over the mine and hit a detonator, such as one of the horns on a horn mine. The detonation caused direct damage by blowing a hole in the ship's hull at, or slightly below, the waterline. Crew members were most often injured by fragments from this blast. Typically, one or more watertight bulkheads became water-filled, causing smaller ships to sink and damaging larger ships.

The bottom mines were distance mines and were effective in water depths of 10–50 metres, and worked via the pressure wave from the explosion when the mine detonated.

8 Permalloy is the name for an iron-nickel alloy, also known as 'nickel steel', whose nickel content is 70–80 percent. The alloy is non-magnetic and therefore very useful in an induction coil.

9 Gerhard Frhr. v. Ledebur, *Die Seemine* (Munich: 1977), pp.92–93; Stephen W. Roskill, *The War at Sea 1939–45*, vol. 1 (London: HMSO, 1954), p.123.

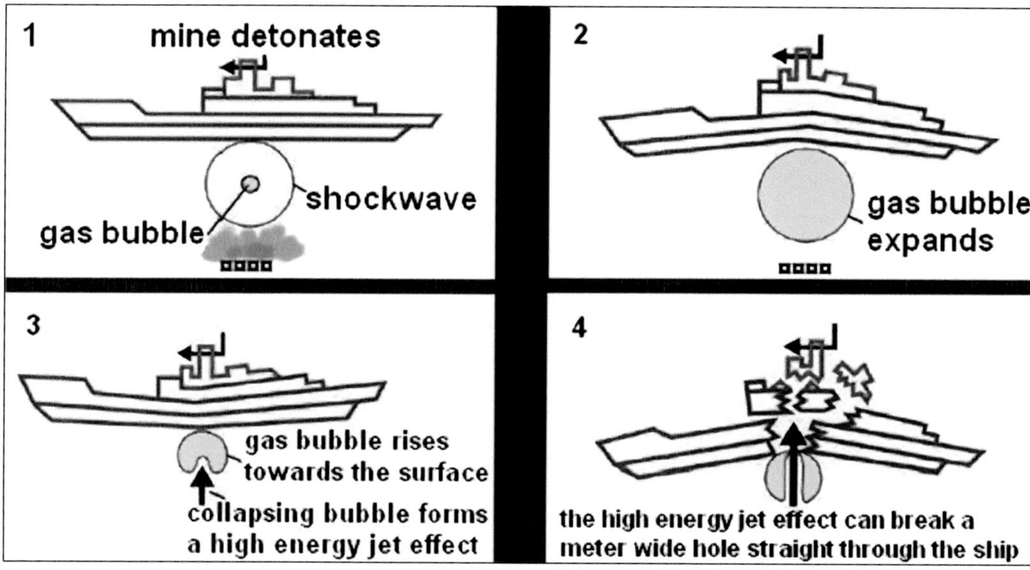

The potential devastating effect of a detonating bottom mine on a ship.

When the bottom mine detonates, an enormous pressure is created that sends a shock wave travelling at a speed of approximately 600 km/h through the water in a matter of milliseconds. This shock wave will have an initial damaging effect on the ship, destroying welds, affecting riveted plates and generally weakening the supporting structures, fig. 1. shows the explosion creates a high-pressure gas bubble that expands very quickly. The gas bubble will push the ship upwards, deforming its keel and further weakening the hull. Significant damage will occur to major mechanical parts and communication, weapon and control systems will be destroyed, fig.2. After reaching its maximum volume, the gas bubble will eventually collapse due to the inertial effect. The pressure will now be lower than the surrounding water pressure, causing the ship's hull to bend downwards, fig.3. In the final stage of collapse, when the gas bubble is close to the hull, a high-speed jet effect is created with a concentrated burst of energy that can easily cut a metre wide hole all the way up the ship's body. This mechanism has been identified as a third cause of damage to mine-blasted ships, and probably the most devastating. In cases where the jet effect occurs near the surface of the sea, next to a ship, it can raise a water column up to 100 metres high. The whole process lasts about 2 seconds.[10]

At the request of the British Bombing Survey Unit, Coastal Command Headquarters assembled a team of specialists just after the end of the war in Europe, who left on 15 June 1945 to investigate the effects of bombs, mines, rockets and machinegun fire on ships. The team included representatives from the Royal Air Force: Bomber Command, Coastal Command and 2nd Tactical Air Force, as well as a representative from the Admiralty's Department of Naval Architecture. The initiative was supported by the Aircraft Anti-shipping Committee

10 B. C. Khoo, 'Devastating Bubble Power' <http://www.eng.nus.edu.sg>.

and a total of 52 ships were to be examined in Kiel, Travemünde and Neustadt in Germany, and Aarhus, Aalborg, Frederikshavn and Nakskov in Denmark. After inspecting the ships and interviewing witnesses to assess the effectiveness of the weapon types mentioned and analysing the tactics used, the team returned home a month later.[11] In the report that followed, the fate of each vessel was analysed in detail. There was a brief description of the attack itself, sketches indicating the damage, accompanied by black and white photos and, in several cases, photos taken from the aircraft during the attack. Aerial photos taken by the RAF's photo reconnaissance unit P.R.U. were also included in some cases.[12]

The short version of the report's conclusion was:

> ... of all the weapons whose effects were studied, mines caused the most widespread damage. This is only to be expected since the weight of the explosive (about 1,000lb) is greater than that for most other airborne shipping weapons and the effect of the explosion is enhanced by the presence of the seabed. When a mine detonates under the bottom of a ship, both structural and shock damage may be caused..[13]

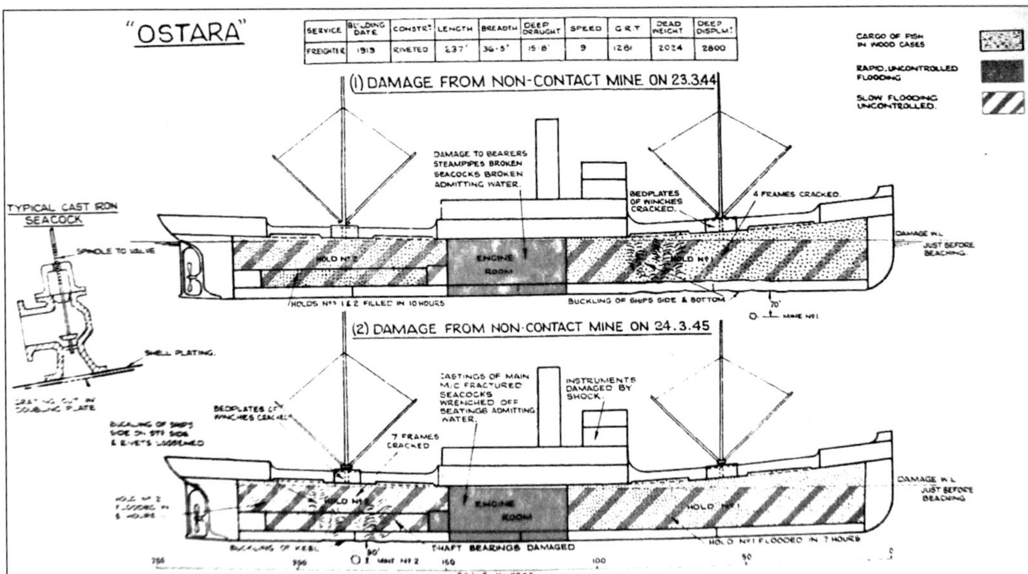

The fishing vessel *Ostara* had the misfortune to set off British bottom mines two days in a row in March 1945. Luckily for the ship's crew, it happened at depths of 23 and 30 metres respectively, and in both situations the ship was able to stay afloat because the cargo of fish was thrown overboard and all pumps were activated.

11 Air Historical Branch: 'A Survey of damaged Shipping in N. Germany and Denmark' Introduction a) and b), June 1945, p.1. It was only possible to compile a detailed survey of 42 vessels.

12 Air Historical Branch: 'A Survey of damaged Shipping in N. Germany and Denmark' Introduction e), June 1945, p.1.

13 Air Historical Branch: 'A Survey of damaged Shipping in N. Germany and Denmark' Weapon effectiveness, June 1945, p.2.

4.5 Aircraft as Minelayers

In 1930–1931, the *Kriegsmarine* began experimenting with laying bottom mines using bombers. While the prototype RMA contained 800kg of explosives, two smaller 'air mines', the LMA and LMB, containing 300kg and 700kg of explosives respectively, were constructed.[14] As the BIK mechanism was relatively vulnerable to shocks, the air mines were equipped with parachutes that could slow their fall speed from the aircraft's approximately 300km/h to about 70km/h. During transport in the aircraft, the mines were fitted with safety devices that were either removed automatically when dropped, or by a water pressure switch when the mine was on the seabed. During trials of dropping the mines from aircraft, it was discovered that this could not be done from a height of more than 500 metres above the water. Otherwise, it would be more difficult to place the mines accurately in the target area and there was a high risk that the mines would be destroyed on impact with the surface of the water. Once the mine was in the water, the parachute was released using a melting fuse, after which the mine slowly and quietly settled on the seabed.

A German LMB magnetic mine going astray, retrieved from the Warwick water reservoir in Walthamstow about 8km north of central London.

After two years of development and testing, the two types of air mines were handed over to the *Luftwaffe*. They did not like the idea much, so no further action was taken. Hermann Göring, *Oberbefehlshaber der Luftwaffe*, did not think much of the mine weapon. He believed in the superiority of the air force as a means of threat and suppression, the strategy of blitzkrieg and of quick victories. In his opinion, there was no need for such outdated

14 The total weight was 520kg for LMA and 1,000kg for LMB.

weapons that were based on a long-term blockade war. In addition, he was a sworn enemy of the Navy Chief, *Admiral* Erich Raeder, who in turn prioritised the mine weapon. In the dispute over who would have operational control of the minelaying bombers, Göring won a clear victory. Hitler made it clear to the naval component that minelaying by aircraft, air attacks on ships in the open sea, on naval bases and harbours were entirely the domain of the *Luftwaffe*.[15]

As a result, the Luftwaffe shelved the new types of mines in 1935, which meant that this tactical advantage could not be fully utilised when war broke out. During the 'Phoney War' from 3 September 1939 to 9 April 1940, the German Navy managed to lay approximately 1,000 RMA mines, while the Luftwaffe only dropped a total of 68 LMA mines![16] While the *Luftwaffe* did not prioritise mine warfare very highly, the RAF began to see the potential of the new weapon.

15 Erich Raeder:' My Life', Annapolis, Naval Institute Press, 1960 pp.102–105, 117–119

16 Gerhard Frhr. v. Ledebur, *Die Seemine* (München: 1977), p 91; Friedrich Ruge, *Im Küstenvorfeld* (Munich: 1974), p.22.

Chapter 5

5.1 RAF Minelaying Operations – The Prelude, 1936 to April 1940

The idea that a magnetic mine could be delivered to the target by a bomber was included from the start as part of the widespread rivalry between the RAF and the RN. Neither the Royal Navy nor the British Army were particularly willing to hand over all air operations to the RAF. The two services wanted their own air forces at the expense of the RAF. However, the navy was the most ardent opponent of a unified and expanded RAF.

On 2 June 1936, the Deputy Director of Plans, Air Ministry, Group Captain Arthur T. Harris, sent a proposal to the British Admiralty. It was for the RAF and RN to jointly develop what Harris called an 'H' bomb, but which was in fact a distance-type magnetic mine, a bottom mine. His proposal stated that the 'H' bomb should be deliberately dropped near ships in harbours, anchorages, canals and in shallow waters where there was ship traffic. There did not need to be any significant requirement for precision, as the 'bomb' would simply lie on the seabed and wait. A time-delay device would arm it after a set period of time. Then the 'bomb' would be activated by the magnetic field of a passing ship at a certain distance.

Harris explained the potential uses of the 'H' bomb and also pointed out that it would be difficult to neutralise by 'magnetic sweep', as only those 'H' bombs that were armed would detonate. Therefore, the enemy could not be sure that other 'H' bombs would not be armed immediately or shortly after a strike had been made. Finally, Harris gave suggestions on how to prevent divers from removing the bombs.

On 30 September, the Admiralty replied that although the weapon in question could be deployed from aircraft, they firmly believed that it was unmistakably the development of a new type of mine. The Air Council therefore realised that the development of the weapon should naturally be carried out by the Admiralty. At an internal meeting held on 8 October, it was also made clear that the operational control of the new mine weapon must unconditionally be placed under the authority normally responsible for shipping. The use of the mine would affect shipping traffic regardless of whether it involved allied, enemy or neutral ships. The discussion is recognisable from the dispute between the Luftwaffe and the German naval leadership, although the positions taken by the two services' leaders were diametrically opposed![1]

1 Dudley Saward, *'Bomber' Harris': The Story of the Marshal of the Royal Air Force Sir Arthur Harris* (London: Cassell Ltd, 1984), p.55.

In February 1937, the Admiralty made a more formal proposal for a type of mine that could be laid from aircraft. Harris, who had been awaiting the Admiralty's response for over six months, expressed his satisfaction with, and support for, this proposal in a letter on 2 March. He added that the development of such a type of mine should be a joint responsibility of the RN and RAF as the potential users of the mine, either separately or jointly. Harris mentioned inland waterways, rivers and canals, such as the Kiel Canal, as obvious RAF targets. On the other hand, the German Baltic Sea harbours were considered common targets, as the mines could be part of the RN's blockade weapons and only the RAF was able to place the mines. Therefore, for obvious reasons, it would be most expedient for both the RAF and the RN to work together to develop this type of mine.

Despite the good arguments and the offer of cooperation, the Admiralty was not willing to change its position. The development of the mine and later its use was solely a matter for the RN. This 'dog-in-the-manger' attitude[2] prompted Marshal of the Royal Air Force, Sir Edward Ellington, who was Chief of Air Staff, to write an unusually sharp note to Secretary of State for Air, Lord Swinton, on 24 June 1937. He wrote, among other things:

> The whole affair is an outstanding example of the deplorable result of interdepartmental bickering, and provides further proof of the Admiralty's determination to maintain naval 'autarky' at all costs. It is very probable that the Admiralty realises quite well that the 'bomb-mine' will normally have to be used by shore-based bomber squadrons, and that their claim for 'operational control' over the weapon is therefore yet another attempt by back-door methods towards the attainment of a separate Naval Air Force[3]

Along with the letter, Ellington enclosed a memo from the Air Staff in which Harris, who had written the memo, pointed out the foolishness of the Admiralty's claim that the element, land, air or water, in which the weapon/projectile exploded, should be decisive for which defence force had the right of disposal over it. Should the coastal forts, which mainly targeted enemy ships, also be under the command of the Admiralty? Would the guns on British warships, which could also fire at land targets, be under the command of the army? And what about the anti-aircraft batteries on land and aboard navy ships – should they be under the Air Ministry because the targets were enemy aircraft? Above all, Harris was determined that the mine should be developed in close cooperation between the two services, being delivered by, and dropped from, an aircraft just like a bomb, and then working in water, like a sea mine aimed at ships. However, if the Admiralty would not accept such cooperation, and it came to a decision as to which service should have operational control of the mine, it would clearly have to be the Air Ministry, according to Harris. From the moment the 'mine bomb' boarded the aircraft it would be air tactics that would be used to deliver it to its target. Threats to the weapon would be enemy aircraft and anti-aircraft fire

2 Someone who prevents others from enjoying something despite not needing it. The term refers to Aesop's fable from the mid-sixteenth century about a snarling dog that prevents horses from eating food that is unpleasant for the dog itself.

3 Dudley Saward, *'Bomber' Harris': The Story of the Marshal of the Royal Air Force Sir Arthur Harris* (London: Cassell Ltd, 1984), pp.55–56.

and it would be RAF trained observers using a bombsight to trigger the mine. Until it hit the water, the 'mine' would therefore be considered a 'bomb'.[4]

After further long and heated correspondence between the two services regarding who would lead the development of the mine and who would eventually have operational control over it, Harris was finally vindicated. The RAF and RN began working closely together on the joint project. A certain division of labour was natural, with the RN developing, constructing and testing the mine, while the RAF developed and tested various mine suspension and minelaying methods.[5]

On 1 September 1939, the Air Ministry presented a list of the tasks the RAF could be expected to perform in the event of war with Germany, the so-called 'Western Airplans' (WA). Among other things, it appeared that the laying of magnetic mines by bombers, aimed at enemy shipping, was included as WA No.15.[6] The purpose of the minelaying was formulated as follows:

> To contribute to the protection of the sea communications of the Empire by the destruction or threat of destruction of the naval forces of the enemy and to assist to the maximum possible extent in the dislocation of his war effort.[7]

Although the war became a reality just two days later, work on the development of, and training with, magnetic mines was not accelerated for this reason. It was not until six months later that the WA No.15 began to be looked at more closely.

5.2 The Mysterious Mines

In November 1939, an event occurred that was both significant in the mine war and at the same time illustrated a very important aspect of this type of warfare: the technological race.

From 16 October 1939, mysterious sinkings of ships began to occur off the English ports on the south coast.[8] Ships were mined in waters that had already been searched and swept by British minesweepers. In early November, six ships were sunk in the Thames Estuary and the British naval command began to consider closing London harbour. It was suspected that some form of magnetic mine was probably at work, but until the exact mechanism and behaviour of this type of mine was known, the necessary countermeasures could not be taken. Rear Admiral Lyster of the Admiralty Mines Section was summoned by the First Sea Lord, Sir Dudley Pound, to discuss what further measures could be taken against these mysterious mines. However, despite a great deal of effort to gather all the information

4 Dudley Saward, *'Bomber' Harris': The Story of the Marshal of the Royal Air Force Sir Arthur Harris* (London: Cassell Ltd, 1984), p.56.
5 Dudley Saward, *'Bomber' Harris': The Story of the Marshal of the Royal Air Force Sir Arthur Harris* (London: Cassell Ltd, 1984), p.57.
6 Charles Webster and Noble Frankland Webster, Charles & Frankland, Noble, *The Strategic Air Offensive Against Germany, 1939–1945* (London: HMSO, 1961), vol. 4, App. 6, p.102.
7 J. S. Cowie, *Mines, Minelayers and Minelaying* (Oxford: OUP, 1949), p.121.
8 Brigadier Peter Young (Ed.), *The World Almanac Book of World War II* (New York: Bison, 1981), p.43.

available about the mine blasts, Lyster was unable to contribute significantly to solving the mystery. HMS *Vernon*, the Royal Navy's mine research centre in Portsmouth, was also unable to provide more than an educated guess.

On the evening of 20 November 1939, a mine-damaged ship managed to enter the River Humber. At the same time, reports were received at the Admiralty that German aeroplanes had dropped some large objects from low altitude in the waters off Hull and Southend. An expert from HMS *Vernon*, Lieutenant Commander Lewis, was immediately sent to the area to interview eyewitnesses, including the captains of the ships that lay anchored in a place off the coast. Several of them reported that they had seen German planes dropping objects that looked very much like the bunk bags that sailors carry. These observations were confirmed by the naval officer in charge of coastal defence in the area. His anti-aircraft batteries had not opened fire on the German aircraft, as their firing was to be directed from a central command centre in Uxbridge, based on a radar plot. This was obviously unsatisfactory in the given situation, and the naval officer had therefore asked for a number of well-trained anti-aircraft gunners from the Naval Artillery School on Whale Island on his own initiative. While Lewis was writing up the final reports, the sharpshooters from Whale Island arrived and were posted at suitable intervals on the Southend pier.

Lewis returned to London on 22 November and immediately began writing a report to the Admiralty. Late in the evening, while he was still at work, a message came from Southend that the anti-aircraft gunners on the pier had just fired on an enemy aeroplane, which had then 'dropped' an object. The artefact had fallen on one of the mud banks off Shoeburyness, east of Southend. Lewis asked the Chief of Coastal Defence to summon a photographer and set off again, this time accompanied by a colleague, Lieutenant Commander Ouvry. After 45 miles of driving through dense fog, they reached Southend, where the photographer joined them in the car. They drove down to the beach at Shoeburyness and quickly found the mine. The high tide was coming in and would cover the mine within half an hour, so they settled for photographing it from all angles and taking a survey. With a pencil and a piece of paper, they made an impression of a silver-coloured 'gizmo' attached to the side of the mine container. On the way to the beach, they found the parachute that had been attached to the mine.

A preliminary report was sent to the Admiralty, and the next morning the team headed back out to the mud bank where the mine was now above water. They had about 4 hours to work before the water would cover the mine again. First, they took a good look at the mine container. Then they decided to remove the small silver-coloured 'thing' that they had taken impressions of the night before. In their immediate opinion, it must contain the

The German mine found off Shoeburyness in November 1939.

detonating cartridge. Ouvry, who had more seniority than Lewis, would try to unscrew the thing with a special spanner that they had made during the night from the pencil impression. Meanwhile, Lewis was to stay 300 yards away and use a field telephone to monitor and record Ouvry's observations and efforts to defuse the mine. To help him, Ouvry had a Quartermaster Baldwin.

Slowly, the thing was unscrewed and now that the detonator had been removed, the mine should be harmless. They wondered why the detonator seemed to have no direct connection to the mine. There were no wires or anything else that could connect to a mechanism inside the container. Nevertheless, it had to be the detonating cartridge they were carrying, as there was a so-called 'gaine' at the bottom, a small detonator capsule that amplifies the explosive power of the fuse. They carried the primer onto the beach, and now all three of them and a non-commissioned officer went to the mine to see if there were any more parts that could be removed on site. The high tide was coming in quickly. First they removed the spring mechanism that had triggered the parachute. Then they rolled the mine over to the other side. Here they found another 'thing' that could apparently be unscrewed. With a screwdriver and a hammer, they eventually got the thing free – a mine fuse container with two detonators at the bottom! For a few seconds they were all paralysed by shock!

After this scare, they carefully cut the wires and pulled out the detonators. At one end of the mine were four metal discs, about 15cm in diameter. However, when the mine was finally defused, they saw no need to dismantle the mine any further. It was loaded onto a lorry and while Ouvry took the mysterious 'gizmo', which they had first thought to be the fuse, to Woolwich Arsenal for examination, Lewis drove to London to report to Rear Admiral Lyster.

In the Admiralty, there was great excitement. The efforts of the four men had seemingly saved the British Fleet from disaster. By this time, the German magnetic mines had already cost British losses totalling 50,000 tons of shipping. Once the German mine had been thoroughly investigated, the right precautions could finally be taken.

Secretary of State for the Navy Churchill called a meeting of all the admirals and chiefs of the Admiralty at 23.30 that night. Lewis, who had not slept for two days, had to tell the whole story from the beginning. When he had finished, Churchill asked him if he had been

The mine is placed on the lorry. From left: A. B. Vearncombe, Lieutenant Colonel Lewis, C.P.O. Baldwin, and Lieutenant Colonel Ourvy with his back half-turned to the photographer.

afraid. Before Lewis could answer, First Sea Lord, Sir Dudley Pound, who apparently considered the question to be an insult to a naval officer, angrily exclaimed," Scared? Of course he wasn't scared!" Churchill then asked Lewis what type of mine he thought it was. Lewis was of the opinion that the Germans were unlikely to use a type of mine that the British Navy had known about since 1918, so he thought it was probably not a magnetic mine, but rather an acoustic mine, and that the mechanism must be behind the four metal discs. Churchill then closed the meeting and Lewis was able to get a well-deserved night's sleep.

King George VI visited HMS *Vernon* on 19 December 1939 to honour Commander John Ouvry DSO and the rest of the team for their efforts in securing an intact German mine. These were the first medals awarded to naval personnel during World War II.

However, after a few days of investigation, the experts at HMS *Vernon* announced that the 'mysterious' German mine was in fact an improved version of the twenty-year-old British magnetic mine. One of the new refinements of the German version was the incorporation of an aerial bomb fuse that could be set to detonate at a depth of two metres or less. This meant that the mine would automatically explode if it fell in shallow water or on land. It was this 'gizmo' that Ouvry and Lewis had first removed and did not know what to do with. The device had failed on this occasion, probably because the crew of the German aircraft had been surprised by the anti-aircraft gun on the pier. The mine had been thrown so quickly that the crew had forgotten to set the mechanism to detonate in their haste. But because Lewis mistakenly thought it was an acoustic mine, Churchill had already started research work to develop a device for sweeping acoustic mines. So when the first British ship was sunk by an acoustic mine some four months later, the Royal Navy was ready with a countermeasure.[9]

9 Gerald Pawle, *Churchill i krig* (Gentofte, 1964), pp.37–41. At the end of 1940, the first German mines appeared with a built-in counting mechanism and clockwork that could delay the armouring of the mine until after 1–16 passes or impacts and/or after a preset time. When the first German acoustic mines appeared, they were in such small quantities that the British countermeasures then in place could provide reasonable protection in the form of electric hammers on the ships' bows and similar sound machines in tow. J. S. Cowie, *Mines, Minelayers and Minelaying* (Oxford: OUP, 1949), p.136.

5.3 The British Planning

On 15 March 1940, a meeting was held at the Admiralty, attended by the Director of Plans J. C. Slessor of the Air Ministry. The final list of potential target areas for the RAF's laying of magnetic mines had not yet been finalised. It was therefore decided that, before such a list could be drawn up, more reconnaissance had to be carried out over the German estuaries, which at the time were the target for the new mines. In the RAF, the test team had not yet fully completed the testing of the new weapon. Among other things, they had not finished measuring how much water spray the mine caused when dropped from different heights. However, all the participants agreed that the matter should be expedited, and a date was set for another meeting regarding WA No.15. The meeting was to be held at the Air Ministry on 8 April.[10] Until then, the primary task of the five groups in Bomber Command would be reconnaissance of the German estuaries, canals, coastal routes and harbour mouths, with a view to the final selection and mutual prioritisation of the future target areas.[11]

The magnetic mine drop tests continued in the following weeks. It was found that a mine dropped from a height of 500 feet produced a water spray that was difficult to see from a distance of 1 mile. The drop trials and the rest of the training with the new weapon type were conducted by 5 Group Bomber Command, which was equipped with Handley Page Hampden bombers. This aircraft was found to be the most suitable for the specialised task. Although it could only carry a single mine, whereas aircraft such as both the Vickers Wellington and Armstrong Whitworth Whitley could load two mines, a Hampden was faster, more manoeuvrable and had a longer range than the two heavier bombers. However, the main argument was that it was relatively easy to install the special mine suspension in the Hampden's cargo hold. To prevent the *Kriegsmarine* from discovering where the mines were laid, it had also been decided that the minelaying raids would take place at night. Shortly after the outbreak of war, the Hampden had already been found totally unsuitable for daytime attacks, partly due to the many blind spots of the rear gunner. There was therefore no doubt that it had to be 5 Group Bomber Command, where all Hampden squadrons were gathered, that would eventually also be responsible for the operational use of the mines.

The commander of 5 Group was fully committed to the task that had been assigned to his unit. Since 11 September 1939, the commander had been the same A. T. Harris, who in 1936 had sent the Admiralty a proposal for the development of an airborne magnetic mine. Now he was responsible for introducing and implementing the operational use of the new weapon in practice.[12]

The Admiralty demanded that Coastal Command should participate in the minelaying operations. However, it was also recognised that 5 Group Bomber Command with its Hampdens would be responsible for the main effort. It was therefore agreed to order crews from 5 Group to reconnoitre the planned minelaying areas. Considering the prevailing state

10 National Archives, Air 15/245 D.of Plan's minutes of the meeting to AOC-in-C, Coastal Command on 1 April 1940.

11 Denis Richards & Hilary St George Saunders, *Royal Air Force, 1939–1945* (London: HMSO, 1953), vol.1, p.53.

12 Bryan Philpott, *RAF Bomber Units, September 1939–June 1942* (Oxford: Osprey, 1977) Airwar Series no.5, p.44

Three Hampdens from 408 Squadron RCAF are loaded with one magnetic bottom mine each.

of war between the United Kingdom and Germany, it is surprising that the order to carry out reconnaissance was not issued until 24 March, nine days after the decision was made at the above-mentioned meeting of the Admiralty![13]

On 8 April, the Air Ministry met as agreed. Harris was able to inform the assembly that 5 Group crews had been reconnoitring the areas around the German estuaries for the past fortnight as planned. Moonlight had been scarce during this period, but they had still managed to make the necessary observations. Flyers had been dropped during the raids to conceal the real purpose of the overflights. Contrary to previous assumptions, Harris now believed that it would be possible to lay mines in similar low light conditions. In his opinion, it was therefore not absolutely necessary to wait for full moonlight to begin laying mines.

During the course of the day, it became even more urgent for the meeting participants to make a decision regarding the deployment of the RAF's minelaying aircraft. That morning, the Royal Navy had launched 'Operation Wilfried', the laying of minefields on the Norwegian coast.[14] A German reaction was therefore to be expected over the next 48 hours.

13 National Archives, Air 14/701 Mentioned in letter from HQ 5 Group to HQ Bomber Command, 3 June 1940.

14 'Operation Wilfrid': Early in the morning of 8 April, British destroyers entered Norwegian territorial waters and began laying mines. At 0600 hours, an Anglo-French note was delivered to the Norwegian Ministry of Foreign Affairs stating that mines had been laid in Vestfjorden, the entrance to Narvik, and two other places on the Norwegian coast between Trondheim and Bergen. According to the note, the laying of mines was intended to deny the enemy the continued use of Norwegian waters. In reality, mines had only been laid at Narvik, while the manoeuvres of the British naval vessels at the other two locations had been feigned. The Norwegian government protested, but decided not to use force against the British ships. Stephen W. Roskill, *The War at Sea 1939–45*, vol. 1 (London: HMSO, 1954), pp.157–158.

Although Harris believed that the operation could begin immediately, there was a majority in favour of postponing the first minelaying raid until the night of 17/18 April, when there would be a chance of optimal moonlight conditions.

Another, and very important, reason for this decision was that only 200 ready-to-distribute magnetic mines were in stock at the time. By waiting another 10 days or so, it would be possible to start with a slightly larger number of mines in the first phase of minelaying. It would not be a significant increase, but it would be a better starting point. There would be no risk of making the same mistake that the Germans had made six months earlier. When German aircraft began laying magnetic mines along the south coast of Britain in October 1939, they had done so on such a small scale that, as mentioned, after the Royal Navy had recovered an abandoned German magnetic mine on 22 November, they were able to develop mine sweeping techniques and equipment relatively quickly. As the mines were produced in larger quantities and the Germans increased the number of mines laid, the Royal Navy's minesweeper organisation was better equipped to neutralise a large proportion of the new type of mine.[15]

Although the Germans only slowly increased the number of mines laid over a long period of time, giving the Royal Navy a good opportunity to develop appropriate countermeasures along the way, it was even slower to build up a well-functioning and effective minesweeper organisation. In the period from November 1939, when the German magnetic mine was first investigated, up to and including March 1940, an average of a dozen British ships were mined every day in the areas where the German magnetic mines were laid.[16] It was an expensive lesson that clearly showed how effective a weapon the magnetic mine was, even though this German 'secret' weapon had been revealed. The RAF and RN believed that it was precisely the element of surprise that the Germans had missed. They did not want to repeat that mistake.

The Air Ministry would have liked to wait a few more weeks, but due to the tense situation on 8 April 1940, they were forced to launch the minelaying operations with the 200 mines at hand. Bomber Command, and thus 5 Group, would have 155 mines, while Coastal Command, and here it was 22 Squadron that would lay the mines, could dispose of the remaining 45 mines.

Based on the last 14 days of aerial reconnaissance, it was agreed to prioritise the distribution of the mines to the individual target areas according to the following table (see next page).[17]

After the Air Ministry meeting, an operation order was issued the next morning, 9 April, from Bomber Command Headquarters to 5 Group. It outlined the priority of the selected target areas and the key data of the 'secret' mine weapon. The aircrews were to be informed that the mine weighed approximately 1,500 pounds, half of which consisted of the explosive TNT. They were also to be instructed that the mines had to be dropped very precisely from a height of between 400 feet (about 120 metres) and 1,000 feet (about 300 metres) and at a

15 Peter Elliott, *Allied Minesweeping in World War 2* (Annapolis: US Naval Institute, 1979), pp.31–32.

16 *Historical Overview Of The Sea Mine And Its Utilisation* (without place and year of printing), Marinens Bibliotek, p.3.

17 National Archives, Air 15/245, 'Minutes of a meeting held at Air Ministry on Monday 8 April, to discuss plan WA 15.' Dated 9 April 1940.

Target Area	Number of mines	Command
Ems estuary	20	Coastal
Jade and Weser estuaries	28	Coastal
Elbe estuary	38	Bomber
Kieler Bay	38	Bomber
Lübecker Bay	38	Bomber
Waters off Warnermünde	10	Bomber
Waters off Swinemünde	28	Bomber

Plan for the distribution of magnetic mines to the individual target areas on 8 April 1940.

maximum speed of 150–200 mph. During the month of May, some mines would use long delay ignition rates of 6, 36, 72 or 144 hours.

From 5 Group the messages were immediately passed on to the three operational air stations – Waddington, Hemswell and Scampton. They were told that 50 mines would soon be delivered to each airfield. The station commanders were also told that the first mine-laying was likely to be carried out on the night of 18 April. The last point of the message read: 'Neutral territory and territorial waters is to be avoided.'[18]

But that morning, the military situation changed completely – German troops had landed in Denmark and Norway.

18 National Archives, Air 15/245 Bomber Command operations order no.93, 9 April 1940.

Chapter 6

6.1 Minelaying in Danish Waters, April 1940

On 9 April, when the Air Ministry learnt that German forces had launched an offensive against Denmark and Norway that morning, Wing Commander Pendred of the Air Ministry's Directorate of Plans immediately contacted Bomber Command Headquarters. He was able to announce that the existing minelaying plans had to be changed immediately. It was no longer the German estuaries that had first priority, now it was primarily the Danish waters.

By this time, the first 20 mines had already been delivered to 5 Group. Theoretically, they could have been prepared and laid already on the evening of 11 April. However, Danish waters had not been reconnoitred for minelaying operations. Pendred therefore suggested that the parties involved in the Admiralty and Bomber Command should be summoned to a meeting as soon as possible to determine which suitable target areas existed in Denmark. However, neither the head of 5 Group, A. T. Harris, nor SASO Bomber Command, Air Vice-Marshal Norman Bottomley, could make time for such a meeting. The new developments in the war meant extensive changes in the RAF's strategy. An easy and quick, but rather unconventional way out was therefore chosen. It was simply agreed that a naval officer, Commander Nichols, would visit Harris the next morning so that the two of them could jointly find the strategically most important Danish waters![1]

The next morning, 10 April, Nichols and Harris had the new target list drawn up. Nichols then contacted the Admiralty to request maps of the new target areas. Meanwhile, Harris telephoned AOC-in-C Bomber Command, Air Marshal Charles Portal, and asked his permission for 5 Group to carry out a reconnaissance over, and later a minelaying operation in, Danish waters as soon as possible. He assured Portal that the aircrews could easily accomplish this task, even though the nighttime light conditions were not yet optimal. Portal passed this request on to Deputy Chief of the Air Staff (DCAS), Air Vice-Marshal Richard Peirse, and at the same time asked to be told how many mines, according to the Air Ministry's estimate, should be available before the green light could be given for the deployment. Bomber Command could then initiate the first minelaying operation itself when the stated number of mines was ready.

---

1 Air 14/700. Bomber Command HQ to SASO, Bomber Command, 9.4.1940. Air 14/2064 Draft by SASO, Bomber Command, 10 April 1940.

At noon Peirse was able to report back to Portal that the Air Ministry had come to the decision that as soon as the first 8 mines were ready, the first mine laying could be ordered. Portal immediately passed this message on to Harris in 5 Group. But knowing that Harris was more than eager to get started, Portal emphasised that this message from Bomber Command Headquarters was not an actual operation order to leave immediately. It was just a forewarning that the order would probably arrive in the next few days, and that 5 Group could start getting ready.

At 15.00 a telephone order came from Bomber Command to 5 Group that the Øresund, Great Belt and Little Belt were to be reconnoitred that evening. This time, no leaflets were to be dropped as cover, as they simply did not have leaflets intended for the Danish population and because dropping German-language leaflets outside Germany might reveal the real purpose of the raid.[2]

As ordered, 6 Hampdens set off on a reconnaissance mission to Denmark that evening. Two from each of the three operational air stations in 5 Group were assigned to the task. The reconnaissance of the Danish Straits and Belts took place under the cover of an ordinary patrol to the German island of Sylt.[3]

On the afternoon of 11 April, a precautionary order was received from the Air Ministry to Bomber Command regarding the priority of the target areas and the extent to which they should be mined. At the same time, the Admiralty and Coastal Command were informed of the contents of the order. It had been decided that the first 8 mines, when the operation order arrived, would be distributed with 4 in each of two areas, 'A' and 'B', in the Great Belt, off Korsør and Nyborg, respectively. Then the subsequent mines were to be dropped in 'C', Snævringen in the Little Belt, between Fredericia and Middelfart. Once a total of 20 mines had been laid in each of these three areas, the originally selected target areas in German waters were to be mined. The only change was that the total of 60 mines laid in Danish waters were deducted from the number of mines planned for the German Baltic Sea ports.[4]

During the day, Harris sent a letter to Bottomley at Bomber Command Headquarters suggesting that a common nomenclature or code for the use of the magnetic mines, which at this early stage of the war were still labelled a 'secret' weapon, be introduced immediately. In his opinion, the mines had been too often referred to in plain language in various letters in recent days, and if this continued, the mine would not remain a secret much longer. Harris suggested that the following code be adopted: the laying of the magnetic mines should be called 'gardening' and the mines should be called 'vegetables'. As the minelaying areas had already begun to be given code letters in alphabetical order as they were identified, it would be natural to call the mines to be laid in e.g. 'A', 'B' and 'C' 'Asparagus', 'Broccoli' and 'Carrots' respectively. If an operation order then stated that 'five gardeners on gardening duty were to plant five broccoli', this meant in plain language that five minelaying aircraft were to lay five mines in area 'B' off Nyborg.[5]

2 Air 14/700. Minutes of telephone conversations between the mentioned persons in the period 11.00–15.00, 10 April 1940.

3 Air 25/109 A. 5 Group ORB, 10.4.1940.

4 Air 15/245. Original order no. X.121 from AM to BC, CC and ADM, sent on 11.4.40 at 15.30 and received at 16.42.

5 Air 14/700. Letter from Harris, 5 Group HQ to SASO, Bottomley, Bomber Command HQ.

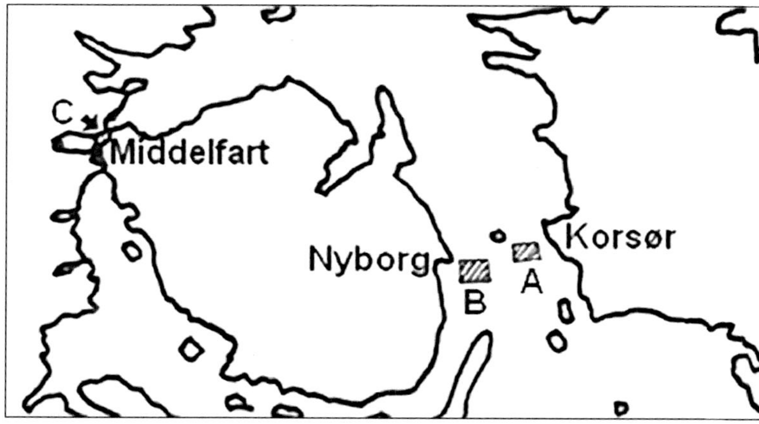

Bomber Command's first three minelaying areas in Europe, 10 April 1940.

Bomber Command Headquarters, the Air Ministry and the Admiralty thought the idea behind 'Operation Gardening' was a good one and the proposal was immediately put into action when the first operation order was sent from Bomber Command to 5 Group two days later.[6]

However, Harris thought it appropriate to use the waiting time to reconnoitre the three selected minelaying areas in Denmark once again. Twenty of his most experienced aircrew – 2 from Hemswell, 14 from Scampton and 4 from Waddington – were therefore ordered to the Danish belts. Armed with explosive bombs to attack any ship targets en route, the force departed that evening. One of the crews from Hemswell experienced navigational problems and turned back across the North Sea, and two crews from Scampton also had to turn back before they reached the Danish coast. In one aircraft, the pilot had fallen ill and the other aircraft had instrument failure. The remaining 17 aircraft completed the reconnaissance as ordered.

Harris had instructed them to specifically locate clear landmarks, characteristic coastlines, rivers, lakes and the like. This would give them a better chance of reaching the target areas when they were sent out on a minelaying mission. Area 'C' in the Little Belt had been added to the target list at the last minute, and so the 14 crews from Scampton had to specifically survey this area. They followed the route: Scampton – Fredericia – Middelfart – Lille Bælt – Kattegat – Scampton. None of the crews observed ships of any kind, and all the aircraft returned safely to their respective air stations during the morning of 12 April.[7] During the day, the observations from the reconnaissance were collated and discussed at 5 Group headquarters. The best approach routes to the target areas 'Asparagus', 'Broccoli' and 'Carrot' were determined.

6 Air 14/700. Operation order no. A 95 from Bomber Command HQ to 5 Group, at 17.58 on 11.4.40. The official approval of the code was not received until 20.15 on 13.4.40.

7 Air 14/669. Bomber Command opr. draft dispatch by Portal; Air 25/109A. 5 Group ORB, 11.4.40; Air 27/686. 83 Sqdn. ORB, 11–12.4.40; Air 28/681. Scampton ORB, 11–12.4.40. Guy Gibson states that the first mine laying was on the night of 12 April. So does military historian Chaz Bowyer *Hampden Special*, but it is clear that he has confused the laying of mines with 12 Hampden's fatal attempt to attack a German ship near Kristiansand. The German fighters from Kjevik shot down half the force and the rest returned home with unfinished business. Guy Gibson, *Mål i sigte* (Haderslev: 1963), p.49; Chaz Bowyer, *Hampden Special* (Shepperton: Ian Allan, 1976), p.22

On the morning of 13 April, Portal called Harris and asked if 5 Group was ready to carry out the first mine laying. Harris replied that only 10 mines had been prepared so far, while the remaining 190 mines were still missing vital parts. Portal then asked if it was possible to carry out bombing attacks on ships in connection with the minelaying operations and if so, how many aircraft Harris could provide. Harris promised to look into this.[8]

At 16.10 the first mine laying order of the war was received by 5 Group, Bomber Command. Only two squadrons were to be equipped with the necessary mine suspension. The remaining squadrons would be loaded with bombs for possible use against ships in the waters between Kieler Bay in the south and Oslo Fjord in the north, while the mine laying was in progress. All aircrews were to keep a close eye on the movement of ships in Danish waters and take note of the blackout conditions over Denmark, especially in the harbour towns.[9] The order to 5 Group also stated that the aircrews were to be instructed that if they had the slightest doubt as to whether they were over the correct target area, they were to take the mines back home.[10] At about the same time, an additional order was issued to 5 Group that the target areas in order of priority would be: 'A', 'B', 'C', 'D', 'E' and 'F'. In addition, the order was repeated that when the first eight mines were ready to be laid, four would be laid in each of the areas 'A' and 'B'.[11]

Nevertheless, Harris decided to send only six aircraft to the same target, namely 'B', the waters off Nyborg. A few hours later, three Hampdens from 61 Squadron and three from 144 Squadron took off from Hemswell bound for Denmark. One of the aircraft quite quickly turned back because of instrument failure, but the other five continued over the North Sea.

After 3 to 4 hours, they reached the German island of Sylt, where powerful searchlights at Hornum and Westerland air bases began searching for the intruding enemy aircraft. The small force managed to avoid the illuminated tentacles and soon reached the South Funen archipelago. When the five Hampdens were off Svendborg, they turned north and the observers readied their scopes. A few minutes later, when they sighted Knudshoved Lighthouse and, at the bottom of Nyborg Fjord, the slightly smaller Lindholm Lighthouse, the bomb bays in the five aircraft opened. The target area was now straight ahead. At the prescribed altitude of 5–600 feet, one by one the planes dropped their mines.

A total of four mines quickly floated down towards the dark water. One of the pilots was not sure that he was in the correct position, so he circled the area for about 20 minutes. As he was still in great doubt about his position, he turned his nose homewards without having dropped the mine. The other aircraft were already on their way home over the North Sea, where fog and rain forced the pilots to fly completely by instruments for the next 3 to 4 hours. All but one aircraft landed safely at Hemswell.

The last plane took an unintentional detour. The bad weather had caused static electricity inside the aircraft, and the crew was not too keen on the light show of bluish flashes that for almost two hours lit up the aircraft's interior with a ghostly glow. Worse, the aircraft's instruments were affected by the static electricity to such an extent that, to his horror, the pilot suddenly saw the French coast ahead. He followed the coastline northwards to the Belgian

8 Air 14/700 Cf. conversation between AOC-in-C, BC, and SASO,5 Group, 13.4.40.

9 Air 14/700. Bomber Command Opr order A.96 to 5 Group, 13.4.40.

10 Air 14/700. Bomber Command Opr order A.97 to 5 Group, 13.4.40.

11 Air 14/700. Bomber Command HQ ops. 827 to 5 Group, 13.4.40.

The map that accompanied the British press release on 14 April 1940! Somewhere the four bottom mines were lurking!

coast and then, heading due west, he reached Manston airfield in south-east England. With almost empty fuel tanks and tired, the last of the crew landed safely.[12]

During 13 April, three more target areas were added to the list: 'Daffodil' in the Sound, 'Eglantine' at the mouth of the Elbe and 'Flax' in the Bay of Kiel.[13] At this point, only 4 mines had been laid in one of the six designated areas. Nevertheless, the military authorities issued a press release to the British newspapers announcing that new British minefields had been laid in the Kattegat and along the German Baltic coast. The article stated that the blockade of the German waterways northwards was now complete. The article was accompanied by a map showing the areas that had been mined by Germany and the United Kingdom respectively.[14]

Captain J. S. Cowie, who for most of the war was head of the staff that planned British mine warfare, had to admit after the war that the publication of this 'fake map' had been a stopgap measure. By publishing the article and map, it was hoped that the German naval leadership would take certain security measures that could, at best, cause delays in German transports to and from Norway. It had been learnt during World War I that 'paper minefields' did not fool the enemy for long. After a short period of unhindered navigation through the alleged minefields, the Germans would be able to expose such a bluff.[15] It was therefore of crucial importance for the credibility and effect of the declaration that Bomber Command laid as many mines in Danish waters as possible within the next few days.

Already on the morning of 14 April, Bomber Command issued an order to 5 Group to lay mines in the Great and Little Belt that evening. The order emphasised that no mines were to

12 Air 28/351 Hemswell ORB, 13–14 April 1940. Raid DEH 221–226; Air 28/353 Hemswell ORB, 13–14 April, app.

13 Air 15/245. Addition to X121: X377 'Daffodil'; Air Ministry to BC, CC and Adm, 13 April 1940 at 11:15.

14 Keesing's Comtemporary Archives, 1940–43, p.4013 + map p.4012

15 J. S. Cowie, 'The British Sea-Mining Campaign, 1939–1945' in *Royal United Services Institution. Journal*, volume 93, no.569 (1948), pp.22–39.

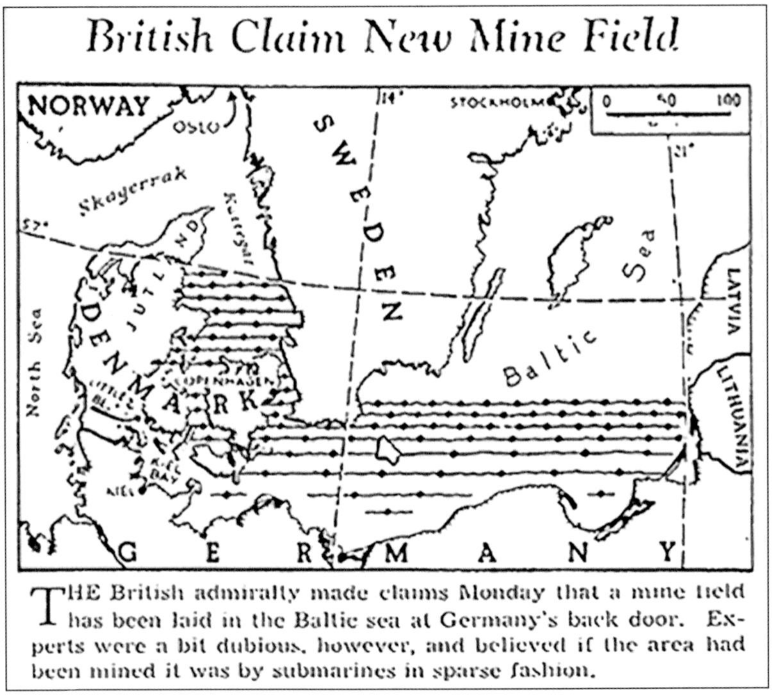

British Claim New Mine Field

THE British admiralty made claims Monday that a mine field has been laid in the Baltic sea at Germany's back door. Experts were a bit dubious, however, and believed if the area had been mined it was by submarines in sparse fashion.

American newspapers questioned whether it had even been possible for British minelayers or submarines to lay mines in Danish waters. Apparently laying mines from aeroplanes was not an option that was considered.

be laid in 'Eglantine' and 'Flax'[16] until 'Asparagus', 'Broccoli' and 'Daffodil' had been mined. Although the plan was to lay the most mines in 'Daffodil' [Øresund], 36 compared to 20 in each of the other two, the initial focus would be on mining the belts.[17]

The decision not to send Gardeners over the Sound on the night of 15 April was made so as not to disturb 22 Hampdens, whose task that night was to find possible ship targets in the waters from Kieler Bay via the Sound to the Oslofjord.[18] In addition, seven Wellingtons from 3 Group would be in the eastern Kattegat, also looking for targets. British naval command had received intelligence that a large German convoy would sail from Kiel during 14 April, heading north towards Oslo. All aircraft from Bomber Command had orders to attack any surface ships they saw, whereas they were forbidden to attack U-boats, as British submarines were still operating in the Skagerrak and Kattegat at this time.[19]

The mine laying was to be carried out by seven Hampdens from 61 Squadron and seven from 144 Squadron, all of whom were to lay mines in 'Broccoli' near Nyborg. The two squadrons had shown their abilities the previous night, when four out of five aircraft had found their way to this area. It was therefore natural to give them this task. In Lillebælt, four

16 The 'Flax' mining area, the mouth of the Elbe and the Kieler Bay, was later divided and given the code names 'Eglantine' and 'Forget-me-not' respectively.

17 Air 14/700. Bomber Command HQ to 5 Group. Ops. 840, 14.4.1940.

18 Air 28/353. Hemswell ORB, 14.4.1940. Raid DEH 228-41; Air 27/686. 83 Sqdn. ORB, 14.4.1940.

19 Air 28/549. Mildenhall ORB, 14.4.1940.

Hampdens from 83 Squadron were to lay their mines, while a further 22 Hampdens from the three squadrons were to lay mines in areas such as 'Asparagus' near Korsør.[20]

At Bomber Command HQ, doubts were beginning to arise as to whether Harris was following the guidelines he had been given regarding the minelaying operations. Just after noon, Air Commodore D. F. Stevenson, Director of Operations (Home), called Portal. He wanted to complain that the orders issued by Harris meant that all three areas, 'A', 'B' and 'C' would be mined simultaneously. Stevenson pointed out that this clearly contradicted Bomber Command's order that the areas were to be mined in order of priority. It was only when 'A' had been mined with 20 mines that you could start mining in 'B', then 'C' and so on. He asked for an explanation as to why these guidelines were not being followed. Portal immediately called the Air Ministry and was told that they had ordered mines to be laid at Nyborg as the first priority, in order to hit German shipping through the Great Belt and the Korsør-Nyborg ferry connection. Portal was then able to call Stevenson and reassure him that Harris had simply followed the orders from the Air Ministry. Portal took the opportunity to state that in the future it would of course be the task of the Air Ministry and Bomber Command to give the head of 5 Group clear and unambiguous guidelines for minelaying operations.[21]

On another point, however, Harris had clearly exceeded his authority. Despite Bomber Command's order that only two squadrons were to be equipped with the special mine suspension, Harris had ensured that all aircraft in 61, 83 and 144 Squadrons received it. On reading the order Harris had issued for the night, Bomber Command HQ now realised that aircraft from all three squadrons were to participate. A telex was immediately sent to 5 Group reminding Harris of the orders he had received. However, it was sent so late in the evening that Harris 'unfortunately' found himself unable to change the operational plans.[22]

Hampden bomber crews of 61 Squadron at Hemswell putting on their flying kit, 1940.

20 Air 28/353. Hemswell ORB, 14.4.1940; Air 27/686. 83 Sqdn. ORB, 14.4.1940.
21 Air 14/700. Bomber Command ORB. BC to 5 Group. 12.20, 14.4.1940.
22 Air 14/700. Bomber Command ORB. BC HQ to 5 Group. Ops. 845. 19.50, 14.4.40.

Meteorologists had warned all squadrons that a warm front with rain, fog and possible thunderstorms was heading east across the North Sea towards England. Nevertheless, 40 Hampdens took off from their bases on schedule and were soon on course for Denmark. Before long, however, the pilots realised that the meteorologists' prediction was correct. The weather was extremely bad over the North Sea. Most of the planes had to turn back after a few hours of flying. However, the 14 crews that were to lay mines in the Great Belt and one of the four crews that were to lay mines in the Little Belt continued towards their targets. Almost blindly, they reached Denmark. Ten of the fourteen pilots could not locate the target area 'Broccoli'. As there were clear and very strict orders that the mines had to be taken back home in such cases, they turned back after a few minutes of searching. The last four laid their mines and then followed the others home.[23]

In cases where a crew found it necessary to drop their mine, for example if the aircraft had been damaged by flak or enemy fighters, the mine had to be dropped in as deep water as possible. This would prevent the Germans from being able to recover a mine intact. If the crew was over land, unable to reach open water and forced to parachute out of the aircraft, it was the pilot's job to keep the aircraft's engines running for the duration of the drop. This significantly increased the chance that the plane would explode on impact, removing any trace of the secret weapon that the magnetic mine was still considered to be.[24]

Of the 4 aircraft from 83 Squadron that were to lay mines in Lillebælt, only one reached the target area. The later famous Guy Gibson, was the pilot of this aircraft.[25] Through rain and fog, his navigator, Jack Winthers, suddenly made landfall on the island of Sylt. From Gibson's hand we have a vivid account of what happened next:

> We flew on the instruments all the way to our destination, but then it cleared up a bit and we spotted Denmark ahead. It did not take Jackie Winthers long to locate the southern tip of Sylt, after which we headed for the Little Belt. As we roared off at 700 metres above Denmark, we ran into low cloud cover again. We were right on the edge of the cloud cover, which must have gone right down to the ground ... Shortly afterwards Jack told me to reduce altitude and the old Hampden slid slowly into the darkness at a speed of 90 metres per minute ... There was silence for a while, while we were still losing altitude; outside there were only the dancing clouds, inside the dim light from the instruments. It got darker and darker. I looked at my own altimeter; it was almost at zero.
>
> Come on, Jack, what's the height?
>
> I said and pressed the button for the backup intercom. His voice reached me after a small click.
>
> I'm sorry! The plug fell out. Jesus Christ, if my altimeter is right, we're a bloody submarine!

23 Air 28/353. Hemswell ORB. Raid DEH 228-41. 14.4.1940.

24 Air 28/882. 5 Group operation order no. B.57. 11.4.1940.

25 Guy Gibson was a wing commander at the time and on 16 May 1943 led an outstanding attack on two German dams, Möhne and Eder, earning the crews the nickname 'The Dam Busters'. For his efforts, he was awarded the Victoria Cross. He was killed while flying back from a mission over The Netherlands on 19 September 1944.

Flying Officer Guy Gibson earned a reputation as a fearless and brave pilot as early as 1940, at the age of 22, after his trip under the Little Belt Bridge.

> I immediately levelled the machine; and then I saw the bridge. It was indeed the Little Belt Bridge; right in front of us. There was nothing to do but stay down here. So it was that Mac [the rear gunner] was suddenly astonished to see, from his place amidships, a bridge whizzing by above him.
>
> And then …
>
> Bomb doors open. Here we are.
>
> All right! Stay the course.
>
> Steady, steady, not too early.
>
> Ok! The mines – gone!
>
> There was a slap and a clonk as the mines slipped out through the hatch.[26]

The plane had descended to an altitude of just 90 feet above the surface of the water and suddenly a German flak ship opened fire at the plane. The rear gunner opened fire at the ship while Gibson pulled the aircraft up and out to the west. A south-westerly gale meant

26 Guy Gibson, *Mål i sigte* (Haderslev: 1963), pp.50–51. Gibson's book does indeed say 'mines', but as mentioned, Hampdens only carried 1 mine per sortie!

that he could not push the aircraft's ground speed to more than 95mph, or about half the normal speed. In addition, the unsettled weather affected the aircraft's instruments, so Gibson and his crew also involuntarily took a 'small' detour home. After a couple of hours of flying, much to their surprise, they passed close to the Dutch coast, after which Gibson quickly set his course westwards. After a total of 9 hours of gruelling flight, Gibson was able to set the plane down at the home base. Some of the other crews were not so lucky. During the night, one of the planes passed Manston airfield apparently without realising it. The aircraft continued over the Atlantic Ocean and no trace of either aircraft or crew was ever found. Several of the other aircraft had to make emergency landings at the nearest airfields, during which a number of crew members were killed.[27]

Considering the relatively small number of aircraft that reached the target areas and the extremely bad weather, it is quite understandable that the German reports regarding the overflights that night were 'Reconnaissance aircrafts over Sylt, Schleswig-Holstein and southern Denmark.' A single German fighter was sent up to get at the British planes, but it failed to find, let alone make contact, with any of the intruding aircraft.[28]

Gibson and his crew's 'aerial act' under the Little Belt Bridge had consequences for German-Danish relations, as the German military authorities in Denmark immediately demanded the handover of a total of 24 machine guns from the Danish Army for the defence of strategically important traffic routes. The machine guns were to be distributed with eight guns at the Little Belt Bridge, eight guns at the Storstrøm Bridge and eight guns to protect the ferry berths at the Great Belt crossing. After some discussion in the Danish Government, the required weapons were eventually handed over.[29]

Guarding the Little Belt Bridge April 1940.

In this way, the Germans freed up a similar number of their own machine guns, which were quickly relocated to Norway.[30]

27 Air 27/686. 83 Sqdn ORB. 14–15.14.1940; Air 28/681 Scampton ORB. 14–15.14.40.

28 Adm. Dän, 12/206. 14.4.1940, 21.39-01.04.

29 Palle Roslyng-Jensen, *Værnenes politik – politikernes værn* (Gyldendal: 1980), p.53. See also the section on Danish-German relations.

30 Børge Outze, *Danmark under den anden verdenskrig*, (Copenhagen:1962–1968), vol. II, pp.102 & 110.

Bomber Command's lesson from the night raid was clear. Harris had probably overestimated the aircrew's ability to find their way in bad weather. On the afternoon of 15 April, the Air Ministry issued a precautionary order to both Bomber Command and Coastal Command. It was short and to the point: 'Mining operations shall not, repeat, not be carried out unless weather and light conditions are good enough for the satisfactory performance of the tasks.'[31]

Gibson's encounter with the German flak ship in the Little Belt, as well as information that the Little Belt Bridge would probably be further protected by anti-aircraft fire in the future, led Harris to decide on a slightly more southerly location for the 'Carrot' target area.[32] By this time, Harris was getting tired of all the talk and letters that still referred to the secret magnetic mines in plain language. In a memorandum to Bomber Command Headquarters dated 15 April, he informed the leadership that in order to maintain the secrecy surrounding 'Operation Gardening', it was necessary to enforce the use of the agreed code. He had therefore compiled a complete list of code names, so that there was a code name for each letter of the alphabet. The list started with the six mining areas that had already been adopted: 'Asparagus' (Korsør), 'Broccoli' (Nyborg), 'Carrots' (Lillebælt), 'Daffodil' (Øresund), 'Eglantine' (Elbe) and 'Forget-me-Not' (Kielerbugten).[33] On 17 April, Bomber Command HQ accepted this list of code names and communicated this to the Air Ministry and Coastal Command.[34] During 1940–1941 the list was expanded to a total of 64 minefields from Archangel in the north to Gibraltar in the south.

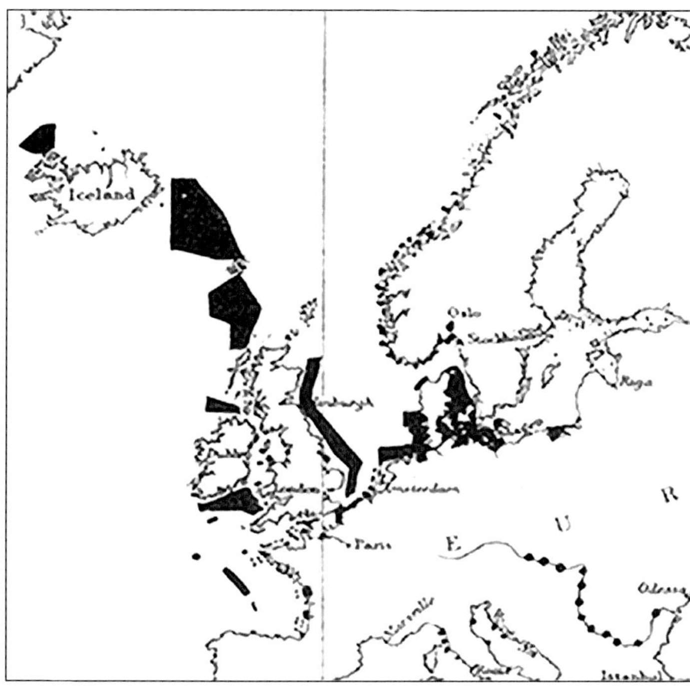

British minefields 1940–1945.

31 Air 14/700 Air Ministry to Bomber/Coastal Command. 15.4.1940, 15.50 hrs.

32 Air 14/700. Minutes of Portal's conversation with Bottomley (SASO BC) regarding conversation with Naval Liaison Officer 5 Group about the minefields. The mining areas. 15.4.1940.

33 Kieler Bay had previously been codenamed 'Flax', but Harris apparently thought 'Forget-Me-Not' was more appropriate for this area; Air 14/700. Minutes of Portal's conversation with Bottomley (SASO BC) regarding conversation with Naval Liaison Officer 5 Group about the minefields. The mining areas. 15.4.1940.

34 Air 15/245. Bomber Command HQ to Air Ministry and Coastal Command. 17.4.1940.

Asparagus – Great Belt	Pollock – Bornholm-area
Broccoli – Great Belt	Pumpkins – Great Belt
Carrots – Little Belt	Quinces – Great Belt/Kiel Bay
Daffodil – The Sound	Radishes – Kiel Bay
Endives – Little Belt	Silverthorn-Kattegat Areas (1941–)
Forget-me-Nots – Kiel Canal	Sweet Peas – Rostock and Arcone Light
Geranium – Swinemunde	Undergrowth – Kattegat (1940-1941)
Hawthorn – Esbjerg Approaches	Verbena – Copenhagen Approaches
Jasmine – Travemunde	Wallflowers – Kiel Bay
Krauts – Lim Fjord	Willows – Arcona River Dievenow
Lettuces – Kiel Canal	Yewtree – Kattegat (Læsø Rende)
Nasturtiums – The Sound	

19 minefields in Danish waters and 4 fields in the western part of the Baltic Sea that are often included in the count of mines in Danish waters.

In cryptanalysis, 'Gardening' became a term used by the British code experts at Bletchley Park. The method was used to lure the Germans into including known plaintext, which the British called 'Cribs' in their encrypted messages. The technique is claimed to have been the most effective at intercepting messages produced by the German Navy's Enigma encryption machines. If the Germans had recently swept a particular area for mines and analysts at Bletchley Park needed to lay some 'cradles', they would request the Admiralty that the area be re-mined as soon as possible. This often caused encrypted messages from the local German naval command, with the word *Minen* or the geographical location included in a message to the minesweeper service that the area would be swept again. It often worked as intended and to the great satisfaction of the codebreakers.[35]

Bomber Command was naturally very interested in finding out how effective the laid mines were. The day after the first mine laying, on 14 April, a Hampden was sent out on a reconnaissance mission over the southern Danish waters. The crew was to make ship observations over Fredericia, Middelfart, Nyborg and Esbjerg. However, there were no wrecks to be seen in the Great Belt that day.[36]

After being subject to an enforced 'German sailing plan' since 9 April, the Korsør-Nyborg ferry service was only stopped at 16:00 on 14 April, as Danske Statsbaner (Danish State Railways/DSB) management had heard on Swedish radio that the RAF had laid mines in the Kattegat, Baltic Sea and the Belts. The Ministry of Industry, Trade and Shipping could confirm this, as they had listened to the British radio.

Two hours later, Peter Knutzen, Director General of the DSB, was summoned to an interview with the German railway representative, who demanded that the voyage be resumed as there was no danger of mines. Knutzen let the order go ahead, but noted in his report that sailing was now resumed 'on the Germans' responsibility! The first crossings went

35 <https://en.wikipedia.org/wiki/Gardening_(cryptanalysis)>.
36 Air 22/8. War Room Daily Summaries, April 1940.

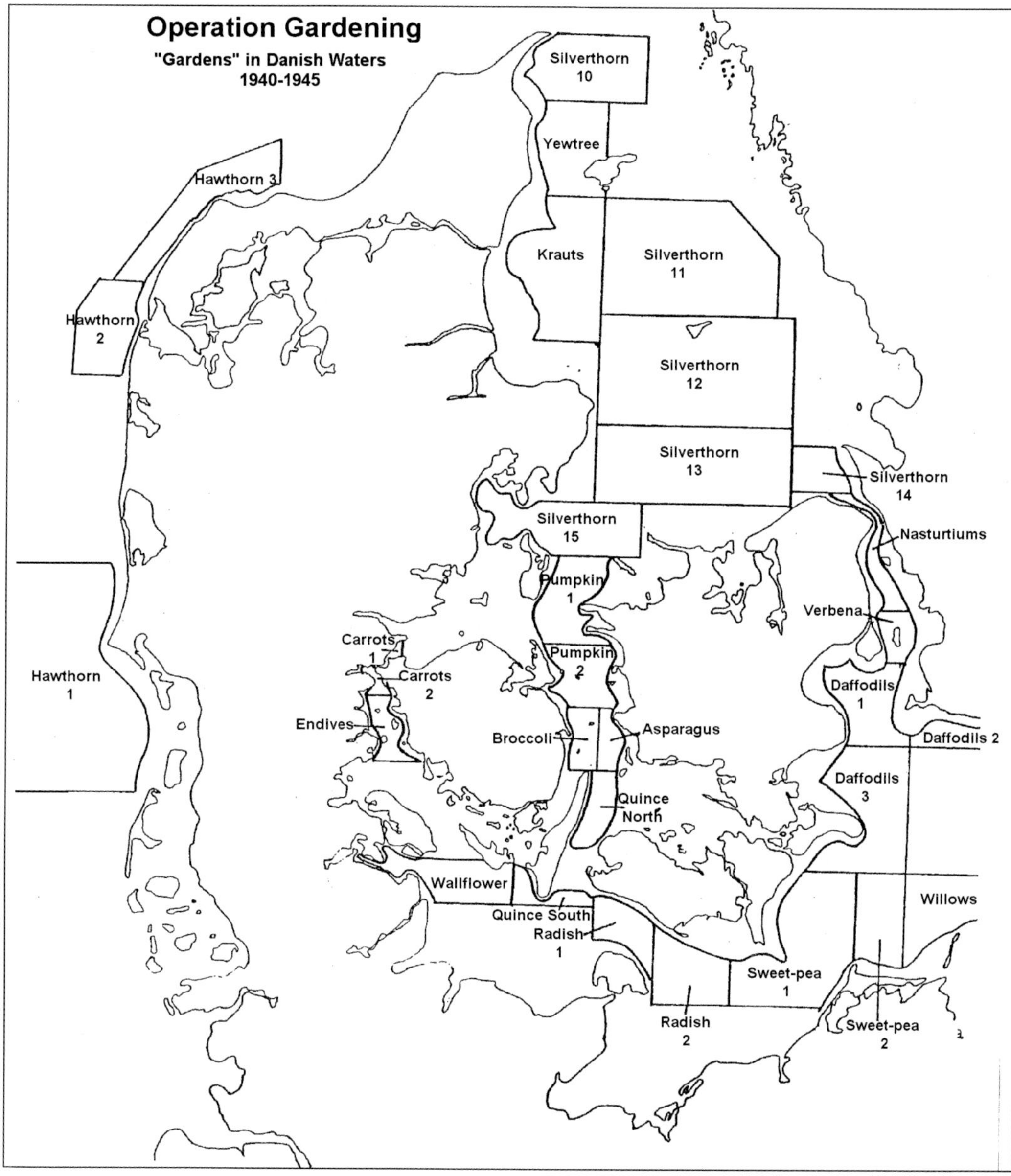

Mine map with 'Gardens' in Danish waters. Based on data from AIR 24/ 728 'July 42-July 44. Mining: Operation orders and instructions'.

according to plan, but at 23.00, the freight ferry *Nyborg* ran into a British mine just south of Sprogø. The Danish newspaper editors were strictly instructed by the Danish Ministry of Foreign Affairs not to mention the incident in any way.[37] The detonation destroyed the ferry's rudder, while the hull and engines were not damaged. The cargo of 29 freight wagons was also intact. *Nyborg* was towed to Korsør and DSB decided to suspend ferry services on the Great Belt, including the Aarhus – Kalundborg connection, until further notice.[38]

The German minesweepers immediately searched the Great Belt and by the evening of 15 April, DSB was informed that the route could be sailed again and that the first ferry would have a minesweeper ahead all the way. However, at the last minute, the sailing was postponed, which was just as well! A few hours later, one of the British mines struck an even bigger prey – a German mine sweeper of the *Sperrbrecher* class.

In the spring of 1940, the German Navy only had 12 of these large minesweepers, 9 of which were in active service during the German occupation of Denmark. All 9 *sperrbrechere* operated in Danish waters, including the only example of the *VES-Sperrbrecher* class. VES stood for *Voraus-eigenschutz* (advanced self-protection). The *Sperrbrecher IV* was able to strike magnetic mines using an extra powerful forward magnetic field. After the *Nyborg* mine blast, three *Sperrbrechers*, Nos *X*, *XI* and *XII*, were deployed on the route.

Shortly before 20:00, *Sperrbrecher XI* was hit by a violent detonation while anchored off Korsør harbour. The explosion hit the bow of the minesweeper and it was badly damaged. The next day, the ship barely managed to make it to Kiel under its own power, but it was not worth the effort to repair the damage immediately.[39] Despite their diligent efforts, the German minesweepers found no further mines.

On 16 April, the route was again searched by the two remaining *sperrbrechere* and again without success. The ferry service was then resumed, but with the new safety measure that a *sperrbrecher* would sail ahead of every ferry crossing.[40]

Through interception of German radio communications, it quickly became clear to the British what had happened to *Sperrbrecher XI*.[41] Through Swedish press sources, the news of the *Nyborg* mine blast and DSB's precautions in this connection also became known in the British Admiralty. Based on these two successes, Director of Operations (Home), Air Commodore Stevenson, decided on 16 April that all operational squadrons in 5 Group should be involved in 'Operation Gardening'. He informed Air Commodore Bottomley, Senior Air Staff Officer Bomber Command, that the restriction of a maximum of two

---

37 Steen Ousager, *På sporet 1847-1997*, vol. 2 (Odense: 1997), p.306; 'Confidential messages from the Ministry of Foreign Affairs to the editors', unpublished Statsbiblioteket i Aarhus, p.68, 15.4.1940. KTB Naval Commander Denmark, 14/4 1940.

38 *Avisårbogen* 1940 & Mogens Lebech, *Bæltoverfart i tusind år* (Copenhagen: 1965), pp.126–127.

39 Peter Arndt, *Deutsche Sperrbrecher, 1914-1945* (Stuttgart: 1979), pp.98 & 294; KTB Naval Commander Denmark, 15/4 1940. *Sperrbrecher XI* was originally named *Berengar* and was commissioned by a German owner in 1911. In 1919, it became British spoils of war, and was renamed *General Botha* in 1923. In 1926 it was sold to Germany and renamed *Berengar*, before being renamed *Petropolis* in 1938 and *Sperrbrecher XI* the following year. After the mine blast on 15 April 1940, it was repaired and then used as a cargo and troop transport ship. <https://www.kbismarck.com/mine-barrage-breakers.html> (04.02.2025).

40 KTB Naval Commander Denmark, 16/4 1940.

41 ADM 223/82 Operation al Intelligence Centre, Daily report, 16.4.1940.

Sperrbrecher XI.

minelaying squadrons could be lifted immediately and that areas 'A-D' would be mined with the agreed number of mines.[42] Bottomley immediately informed Harris of this new decision,[43] and the Air Council agreed that the sooner the whole 5 Group was involved in laying mines the better. It was hoped that the weather would allow these waters to be mined as soon as possible. Of course, it was still intended that 5 Group would return to carrying out bombing raids once the planned mining had been completed.[44]

For the time being, however, there was plenty for the unit to do in Danish waters. On the night of 18 April, mines were dropped in the waters around Aalborg. Two Hampdens from 83 Squadron who carried out this raid made a short reconnaissance over Ålborg after dropping their loads. The two crews' observations of the activity at the two airfields gave a cause to the first air attack on Rødslet airfield.[45]

The following day, 19 April, Bomber Command sent an order to 5 Group to conduct a reconnaissance over Aalborg to determine whether the mines had inflicted losses on the Germans. At the same time, three Hampdens were to be prepared to carry out an air strike on Rødslet airfield near Aalborg that evening. However, both of these tasks were only to be carried out if they did not interfere with 5 Group's main task of mine laying.[46] Neither of these missions was carried out until the following day.[47]

42 Air 141700 Record of telephone conversation between Stevenson and Bottomley, 17.00, 16.4.1940. Norman Bottomley was Senior Air Staff Officer at Bomber Command Headquarters from 1938–1940, and was appointed Air Officer Commanding 5 Group in November 1940, succeeding Harris. In 1943 he was promoted to Deputy Chief of the Air Staff and at the end of the war succeeded Harris again, this time as Commander-in-Chief Bomber Command.

43 Air 141700 Record of telephone conversation between Bottomley and Harris, 17:15, 16.4.40.

44 Air 9/446 Report from Peirse (Air Council) to Directorate of Plans, 16.4.1940. .

45 Air 27/686 83 Sqdn. ORB, 17/18.14.1940.

46 Air 24/200 Bomber Command ORB, Ops. order to 5 Group, 19.4.40.

47 Air 28/681. Scampton ORB, 17/18.14.1940, 20/21.4.1940

Over the next few days, mines continued to be laid in several Danish waters, but from 25 April to 1 May operations were suspended. Officially, the weather was blamed,[48] but during the same period Hampdens participated in several bombing raids. Among other things, 20 Hampdens were to have been sent to Aalborg on 30 April, a force that was ultimately somewhat reduced due to the threat of invasion of The Netherlands and Belgium. It seems that air support for the evacuations in Norway was prioritised over the laying of mines. At the same time, the anticipated German campaign in Western Europe meant that every effort was being made to economise on the use of the aircrews and the number of aircraft.

After Bomber Command, Coastal Command, Fleet Air Arm and British submarines had been laying mines in Norwegian and Danish waters for about two weeks, the outcome was eagerly awaited.[49] On 24 April, Portal wrote to Peirse that he could see that it was difficult to obtain sufficient information. The British Secret Intelligence Service had largely given up on getting information from Germany and Denmark. But Portal believed it was vital to find out whether the mines worked at all. In his opinion, information had to be obtained from Swedish and Finnish harbours.[50] On 27 April, information was received from Sweden that two merchant ships had sunk on the night of 25 April in the southern end of Øresund. In addition, a ship was seen blowing up near Drogden Lighthouse on 27 April.[51]

With such meagre intelligence, consisting mainly of the above-mentioned report from Sweden, Harris took stock of the progress and outcome of the minelaying operations from 14 to 27 April, complaining about the lack of information on the effects of the mines. In particular, he criticised the Admiralty, which he felt must have the necessary connections to obtain information.

As mentioned, DSB had stopped ferry traffic after the Storebælt ferry *Nyborg* hit a mine on 14 April. A total of three ferries were held back, including the damaged one. In Harris' interpretation, all three ferries had been blown up by mines.[52]

It seems that the crossing had apparently been resumed within a few days, because already on 17 April, the steam ferry *Odin* was also damaged by a mine in the Great Belt. On 19 April, DSB therefore suspended the crossing again. However, it was resumed the following day, but now only during daylight hours. The steam ferry *Christian IX* was hit by a violent explosion on 20 April at 18:30 on the trip from Nyborg to Korsør, even though it was sailing 400 metres behind two German minesweepers. Water entered the engine room and the passengers and some of the crew were transferred to the escort ship in lifeboats. A German surveillance and pilot vessel ship arrived immediately afterwards and transferred mail and goods, after which it began towing the ferry towards Korsør. At 23.00, the ferry sank at a depth of 8 metres on Nygrund. The next day, ferry traffic was stopped again. On 22 April, the Aarhus-Kalundborg route was resumed, while traffic between Zealand and Funen-Jutland now ran via Nakskov-Spodsbjerg.[53]

48 T. K. Derry, *The Campaign in Norway* (London: HMSO, 1952), p.54.

49 Denis Richards & Hilary St George Saunders, *Royal Air Force, 1939–1945* (London: HMSO, 1953), vol. 1, p.89.

50 Air 14/1929 AOC-in-C BC correspondence with D.C.A.S. 24.4.1940.

51 Air 14/3413. Bomber Command Intell. Sum, 27–29 April 1940.

52 Air 14/2064. Bomber Command opr. 'Gardening'. Report 29.4.1940.

53 *Avisårbogen*, 1940, p.35–36. www.vragguiden.dk/wreck.asp?wreckid=1310> 28.10.1908: *Christian IX* was deployed on the crossing between Korsør and Nyborg. 20.04.1940: The ferry hit a mine in the Great Belt and sank in 8 metres of water. The ferry was recovered after some time and towed to

The steam ferry *Christian IX* after the mine blast on 20 April 1940.

After the Great Belt ferry *Nyborg* was damaged on 14 April, the German authorities initially referred to it as sabotage. When rumours began to emerge that it was a mine blast, the explanation was changed to that it had probably been one of the German laid mines that had broken loose. Harris took these excuses as a sign that the Germans had probably suffered greater losses, but were stubbornly trying to deny that it could be the result of a British mine laying effort.[54]

German ships had actually laid mines in the Skagerrak as early as 9 April.[55] But it was a long way from Skagerrak to the Korsør-Nyborg route, and the consistent British mining of these waters makes it likely that it was British mines that caused the damage to the two ferries on the Great Belt. The report, which was based on intelligence from Sweden on 27 April, stated that a ship had sunk in Drogden, the waters between Amager and Saltholm, after a powerful explosion. In the report, the ship was mentioned as the fifth ship to sink near the Drogden Lighthouse in the last three days.

The results from Øresund and the Great Belt showed, again according to Harris, that 16 percent of the dropped mines had been effective. Within the last two weeks, a total of 110 mines had been laid in Danish waters. As the Swedish data only covered three of the nine minelaying areas that had been mined, Harris calculated the overall result to be 10 percent effective mines of the total amount. He assumed that the missing information could cover a larger number of mined ships than they knew.

Nakskov shipyard for provisional repair. Later towed to Copenhagen for permanent repair. 06.1941: Back in traffic. 14-10-1944: The ferry was seized by the German Navy to be used as a troop transport ship – primarily in the Norwegian fjords. 1945: After the end of the war, the ferry was found in Narvik and returned to DSB in July. Towed to Copenhagen for renovation. 1946–1964: The ship was deployed on the route between Korsør and Nyborg.

54 Air 14/2064. Bomber Command opr. 'Gardening', Report 29.4.1940.

55 *Avisårbogen*, 1940, p.112.

When we know the total number of mines dropped, totalling 110, the number of flights must also be at least 110. Only seven aircraft were lost during this period, which showed that, also in terms of maintaining air power, mine laying was the best method of preventing German reinforcements from reaching Norway by sea. Harris therefore pleaded for an increased effort with the participation of aircraft from some of the other Groups, as well as an increased production of magnetic mines. The latter was necessary if new areas were to be mined while the 'old' areas were still to be maintained. Tactically, an increased mine threat would force the Germans to accelerate their plans and operations in Norway. This pressure would ultimately be devastating for German warfare. Extensive mining of the routes that German ships were forced to follow might prove to be the best support for the Allied troops in Northern Norway, as German supplies of especially aviation fuel could then be delayed or, at best, destroyed.

Harris also pointed out that it was necessary to take advantage of the fact that the Germans did not have sufficient knowledge of the British magnetic mines to develop countermeasures. However, it would not be long before such measures could be expected. Harris was quick to cite horrifying historical examples of how the benefits of introducing a secret weapon had been squandered by hesitating too long before using it on a full scale.

In his final report, Harris promised that with six Hampden squadrons, including a squadron equipped with extra tanks, he would be able to hold enemy ships in their ports of departure. If the German ships did attempt to reach Norway, Harris' mining would inflict heavy losses on the German merchant and naval fleet – weather permitting, of course! In reality, the Germans 'only' lost 8–9 percent of their shipping tonnage and about 1 percent of their troops during the sea transport to Norway.[56]

The report came at an unfortunate time for Harris. The decision to withdraw and evacuate Allied troops at Åndalsnes and Namsos in Norway had already been made and would be implemented in the first few days of May. At the same time, forces were beginning to gather to counter the expected German advance in Western Europe. Instead, the minelaying continued with a reduced force of 4–6 aircraft from each of the operational squadrons in 5 Groups, totalling 24–36 aircraft out of a total force of 55–60 operational aircraft.

On 3 May, Peirse sent a warning to Portal that he could soon expect a request from the Air Ministry for 5 Group's Hampdens to be used for air strikes on the German-occupied airfields at Trondhjem and Værnæs in Norway. These attacks would help ease the pressure on the Allied forces at Narvik. The warning prompted Portal to send a report to Peirse the following day, outlining the action that would be required. In order to reach the targets, and back again, the planes would have to take off from Lossiemouth in northern Scotland. To prevent the *Luftwaffe* from using the two airfields, at least 25 Hampdens and 30 crews would be needed for this purpose. As 5 Group at this time had 55 operational aircraft and 76 crews, approximately half of the Group would have to be given up. Over such a long distance that the aircraft would have to cover, approximately 750 miles, a high loss rate was to be expected. Add to that the fact that the crews would be far from their home base, and morale would drop pretty quickly.

56 Air 14/2064. Bomber Command Op.'Gardening', Report 29.4.1940. Denis Richards & Hilary St George Saunders, *Royal Air Force, 1939–1945*, vol.1 (London: HMSO, 1953), chap. IV, p.89.

Portal questioned how much the Air Staff really valued mine laying? After attacks on industrial targets, Portal considered minelaying to be the most profitable method of inflicting losses on the Germans. He therefore thought it would be a waste of good effort to assign experienced minelaying crews to bomb airfields in unfamiliar territory. In Portal's opinion, attacks on airfields were rarely a good solution. He therefore intended to reject any Air Ministry proposal of this nature as uneconomical and unhealthy for morale, as well as being against the existing conservation policy, which was to preserve and strengthen the long-range bombing force.[57]

It was not a general opposition to attacks on airfields that Portal was expressing here. His main argument was that, as far as possible, one should try to preserve and utilise the experienced minelaying unit one had, rather than throwing it into a, at that time, risky attack attempt. Portal could not be interested in having his 5 Group decimated in this way. This is also emphasised by his final argument, namely the conservation policy. Since 1 May, Bomber Command had kept large parts of the air force on standby, which, for example, had an impact on the last air raids on the German-occupied airfields in Ålborg and Rye in early May. It was expected that the Germans would soon move into The Netherlands and perhaps France. Therefore, Portal's use of this particular argument was a trump card to conclude his defence of the preservation of 5 Group as a minelaying unit.

With this content of the letter in mind, it is clear that the British military historian Max Hastings, in his book *Bomber Command*, has misinterpreted and misused the extract of Portal's letter to Peirse quoted by him.[58] Hastings does not mention anything about Portal's main argument that mine laying should be prioritised over attacks on German and German-occupied airfields, but only that Portal considered it risky to risk the loss of bombers in this type of attack, and used it to criticise the conditions surrounding the disastrous air raid on Aalborg airfield on 13 August 1940.

Peirse's ulterior motives in warning Portal must be seen in light of the discussion in Bomber Command on 19 April, where Peirse had been a strong advocate of prioritising attacks on German shipping. In the Air Council, where Peirse also sat, there was also a majority in favour of a major effort in this area. It therefore seems that Peirse, through his warning to Portal, wanted to get backing from Bomber Command before the request for 5 Group's efforts in Norway was made by the Air Ministry. With the letter from Portal, Peirse was able to take the proposal off the table before it was passed on to Bomber Command. In the end, the last attack Bomber Command carried out during the Norwegian Campaign until 10 May was not carried out at the two airfields mentioned, but at Sola, near Stavanger, on 7–8 May.[59]

Minelaying operations continued from 1 to 15 May. After this, 5 Group became involved in the evacuation of troops from Dunkirk. Due to the aforementioned vulnerability of the

57 Air 14/194. Letter from Portal to Peirse, Air Ministry, 4.5.1940.

58 Max Hastings, *Bomber Command* (London: Pan Books, 1982 2nd edition), p.82.

59 Air 14/669. Bomber Command ops. during the Norw. Camp: Draft dispatch by Air Marshal Portal. This last attack was carried out by the Wellingtons from 3 Group. Air 28/520. Narrative report. Attack on Stavanger aerodrome, 7/8. May 1940. About the fatal air raid on Aalborg airfield on 13 August 1940 see Frank Weber et al, *Vestallierede luftangreb i Danmark under 2. Verdenskrig* (Viborg: Aarhus Universitetsforlag, 1988), vol. 1, pp.150–178.

Hampden aircraft during daylight raids, 5 Group's task was mostly to conduct night raids and patrol flights while the evacuation was in progress. The evacuation of the British troops, as well as many French and Belgian troops, was completed on 2 June, and two days later the last French troops in the area surrendered. On 6 June, minelaying resumed, but initially only with a single squadron. The rest of 5 Group still participated in the defence of France. In the nights between 10 and 13 June, direct air support was provided to the French forces through attacks on German lines of communication.[60] But after almost two weeks, the armistice between France and Germany, signed on 22 June, came into effect on 25 June, and 5 Group's future efforts had to be re-planned.

6.2 The Consequences of the First Mine Laying, 1940

In the aforementioned mine laying report issued by Harris on 3 June, covering the period 13 April to 7 May, it was stated, among other things, that approximately 40 percent of the aircraft deployed placed their mines at the designated location. In June this rose to 70 percent, which Harris attributed to the crews' increased experience in night flying and knowledge of the individual minelaying areas. Of course, the light nights also made it easier for the navigators to find their way over enemy territory.[61]

At the end of 1940, the preliminary results of the minelaying programme were calculated. A total of 1,117 mines had been laid, 765 of them by 5 Group, Bomber Command. A total of 1,029 Hampdens had been launched and only 21 aircraft had been shot down or otherwise lost. The total loss for the entire RAF minelaying effort was 31 aircraft.[62] This shows how effective this weapon was, especially when we now know that 86 German, or German-controlled, ships were sunk and 10 damaged to various degrees during that first year.[63] Just under half of the mines, 300, had been laid in Danish waters. [64]

The reason why so many planes turned back with unfinished business was usually the weather. It almost always failed in one of the places: over the airfields in Great Britain, over the North Sea or over Denmark. A small number of aircraft turned back after being hit by German fighters. A slightly larger proportion were hit by German flak.

It is difficult to say how many losses the German Navy actually suffered from the British mines in the early period. The British themselves estimated that the German Navy had only lost 8–9 percent of their ships on the Norway route in the period from the start of minelaying in mid-April to mid-June 1940. Out of the approximately 100,000 officers and soldiers who had been transported through Danish waters during this period, only around

60 Air 14/673. Report on operations for the period 5 June to 16 June 1940. HQ 5 Group to HQ Bomber Command, 16.7.1940.

61 Air 14/673. Report on operations for the period 5 June to 16 June 1940. HQ 5 Group to HQ Bomber Command, 16.7.1940. pkt. 6.

62 Chaz Bowyer: 'Hampden Special' Published by Ian Allan, 1976 p.22. Stephen W. Roskill, *The Navy at War 1939–1945* (London: HMSO, 1960), p.125.

63 Stephen W. Roskill, *The Navy at War 1939–1945* (London: HMSO, 1960), p.336.

64 Bomber Command and Admiralty Mining Dept. Records, 1940 (number of mines in the 19 Danish fields).

1,000 men lost their lives.[65] The term 'only' in the British report suggests that the result was not satisfactory. From the German side, the losses for the same period were calculated at 1,317 killed, 1,604 wounded and 2,375 missing at sea or elsewhere. The German Navy had lost 3 cruisers, 10 destroyers, 1 torpedo boat and 6 U-boats. In addition, 15 smaller naval and auxiliary vessels were lost.[66] Furthermore, as previously mentioned, the *Sperrbrecher XI* was hit by a mine near Korsør on 15 April. On 30 May, a German speedboat and a mine-sweeper *M 75* was damaged by mines in Øresund.[67] However, the damage was limited in that in mid-July the *M 75* was able to take part in the firing at two British aircraft over the Sound.[68] Nevertheless, the ship was sent to the shipyard 15 days later to have the boiler repaired.[69] Another minesweeper, *Sperrbrecher 11*, was hit by a mine on the night of 9 September at Halskov Rev Fyrskib, off Korsør.[70]

In addition to the three ships mentioned above, there were a further eight German naval vessels that were severely damaged by magnetic mines in Danish waters. In addition, 12 Danish vessels, ranging from motor ships and galleasses to steamers and motor ferries, were hit by mines in the period from May to December 1940.[71] A single Swedish steamer was among the casualties when it struck a British mine at Drogden Lighthouse on the morning of 21 July.[72]

The mine blasts occurred precisely in the areas where British aircraft laid mines, both in the southern waters and near Sæby and Aalborg. In the North Sea and Kattegat/Skagerrak, fishing boats were occasionally shaken when they caught a mine in their nets. But these were usually German contact mines, which were, after all, in the majority. Few fishermen would behave like the two men who caught a mine in their net on 2 December. They fished it out and hauled it in. During the process of placing it on deck, it detonated and both fishermen were killed.[73]

The immediate result of the mine laying seemed to be fairly minor. The indirect effect on shipping traffic, however, was not insignificant. For example, ferry routes were repeatedly cancelled for fear of the danger of mines. Several times it took more than a week before both the German and Danish authorities dared to allow the waters to be navigated again. As soon as a British overflight was suspected of being a minelaying operation, traffic was again

65 Denis Richards & Hilary St George Saunders, *Royal Air Force, 1939–1945*, vol.1 (London: HMSO, 1953), p.89.

66 *Avisårbogen*, 1940, p.114: 'A German account of the course of the war in the Nordic countries is published', 13.6.1940.

67 Adm. Dän. 18/249, 31.5.40.

68 Adm. Dän. 18/249, 15.7.40.

69 Adm. Dän. 18/249 30.8.40. Then mine sweeper training ship until it sank during a storm in the Sound, 2.3.1945. Walther Lohmann and H.H. Hildebrand, *Die Deutsche Kriegsmarine 1939–1945*, Vol. 1 (Bad Nauheim: 1956), pp.23 & 34.

70 Adm. Dän. 18/249, 8–9 September 1940. *Sperrbrecher 11* – former M/S *Zeus*.

71 *Avisårbogen*, 1940. Adm. Dän. 18/2491940. 'Confidential messages from the Ministry of Foreign Affairs to the editorial staff' unpublished Statsbiblioteket i Aarhus. Poul Bech, *Søkrig i danske farvande under Anden Verdenskrig 1939–1942* (Schønberg: 2008), pp.270–272 – a list of mined ships in the inner Danish waters 1940, which shows that 11 German ships were damaged or sank, probably as a result of British bottom mines. In total, 70 ships were hit by mines in 1940.

72 'Confidential messages from the Ministry of Foreign Affairs to the editors' unpublished Statsbiblioteket i Aarhus, pp.96–98.

73 *Avisårbogen*, 1940, pp.99–100, dd 2.12.1940.

stopped for a period. A few times, ferries were even directed back to the port of departure after having sailed. Several times, harbours were closed for one or more days when it was suspected that they had been mined. After the three ferries were mined between Korsør and Nyborg on 14–20 April, ferry traffic came to a standstill for a week, with around 1,400 wagons gradually piling up on both sides of the Great Belt. It was not until 28 April that services resumed, and then only with a single double trip per day. After a week, the lorry congestion was cleared. Even a port as important to the Germans as Frederikshavn was closed several times in 1940, for example on 6 and 7 September.[74] When Danish shipping traffic was disrupted to such a relatively high degree, it is reasonable to assume that German shipping traffic was also affected.

The British saw the minelaying as the main reason why German troop transports to Norway from 13 April until 10 May increasingly shifted the emphasis from ships to rail. By transporting troops and supplies to Frederikshavn and Sæby, the sea journey was significantly shortened.[75]

However, the mines could not have been the cause until 25 April at the earliest. In the intervening days, from the first mine laying on 14 April and 10 days later, the Germans did not link the damage reports to the British overflights. It was assumed that the explosions were caused by sabotage or torpedoes from British submarines. Only after the ferry on the Great Belt crossing on 16 April was damaged by a mine that was not supposed to be there did the German Navy's leadership realise that there might be such a connection. It was not until 25 April that they became certain that the RAF was behind the mine laying. On that day, a German minesweeper managed to get hold of an intact mine that had landed in shallow water. It had possibly been damaged or for some other reason had not been armed. The next day, the mine was sent for closer examination at the *Kriegsmarine*'s mine testing station in Kiel. They were convinced that it was a combined acoustic and magnetic mine. However, it later turned out to be a pure magnetic mine, similar to the type the Germans themselves had used against British shipping since the beginning of the war.[76]

In his report to Hitler on 26 April, the Commander-in-Chief of the *Kriegsmarine*, *Grossadmiral* Admiral Raeder, announced that mine warfare was now of great importance. Only one British mine of the new type had been captured and it was not yet certain whether it was a magnetic mine. Raeder believed that the best weapon against the British minelayers would be to bomb their bases. The RAF had previously used this method with great success against the German minelaying aircraft.[77]

On 7 May, he again reported to Hitler and again stressed the importance of combating the airborne mining of German ports and shipping lanes. However, Göring would not grant Raeder's request to conduct air strikes on the bases of the British minelayers. He would not even provide the *Kriegsmarine* with more minelaying aircraft than it already had at its disposal. Göring justified this with the need to save *Luftwaffe* resources for the upcoming

74 Steen Ousager, *På sporet 1847–1997* (Odense: 1997), vol. 2, pp.307–310. Adm. Dän. 18/249, 6–7 September 1940.

75 T. K. Derry, *The Campaign in Norway* (London: HMSO, 1952), p.55

76 Michael Salewski, *Die Deutsche Seekriegsleitung 1935–1945*, vol. 1 (Frankfurt am Main: 1970), p.214; Poul Bech, *Søkrig i danske farvande under Anden Verdenskrig 1939–1942* (Schønberg: 2008), p.182.

77 Gerhard Wagner, *Lagevorträge des Oberbefehlshabers der Kriegsmarine 1939–1945* (Munich: 1972), p.100.

campaign in the west.[78] Hitler supported Göring on this issue.[79] On this point, both the German and British military leaders of the respective air forces saw the situation in the same way. They were saving their energies for the anticipated confrontation. The *Kriegsmarine* was therefore largely left to come up with its own countermeasures against the British minelaying, as the next Chapter shows.

In 5 Group, which was still responsible for RAF mine laying, the weak fighter air defence over Denmark had been noted, and in a report to Bomber Command on 16 July 1940, it was pointed out that the flak and searchlight activity in Denmark was also very weak.[80] But in the end, it was the Air Ministry that decided how large the minelaying effort should be. During the autumn of 1940, there was an increasing need for long-range aircraft for escort and anti-submarine activities, which contributed to a further reduction in mine laying efforts. At the same time, more and larger bombing raids were needed to hit targets inside Germany itself, and the Air Ministry needed everything that could be spared for this purpose. Nor had it yet been realised how much damage was being inflicted on the enemy by a relatively small minelaying operation. The consequence of all this was that during the last three months of 1940 only 134 mines were laid by Bomber Command, while during the month of July 1940 alone 156 had been laid. However, the Air Ministry promised that the first new Stirling and Manchester squadrons would be assigned to minelaying work.[81]

6.3 Bombs Dropped During Minelaying Operations, 1940

For the first few months after 9 April, the mining planes carried no or very little bomb load on board. It was up to the individual station commander at the airfield to decide whether or not bombs could be carried. The mines weighed around 1,500 pounds each, and since a Hampden could only carry a maximum of around 4,000 pounds on a trip as long as to Denmark, each aircraft only carried one mine. The weight of the extra fuel of around 1,500 pounds also had to be taken into account. The author has found no example of a Hampden being fully loaded, i.e. with fuel (1,500 pounds), 1 mine (1,500 pounds) and four 250 pound bombs, to a total of 4,000 pounds. That would have been pretty risky too. Therefore, when the planes were 'allowed' to carry bombs, it was usually only two 250 pound bombs.

On the night of 20 July, five Hampdens from 44 Squadron were each equipped with two bombs in addition to the mine on their way to Denmark. Three of the planes were to lay their mines in 'Undergrowth' off Frederikshavn, while the other two were to lay theirs in 'Pumpkin', Sejerø Dyb. The planes at Frederikshavn dropped the mines as planned, but the first plane to arrive was quickly shot down. As the lead aircraft, it was to drop a flare to mark the target area. This illuminated the aircraft itself, making it an easy target for the powerful flak batteries that the Germans had placed near Frederikshavn.[82] It therefore had to make an emergency landing in Tannis Bay off Kandestederne. The two aircraft at Sejerø

78 Gerhard Wagner, *Lagevorträge des Oberbefehlshabers der Kriegsmarine 1939–1945* (Munich: 1972), p.102.
79 Michael Salewski, *Die Deutsche Seekriegsleitung 1935–1945*, vol. 1 (Frankfurt am Main: 1970), p.215.
80 Air 14/673. Memo. Minelaying, 5 Group to Bomber Command 16.7.40.
81 Stephen W. Roskill, *The Navy at War 1939–1945* (London: HMSO, 1960) p.336.
82 Air 28/879. Waddington ORB, 19–20 July 1940.

also dropped their mines as planned, after which the crews observed two cargo ships in the waters. The planes attacked each ship with their bomb load. The bombs were dropped from a height of 2,000 feet and all four missed their targets. However, both pilots later reported how violently the ships had been tilted when the bombs detonated. From one aircraft, the tail gunner had opened fire on the ships, but neither the result of the firing nor the bombs could be determined with certainty.[83]

It was probably because of this somewhat unsuccessful bombing attempt that an order was issued from 5 Group the next day that bombs, which were then carried with the permission of the station commander, had to be fitted with an 11-second delayed fuse. This made it possible for the aircraft to attack merchant and naval ships from a lower altitude without the risk of being hit by the detonation.[84]

A month later, the authorisation to attack ships on the high seas was extended as a last resort to any airfield or other military targets on land.[85] However, the authorisation came a little too late. Hampdens from 5 Group had already bombed airfields in Denmark on several occasions. The first time was on 3 July when six Hampdens were to lay mines in 'Quince', Langelandsbæltet. The four aircraft dropped their bomb loads on Rødby Airfield, a former Danish emergency landing site, and Marslev Airfield, also a former emergency landing site east of Odense, both of which had been taken over by the Germans. Finally, they dropped bombs on Husum Airfield, a North German base west of Schleswig. Along the way, a flak ship was also attacked with machine gun fire. However, hits were only detected at the landing site at Rødby Harbour.[86] In addition to these military targets, two inns in the northern part of Funen very close by were bombed, namely Hindevad Kro and Mørkenborg Kro. The last bombs fell on Kelds Sand, east of Sønder Ho, and were aimed at the German installations in the Esbjerg area. [87]

July was also a month with a number of bombs dropped in connection with raids. For example, the following night, 4 July, bombs were dropped on the southern tip of Langeland and an attack was made on a ship at Kjels Nor off the southern coast of Langeland. Again, this was in connection with a minelaying operation.[88]

The same seems to apply to the bombing raids on the night of 7 July, when 15 or 16 aircraft crossed the Danish coast from the west over a stretch from Henne Strand in the north to Rømø in the south. Wellington and Hampden aircraft were observed near Ribe. Most of the aircraft were at an altitude of 3,000 to 9,000 feet, but even though the German flak batteries opened fire, including with the dreaded 88mm flak guns, no aircraft were hit because the searchlights could not maintain the targets. Two Hampdens came in over Esbjerg at an altitude of only 900 to 1,500 feet and were met by the light flak from machine guns. The Germans themselves believed that this fire caused the planes to turn off. Most of the planes headed south, while a few continued eastwards.

83 Air 27/453. 44 Squadron ORB, 19–20 JULY 1940.
84 Air 14/2064. Ops order 813, from 5 Group to Waddington, Scampton. Hemswell and Lindholme. 21.8.1940.
85 Air 14/2064. Ops. order 813, from 5 Group to Waddington, Scampton. Hemswell and Lindholme. 21.8.1940.
86 Air 24/222nd Bomber Command ORB, 2–3 July 1940.
87 Danish Civil Air Defence, SCL, 2–3 July 1940.
88 Danish Civil Air Defence, SCL, 3–4 July 1940.

From the aircraft types alone, we can see that the two groups of aircraft were on separate missions. The large group of high-altitude Wellingtons were to attack Kiel,[89] while the two Hampdens were to lay mines. It was they who continued eastwards. Via Fåborg, one came south of Funen and up to Nyborg. There it dropped a flare on Avernakke, where the petrol depots had been bombed on 28 June. The Germans had moved more flak to the area and a heavy fire was opened against the aircraft. After laying the mine off Nyborg, the bomb load was dropped a little later in the centre of Langeland, specifically at Frellevig. As there was no immediate target there, the bombs must have been dropped to lighten the aircraft. Perhaps it was damaged by the intense flak over Avernakke. Meanwhile, the other minelaying aircraft had laid its mine in Lillebælt, off Kolding. The bombs from this aircraft were dropped at Marstrup south of Haderslev. Again, it is difficult to determine whether it was to lighten the aircraft or if the pilot thought he saw a military target. In any case, the two planes then headed for home. One dropped two flares over the southern part of Fanø, which of course triggered a flurry of activity in the German air defence system. Searchlights began looking for the aircraft, but it quickly dived to the lowest possible height above the water, making it impossible for the Germans to locate its position.

That same night, 10 bombs fell in a row at Genner Strand, midway between Haderslev and Åbenrå. The bombs must have been dropped by one or two Wellingtons on the way to Kiel, as the time of impact lies between the time of approach at Esbjerg and the time of attack at Kiel.[90] Perhaps it was a coincidence that the bombs fell right at Genner Strand, but as there was a charging station and several small repair workshops for German U-boats at this location, it may have been a well-planned bombing raid on a 'last resort' target.[91]

At the end of the month, minelaying aircraft were again flying over Denmark. On the night of 29 July, bombs were dropped in various parts of the country. According to reports from the *Statens Civile Luftværn*,[92] there was anti-aircraft fire near Esbjerg in the early evening as the British planes approached. Later, there were reports of anti-aircraft fire near

---

89 Detlef Boelck, Detlef, *Kiel im Luftkrieg 1939–1945* (Kiel: 1980), p.1: 'Lebhaftes Flakfeuer. Through nervousness and uncertainty? What will happen? Was kommt?' It is confirmed that they came!

90 Danish Civil Air Defence, SCL. 7.7.40 and 8.7.40. Adm. 22/263A, 7.7-.40.

91 Ebbe Muncks supplement sheet, 2/2.

92 The *Statens Civile Luftværn* (The State Civil Air Defence) was established in 1939 and was given the responsibility of installing sirens to warn the population in all major cities, of building shelters and of training personnel who could be deployed with fire and rescue equipment against war damage. The *Statens Civile Luftværn* was a humanitarian and non-military organisation.
It was a large and challenging task, as they had no experience to build on. However, after the outbreak of War in September1939, they received information from England and Germany about air raids on cities and the effect on the civilian population. They also ordered the blackout of all light that could be seen from the air and made plans for the evacuation of the population from threatened urban areas, especially where the Germans were expected to invade.
Denmark was spared major war damage, but some cities were subjected to minor attacks, including Aalborg when British planes attacked the German airfield there. The *Statens Civile Luftværn* was also responsibly for early warning regarding aerial threats from balloons and aircraft. There was no direct cooperation between the German *Fluko* and *Statens Civile Luftværn*. To assist in the event of major air attacks, several mobile relief columns with conscripted personnel – CBU columns – were established. The total strength of the force in 1945 was approximately 250,000. After the end of World War II, the *Statens Civile Luftværn* was disbanded,

Copenhagen, while the planes laid mines in either 'Daffodil' or 'Verbena'. Bombs were dropped on Gedser Odde, a little further north at Bøtø, a German emergency landing site, and at the airfield at Rødby Harbour. The planes probably laid mines in 'Radish' south of Lolland and in 'Sweet Peas' south of Falster. The last report on the planes reported anti-aircraft fire near Esbjerg, so the British planes were followed to the end.[93]

In the German archives, it was mentioned for July as a whole that the enemy shelling of the flak troops' barracks on Fanø, as well as the German flak batteries' own heavy firing in particular, had caused major damage to the equipment. The windows were smashed in several barracks, and kitchenware and crockery were broken. One of the barracks, belonging to *Flak-Division Nr 3*, had its walls caved in, and there was an imminent danger that the roof would fall into the building. On the last day of the month, 31 July, work began to repair the damage.[94] So it seemed that it was the German flak crew that suffered the most from their own heavy flak fire.

On the night of 30 July, another bombing attack was carried out on the airfield at Rødby Harbour. Three Hampdens out of five that had laid mines in 'Sweet Peas' were responsible for the attack. A total of 12 Hampdens had gone on a raid that night, seven from 61 Squadron and five from 144 Squadron. The plan was to lay mines in 'Daffodil' near Copenhagen and in 'Sweet Peas' south of Gedser. During the approach, one of the planes suffered an overheated engine, and the pilot chose to drop the bombs over a flak battery in southern Denmark – or so he thought. The plane was over the northern German town of Nieböll, about 15 kilometres south of Tønder. However, the pilot continued on the wrong course and later mistook the German island of Fehmarn for Falster. Only when he tried to find the minelaying area south of Gedser did he realise his mistake. It was too late to correct the mistake and the mine was brought back home.[95]

One of the other aircraft entered the correct target area, but the pilot continued until he reached the North German peninsula of Zingst. The error was detected, but there was not enough fuel to find his way back to the target area. The bombs were dropped on an airfield near Barth and the mine was brought home. The remaining 10 aircraft managed to lay their mines without difficulty. The crews of the aircraft that had been in the vicinity of Copenhagen unanimously reported that the area was almost clear of flak.[96]

The Danish newspapers explained the night's overflight in a slightly different way. British aircraft had approached the Danish Capital, but had been driven off by German anti-aircraft artillery.[97] Something had to explain the air raid warning! All six aircraft returned safely. Of the four that laid their mines in 'Sweet Peas', one aircraft attacked the airfield at Rødby Harbour. These aircraft also returned without further incident.[98]

Another attack on the small airfield at Rødby should it come to this time. On the night of 1 August, 12 Hampdens set off to lay mines in 'Radish' south of Lolland and 'Forget-me-not' at the entrance to Kiel. However, one of the planes turned back relatively quickly due to

93 *Avisårbogen*, 1940, p.65; *Luftbogen*, pp.10–11.
94 Adm. 22/263a. 'Experiences' for July 1940.
95 Air 24/200. Bomber Command ORB, 29/30.07.1940.
96 Air 27/980. 144 Sqdn. ORB, 29-30.7.1940.
97 *Avisårbogen*, 1940, p.65, 30.7.1940.
98 Air 28/355. Hemswell ORB. 'Gardening … on the night of 29/30 July 1940'.

strong vibrations in the fuselage. Another two aircraft were unable to find the target.[99] Of the remaining nine aircraft, four laid their mines in 'Radish', while four or five laid theirs in 'Forget-me-not'. We do not know if the last plane laid its mine, as for unknown reasons it crashed into the sea 40–50 miles from the English coast on its way home. Aircraft and ships were sent out to search for survivors, and 15 hours after the crash, a rubber dinghy with four men on board was spotted from one of the search planes. It was then only 32 miles off the coast. But the aircraft again lost contact with the survivors and they were never found again.[100]

After the mines had been laid in the two waters as ordered, five of the planes carried out a 'special reconnaissance' during which they attacked the airfield at Rødby. The lights on the airfield were switched on until just before the first British aircraft dropped its two bombs on the target. The five aircraft continued westwards, where they attacked another airfield. Further west, a couple of the planes attacked a searchlight and flak battery near Toftlund. The rest of the aircraft attacked a similar German battery about 75 kilometres south, near Schleswig. All 10 crews reported very little flak, even over Kiel where only moderate light flak had been fired, but the salvos fired had been quite accurate.[101] At Esbjerg, fire had also been opened with the dreaded 88mm flak guns. But dense cloud cover from 600 to 2,400 feet prevented the searchlights from finding the aircraft. The anti-aircraft gunners therefore fired blindly at the sound of the aircraft engines.[102]

A week later, on the night of 8 August, five Hampdens from Hemswell and seven from Hatfield Woodhouse (renamed Lindholme 10 days later) went on a minelaying mission to 'Quince', the Langeland Belt.[103] One of the pilots fell ill after half an hour's flight, after which the aircraft returned. All five aircraft failed to reach the target area due to dense cloud cover over Denmark. The last six aircraft managed to lay the mines, only bothered by some light flak from batteries at Svendborg and Korsør. However, the shooting was far too inaccurate for the pilots to take it seriously. One of the planes dropped its two bombs on a lit area just south of Svendborg, which the crew thought was a ship. In any case, the lights were switched off after the bombs were dropped.[104] However, the crew was mistaken, as it was a residential building.[105] It seems that two of the planes that did not find the 'Quince' thought they were bombing Rødby Airfield when they dropped their bombs in the south-west of Lolland, near Fredsholm. During the night, bombs were also dropped on Langeland, Als and in Jutland.

The last 'illegal' bomb drop by crews from 5 Group was carried out on the night of 13 August. Nine Hampdens from Hatfield Woodhouse (Lindholme) took off for 'Quince' in the Langeland Belt, while three aircraft from Waddington headed for 'Wallflower' in the southern Little Belt.[106] Of the first nine, only seven made it to the target area. One turned back due to a leak in the hydraulic system, while the pilot of the other had taken the wrong course. He had been flying after some flashes of light that he thought were the

99 Air 28/478. Lindholme ORB, 31.7.1940.
100 Air 28/478. Lindholme ORB, 1.8.1940.
101 Air 24/222 Bomber Command ORB, BC Intell. Sum. rep. 1.8.1940.
102 Adm. Dän. 22/263a, 1.8.1940.
103 Air 24/200. Bomber Command ORB, 7–8 August 1940; Air 25/109A. 5 Gr. ORB.
104 Air 28/478. Lindholme ORB, 8.8.1940.
105 Bent Andersen: Andersen, Bent, *En dråbe I havet* (Rudkøbing: 1994), p.97.
106 Air 25/109A. 5 Group ORB, 12.8.40.

other aircraft's navigation lights. It later turned out to be reflections of moonlight on the sea surface. He then turned around. (I wonder how difficult it must have been to have to report such a blunder back at base?) The other aircraft found their way to the two minelaying areas without difficulty. Among other things, they had navigated according to the signals from the German direction finding stations! In addition, the weather was good throughout the trip and none of the crews noticed any flak. One of the pilots reported on his return that he had dropped his two bombs on Haderslev station and was certain that one of the bombs had hit the railway embankment,[107] but no Danish or German sources confirm this.[108] However, there are reports of two bombs at Foverup, 15 kilometres west-southwest of Åbenrå, and one bomb at Otterbøl, 22 kilometres north-northwest of Tønder. Finally, two bombs fell at Nældemose south of Assens on Funen.[109]

Only now, after all the above-mentioned bombing of airfields in Denmark – especially, of course, Rødby Airfield – did the Air Ministry authorise such attacks. In military terms, a couple of 250-pound bombs here and there would not make much difference, of course. The authorisation to carry bombs and use them against ship targets, airfields and other military land targets must therefore be seen primarily from the point of view of crew morale. They had clear and strict orders to bring the mines home as far as possible if the weather, flak or other conditions made it impossible to place them in the right place. As mentioned, this happened regularly during 1940. With the bombs on board and the knowledge that a suitable target would appear, the crews would not feel as much of a waste of time and effort on the long journey. The fact that there was absolutely no attempt to achieve any particular military results when 5 Group ordered all mine planes to be equipped with two 250-pound bombs on 2 September is underlined by the fact that it was also emphasised that ships were still the primary target. [110]

Perhaps that is why the next attack on Rødby Airfield was not carried out by Hampdens in the minelaying role. On the night of 6 September, 26 Hampdens were on their way to bomb an oil refinery in northern Germany.[111] One of the aircraft stood out and attacked the airfield with four 250-pound high-explosive bombs and 60 four-pound incendiary bombs.[112] The pilot reported a lot of activity at the airfield, but could not say anything about the outcome of the attack.[113] The activity can probably be attributed to the fact that, due to the repeated overflights, the Germans set up a lot of flak on the site from 27 August onwards.[114] On the other hand, the airfield at Rødby also served as a decoy for the British bombers. Some of the activity may therefore have been created with this purpose in mind.

However, it was not long before the minelayers were on the move again. On the night of 3 October, three Hampdens from 61 Squadron and three aircraft from 144 Squadron were to lay mines in 'Quince', the Langeland Belt. On the same night, four aircraft from each of the

107 Air 28/478. Lindholme ORB, 13.8.1940.
108 No newspapers mention this and the Civil Air Defence reports are missing for the period: 20.7 to 26.10.
109 'Air Book', p.13.
110 Air 14/2064. Operation Gardening. Order of 2 September 1940.
111 Air 24/200. Bomber Command ORB, 5–6 September 1940.
112 Air 14/3414, Bomber Command Intell. Sum. 6.9.1940 (No. 407).
113 Air 24/223 Bomber Command Intell. Sum. 6.9.1940 (No. 408).
114 Adm. Dän. 17/248, 27.8.1940. This is the first time I have come across an announcement that flak would be installed at Rødby Airfield.

two squadrons were to bomb an oil refinery near Hamburg. The planes took off from their base, Hemswell, every few minutes. Two of the planes turned back shortly afterwards. One with a damaged wing, probably due to a collision with a flock of birds. The other returned with a faulty radio. The other 12 aircraft followed in formation over the North Sea and came in over the west coast in four waves of three aircraft each. Shortly afterwards, the bomber force turned south, while the minelayers continued towards Langeland.

Five of the six minelayer planes managed to place their cargo in the right place. The last one brought the mine back home, as the trigger mechanism did not work. Only one of the 'Hamburg aircraft' managed to drop the bombs on the target. The others bombed alternative targets, partly in Denmark and partly in northern Germany. For example, five German airfields were attacked. Apart from the fact that one of the minelayer planes suddenly found itself near Copenhagen, none of the planes experienced any unpleasant incidents. It can therefore be assumed that the crews were very satisfied with the outcome of the night. However, they must have been in for quite a shock when they landed at Hemswell. Close to the runway, a few wrecked aircraft stood next to a couple of heavily damaged buildings. Half an hour earlier, a sea mine had been detonated during transport from the ammunition depot to one of the planes. Six men had been killed and many more of the ground crew had been badly injured.[115]

After this raid, mines were only laid a dozen times until the end of the year. This was partly due to 5 Group's extensive experience as a long-range night bomber unit. During the Battle of Britain, the number of potential targets in Germany itself had grown considerably; targets that could not previously be attacked. From Danish and German sources, you can see how the number of overflights continued to increase, while the size of the formations grew steadily. The targets were just not in Denmark but in northern Germany.

A few mines were laid anyway. For example, on the night of 10 October, a single Hampden set off on a course for Sylt. It was to lay its mine in 'Forget-me-not' off Kiel. As the aircraft passed Sylt at an altitude of 8,000 feet, light flak opened fire from the island. However, it could in no way threaten the British aircraft. Once it arrived at the target area, the pilot dived to just 300 feet above the water. The mine was dropped and the plane immediately climbed again. As the plane was travelling west at 6,000 feet, it passed the airfield at Tønder. The pilot dropped the two 250-pound bombs on this target. By his own estimation, they probably missed a little. The aircraft then returned safely to Mabelthorpe.[116]

Another reason why minelaying operations were less frequent was that it was assumed that the relevant waters were now fully mined. From then on, they only needed to be maintained from time to time. At the end of October, a plane from Waddington was ordered to carry out a minelaying mission near Copenhagen. The aircraft took off, but quickly turned back again. Major vibrations in one of the engines made it impossible to complete such a long trip. The trip was then cancelled completely. It was perhaps fortunate for the pilot that he and the crew did not make it to the finish line. He would have had great difficulty locating it. The order stated that a mine was to be laid in the strait west of Copenhagen![117]

---

115 P. Chr Dahl, *Strandinger og trandingsgods* (Esbjerg: 1974), vol. 2, pp.40–41; Adm. Dän. 171248, 3.10.1940. Luftbogen, p.17, 3.10.1940; Air 27/576.61 Squadron. ORB, 2/3.10.1940; Air 28/35I. Hemswell ORB, 3.10.1940; Air 28/355. Hemswell ORB, Opp. 'Gardening', 3.10.1940.

116 Air 27/980. 144 Sqdn. ORB, 10.10.1940.

117 Air 28/879. Waddington ORB, 29–30 October 1940.

Hampdens from 44 Squadron (Rhodesia).

Chapter 7

7.1 Danish-German Naval Arrangement, 1940 and Minesweeping in Danish Waters, 1940–1941

During the occupation of Denmark, the *Kriegsmarine* was organised as follows:

1) Navy High Command: *Grossadmiral* Erich Raeder
   a) Fleet Command: *Grossadmiral* Otto Schniewind
      i) Commander of the battleships
      ii) Commander of the submarines
      iii) Torpedo boat group commander
      iv) Destroyer group commander
   b) Naval Group Command North
      i) Baltic Sea Naval Station, Kiel : *Generaladmiral* Rolf Karls
      ii) Chief of Staff for Naval Station Baltic Sea Vice Admiral Wurmbach
         (1) Commander of the Baltic Sea Defence Command
         (2) Commander of the Air Force (*General* of the *Luftwaffe* under the Commander-in-Chief of the *Kriegsmarine*)
         (3) *Admiral* Norway
         (4) *Admiral* Denmark: *Admiral* Raul Mewis
         (5) *Admiral* North Sea
      i) North Sea Naval Station, Wilhelmshaven
         (1) Commander of North Sea Security

From the beginning of the occupation, the *Kriegsmarine* in Denmark was commanded by *Admiral* Raul Mewis, most of the time with the title *Marinebefehlshaber Dänemark. Admiral* Mewis initially held the title *Küstenbefehlshaber Dänemark* and, unlike, for example, his Norwegian *admiral* colleague, had little say in Danish waters. His responsibility was the safety of the harbours, which in practice was handled by port captains in: Skagen, Frederikshavn, Hirtshals, Thyborøn, Lemvig, Aalborg, Grenaa, Aarhus, Fredericia, Esbjerg, Odense, Nyborg, Svendborg, Nakskov, Korsør, Kalundborg, Nykøbing S, Hundested, Helsingør, Copenhagen, Gedser and Rønne. In addition, in the strategically most important harbours – Skagen, Frederikshavn, Hals, Aalborg, Fredericia, Esbjerg, Nyborg, Helsingør and Copenhagen – so-called harbour protection flotillas were established.

The flotillas were responsible for protecting the harbour and the nearby sea area, and primarily consisted of up to 40 small vessels, mainly cutters, tugs and guard ships. The coasts were guarded by the Danish police – and certain stretches of coastline on Zealand were monitored by Danish naval vessels.

Everything at sea in the Baltic Sea, the Sound, the Belts, the Kattegat and the Skagerrak was controlled by an admiral of the Naval Station Ostsee in Kiel and an admiral of the Befehlshaber der Sicherung Ostsee (BSO), while activities in the North Sea were under the command of the Befehlshaber der Sicherung Nordsee (BSN) in Wilhelmshaven. Mewis was only responsible for the command of the maritime forces on land and coastal defence. However, this did not include the defence positions on the west coast, which were under the BSN. Initially, the Kriegsmarine in Denmark was divided into two independent geographical sections, the West Coast and North Jutland, which were led by a commander in Esbjerg and Frederikshavn respectively. The North Jutland commander reported to Mewis, while the commander in Esbjerg had the admiral of BSN as his boss. This division was not particularly appropriate, and after a few years this was recognised in the German Kriegsmarine! In October 1942, *Marinegruppenkommando Ostsee* (MOK Ost) was therefore given total responsibility for the entire coastal defence in Denmark. In light of the fear of invasion, a third section was established covering the east coast of Jutland and the Danish islands with a commander located in Copenhagen.

After the Danish Government accepted the German peaceful occupation of the country on 9 April, senior officials from the Danish armed forces met with Defence Minister Alsing Andersen and Foreign Minister Munch to discuss what position to take on the German demands regarding military issues. It was not immediately possible to agree on a common position. Later that day, representatives of the Danish military met with the German authorities to agree on practical measures regarding the peaceful occupation. These were not negotiations, but both sides tried to find pragmatic solutions to the German orders. The German forces took over all Danish fortifications and airfields, as well as a few barracks, to ensure the defence of Denmark. The Danish forces were demobilised, with the exception of a few thousand men, and the practical solution of the blackout, German use of Danish means of transport, border patrols and mine barriers were discussed. The last issue was left for discussion between the Danish and German naval authorities the following day.[1]

The next day, the naval negotiations started. For the Danish side, the Danish Navy Commander *Viceadmiral* Rechnitzer, Deputy Chief of Naval Staff *Kommandørkaptajn* Vedel and *Orlogskaptajn* Pontoppidan participated.[2] For the German side, the head of the German naval forces in Denmark, *Admiral* Mewis, and *Kapitän zur See* Henning, the naval attaché of the legation, took part.[3] They began to make agreements regarding the Danish Navy's training activities, the German takeover of Danish coastal forts and the maintenance of the

1 Palle Roslyng-Jensen, *Værnenes politik – politikernes værn* (Gyldendal: 1980), pp.32–36.

2 *Orlogskaptajn* Svend Erik Pontoppidan: 2 December 1939 – 30 April 1940, Chief of Staff and Barracks Commander, Slipshavn Naval Station. 15 May 1940 – 21 October 1947, on the naval staff. May 1940 – 5 May 1945, Ministry of the Navy liaison officer to the German commanding admiral in Denmark during the occupation and thus daily negotiator in all matters concerning the navy, lighthouse and guard service, pilotage, rescue services, merchant shipping and fishing. 5 May 1945 – 1 October 1945, Ministry of the Navy liaison officer to the British Admiral after liberation. <http://www.navalhistory.dk/danish/officererne/>.

3 Palle Roslyng-Jensen, *Værnenes politik – politikernes værn* (Gyldendal: 1980), p.37. Later, the assistant naval attaché *Korvettenkapitän* Hashagen handled the negotiations from the German side.

Danish and German mine barrages, 1939–1940.

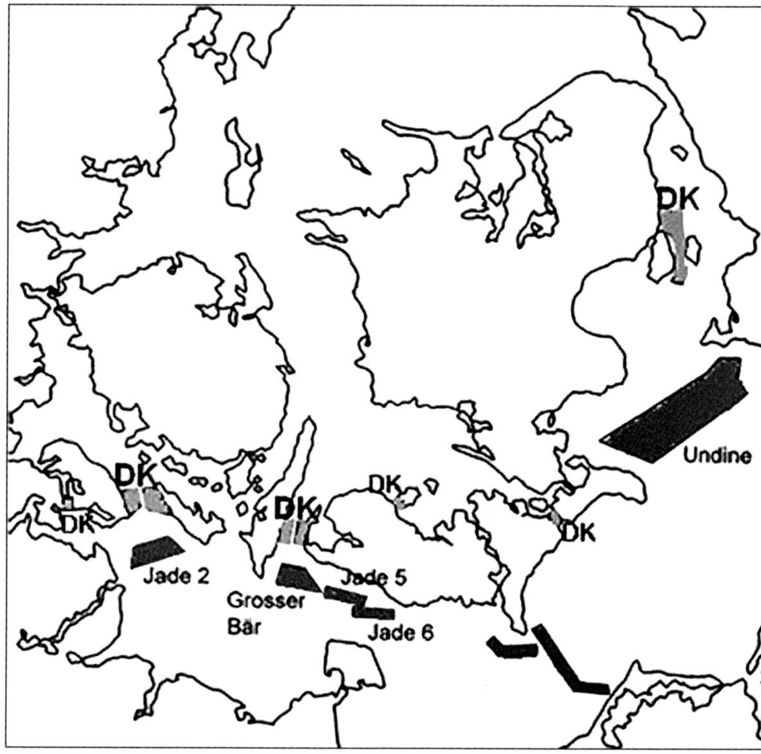

Danish mine barrage rings in the Great Belt. After some tug-of-war back and forth, it was agreed that Danish cadets and maths students[4] could be trained at sea in the Isefjord, the Småland Sea and the South Funen Archipelago. Of the coastal forts, the Germans immediately took over Flak Fort, Dragør Fort and Mosede Battery. The majority of the Danish Navy's ships were to be based at the naval harbour Holmen in Copenhagen, but also in a number of provincial harbours to avoid being a potential target for British bombers.[5]

A few weeks later, Mewis received orders from his commander, *Admiral* Carls of Naval Station (later *Marineoberkommando) Ostsee*, that the Danish mine barriers in the Great Belt should be repaired and maintained by the Danish Navy. After a few days of reflection, this demand was flatly rejected by the Danish on 6 May. It could be perceived as direct Danish support for the German war effort. The German negotiators tried to push the demand through, but were again rejected. After a dozen days, the Germans gave in and removed the mine barriers themselves on 17 May 1940. At that time, the fear of a British naval advance into the Baltic Sea was probably minimal, but behind the scenes there had been a change. As early as 13 April, the German Navy's commander-in-chief, *Grossadmiral*

4 In the period 1932–1951, 'math' denoted a military rank in the Danish Navy, which was a private conscript in voluntary service and a non-commissioned officer trainee.

5 C. A. S. Westermann, 'Flaaden fra 9. April til 29. August' in *Denmark under the Occupation* (Copenhagen: 1946), p.403.

Raeder, had asked Hitler's permission to take over the Danish Fleet, possibly for a payment! Hitler gave the go ahead, but within a week, the German naval leadership changed its mind. They now asked Hitler to postpone a possible takeover of Danish naval vessels, as they would rather try to establish a cooperation with the Danish Navy for surveillance and escort tasks in Danish waters.[6]

The *Kriegsmarine* did not have nearly the required number of minesweepers itself. In January 1940, Germany only had 12 minesweepers. In addition, there was also a fleet of observation and flak ships that were part of mine countermeasures. By comparison, in May 1940, the navy calculated that 18 minesweepers and 9 in reserve were needed for Danish waters alone. In addition, 4 minesweepers with 2 in reserve were needed to accompany the German U-boats from Kiel and Flensburg out into the North Sea, a total of 22 vessels with 11 in reserve to secure the passage of the Danish waterways. If we compare this to what the navy had calculated was necessary in Norway, for example, it had only allocated 6 minesweepers with 3 in reserve. This shows how important it was for the Germans to keep Danish waters clear of enemy mines. For these two Nordic countries alone, the estimated need was 28 minesweepers. At the end of 1940, there were only 36 minesweepers in the entire *Kriegsmarine*.[7]

Against this background, the *Kriegsmarine* presented the Danish Government with a new demand. It was that the Danish Navy take over the mine sweeping service in the inner Danish waters, including establishing observation posts and contributing to the neutralisation of mines driven onto the shores. The Danes fully agreed with the last two points, but with regard to mine sweeping, it was crucial for *Kommandør* Vedel to emphasise that it should in any case be established by the Danish Navy only to maintain Danish shipping, and was therefore a relevant activity for the Danish crews. He also stated that the navy's minesweeping capacity was very limited, and that the area of operation had to be restricted to the east–west routes between the parts of the country. The *Kriegsmarine* had to take care of the north-south routes through Straits and Belts. The six old minesweepers, *Springeren, Støren, Søridderen, Søhunden, Havørnen* and *Narhvalen* could not be used against magnetic mines. It was therefore decided that three newly built minesweepers of the *Søløven* class, *Søløven, Søbjørnen* and *Søulven* should be equipped for this purpose. In addition to the nine vessels mentioned above, a number of hired fishing cutters were used for mine detection and as auxiliary vessels for the minesweepers. The mining vessel *Kvintus* also participated in minesweeping.[8]

Doctor Jørgen Røjel, who later became a saboteur in the resistance movement, was on board the minesweeper *Søulven* and in his memoir, *Kæft, trit og retning*, he described how the minesweeping took place and what the atmosphere was like on board, as well as what the crew of around 50 men thought about their task. Among other things, the first British mine they found was swept a little too close to *Søulven*, which, when detonated, tipped the stern

6 Palle Roslyng-Jensen, *Værnenes politik – politikernes værn* (Gyldendal: 1980), p.38. A week earlier, on 10 May, Germany had attacked France, where the fighting on both sides was now focussed.

7 Peter Arndt, *Deutsche Sperrbrecher, 1914-1945* (Stuttgart: 1979), pp.126–130.

8 Palle Roslyng-Jensen, *Værnenes politik – politikernes værn* (Gyldendal: 1980), p.39; Gunnar Olesen.'MS-bådene' in *Marinehistorisk Tidsskrift*, 1991, no. 1 p.27. The six old minesweepers were originally built as torpedo boats during World War I.

of the ship clear of the sea surface, while the bow was pressed down so that the ship was at an angle of 25–30 degrees to the water surface. None of the crew members were seriously injured, but the ship's demagnetising equipment was damaged, and thus they had to go to Korsør to have it repaired:

> In the quartermaster's mess in the evening we felt sorry for ourselves, partly because we did not like the job and partly because we agreed that this kind of mine sweeping was helping the Germans.[9]

It helped a little when, a few days later, they witnessed one of the Germans' *Speerbrechere* being hit by a mine in Østerrende. In addition to the danger of getting too close to a mine, there was the danger of being attacked by British aircraft, which could not distinguish between German and Danish minesweepers. Therefore, *Søulven* anchored in hiding between Omø and Agersø at night. In the latter half of September 1940, the crew succeeded in sweeping mine no. 2 just south of Bagenkop on Langeland. This time it went perfectly by the book, and *Søulven* was able to sail on. Shortly afterwards, the heavy German cruiser *Admiral Hipper* came in on a northerly course at full speed exactly over the spot where *Søulven* had just swept the mine. The large warship was accompanied by three former Polish destroyers and was on its way to Norway and then onwards into the Atlantic in search of British convoys and other prey. Røjel was shaken,

> It was an unpleasant sight to see the German naval forces unfold where we worked – and we felt that Danish marines were taking part in the German warfare against the United Kingdom that stood alone as the slim hope the free world had to build its future on.[10]

Something had to be done. Røjel took the initiative to draft a letter of protest to the Danish Ministry of the Navy, which, signed by all the conscripts on board, was to be sent through the chain of command to the Ministry. There were three points in the letter. Firstly, the crew applied for a risk allowance in the same amount as the crews of the guard ships at the Danish minefields received, namely DKK 1 per day. Secondly, the crew wanted to clarify the limits of their tasks in the southern part of the Great Belt, as it was difficult to see them as solely to secure national shipping. Thirdly and finally, the crew wanted to make it clear to the Ministry that they would not sweep mines for foreign powers, as it went against their national beliefs and honour as Danish men.

Big fuss. The ship's captain had the entire crew assemble on deck that evening. The letter was read out, and the chief pointed out that the signatories could risk imprisonment for mutiny and insubordination. But Røjel could only confirm on behalf of the crew that the protest letter should be passed on as it was. A little later, in his cabin, the chief once again tried to emphasise to Røjel and one of the other signatories the criminal nature of the last

---

9 Jørgen Røjel, *Kæft, trit og retning. En sabotørs erindringer* (Copenhagen: 1973), p.14. Life on board a German minesweeper in Danish waters during the war is vividly described in Johannes W. Studts, *Als Matrose auf einem Minensucher, 1940–1945*, (Hamburg: 2004).

10 Jørgen Røjel, *Kæft, trit og retning. En sabotørs erindringer* (Copenhagen: 1973), p.16.

The Danish minesweeper M3 *Søulven*, 1940.

two points in the letter. They insisted on their freedom of speech and were ready to face the consequences. The next day, *Søulven* sailed to Svendborg, from where the letter was sent to the Ministry of the Navy. Røjel sent a copy to the *Danish Crown Prince* Frederik, whom he had befriended in the Danish Students' Rowing Club, in the hope that Frederik might be able to put pressure on the Ministry. The *Danish Crown Prince* replied in a letter a week later. After some initial small talk and a comment that a request for a risk allowance was fine, he set about reprimanding Røjel.

> There is a rule, both at sea and on land, to keep one's mouth shut, step and direction, and it's not so bad after all … The ship sails under the Danish flag, and the crew serves the flag; ship and crew together serve the country, and there is no such thing as whether it suits you or not. Once the crew starts talking to you, you have gone too far and it all ends in a mess … A ship is not a discussion club.

Then rounded off the letter with some small talk.[11]

The Ministry of the Navy, however, did not respond to the letter. The crown prince Frederik had informed his old officer friends in the Ministry that he had reprimanded Røjel in writing and thought it could stay that way. Nevertheless, the letter may have made an impression. *Søulven* was moved from its service in the north-south route in the Langeland Belt to mine sweeping on the Aarhus-Kalundborg ferry route. A month after the incident, Røjel was ordered ashore for duty at Holmen Barracks' infirmary.[12]

The fact that Danish minesweepers sailed on routes that also benefited German shipping was generally a very sensitive issue. When the newspaper *Nyborg Socialdemokrat* mentioned in a notice on 1 November that Danish minesweepers were sailing on the Great

11 Jørgen Røjel, *Kæft, trit og retning. En sabotørs erindringer* (Copenhagen: 1973), pp.18–19.
12 Jørgen Røjel, *Kæft, trit og retning. En sabotørs erindringer* (Copenhagen: 1973), p.19. Throughout, Røjel has some problems with timing events correctly.

Belt crossing, the Ministry of Foreign Affairs immediately sent a letter to all of the country's editorial offices stating that under no circumstances could the publication of any information about the position, movements and activities of Danish warships be allowed.[13] The Germans, however, exploited the situation in propaganda via the news media *Ritzaus Bureau*, which they controlled. For example, after the passenger steamer *Hammershus* was hit by a mine shortly after leaving Copenhagen harbour, it was said that it was probably one of those mines:

> ... which English airmen have recently dropped uncritically several times in Danish waters. They have not caused any damage to objects of military importance, as the British are not aware of them. The Germans, in cooperation with the Danish Ministry of the Navy, are doing everything possible to protect shipping from this traffic.[14]

Another example is from the end of the same month, on 31 August 1940, when another passenger steamer, *Rise*, hit a mine and sank during the crossing between Svendborg and Ærøskøbing. Several people died, and the Germans claimed that:

> ... The deplorable accident shows that the British airmen from dropping mines on the main sea routes to the Baltic Sea have now switched to dropping them in such inner Danish waters, which are used solely for peaceful Danish merchant shipping and fishing.[15]

It was also of propaganda value when two ferries carrying Copenhagen schoolchildren returning from holiday in Jutland were escorted by two ships of the *Kriesmarine* from Aarhus to Kalundborg to avoid the danger of mines.[16]

The *Kriegsmarine* had developed an effective minesweeping method to remove the British magnetic mines. Large steel barges were rendered highly magnetic by winding them around with powerful cables. However, the barges, which were towed at a safe distance behind the minesweepers, were vulnerable to the powerful detonations and were often blown apart or severely damaged during the sweeping.

Orlogskaptajn H. J. Bahnsen, head of the navy's radio section at the naval harbour Holmen in Copenhagen, had invented some floating ironing magnets of 12, 18 and 24 metres in length in divided pontoons, with a current-carrying cable wrapped around the middle. The current was supplied by one of the tug's dynamos, and the current was reversed a variable number of times per minute to affect the magnet mines' counting mechanism.[17] The

13 'Confidential messages from the Ministry of Foreign Affairs to the editors', unpublished Statsbiblioteket i Aarhus, p.69, 12.11.1940.

14 'Confidential messages from the Ministry of Foreign Affairs to the editors', unpublished Statsbiblioteket i Aarhus, p.99, 4.8.1940.

15 'Confidential messages from the Ministry of Foreign Affairs to the editors', unpublished Statsbiblioteket i Aarhus, p.101, 31.8.1940.

16 *Avisårbogen*, 1940, p.67, 5.8.1940.

17 S. A. Nielsen, *30 år i Orlogsværftets Elektroafdeling 1940–1970 – uddrag af oplevelser, hændelser og episoder* (2003), unpaginated. Bahnsen's current reversers were constructed at the shipyard's electrical

sweep width of the 12 metre floating magnets was 30 metres to each side, at a distance of 100–200 metres behind the tug. Normally 12 sweeps were made, as this was reportedly the maximum number of passes the British mines could be set for.[18] At the end of June 1940, the German naval command in Kiel invited Bahnsen and a colleague to its research unit in Kiel, where they were updated on German research on sweeping magnetic and acoustic mines with FRG (*Fernräumgerät*) and KFRG (*Kabelfernräumgerät*), and were shown an English magnetic mine and an early model of the German magnetic mine. After returning home, Bahnsen received the German drawings and records to FRG and KFRG.[19] It was a good investment, as *Admiral* Mewis was pleased to note the following on 15 July:

> The confidence demonstrated by this has had the most favourable influence on the Danish Navy's initiative on the issue of mine clearance.[20]

On 6 October, he informed Wurmbach that:

> It turns out that the Danish FRG (3 floating magnetic rods without a boat) is far superior to the German FRG in terms of towing speed (12–13 nm) and seaworthiness (up to sea state 5). Towing speed (12–13 nm) and seaworthiness (up to sea state 5) is considerably superior to the German device.[21]

The new and more efficient minesweeping equipment was henceforth called *Bahnsengerät* by the Germans.[22]

Bahnsen and his colleague, engineer Ingerslev, had also been introduced to the German equipment for mine-proofing ships against magnetic mines *Magnetischen Eigenschut*. In the autumn of 1940, Bahnsen developed a similar mine protection cable, which the Danish naval vessels were immediately equipped with. By sending current through a cable placed along the side of the ship all the way around the ship, the vessel could be 'demagnetised'. By measuring the ship's natural magnetic field, the right amount of current could be determined, making the ship almost non-magnetic. Bahnsen was, not undeservedly, awarded one of Denmark's highest awards, The Royal Knights Cross of the Order of Dannebrog, by the King of Denmark.[23]

---

workshop, which supplied them to the radio section. The minesweeping magnets were built at Elsinore Shipyard because the management of the navy yard did not initially believe that Bahnsen's invention would work.

18 'Lieutenant Colonel P. E. Rye Hansen: Memoirs of a Lieutenant Colonel (1943–46)', <http://www.navalhistory.dk/danish/Orlogsliv/Beretninger/MS_baadene.htm>. The invention was named 'Bahn's floating magnets.' It is a good thing they did not realise that the British mine countdown clock went up to 14!

19 KTB MarBef 16–30.6.1940, Cooperation with Danish Navy.

20 KTB MarBef 1–15.7.1940, Cooperation with Danish Navy.

21 KTB MarBef 6.10.1940 p.142 Danish long-range clearing equipment.

22 KTB MarBef 23.10.1940, p.162. As a thank you, the navy received an English magnetic mine from the German naval authorities in February 1941. 'Naval Staff – Negotiations with the German naval authorities 4.2.1941', p.53.

23 Handbook for the Navy 1956, <http://www.marinehist.dk/hfs/1956-HfS.pdf>.

The Danish minesweeping unit was deployed from August 1940 on the domestic ferry routes between Kalundborg-Aarhus, Hundested-Grenå, Nakskov-Spodsbjerg and others. During 1941, 3 more newly built *Søløven* class minesweepers joined the service, along with 10 new wooden minesweepers. The minesweeping service was under constant pressure from the German naval leadership to be included in the sweeping on the north-south routes. This was therefore done to a certain extent. A geographical division was eventually established, so the Danish minesweepers took care of the magnetic mines in the Great Belt and Kattegat, while the Germans were responsible for sweeping in the Sound and the Baltic Sea, where the Swedish Navy also participated. A newly created section under the Danish naval staff, called the Naval Command Office at Holmen, was tasked with keeping track of all important incidents in Danish waters. All mine barrages were to be mapped and, in particular, all British minelaying operations were to be recorded in order to organise mine sweeping and warn shipping.[24]

British mines detonated or swept in Danish Waters	**1940**		
	April-June	**July-Sept**	**Oct-Dec**
Danish ships detonated	10	17	10
German ships detonated	18	10	2
Other ships detonated	5	1	2
German minesweeping	9	20	13
Danish minesweeping	0	2	2
Swedish minesweeping	0	0	6
In total	42	50	35

British mines detonated or swept April-December 1940.

Between April and December 1940, 52 British mines were disarmed while 75 were detonated, causing minor or major damage to ships.[25]

On 12 November 1940, one of the mines that had not been cleared struck the German steamship *St. Jürgen* in Lillebælt. The ship was carrying 812 tonnes of pork from 14,000 pigs, which was intended to supply Berlin's population for five days. The 4.5 million Berliners now had to make do with around 290 tonnes of pork, which was deemed good enough for human consumption after Svitzer's salvage vessels removed the cargo from the wreck on 30 November. But lightly salted pork, with sea salt even, was not to be despised! The Chief of Staff of *Marinebefehlshaber Dänemark, Admiral* Mewis, noted in the war diary that this again emphasised the importance of keeping the waters free of mines.[26]

24) Palle Roslyng-Jensen, *Værnenes politik – politikernes værn* (Gyldendal: 1980), pp.39–40; E. J. Saabye, *I medvind. En søofficers erindringer* (Copenhagen: 1981), pp.86–88. The United Kingdom got some sketches of Bahnsen's inventions in 1941, but not until after 29 August 1943 was the actual technical information obtained. Daniel G. Harris,'Den danske Flåde 1940–43' in *Marinehistorisk Tidsskrift*, 1989, nr.2.

25 Monthly accounts for laid and detonated British bottom mines, April 1940-July 1943, Naval Weapons College.

26 *Admiral Dänemark* war diary, 1940 p.218.

7.2 Forced Routes

When the German authorities realised that the RAF had laid bottom mines in Danish waters, the BSO in Kiel issued an order to *Admiral Dänemark* on 26 April 1940 to establish a network of forced routes in Danish waters. The routes were to connect the major harbours with each other via the usual waterways.[27] The forced routes were to be marked and then kept free of enemy mines. The only problem was that *Marineoberkommando Ost/Ostsee* at this time only had eight ships with FRG, four of which were assigned to the Kiel Canal and Kieler Bay, one to Travemünde and one to Warnemünde. The remaining two minesweepers with FRGs were to cover Danish waters. It was recognised that this was an impossible task and that the forced route network had to be built up and expanded as more minesweepers with either KFRG or FRG were added. *Sperrbrechere* with VES, the most effective minesweepers against magnetic mines, were not yet an option.[28]

On 8 May, the Danish naval staff received a request from the German naval authorities to borrow 30 ordinary sea marks to mark a 200-metre wide shipping lane down the Øresund. As the Germans did not have ships with the equipment to lay the marks themselves, they asked the Danish Navy for help. This was granted on the condition that the Germans would sweep for magnetic mines in front of the ship that was to lay the marks. This was granted.[29] In the following three weeks, the forced route in the Great Belt was marked, including the Korsør-Nyborg ferry route.[30] By the end of July, the two minesweepers with FRGs had been supplemented with nine more FRGs, four KFRGs and two *sperrbrecher* VES, one of which, *Sperrbrecher X*, had been slightly damaged by a British mine and was therefore sent south after a few days. They had therefore come closer to the force that *Küstenbefehlshaber Dänemark* considered to be the minimum required to fulfil the task of keeping the Danish waters free of British mines, namely: 16 FRG, 10 KFRG and four *Sperrbrecere* VES.[31] During September, the route between Aalborg and Frederikshavn was marked out, and the Germans asked the Danish authorities to emphasise to smaller ships in particular that they should sail in the mine-cleared routes whenever possible. The Danes believed that this had been done to a sufficient extent, and that it would be useless to emphasise this, as the ships in question had the legal right to sail as they pleased![32] Eventually, the network was expanded to around 300 sea bouys with signalling lights, for a route system that was also used several years after the war.[33]

As all civilian ships passing through Danish waters had to follow the forced routes, the location and extent of the routes became known to the British during 1941, and Bomber

27 KTB Marine station of the Baltic Sea 26.4.40.

28 KTB Marine Group Command East 28.4.40.

29 Naval Staff, 1926–1947, A. Group-ordered cases. Negotiations with the German authorities 1940–1941. Danish National Archives 0008 . 8.5.40.

30 Naval Staff, 1926–1947, A. Group-ordered cases. Negotiations with the German authorities 1940–1941. Danish National Archives 0008. 21.5.40 + 22.5.40 + 24.5.40 + 30.5.40.

31 KTB Marine station of the Baltic Sea, summarised situation assessment on 31.7.40

32 Naval Staff, 1926–1947, A. Group-ordered cases. Negotiations with the German authorities 1940–1941. Danish National Archives 0008. 10.9.40.

33 John Nielsen, 'De danske farvande i fred og krig' M/S Museet for Søfarts årbog, 5, p.116. <https://tidsskrift.dk/mfs_aarbog/article/view/96004>.

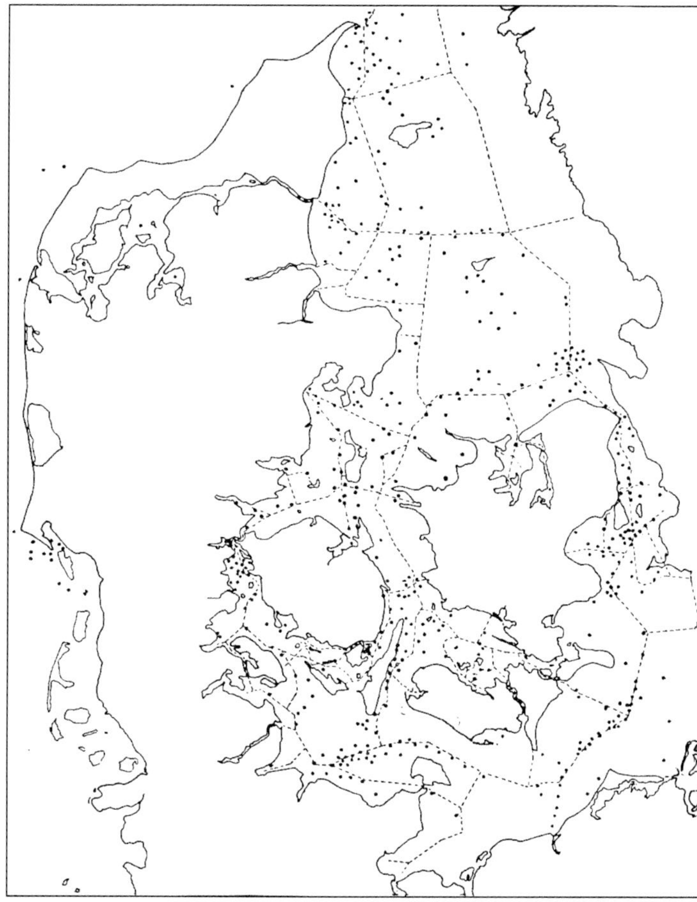

Map of forced routes in Danish waters. The many dots are mined ships. The RAF laid mines in the forced routes with reasonable success. The map shows all shipwrecks up to and including March 1946.

Command then set out, with great determination, to mine them. In 1945, the Danish newspaper *Nationaltidende* compiled a list of all the known war-lost ships from September 1939 up to and including May 1945, with their approximate position indicated on a map. This list forms the basis for the map seen here, on which the forced routes are plotted on the basis of the Lighthouse Directorate's catalogue.[34]

7.3 Sweden's Situation 1939–1940

Between 1933 and 1938, the military leadership of the two Nordic countries explored the possibilities of Danish-Swedish military cooperation, under which Sweden would come to Denmark's aid in the event of German aggression. For mainly political reasons, this did not materialise.[35] The Swedish Government therefore declared its continued neutrality in accordance with international law on 27 May 1938, after consultation with the other Nordic countries.

34 John Nielsen: 'De danske farvande i fred og krig' M/S Museet for Søfarts årbog, 5, p.121.

35 Gregersen, Jens J. K., 'Et svensk ekspeditionskorps til Sjælland?' in *Historisk tidsskrift*, series 6, volume 15 (1991), pp.429–458.

Immediately after the outbreak of World War II, on 18 September 1939 the Nordic countries issued a joint statement, stating that they would continue to trade with all warring parties to protect their own economies. A month later, the heads of state of the four countries, i.e. the Kings of Denmark, Norway and Sweden and the Finnish President, met in Stockholm. The reason for the meeting was the Soviet demands for Finland to move its borders, and the purpose of the meeting was to show the Nordic countries' unity and unity in the defence of their neutrality. The meeting received a lot of attention both at home and abroad.[36] In connection with the German establishment of minefields south of Danish waters, there was a disagreement between Germany and Sweden about the width of Swedish territorial waters. This led to the construction of the Falsterbo Canal.[37] Germany wanted to block access to the Baltic Sea with the minefields, but at the same time they were used to control all merchant ships passing through the waters. German warships and aircraft patrolled the international waters around Denmark and investigated merchant ships suspected of carrying contraband. Swedish ships were therefore advised to stay within neutral territorial waters as far as possible. In addition, the Swedish Coast Guard increased its patrols at sea and in the air over Swedish waters.

On 30 November, war broke out between Finland and the Soviet Union (the 'Winter War'). In this situation, Sweden chose to declare itself as a 'non-combatant' in order to maintain its neutrality while sending humanitarian and material aid to Finland. Fearing that Sweden could be threatened by this conflict, a coalition government was formed a fortnight later with the participation of all parties except the Communist Party. This government continued until the summer of 1945.

The harsh winter of 1939–1940 meant that patrolling and escorting Swedish merchant ships ceased in February and could only resume when the ice broke up in early April. The Swedish intelligence service had, like the Danish, registered the large German military concentration leading up to the occupation of Denmark and Norway. On 8 April, the alert on the Swedish west coast was raised to the highest level. A large German naval force was observed in the Kattegat on a northerly course, so Swedish destroyers were sent to patrol outside the southern Gothenburg archipelago. All Swedish Navy warships were armed and placed at strategic locations along the coast. That same evening, all merchant ships were advised to remain in harbour until further notice. In the following days, as German troops attacked Denmark and Norway, two more destroyers were sent on patrol along the west coast of Sweden. The waters between Varberg and Lysekil were mined and some harbours were closed. For a short period, all lighthouses on the west, south and east coasts of Sweden up to north of Öland were switched off. However, the most important lighthouses were switched back on when it became clear that Sweden was not part of the German occupation plan.[38]

36 Swedish foreign policy during the Second World War. International Politics 24, published by the Swedish Institute of International Affairs, Kooperativa förbundets bokförlag, Stockholm, 1946. <https://www.histdoc.net/history/1939-10-18-19.html>.

37 Bertil Lagvall, *Flottans neutralitetsvakt 1939–1945* (Stockholm: 1967).

38 Rolf Vallerö, *Svenska handelsflottans krigsförluster under det andra världskriget* (Stockholm: 1963), pp.13–14.

On the morning of 9 April at 06:00 and again at 08:00, Swedish Foreign Minister Christian Günther was visited by the German envoy in Stockholm, the Prince of Wied, who had already been tasked by German Foreign Minister Joachim von Ribbentrop on 7 April to inform the Swedish Government of the following demands:

1. The German Government expects Sweden to observe the strictest neutrality and to refrain from any action directed against the German occupation of Denmark and Norway, especially military mobilisation and troop movements.
2. The German Government has requested that the Swedish warships, in their own interest, for the time being do not move outside Swedish territorial waters (3 nautical miles) in Kattegat, Øresund and along the Swedish south coast to Karlskrona. This obstacle to the free movement of Swedish warships will be lifted again when the situation warrants it.
3. The German Government expects that telegram and telephone traffic to the German authorities in Norway from Germany via the Swedish lines will not be prevented.
4. The German Government expects iron ore deliveries to Germany to be maintained and any English-inspired sabotage actions to be prevented.

As early as 09.00, the Swedish Government met briefly before going to the King's apartment, where the *crown prince* and his son, *prince* Gustaf Adolf, were also present. In the afternoon, the Swedish Foreign Minister informed Germany of the government's response. Sweden maintained the same neutrality that had already been declared several times during the war, and would therefore take the necessary measures to defend it. Otherwise, the government agreed to the four German demands mentioned above.[39]

Prior to 9 April, Swedish intelligence had received clear indications that the German occupation only concerned Denmark and Norway, and that Sweden was not immediately threatened this time around. Therefore, the first item on the German 'wish list' was violated just two days later. They secretly mobilised the Swedish force under arms from 60,000 to 320,000 men within a few weeks. In order not to provoke Germany unnecessarily, this was done by letter and not in a radio broadcast.[40] The third item on the list was complied with, insofar as the Swedish intelligence service listened in on the telephone lines. The German military used a special encryption machine on their teleprinters, but due to the poor standard of the telecommunications network, that was the official explanation, the telegrams were often interrupted. Due to the large amounts of telecoms traffic that had to be sent back and forth under great time pressure, the German operators reused the used code keys. This enabled a Swedish mathematician, Arne Beurling, to crack the code system in a few weeks using paper and pencil. The Swedes were then able to eavesdrop on German telecoms traffic for the following years.[41]

After the German occupation of Denmark and Norway, the Swedish Government was faced with new German demands for the transit of German personnel and equipment

39 <https://sv.wikipedia.org/wiki/Sverige_under_andra_v percentC3 percentA4rldskriget>.
40 Bertil Åhlund, *Svensk marin säkerhetspolitik 1939–1945* (Stockholm: 1994), p.261.
41 'Svensk knäckte nazisternas hemliga koder,' *Svenska Dagbladet*, 25 October 2010.

through Sweden to the German troops in Norway. The Swedish Government initially said no to this traffic, but before negotiations were concluded, approximately 300 German doctors and nurses and 400 tonnes of equipment were allowed to be sent to Norway between 16 April and 10 June 1940. In retrospect, it turned out that many of these medical assistants were actually weapons and radio specialists. The Swedish Government also allowed the transport of German sailors off sunken warships from occupied parts of Norway to Germany, despite Norwegian protests. Norway even had a request for military equipment from Sweden rejected on the grounds that support for Finland had depleted Swedish readiness stocks to the point where there was barely enough for their own troops.[42]

When Germany had gained full control of Norway and the Norwegian Government had fled into exile, negotiations between the Swedish and German Governments resumed. On 17 June, Germany demanded free transit of troops to and from Norway via the Swedish railways. It was emphasised from the highest level to the Swedish Ambassador in Berlin that a negative reaction to the German request for transit would result in sanctions and these would probably be of a military nature.[43]

On 26 June, the so-called 'horseshoe traffic' (the route looked like a horseshoe on the map) began from Trondheim to Narvik via the Storlien-Östersund the national border. However, this first traffic was not soldiers on leave, but regular troop movements.[44] On 8 July 1940, Sweden and Germany had agreed to allow German soldiers on leave to travel to and from Germany on the Swedish railways. However, the traffic was quickly expanded to include other forms of transport, including weapons. This traffic lasted more than three years and came to a total of around 2.1 million soldiers, around 100,000 wagonloads of military equipment and accounted for around 10 percent of the Swedish railway's transport capacity. In one case, a fully equipped German division, the 163rd Infantry Division of approximately 15,000 men, was allowed to travel through Sweden from Southern Norway to Northern Finland after Operation Barbarossa, the German attack on the Soviet Union in June 1941. This transport, unlike the 'leave traffic', was closely monitored by the Swedish military.[45] Germany demanded the transit of another division, but the Swedes refused. In return, they offered to transport the division by water through Swedish territorial waters and escorted by Swedish naval units. Thus, 10 German troop transport ships ensured that another combat-ready division could be brought to the Eastern Front in July 1941. This traffic, through Swedish waters and with a further 93 larger German vessels in the autumn of 1941, protected by Swedish destroyers and with Swedish pilots, was kept secret for many years. The transports continued in 1942 with a further 25 transport ships. The German ships initially returned without cargo, but soon they began to function almost as hospital ships, filled with wounded soldiers.[46]

42 Lennart W. Frick, *Bakom hemligstämpeln: hemlig verksamhet i Sverige i vår tid* (Lund: Historiska Media, 2004), p.99–101. Bo Hugemark (ed.), *I orkanens öga. 1941 – osäker neutralitet* (Probus: 1992), pp.194–198.

43 Erik Boheman, *På vakt* (Stockholm: 1964), pp.133–134.

44 Lars Gyllenhaal, *Tyskar och allierade i Sverige: svensk krigshistoria i nytt ljus* (Stockholm: 2011), p.47.

45 Lars Gyllenhaal, *Tyskar och allierade i Sverige: svensk krigshistoria i nytt ljus* (Stockholm: 2011), pp.72–79.

46 'Tyst om tyska fartyg genom svenska vatten' *Svenska Dagbladet*, 30 June 2009.

Swedish destroyer *J5 Göteborg* accompanying a German convoy along the Swedish east coast. Photographed by an unknown German soldier on board the troopship *Isar* in August-September 1941.

After the German attack on Denmark and Norway on 9 April 1940, the *Kriegsmarine* quickly laid a mine barrage in the Skagerrak between Lindesnes on the south coast of Norway and Hanstholm in northwest Jutland. The Swedish merchant fleet was thereby split in two. Ships within the mine barrier could only reach Swedish harbours within the territorial border, while those outside the barrier were cut off from Sweden.[47]

At the end of May 1940, the British Ministry of Economic Warfare authorised the limited Swedish shipping traffic to pass through the Kiel Canal. However, as the waters on both sides of the canal were British mined areas, the safety of the ships could not be guaranteed.[48] This shorter route between the Baltic Sea and the North Sea was used by Swedish ore transport ships travelling to Hamburg, Bremen and Emden. After the German conquest of The Netherlands, Rotterdam was included as the furthest unloading point for Swedish iron ore. From here, the ore could be cheaply transported up the Rhine to the highly industrialised Ruhr region, thus avoiding the congested railway network in northern Germany. The steel mills in the Ruhr region were often neighbours to gas works, which supplied a large part of the steel mills' energy needs. The gas was extracted from coal, with coke as a by-product. This coke could then be brought back by Swedish cargo ships to Sweden as return cargo.[49]

The Swedish ore carriers, which were now also included in the German convoys along the west coast of Jutland, were increasingly exposed to attacks by British bombers, Coastal Command fighter-bombers and fast motor torpedo boats. At night, magnetic mines were dropped in Danish waters and the western part of the Baltic Sea by Bomber Command. A total of three Swedish ships were hit by mines in Danish waters in 1940. In the Baltic Sea, Russian submarines also posed an increased threat.

47 Nicolaus Rockberger, *Göteborgstrafiken : svensk lejdtrafik under andra världskriget* (Stockholm: 1973), p.22
48 Nicolaus Rockberger, *Göteborgstrafiken : svensk lejdtrafik under andra världskriget* (Stockholm: 1973), p.30
49 Lennart Lundberg, *Handelsflottan under andra världskriget* (Stockholm: 2007), pp.177–178

The fact that the war years increased the need for minesweepers is best illustrated by the fact that Sweden had a total of 6 minesweepers on 1 September 1939. By May 1945, the number of battleships and cruisers was unchanged, while the number of destroyers and submarines had almost doubled. But the number of minesweepers had increased sevenfold to 42.[50]

7.4 1941 – Hard Times and New Tactics

At the turn of the year, ice formations began to cause difficulties for shipping traffic in the inner Danish waters. January 1941 was the coldest January since 1874. By the middle of the month, Øresund was packed with ice, and by February all waters were closed by solid ice.[51] You would think that it would not be worthwhile to lay mines in these conditions. But on 11 January, mines were observed in two different locations in the Langelands Belt. However, it seems that this expedition was a one-off. The next time a mine hazard was reported in Danish waters was on 13 March in the Great Belt, which by then had been made navigable.[52]

For the rest of 1941, the scattered laying of mines continued, at the rate of 2 to 4 aircraft every fortnight. Although this is an average, it clearly shows that the trend from the last three months of 1940 continued into 1941; maintenance of the laid minefields was carried out 'to keep them sweetened up.'[53]

Although the Western Allies could not know exactly how much damage they were actually inflicting on the German fleet, they had felt the effects of the German aerial laying of mines themselves. The mines had caused confusion and heavy losses in the British Fleet. This should therefore have been a good enough argument in favour of increasing the RAF's efforts in this area. The reverse was actually the case. In the first few months of 1941, Bomber Command Group commanders were no longer obliged to make aircraft available for mine laying operations. Whereas 5 Group's Hampdens used to prioritise mine laying over bombing, it was now the other way round. Mine laying was only to be carried out if it did not interfere with bombing operations. In the end, Coastal Command was the only unit that regularly carried out these operations, and since this unit did not have aircraft that could operate over long distances, the few mines were not even laid in the most profitable areas, such as the Baltic Sea and Danish waters. Although Coastal Command's commander pressed for just one squadron of long-range aircraft at his disposal, or for Bomber Command to reconsider its position on mine laying, both requests were flatly rejected by Bomber Command.[54]

Harris had been promised that 5 Group, as compensation for Hampdens being used for bombing, would be given some of the new large aircraft types: the Short Stirling and Avro

50 Rolf Vallerö, *Svenska handelsflottans krigsförluster under det andra världskriget* (Stockholm: 1963), p.16; Bo Hugemark (ed.), *Neutralitet och försvar. Perspektiver på svensk säkerhetspolitik 1809–1985* (Stockholm: Militärhistoriska Förlaget, 1986), pp.178–179.

51 'Is-og besejlingsforholdene i de danske farvande i vinteren 1940–41' p.3 and the map fig. 3 p.7. www.Forsvaret.dk

52 Adm. Dän. 18/249, 11.1.1941, 13.3.1941.

53 J. S. Cowie, 'The British Sea-Mining Campaign, 1939–1945' in *Royal United Services Institution. Journal*, volume 93, no.569 (1948), p.25.

54 Stephen W. Roskill, *The War at Sea 1939–45*, vol. 1 (London: HMSO, 1954), p.337.

A Short Stirling of 149 Squadron at RAF Lakenheath being loaded with 1,500lb sea mines, March 1944.

Manchester. Harris resigned as head of 5 Group in November 1940 and was succeeded by Air Vice-Marshal Bottomley. It was he who received the first heavy aircraft around the turn of the year. The Short Stirling was excellent for mine laying. The fact that it could carry as many as four mines to Danish waters alone was a major advance.

The Manchester, on the other hand, was a different story. Although it could carry four mines, it had a number of shortcomings right from the start, including insufficient engine power. All too often, these aircraft had to be held back from active flying for shorter or longer periods due to repairs and necessary improvements. One of the squadrons first blessed with this aircraft, 97 Squadron, quickly became known as 'The 97th Foot'.[55]

55 Philip J. R. Moyes, *Bomber Squadrons of the R.A.F. and Their Aircraft* (London: MacDonald, 1964), p.341.

It was therefore decided to keep the now worn-out Hampdens, which the Manchesters would otherwise have helped to replace. The old Hampdens were used for mine laying until September 1942. After that, some of them served for a year in Coastal Command as reconnaissance and torpedo aircraft.[56]

But there was hope for minelaying enthusiasts. On 9 January 1941, a four-engine and greatly improved version of the Manchester flew its first flight as a prototype. After the war, the aircraft was dubbed the RAF's best heavy bomber. It was the later famous Avro Lancaster. However, it would be another year before the first aircraft were delivered to the operational squadrons.[57]

In the summer of 1941, there was a significant change in minelaying tactics. In early 1940, the Germans had lacked minesweepers, so it was sufficient to drop a small but constant number of mines in a waterway. This kept the minesweepers under intense working pressure. However, the *Kriegsmarine* had now built up a well-functioning minesweeper unit and several new minesweepers, the so-called *sperrbrechere*, had been deployed. As a result, the RAF changed tactics and began to drop a mixed cocktail of different mines with time-delay and counting devices. Acoustic mines and magnetic mines were mixed equally. For the first time, mines specifically designed for the German *Sperrbrechere* were also produced. The production of mines had also skyrocketed. There was just one problem: there were not enough aircraft to deliver them to the target areas! In the last month of the year, only 66 mines were laid with the joint help of both Bomber Command and Coastal Command.[58] The fact that there had been less activity in 1941 also affected the number of magnetic mines laid in Danish waters. A total of 33 mines were successfully swept, with German minesweepers taking 27, while Danish vessels swept 4 and Swedish minesweepers the other 2.[59]

If you compare the RAF's efforts against enemy shipping tonnage, divided into minelaying and direct air attacks on ships, the figures for 1940–1941 clearly show the advantage of minelaying. With almost 21 percent of the total number of flights, minelaying aircraft managed to sink 229 percent more ships than air strikes. The rate of loss of aircraft was virtually the same and therefore the loss of mining aircraft was only 20 percent of total aircraft losses. Looking at the total number of ships sunk and damaged per aircraft, the yield was 600 percent more per aircraft in minelaying operations.[60] With the 66 mines laid in December 1941, the level was so low that minelaying activity could only increase from there. The first unit to receive the new large Lancasters was 44 Squadron of 5 Group. The Lancaster's operational debut was therefore a minelaying operation in Helgoland Bight on the night of 3 March 1942.[61] From then on, mines would be laid in greater quantities than ever before.

---

56 Kenneth Munson, John W. Wood, et al, *Fighters and Bombers of World War II* (Littlehampton: Littlehampton Books, 1969), p.298.

57 Philip J. R. Moyes, *Bomber Squadrons of the R.A.F. and Their Aircraft* (London: MacDonald, 1964), p.342.

58 Stephen W. Roskill, *The War at Sea 1939–45*, vol. 1 (London: HMSO, 1954), p.510.

59 Palle Roslyng-Jensen, *Værnenes politik – politikernes værn* (Gyldendal: 1980), p.40.

60 Stephen W. Roskill, *The War at Sea 1939–45*, vol. 1 (London: HMSO, 1954), p.125, Table 10 p.336, Table 11 p.339, Table v15 p.507, Table 17 p.511 and Table 18 p.512

61 Philip J. R. Moyes, *Bomber Squadrons of the R.A.F. and Their Aircraft* (London: MacDonald, 1964), p.342.

1940	Direct Attack on Shipping at Sea						
			number sunk	Tonnage sunk	Damaged ships		A/C losses
quarter	Sorties	attacks	ships	BRT	numbers	Tonnage	numbers
apr-jun	2.199	no	4	8.720	2	3.232	53
jul-sept	1.807	Infor-	2	1.655	8	26.254	31
okt-dec	1.034	mation	3	3.156	4	18.176	37
In total	5040		9	13531	14	47662	121

1940	Minelaying						
		Mines laid	Number sunk	Tonnage sunk	Damaged ships		A/C losses
quarter	Sorties	numbers	ships	BRT	numbers	Tonnage	numbers
apr-jun	584	421	32	36.927	2	4.114	15
jul-sept	611	513	40	35.735	5	7.611	9
okt-dec	312	243	14	10.321	3	5.345	7
In total	1507	1177	86	82983	10	17070	31

1941	Direct Attack on Shipping at Sea						
			number sunk	Tonnage sunk	Damaged ships		A/C losses
quarter	Sorties	attacks	ships	BRT	numbers	Tonnage	numbers
jan-mar	1.134		3	9.907	2	1.680	37
apr-jun	2.718		9	11.777	9	56.356	88
jul-sept	1.762		20	18.059	8	20.282	70
okt-dec	1.672		21	35.516	10	19.454	57
In total	7286		53	75259	29	97772	252

1941	Minelaying						
		Mines laid	Number sunk	Tonnage sunk	Damaged ships		A/C losses
quarter	Sorties	numbers	ships	BRT	numbers	Tonnage	numbers
jan-mar	293	235	13	16.356	3	2.369	8
apr-jun	583	473	4	7.248	3	5.982	19
jul-sept	522	416	18	11.674	3	3.731	19
okt-dec	321	261	21	18.669	3	7.894	17
In total	1719	1385	56	53947	12	19976	63

Comparative results obtained by the Royal Air Force from Minelaying and from Direct Attacks on Enemy Shipping at sea, 1940 and 1941.

Arthur T. Harris, the former head of 5 Group, had been appointed commander of Bomber Command on 22 February 1942. Bottomley, his successor in 5 Group, had meanwhile been appointed Deputy Chief of Air Staff in the Air Ministry. With the two chiefs' positive attitude towards the minelaying campaign and the new aircraft, which could carry up to six mines each, the way was paved for an increased prioritisation of minelaying.

During March and May, Harris also got 1 and 3 Bomber Groups respectively involved in the minelaying operation, as both groups had been equipped with the new navigation equipment, GEE.[62] In the meantime, Coastal Command's part in the minelaying operations in April was reduced to being carried out only by the navy's own aircraft.[63] At the same time, operational command of the mine war was moved from Coastal Command to Bomber Command. Harris justified this on the grounds that mine laying now accounted for 10 percent of Bomber Command's total number of operations. However, the practical change was not very significant. Bomber Command had always had the long-range aircraft needed to achieve effective results. Therefore, the work of coordinating the mine and bombing raids between them had also been the responsibility of Bomber Command. Finally, this organisation had, to a much greater extent than Coastal Command, been adapted to strategic warfare, which certainly did not diminish under Harris' leadership.[64] As can be seen from the map, see chapter 6 page 97, where the dark areas show where the Allied naval and air forces laid mines during World War II,[65] Danish waters played a significant role in the overall picture. The dramatic increase in the number of mines laid, which started in 1942 and continued throughout the war, was therefore also very noticeable in Danish waters.

62 Denis Richards & Hilary St George Saunders, *Royal Air Force, 1939–1945* (London: HMSO, 195), vol. 2, p.134; Frank Weber et al, *Vestallierede luftangreb i Danmark under 2. Verdenskrig* (Viborg: Aarhus Universitetsforlag, 1988), vol. 1, pp.286-287.

63 J. S. Cowie, *Mines, Minelayers and Minelaying* (Oxford: OUP, 1949), pp.154–55.

64 J. S. Cowie, 'The British Sea-Mining Campaign, 1939–1945' in *Royal United Services Institution. Journal*, volume 93, no.569 (1948), p.27.

65 J. S. Cowie, 'The British Sea-Mining Campaign, 1939–1945' in *Royal United Services Institution. Journal*, volume 93, no.569 (1948), pp.22–39. The map is between pp.28 & 29

Chapter 8

8.1 1942 Mine Laying Escalates

In late December 1941, British commandos conducted two raids against German positions in Norway. Hitler saw these attacks as preparation for an invasion of Northern Norway. Therefore, in early January 1942, he ordered the two battleships *Scharnhorst* and *Gneisenau*, as well as the heavy cruiser *Prinz Eugen*, to be moved from Brest in France to Trondheim in Norway. *Grossadmiral* Raeder was not keen on sending the three warships through the English Channel under the nose of the British coastal defence guns. At the same time, he believed that the British convoys to North Africa with supplies would be given too easy a ride if the threat from the large German warships disappeared.

But Hitler stood his ground and the audacious project succeeded – almost. The three warships set sail from Brest on 11 February and reached German waters unscathed in the evening of the next day. However, shortly before sailing into the protective harbour of Wilhelmshaven, the two battleships were heavily damaged by British mines. They had been laid by Bomber Command during the day, as the German breakout from Brest had been detected. The *Prinz Eugen* sailed into the Elbe Estuary and therefore reached Brunsbüttel unscathed.[1]

It soon became clear that the big battleships could not continue northwards. Instead, the pocket battleship *Admiral Scheer* was sent off together with *Prinz Eugen*. On the morning of 21 February, the two ships carried out a diversion manoeuvre off the Dutch coast, after which they set course for Norway.[2]

Since the summer of 1941, a large part of the German naval force had been in the Baltic Sea to block a possible Russian breakout attempt to the North Sea. However, no such breakout was attempted. Now that Hitler believed Norway was under threat of invasion, large parts of the Baltic force were directed to the northern Norwegian harbours. In January, the battleship *Tirpitz* arrived in Trondhjem, and on 22 February, the two warships mentioned above, *Prinz Eugen* and *Admiral Scheer*, reached the more southern Grimstad Fjord. At the end of March, the heavy cruiser *Admiral Hipper* also arrived in Trondhjem. These four large warships, together with their escort of destroyers, torpedo boats, minesweepers and others, eventually formed a sizeable naval force.[3]

1 Hans H. Hildebrand, *Die deutschen Kriegsschiffe. Biographien – ein Spiegel der Marinegeschichte von 1815 bis zur Gegenwart*, vols 1–7 (Herford: Koehlers, 1982), pp.100–101; Friedrich Ruge, *Im Küstenvorfeld* (Munich: 1974), p.90.

2 Bruce Robertson, *Beaufort Special* (Shepperton: Ian Allan, 1976), p.34, 'Sink the Prinz. February-May 1942'.

3 John Winton, *Air Power at Sea, 1939–1945* (London: Sidgwick & Jackson, 1976), p.79.

Although the shift in the centre of gravity of the German fleet now threatened Allied convoys in the Atlantic, both German and British naval commanders saw the operation as a strategic retreat for the German fleet. The pressure on the troop and supply convoys to the Mediterranean had now eased enough for the Allies to gain a foothold in North Africa and ultimately seize the initiative in the battles against the German and Italian units.

It was also easier for British air and naval units to keep an eye on the movements of large German warships when they were stationed in German or Norwegian harbours.[4] German shipping traffic through Danish waters was also registered in the British Admiralty. When the battleship *Bismarck* and the cruiser *Lützow* sailed from northern Germany to the Atlantic via the Kattegat in 1941, this was reported surprisingly quickly in England. The German naval command suspected the British naval attaché in Stockholm of being behind the constant monitoring of ship traffic.[5] Danish intelligence also had contact with the British naval attaché Henry Denham via Ebbe Munck, so the German assumption was not entirely off the mark.[6]

Of course, Germany did not realise that the British Admiralty had broken almost all of the *Kriegmarine*'s codes at the same time. To avoid detection, the German naval command allowed the Baltic Fleet to pass through the Kiel Canal and head for Norway along the west coast of Jutland. But when the British were able to decode most German naval orders, Bomber Command suddenly started laying more mines in the North Sea than before. For example, on the night of 27 February, six out of seven Hampdens each laid a mine in 'Hawthorne 2' off the western mouth of the Limfjord.[7]

February was all about minelaying for Bomber Command. Out of a total of 611 operational flights, 327 were mine sorties. The 327 aircraft laid a total of 306 mines, which means that only 21 aircraft took their mine home again. This is a good result considering that the RAF considered the winter of 1941–1942 to be the worst for flying in 50 years.[8] In addition to preventing the increased traffic of German surface vessels, it was also intended to 'stress' the German U-boat crews. From 12 January to 22 March 1942, German U-boats sank British and American ships totalling 1,200,000 GRT off the North American coast. The U-boats had virtually free rein, as the US Navy had not yet organised anti-submarine warfare. The U-boats therefore sank the vast majority of Allied ships using the guns on deck. Approximately 30–40 German U-boats were constantly lying off the American east coast or in transit back and forth across the Atlantic.

The U-boats' home base was the French West Coast, especially Lorient, followed by St Nazaire, Bordeaux, Brest and La Pallice. Bomber Command and Coastal Command laid a

4 John Winton, *Air Power at Sea, 1939–1945* (London: Sidgwick & Jackson, 1976), p.79; Hans H. Hildebrand, *Die deutschen Kriegsschiffe. Biographien – ein Spiegel der Marinegeschichte von 1815 bis zur Gegenwart*, vols 1–7 (Herford: Koehlers, 1982), p.100.

5 F. H. Hinsley, *British Intelligence in The Second World War* (Cambridge: Cambridge University Press, 1979), vol. 2, p.202.

6 For example, 26 large ships with escorts were observed off the west coast in late February 1942. The information was immediately passed on to Henry Denham in Stockholm. Ebbe Muncks ark. pk. 2, miscellaneous sheets, sheet 2.

7 Air 25/109A. 5 Group ORB, 26–27 February 1942; States Civil Air Defence, SCL, 26–27 February 1942.

8 Air 25/109A. 5 Group ORB, 26–27 February 1942.

few hundred bottom mines at each of these bases and maintained them with 20–30 mines per week. Newly produced U-boats from the shipyards in northern Germany made practice runs in the Baltic Sea before travelling via Danish waters north of Scotland and down to the French bases. The mines were intended to put an end to this traffic. At the same time, the danger of triggering a mine during the approach to the home base after a voyage of typically 6–7 weeks would increase the crew's uncertainty and stress and thus break down morale.[9]

8.2 Harris, the Admiralty and the Minefields

As mentioned, Arthur T. Harris became Chief of Bomber Command on 22 February 1942, and Norman Bottomley, also former Chief of 5 Group, had become Deputy Chief of Air Staff in mid-1941. With the two chiefs' particular association with the development of mine laying operations in the early years of the war, it is clear that this side of the RAF's endeavour was coming back into favour. But the Admiralty was still unhappy that Harris continued to follow his own ideas when it came to supporting the British Navy, including the fight against the German U-boats. The Admiralty wanted more of the Bomber Command units allocated to anti-submarine patrols over the Atlantic and North Sea. Specifically, the Admiralty wanted 80 Consolidated B-24 Liberator and Boeing B-17 Flying Fortress aircraft to cover the exposed convoys in the mid-Atlantic. It therefore complained directly to Prime Minister Winston Churchill, who, through his political career as Secretary of State for the Navy during both World Wars, usually had a particularly sympathetic ear for the navy's wishes. In a memo of 1 April 1942, Churchill therefore asked Harris to update him, at this crucial moment, on how Bomber Command intended to participate in the anti-submarine campaign to date and in the future.

Harris replied in his typical polite yet highly ironic manner. In a letter enclosing the requested report, Harris emphasised that the report had been prepared by his Chief Intelligence Officer on the basis of material in Bomber Command and the Air Ministry. He also pointed out that the RAF Intelligence Service was always very conservative in its judgement when assessing what conclusions could be drawn from the available sources, therefore, the Admiralty would probably be disappointed with the answer. On the other hand, their organisation and outlook were probably not used to Air Intelligence either. For example, the Admiralty probably placed more emphasis on warships being sunk by other warships in a naval battle, while apparently finding it very difficult to imagine that the ship may never have been built, and therefore never reached the naval battle, because the shipyard and shipyard workers had been bombed![10]

The report showed that the Air Staff, in collaboration with the naval staff, had prioritised Bomber Command's attacks on the U-boat yards as the best way to damage German U-boat activity. They then totalled up which yards had been bombed and with what result. From destroyed and damaged U-boats, to what delays could be expected in U-boat production.

9 Dudley Saward, *'Bomber' Harris': The Story of the Marshal of the Royal Air Force Sir Arthur Harris* (London: Cassell Ltd, 1984), p.129.

10 Dudley Saward, *'Bomber' Harris': The Story of the Marshal of the Royal Air Force Sir Arthur Harris* (London: Cassell Ltd, 1984), p.126.

Air Chief Marshal Sir Arthur Harris, Commander-in-Chief of Royal Air Force Bomber Command, seated at his desk at Bomber Command HQ, High Wycombe. 24 April 1944.

Finally, Harris discussed the importance of minelaying for anti-submarine warfare:

> Extensive minefields have been maintained and are now being greatly increased by the Command in the Bight, the Belts and the Baltic and the approaches to German ports and to the western bases. Owing to the large numbers of enemy ships known to have been sunk by these minefields, we are confident that they have obtained their quota of submarines sunk and damaged. Interrogation of Prisoners of War tends to confirm this. Unfortunately, whereas trade and insurance sources provide relatively easy and certain confirmation of merchant ship losses, warship losses and perhaps especially submarine sinkings are for obvious reasons much harder to confirm. It is well known that the general dislocation of traffic and necessity for constant sweeping has affected the activities not only of submarines but also of their supply ships.[11]

On this basis, Harris concluded that the strategy was effective. His immediate superior, Chief of Air Staff Charles Portal, one of Harris's predecessors as head of Bomber Command, on 23 March, had already asked for an account of the effectiveness of the mine laying before a meeting with Churchill the following day. Therefore, the Prime Minister was briefed on this part of Bomber Command's efforts before the above enquiry on behalf of the Admiralty. Harris had made it clear to Portal that he was opposed to the Admiralty's wish to let Bomber Command units 'waltz around the Atlantic under naval command looking for a needle in a haystack'.[12] In his memorandum to Portal, Harris had summarised the overall result of the mine laying operations up to 31 December 1941 as follows:

11 Dudley Saward, *'Bomber' Harris': The Story of the Marshal of the Royal Air Force Sir Arthur Harris* (London: Cassell Ltd, 1984), p.128.

12 Dudley Saward, *'Bomber' Harris': The Story of the Marshal of the Royal Air Force Sir Arthur Harris* (London: Cassell Ltd, 1984), p.128.

> 2,569 mines had been laid, 1,757 by Bomber Command and 812 by Coastal Command. The total documented enemy ship losses were 98 with a total tonnage of 211,360 gross tonnes. That's 26.6 mines per ship.[13]

But that was not all. Using a calculation based on the assumption that for every documented ship loss, there was probably another ship loss that was not known, Harris was convinced that around 200 ships had been sunk by Bomber Command mines. The assumption was based on German military charts totalling 300 lost ships. If you excluded ships sunk due to maritime accidents, the British wrecks from Dunkirk, ships sunk by Coastal Command air strikes, torpedo boats and more, there were approximately 200 lost ships left without explanation.

This assumption was, to the best of his knowledge, strengthened by the knowledge of known ship losses in the 60 minefields established by the RAF. The result was from 0 to 8 ships sunk in each field, except for one, where 24 ships had fallen prey to the mines. This field was located in the Sound and was under constant observation by the neutral Swedish Navy, and was therefore one of the fields where the intelligence on the result was considered to be very accurate.

With such success, Harris was also pleased to inform Churchill that whereas the mines laid so far had been laid by Hampdens, which carried one mine each, he had ordered all bomber types in Bomber Command to be equipped with both bomb and mine mounts. This meant that the Halifax and Wellington aircraft could each carry two mines, while the Stirling and Lancaster could each carry six mines. In the future, it would therefore be possible lay 800 to 1,000 mines every month if there were no other, more important targets. They would start by laying 500 to 1,000 mines in the waters off the German U-boat yards in France.

Again Harris emphasised his view of anti-submarine strategy, that the best use of Bomber Command was to lay mines, bomb shipyards and associated industrial targets. The Air Staff took the statement to heart and implemented Harris' strategy in the overall plan. This prevented Harris from having to change his strategy at the request of the Admiralty in the future. Bombers that were not assigned to other missions or had to cancel bombing raids over Europe due to meteorological conditions, as well as all Operational Training Units, could in future be used for mine sorties.[14]

The dispute between Harris and the Admiralty, which had been growing since Harris' time as head of 5 Group and now culminated in the spring of 1942, has been called the most important British strategic debate on warfare during the war, namely how to win the Battle of the Atlantic.[15]

From the time the Anglo-American convoys began in May 1941 until the Admiralty finally wrested some Liberator aircraft from Harris in late 1942, they were beyond the reach

13 Dudley Saward, *'Bomber' Harris': The Story of the Marshal of the Royal Air Force Sir Arthur Harris* (London: Cassell Ltd, 1984), p.128–129. 2569 mines: 98 ships = ratio 26.2, but Harris did not seem to pay much attention to such details!

14 Dudley Saward, *'Bomber' Harris': The Story of the Marshal of the Royal Air Force Sir Arthur Harris* (London: Cassell Ltd, 1984), p.129.

15 Ralph Bennett, *Behind the Battle: Intelligence in the War with Germany, 1939–1945* (London: Pimlico, 1999), p.159.

of British and American air forces in the unprotected stretch of mid-Atlantic; here the German U-boats had almost free rein.

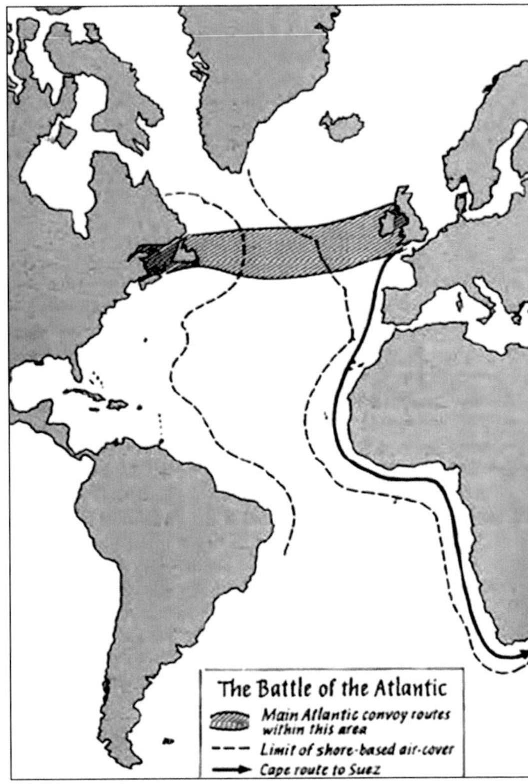

The map shows how far the air support extended from the US and England. In the middle of the Atlantic, the convoys were unprotected.

At the same time, in February 1942, the German Navy changed its 'Enigma' code machine to the type the British called 'Shark'. The British Admiralty, which had cracked the Enigma code in August 1941, had then been able to read virtually all messages from German naval headquarters to all units. By adding a fourth code wheel to the three existing ones in the machine, the Germans had made decryption even more difficult, and for the next 10 months the Admiralty was cut off from this important source of information. There was thus a real risk in the spring and summer of 1942 that Britain's Atlantic lifeline of food, fuel and military equipment would be severed.

Despite warnings from the Ministry of Economic Warfare and the Admiralty, neither Chief of Air Staff Charles Portal nor Harris would recognise the gravity of the situation. They both believed that the danger of U-boat attacks was greatly exaggerated and characterised any transfer of long-range bombers from Bomber Command to Coastal Command as a transfer of aircraft from an active to an uneconomic defensive role. Harris even stated that the Admiralty, Coastal Command and the head of Allied Forces in the Middle East were like 'vultures ripping the entrails out of Bomber Command.'[16]

One wonders why Portal was so supportive of Harris, despite their long-standing friendship, Portal knew the importance of 'Enigma' communications and should have known better. Harris, on the other hand, and therefore Bomber Command, did not receive intelligence directly from Ultra, who read the 'Enigma' messages, until August 1944! Until then, his commander did not allow the information from Ultra to be sent directly to Bomber Command. The former Fighter Command, now Air Defence of Great Britain, the US Strategic Air Force, and the Allied Expeditionary Air Force under Eisenhower's command were all given access to Ultra from 1 January 1944 and benefited greatly from this. Why Portal deliberately failed to provide Harris with such vital information remains an

16 Ralph Bennett, *Behind the Battle: Intelligence in the War with Germany, 1939–1945* (London: Pimlico, 1999), p.160.

unanswered question.[17] In fact, as previously mentioned, Operation Gardening contributed to the deciphering of 'Enigma', as researchers at Bletchley Park pinpointed minelaying areas where they already knew the German coordinates. When Bomber Command laid mines there, the researchers were immediately notified so they could listen in when the positions of the mines were reported by the German observers and the message was passed on to the German minesweeper service via the 'Enigma' codes.[18]

8.3 The Hunt for *Prinz Eugen* 1942

For the time being, however, it was not worthwhile to lay mines in Danish waters. Due to the harsh winter, the ice closed the inland waters and made shipping almost impossible from mid-January to mid-April. Icebreakers had their hands full helping ships stuck in the ice. The ice became up to 80cm thick in some places, and huge ice floes rose up around Denmark at coasts and harbours. Even a west coast harbour like Esbjerg, which is not normally bothered much by ice, was closed by solid ice for most of February in this winter. For the first time ever, an icebreaker had to be stationed in this important harbour.[19]

During April, the ice disappeared more and more from Danish waters. The large German warships went through the Kiel Canal, partly to avoid being spotted too quickly and partly because they could maintain a high speed and make evasive manoeuvres in deeper and open waters.

However, the smaller and slower supply and troop transport ships were still using the Øresund and the belts as a passage to Norway. To put an end to this traffic, a major minelaying operation was carried out in early May. But there was an additional good reason. The heavy cruiser *Prinz Eugen* had been hit by a torpedo from a British submarine when she and the pocket battleship *Admiral Scheer* sailed from Grimstad Fjord on 23 February into Trondhjem Fjord. Outside the entrance to Trondhjem Fjord were four British U-boats, lying in wait for the battleship *Tirpitz*, which was further into the fjord. As the two German warships were about to sail through the net barrier at the mouth of the fjord, a torpedo was fired from the submarine *Trident*. It hit the *Prinz Eugen* at the stern, causing the entire stern of the ship to tear loose and hang down into the water. With great effort, the ship was towed into the centre of the fjord. On 25 February, the workshop ship *Huascaran* began to repair the damage as far as possible. A temporary stern was welded on so that the *Prinz Eugen* would be able to make it to the shipyards in Kiel in one piece, which needed to happen as soon as possible.[20]

17 Ralph Bennett, *Behind the Battle: Intelligence in the War with Germany, 1939–1945* (London: Pimlico, 1999), pp.166–167.

18 Michael Smith, *The Secrets of Station X: How the Bletchley Park Codebreakers Helped Win The War* (Hull: Biteback Publishing, 2011).

19 'Ice and navigation conditions in Danish waters in the winter of 1941–42.' Statens isbrydnings – og ismeldingstjeneste (Copenhagen: 1941), pp.4–11.

20 Hans H. Hildebrand, *Die deutschen Kriegsschiffe. Biographien – ein Spiegel der Marinegeschichte von 1815 bis zur Gegenwart*, vols 1–7 (Herford: Koehlers, 1982), p.68. F. H. Hinsley, *British Intelligence in The Second World War* (Cambridge: Cambridge University Press, 1979), vol.2, p.201.

Prinz Eugen (centre) under repair in Lofjord. On the starboard side is the workshop ship *Huascaran*. *Admiral Scheer* is in the foreground, protected by anti-torpedo nets. March 1942.

One could therefore expect that *Prinz Eugen* would soon attempt to sneak southwards through Danish waters on her way to Kiel. That Harris was determined to get the German warship is evident from the relatively large minelaying force that was allocated for the mission. On 7 May, 89 aircraft took off for Denmark: 10 Manchesters, 12 Lancasters[21] 13 Stirlings, 14 Hampdens and 40 Wellingtons. The aircraft carried a total load of between 234 and 258 mines.[22] They came from both 5 and 3 Group, which together with 1 Group had become involved in mine laying after Harris had become head of Bomber Command.

Since it was obviously not 100 percent certain that the German ship would go through the Kattegat, 20 of the planes were to lay mines in the Heligoland area, 'Eglantine', but all indications were that the damaged ship would take the route through the Great Belt to Kiel. Therefore, 36 aircraft were to lay mines in 'Forget-me-not', at the entrance to Kiel, while the rest of the aircraft distributed the mines in the Øresund, Little Belt and especially the Great Belt.

21 The largest number of Lancasters ever to operate over enemy territory. Bruce Robertson, *Lancaster: The Story of a Famous Bomber* (Letchworth: Harleyford Publications, 1967), p.19

22 The number of mines depends on whether the Lancasters had four or six mines on board

Of the 89 participating aircraft, only two were shot down, a Hampden and a Wellington. Both were shot down over Fanø by the heavy flak in the Esbjerg area.[23] Along the way, some of the aircraft had dropped bombs and fired on German positions in several places. For example, German flak positions at Nyborg, Korsør and Esbjerg were fired upon, while 500-pound bombs were dropped on Nordfyn, Bågø and Esbjerg. The pilot who dropped two bombs on 'Brøndum Airfield' near Esbjerg was probably aiming for a German emergency landing site at Brøndum (Bryndum), 8km north of Esbjerg, which was built in connection with the use of Esbjerg Airfield.[24]

Another pilot dropped bombs on a light glimmer west of Esbjerg. He thought it was some kind of seaplane airfield. In reality, it was a seaside hotel on the northern tip of Fanø, which was thereby damaged. However, as the hotel had been taken over by the Germans it could therefore rightly be characterised as a military target.

Finally, a third pilot was convinced that he had hit close to the dam, which leads from the mainland to the island of Sylt. However, the bombs fell at Skærbæk and Ballum Sluse in south-west Jutland, where the Rømø dam is located.

The Germans opened fire from anti-aircraft batteries at Nyborg, Korsør, Copenhagen, Esbjerg and from an anti-aircraft ship at Middelfart.[25] The German fighter defence was gradually becoming well-developed in Denmark. Among other things, *9/JG 1* had just arrived at Esbjerg Airfield to patrol Southern Jutland with its Me110s.[26] However, the British crews did not see a single German fighter during the entire flight that night; perhaps none were sent up. From *Flugabwehrkommando 'Flakgruppe Dänemark'* in Aarhus, *Fliegerhorst* Esbjerg was discreetly, and perhaps somewhat ironically, made aware that the airfield was actually well located for the fighters to attack enemy bombers.[27] Perhaps this should be seen as a hint to the *Luftwaffe* in Esbjerg that a slightly greater effort was expected in the future. But *9/JG 1* was not intended as a night fighter unit and would not have been able to do much without the necessary equipment and special training for the pilots.

On the night of 9 May, Bomber Command's target was the Heinkel factories at Warnemünde. *Prinz Eugen* had not yet left Trondhjem, so seven aircraft laid mines at Helgoland that night.[28] On the night of 10 May, mines were again laid in Danish waters. A total of 20 aircraft were dispatched, 14 of which laid mines in the designated areas. This time the German fighters were scrambled. The little pep talk from *Flakgruppe Dänemark* in Aarhus might have seemed inspiring. But as mentioned, the German fighter pilots lacked experience in night attacks. All the German fighters observed by the British bombers passed by the assembled minelaying force without detecting it![29]

23 Air 25/109A. 5 Group ORB, 7–8 May 1942; Air 28/375. Honnington ORB, app. Briefing to 3 Group for 7–8 May 1942.

24 Air 27/126.9 Sqdn. ORB, 7–8 May 1942. The result was not seen.

25 Adm. Dän. 8.5.1942.

26 Luftwaffearchiv pk 47/563 Siege at Esbjerg Sept. 41, Dec. 41, Jan. 42 and May-Aug 42.

27 Adm. Dän. 8.5.1942; Air 28/371. Honington ORB, 7.5.1942; Air 27/126. 9 Sqdn. ORB, 7–8 May 1942.

28 Air 25/109A. 5 Group ORB, 8–9.15.1942; Air 28/375. Honington ORB, ops, order to 3 Group 8.5.1942. The force consisted of: two Manchesters from 50 Squadron, three Wellingtons from 419 Squadron, and two Stirlings from 149 Squadron, with a total of 22 mines on board.

29 Air 24/243. Bomber Command Intell. Sum: 'Enemy A/C Observed'.

According to Bomber Command reports, bombs were dropped on military targets on the island of Sylt and at Middelfart.[30] However, there is nothing to confirm that bombs were dropped at Middelfart, but the information that a mine detonated in deep water close to the Little Belt Bridge between 03.12 and 03.30 may cover up a bomb dropped on the bridge.[31]

In the British Admiralty and Bomber Command, the various passages that the *Prinz Eugen* could use en route to Kiel were now considered to be fully mined. Now it was just a matter of waiting. However, on the following two days, the weather was so bad that such a voyage would hardly be possible. Bomber Command could not even carry out a single operational flight due to the bad weather.[32]

On 13 May, something unexpected happened. The British Admiralty received a warning from the British naval attaché in Stockholm that the heavy cruiser *Lützow* would leave Kiel as early as 15 or 16 May to go to Norway to replace *Prinz Eugen*. The Air Ministry decided that Bomber Command should try to stop the *Lützow* as soon as possible using mines in the Sound and in the two belts. However, the following day, 14 May, it was reported that *Lützow* was already on its way through the Great Belt. The RAF sent out reconnaissance and torpedo planes, but *Lützow* made it to Norway unscathed with the help of some fake manoeuvres.[33]

The many dropped mines in the Great Belt had not been a particularly effective obstacle to the German warship, which can largely be attributed to the great efforts of the German minesweeper organisation. Over time, the German minesweepers had gained a good deal of experience in locating and neutralising the British mines. The number of minesweeping vessels had also increased and equipment was constantly being improved.

That is why Bomber Command then got really busy. It would not be many days before *Prinz Eugen* would appear, but before then, new mine barriers had to be established in Danish waters, as it was assumed that the 'old' fields had been neutralised. The first raid was to be carried out on the night of 16 May. Initially, the plan was to send 64 aircraft, of which 17 of the crews would be 'freshmen', i.e. relatively inexperienced mine laying crews. On the afternoon of 15 May, meteorologists predicted that there would be fog over and around the planes' home bases when they returned from the mission the next morning. It was therefore decided to send only the experienced crews, 47 in total. Of this force, 25 Wellingtons would lay mines in the Langeland Belt, 16 Hampdens would lay mines off Nyborg, and 6 Lancasters would lay mines at Korsør.[34] As alternative target areas, mines could be laid in the waters around Helgoland and 'Hawthorne 1', at the entrance to Esbjerg.[35]

At the last minute, it was decided that three of the Lancasters would lay their mines in Læsø Rende, between Læsø and Sæby. However, shortly after take off, one of these aircraft experienced engine trouble, so it abandoned the mines in the North Sea and returned to the airfield. This meant that on the evening of 15 May, a force of 46 aircraft were on their way to Denmark.[36]

30 Air 24/204. Bomber Command ORB, 9–10 May 1942.
31 SCL, message on 10.5.1942 at 19.00 from Fredericia.
32 Air 24/243. Bomber Command Intell. narrative of operations, 10–16 May 1942.
33 F. H. Hinsley, *British Intelligence in The Second World War* (Cambridge: Cambridge University Press, 1979), vol. 2, pp.202–203.
34 Air 24/243. Bomber Command ORB, app. May 1942.
35 Air 24/243. Bomber Command ORB, app. May 1942.'Last resort Targets'; Air 25/65.3 Group ORB, ops. order 15.5.1942
36 Air 28/879. Waddington ORB, 15–16.15.1942.

8.4 The Laying of Mines on 15–16 May 1942

In the following, I will try to illustrate how the pieces of a single minelaying operation in 1942 can be put together into one action. The focus will be on the 14 bombings that took place in connection with the laying of mines, which created a lot of havoc around the country.

Minelaying 15–16 May 1942				
Type of Aircraft	Wellington	Hampden	Lancaster	Lancaster
Number of mines by Take off	50	16	18	18
Number of mines lost	5	3	0	6
Number of mines at target-area	45	13	18	12
The 'Gardens'	*Quince*	*Broccoli*	*Asparagus*	Yewtree
Number of mines planted	At the 'Gardens' Q, B and A 58 of 76 mines			10 mines

Summary of the results of the laying of mines indicating where and how many mines were dropped.

During the approach, a Hampden dropped two 250-pound bombs on what the pilot believed to be the landing lights of a naval airfield west of Fanø. It is clear that, based on the information provided by a pilot on 9 May, it was believed that there was a naval airfield near Fanø. However, it was the straight road from Nordby and due west to the holiday home area that the two pilots saw. The two bombs fell close to the road and uprooted a few trees.

Most aircraft then laid the mines in the predetermined areas. A few of the aircraft laid mines in the alternative areas on their way westward. It was also during the outward flight that the remaining bombing runs took place.

A Wellington dropped two 500-pound bombs on a lightship at Blåvandshuk, but missed. This may be the same trawler or minesweeper that a Hampden tried to hit with its bombs a little later, south-southwest of Blåvandshuk. Another Wellington attempted to target a ship. This time it was a smaller vessel west of Ribe, but the result was not observed. Two Wellingtons had targeted an entire convoy. The convoy was travelling south through the Great Belt. The attack was launched at the southern tip of Langeland. Three 500-pound bombs were dropped on the ships, but the flak from two of the ships prevented the aircrews from seeing the result.

Four Hampdens from 408 Squadron tried their hand at a German minesweeper west of Samsø. On the way home from the Nyborg area, the first Hampden was shot down in the waters south of Samsø by the minesweeper's flak. Shortly afterwards, another Hampden appeared in the arena. The pilot attacked the minesweeper with two 250-pound bombs and turned off. One of the bombs hit the front deck of the ship, but the bomb bounced back up as if from a trampoline and went overboard without detonating. Before the German crew could recover from their fright, another Hampden appeared from the clouds. The German anti-aircraft crew quickly opened fire and hit the British aircraft, which crashed south of Samsø in flames.[37] The aircraft was apparently on the surface of the water for some

37 Report from the navy lookout at Vestborg Lighthouse on Samsø 15–16.15.1942. Informed by Birger Hansen, Copenhagen.

time, as the burning wreckage was observed from a fourth Hampden. However, in the crew's report, the sighting was described as a small ship on fire. Of course, when the two Hampden crews' observations were put together, there was no doubt that a small German vessel had been bombed and was then in flames. Only one of the participating Hampdens appears to have hit a military target on land, namely the 'Maade' searchlight position south of Esbjerg. The gunner on the aircraft sent a shower of bullets towards the lights, which were quickly extinguished.

On the way home, a Wellington came in over Fanø. The pilot dropped his two 500-pound bombs on the 'landing installations', which in reality were not there. However, the bombs fell close to the 'Dora' searchlight position, cutting the power supply to the German installations throughout the island when the main cable from the mainland was torn in half. It was not until 17 May that power was restored to Fanø. Another Wellington attempted to hit the Little Belt Bridge with three 500-pound bombs. It almost succeeded. The bombs hit the water just 150–300 metres from the bridge. A third Wellington pilot had targeted the Alssund Bridge. Two 500-pound bombs were dropped but did not hit the bridge, although they hit very close to the bridge structure. The pilot was pretty sure that one of the bombs had hit the bridge. One pilot thought he had dropped three bombs on some oil tank facilities on Als, probably in Sønderborg. Several bombs did indeed fall in Sønderborg, but according to the German sources, five bombs fell on the railway terrain. A warehouse was completely destroyed and the railway track was torn up. Windows in the immediate neighbourhood were shattered by the blasts.

But who had dropped the five bombs? Part of the answer can be found in a report to the *Statens Civile Luftværn* on the afternoon of 16 May. According to whom, on the night of 16 May, three bombs fell approximately 1km southeast of Lysabild Dairy on the southern part of Als. From the size of the craters, 7–8 metres in diameter and 3–4 metres deep, we can conclude that this must have been where the three 500-pound bombs fell. Perhaps the pilot had seen the dairy's refuelling facilities? But the question remains: which aircraft dropped the five bombs in Sønderborg? Firstly, none of the planes carried more than 3 bombs! It must therefore have been a Wellington that dropped its 3 bombs and 2 mines at the same time. Secondly, only two Wellington pilots reported dropping bombs in Sønderborg itself – the two mentioned above. We must therefore take a closer look at two Wellingtons that did not return home.

One of them belly-landed in Nakskov Fjord for unknown reasons. One crew member was killed on landing, the other four were taken by Danish police for examination at Nakskov Hospital. However, it cannot be this aircraft that was over Sønderborg. The German reports show that the entire bomb load, 3,000 rounds of machine gun ammunition and both mines were found intact. The mines were immediately sent to the *Sperrversuchs-kommando* in Kiel for examination.

Only one possibility remains: a Wellington from 75 Squadron We know that this squadron must have passed right over Sønderborg. It flew on a south-westerly course from the southern Great Belt, with one of the pilots dropping his bomb load towards the dam that leads over to Sylt. If you draw a line from the Sylt dam to the southern Great Belt, it goes through Sønderborg.

The Wellington that bombed Sønderborg with 3 x 500-pound bombs and 2 x 1,500-pound mines was probably shot down by a flak battery on Sylt, which recorded just one

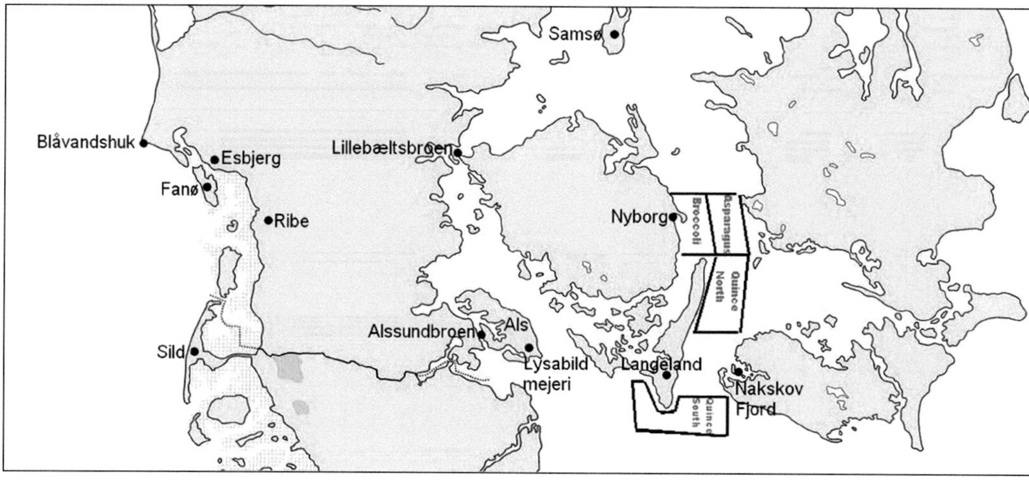

Map with place names and 'Gardens' mentioned.

bomber shot down that night. However, the mines may have fallen out accidentally. One of the other aircraft accidentally dropped a bomb and a mine over the mine laying area instead of both mines at the same time, as there was a problem with the bomb release. The aircraft aiming for Lysabild Dairy was unable to drop the mines over the target area due to a fault in the mine suspension. However, when the pilot prepared to attack the dairy a little later and opened the bomb bay doors again, the mines fell out on their own. They hit the water off the southern tip of Als. [38]

8.5 *Prinz Eugen* leaves Norway

With the above-mentioned laying of mines, Danish waters had once again been heavily mined and the *Prinz Eugen* was still waiting to leave Trondhjem to sail towards Kiel. On the afternoon of 16 May, a reconnaissance aircraft returned from a trip over Trondhjem Fjord, among other places. Coastal Command had the images developed in a hurry. They showed that *Prinz Eugen* and two destroyers had left the fjord and were probably heading south towards the Kattegat. Orders were immediately given for 14 Beaufort torpedo planes to take off at midnight to attack the three German warships. At the same time, six Hampdens were sent to lay mines in front of the ships. However, none of the planes could find the target.

38 The following sources have been used in the above section: Air 24/204. Bomber Command ORB, 15–16 May 1942; Air 24/243. Bomber Command Intell. Sum, 15–16 May 1942; Air 24/243. Bomber Command ops. order, 15.5.1942; Air 25/65. 3 Group ORB, ops. order 15.5.1942 + results; Air 25/109A. 5 Group ORB, 15–16 May 1942; Air 27/126. 9 Sqdn. ORB, 15–16 May 1942; Air 27/538. 57 Sqdn. ORB, 15.5.1942; Air 27/1796. 408 Sqdn. (RCAF) ORB, 15–16.5.1942; Air 28/371 Honington ORB, 15.5.1942; Air 28/791. Swanton Morley ORB, 15–16 May 1942; Air 28/879; Waddington ORB, 15–16 May 1942; Adm. Dän. 15–17 May 1942; Anders Bjørnvad, *Faldne allierede flyvere 1939–1945* (Odense: 1978), pp.143–44,153,157 and 169; SCL, 15–16 May 1942.

Prinz Eugen en route from Norway to Germany, 17 May 1942.

The next day, another reconnaissance was carried out and it became clear that the cruiser was escorted by not two, but four destroyers. The five warships were heading towards the Skagerrak. They could not maintain a very high speed due to the condition of the cruiser. All available Beauforts torpedo planes, 27 in all, were sent against the ships, escorted by 8 Blenheims and 19 Beaufighters. The 54 aircraft were to reach the Norwegian coast at Kristiansand and from there fly west around the south coast of Norway. The plan was to surprise the 5 ships' anti-aircraft defences by attacking from the east, but when the British planes found their target, they were the ones who got a surprise. German Me 109 fighters from I/JG 5 in Stavanger formed a protective umbrella over the ships. The British aircraft were caught in the crossfire between the fighters and the ships' heavy flak protection.[39] None of the German ships were hit. By comparison, seven British aircraft were shot down by the *Prinz Eugen* alone. Eventually, the British aircraft withdrew. After the failed air attack, six submarines were sent after the five German ships, but again without success.[40]

During the night, a total of 107 aircraft had been ordered to lay mines, two-thirds of them in the inner Danish waters and the rest at Horns Rev.[41] The latter because it was feared that the captain of the *Prinz Eugen* was using a deceptive manoeuvre. Perhaps he might decide at the last minute to head down the west coast! Some of the designated aircrew were inexperienced with mine laying and were therefore taken out of the force as the weather over the United Kingdom was not very good. Nevertheless, a sizeable force set off on the night of 17 May.

---

39 Bruce Robertson, *Beaufort Special* (Shepperton: Ian Allan, 1976), pp.34–35; Information about the *Luftwaffe* is from military historian Carsten Petersen.

40 Hans H. Hildebrand, *Die deutschen Kriegsschiffe. Biographien – ein Spiegel der Marinegeschichte von 1815 bis zur Gegenwart*, vols 1–7 (Herford: Koehlers, 1982), p.69.

41 Air 25/65.3 Group ORB, ops. order 16.5.1942. A very detailed account of the drama, plane by plane, has been written by Carsten Petersen. See the report: www.rafcommands.com/archive/03961.php

Short Stirling W7531 LS-F *MacRobert's Reply* gets the mine loaded.

As the crews knew the procedure, most of the mines were placed at the designated locations.[42] The main force of 60 Stirlings was to lay mines in 'Daffodil', the southern part of the Sound. It flew north-east until it approached the Norwegian coast. From there it made a semicircle manoeuvre and flew down the Swedish coast to Malmø and from there to the Øresund. Just as one of the aircraft, named *MacRoberts Reply* from 15 Squadron had reached an altitude of 70 metres and was ready to release the mines, it was hit by heavy anti-aircraft fire. It was from the *Prinz Eugen*, which had sneaked through the Great Belt under cover of darkness and was now heading south on its way to Kiel. Two more of the cruiser's escort ships opened fire on the aircraft, which was badly damaged. The crew did not have time to drop the mines, but tried to evade westwards while the flames were fought. The pilot, Squadron Leader John Hull DFC, attempted to reach the North Sea and a hoped-for rescue. Funen was passed, and with the prospect of soon being able to leave Danish territory, hopes rose. But just as the plane, still burning, crossed the Little Belt Bridge, it was fired upon again and this time luck ran out. The plane crashed at Hindsgavl, and at the same moment one of the mines exploded. The only survivor was the radio operator, who was badly burnt.[43]

For good reason, Bomber Command knew nothing about this, but new reports were constantly coming in from reconnaissance aircraft. The German naval force was seen

42 Air 25/109A. 5 Group ORB, 16–17 May 1942; Air 27/1822. 419 Sqdn. (RCAF) ORB, 17.5.1942.

43 Air 27/1002. 149 Sqdn. ORB, 17–18 May 1942; SCL 17–18 May 1942; Adm. Dän. 17–18 May 1942

Prinz Eugen steering by manual rudder, May 1942.

entering the Kattegat heading towards the Great Belt. Therefore, one last minelaying operation had to be carried out on the night of 18 May, this time by the aircraft that had stayed at home the previous night. Among these aircraft were nine Stirlings from 149 Squadron. Four of them laid the mines in 'Forget-me-not', the entrance to Kiel. One of the aircraft was hit by flak and the mines were dropped in deep water. The bomb load was dropped over the practice area at the home airfield before the aircraft prepared for landing. Another aircraft returned with a full load as the pilot could not locate the target. The last three aircraft all crashed in Denmark. One fell into the water off Asnæs near Kalundborg, one landed near Rise northeast of Åbenrå and one landed in the water south of Lolland.[44] One of the mines from the last plane drilled into the sand in the shallow water.

Throughout most of May, there was hectic minesweeping activity in Danish waters, especially in the Øresund and Great Belt. It must therefore be partly due to these effective efforts that the *Prinz Eugen* and her escort arrived safely at Kiel harbour on 18 May, although Bomber Command had done its best to lay mines in the way of the naval force.[45]

44 *Flyvehistorisk Tidsskrift*, 1973, no. 1, pp.3–10. The author, Palle Sick, makes a few errors in the article, including, among other things, the number of participating aircraft.

45 Adm. Dän, 17–18 May 1942; Hans H. Hildebrand, *Die Deutschen Kriegsschiffe. Biographien – ein Spiegel der Marinegeschichte von 1815 bis zur Gegenwart*, vols 1–7 (Herford: Koehlers, 1982), p.69. While at Lofjord after being torpedoed, the entire stern of *Prinz Eugen* needed to be rebuilt, while the main repair needed was to her rudder. It proved impossible to make adequate arrangements in Lofjord, and so two jury-rigged rudders that had to be operated by hand using capstans were fitted.

In the last week of May 1942, the entire RAF's activity was directed towards the upcoming '1,000 Bomber Raid' on Cologne. This also affected minelaying operations.

8.6 Summer 1942

As previously mentioned, the course was now really being changed in earnest. The Butt Report in 1941, which had revealed how little Bomber Command actually achieved over Germany, helped motivate the RAF leadership to focus more on minelaying. At the same time, the Admiralty had broken the German naval code, and this gave a greater insight into how much was actually achieved by minelaying. Information was collected about German shipping routes, naval training areas, mine swept routes and passages, coastal defences and much more. Some of the information could be read directly from German naval communications, which the British Admiralty could now follow from day to day. When it came to Skagerrak, Kattegat and other inland Danish waters, as well as the Baltic Sea, important information was also obtained from Danish intelligence via the British naval attaché in Stockholm. In addition, some important papers, especially on coastal defence, were captured by two British Commando raids in Norway in late December 1941.[46]

In 1941, as the British Admiralty realised exactly where the mine swept forced routes in Denmark were, a more concentrated laying of mines began here. As mentioned above, civilian shipping and most of the German Navy had to follow these routes, and it was therefore important to find the exact routes. It is clear that the British began to send enquiries to Denmark via Ebbe Munck in Stockholm regarding the results of the minelaying operations to a much greater extent than before. At the same time, they were interested in being kept up-to-date with the number of Danish and German minesweepers, the location of the forced routes, the morale of the German marines and more.[47]

Throughout the war, the British Legation in Stockholm provided information for the Admiralty and Bomber Command. Its naval department collected information on the activities of German warships and merchant ships, as well as on developments in the Danish Navy, through various channels. The British naval attaché H. M. Denham was stationed in Copenhagen from 1939 until the German occupation. He then took up the position in Stockholm until 1946. From his time in Copenhagen, he had got to know the top Danish naval leadership. Through *Orlogskaptajn* Poul Mørch in the Danish naval intelligence service, visits by Danish naval officers to colleagues in Sweden and other good sources, Denham was, until August 1943, extremely well informed about the routes in Danish waters and where it would be most advantageous to lay mines.[48]

In May 1942 *Prinz Eugen* sailed for Germany but was spotted by the RAF and attacked while at sea. Despite her poor steering apparatus, the German cruiser managed to avoid being hit. <https://germanwarmachine.com/free-media/photo-galleries/prinz-eugen.html>.

46 F. H. Hinsley, *British Intelligence in The Second World War* (Cambridge: Cambridge University Press, 1979), vol. 2, p.197.

47 Ebbe Muncks supplement sheet, pk. 2, various sheets. For example, layer 3 has some material on maritime issues from the Admiralty.

48 Daniel G. Harris,'Den danske Flåde 1940–43' in *Marinehistorisk Tidsskrift*, 1989, nr.2, pp.21–24

The forced routes were marked with so-called spar buoys, which had a small flashlight bulb at the top and six large batteries to power it for several months. The buoys were painted red and were visible during the day and flashed every four seconds at night. At route junctions, a yellow-painted buoy was placed, which flashed every six seconds at night. In some places, ships had to sail between two rows of buoys, and in other stretches they had to sail as close to a single row of buoys as possible. On the larger stretches, the markers were spaced 9–10 kilometres apart.[49]

The mining of the forced routes paid off in several places. Especially in the southern routes, many ships were hit by mines, but the mining also concentrated around the points where two or more routes met. Additionally, it should be noted that the northern part of the Great Belt was apparently effectively swept. In the first half of 1942, German minesweepers managed to neutralise 66 British bottom mines, while Danish and Swedish minesweepers swept 9 and 14 British mines respectively, while 36 ships were blown up.[50]

The increased minelaying activity required a reorganisation of operational management and Bomber Command was now given this role. However, the Director of Minelaying Operations, who was based at the Admiralty, was still in charge of mine warfare. Bomber Command's link to this was now through four naval officers, one in each of the three Groups involved and one at Bomber Command HQ. They were to participate in the detailed planning in Bomber Command.[51] The old worn-out Hampdens were replaced with Wellingtons, Halifaxes, Stirlings and, above all, Lancasters. The Manchester was still in use, but was the least useful of these aircraft types. Whereas 5 Group had previously been solely responsible for Bomber Command's mine laying, 1, 3 and 4 Group became involved in this work during 1942. In January 1943, 6 Group had already joined the minelaying work.[52] As a result, not only did the number of flights increase, but also the number of mines laid. In 1941, Bomber Command had laid 1,055 mines with 1,250 minelaying aircraft, but with the new aircraft types, 9,574 mines were laid with 4,743 minelaying aircraft. With the greater effort came a greater loss rate, rising from 1 percent to almost 4 percent, but also a greater profit, as shown in the table on the next page.[53]

The advantages of minelaying over direct air strikes on ships became even clearer than before. In 1942, it took 235 aircraft to sink an enemy ship using direct air strikes, while it only took 26 minelaying aircraft. Ships come in many sizes, but if we look at the total tonnage, an average of 6 GRT was sunk per air strike aircraft, while minelaying aircraft sank an average of 40 GRT per aircraft. From a military point of view, the minelaying programme was therefore a great success. The aircrews may have looked at the loss rate, which was

49 Nielsen, John, 'De danske farvande i fred og krig' M/S Museet for Søfarts årbog, 5, nr 4, p.116. <https://tidsskrift.dk/mfs_aarbog/article/view/96004>.

50 Monthly overview of mine swept and detonated British bottom mines, Jan-Jun 1942. Naval Weapons School, Holmen.

51 Denis Richards & Hilary Saunders, Hilary St George, *Royal Air Force, 1939–1945*, vol. 3 (London: HMSO, 1954), p.16; Air 14/703 Bomber HQ, 9.3.1942; Air 14/703 DCAS to AOC-in-C Bomber Command 25.3.1942. Inexperienced and newly trained crews from Operational Training Units had to be involved in mine laying whenever possible.

52 J. S. Cowie, 'The British Sea-Mining Campaign, 1939–1945' in *Royal United Services Institution. Journal*, volume 93, no.569 (1948), p.31

53 F. H. Hinsley, *British Intelligence in The Second World War* (Cambridge: Cambridge University Press, 1979), vol. 2, p.198; Ken Delve, *Bomber Command 1936–1968 An Operational & Historical Record* (Barnsley: Pen and Sword, 2005), p.131.

not quite as good for the 'gardeners', but it was at what was normally considered an acceptable level in the RAF.[54]

Unlike the *Kriesmarine*, Danish warships escaped sinking due to British mines during the occupation – except for one! On 19 September 1943, the patrol cutter *K1* was hit by one of the first acoustic mines in Øresund off Rungsted. The ship's commander, *Løjtnant* Kaj Nolsøe Bang, described it as 'An infernal rolling bang that felt as if a giant was hammering a huge hammer under the bottom of the ship'[55] Fortunately, the entire crew escaped with only some minor bruises, but the ship sank. It was the first Danish warship to go down in wartime since 1864!

The patrol cutter *K1* which hit a mine on 19 September 1942. During 1942, 155 ships were hit by mines in the inner Danish waters.[56]

Direct attack on shipping at sea

1942	Direct Attack	Direct Attack	Number sunk	Tonnage sunk	Damaged ships		A/C losses
Quarter	**Sorties**	**Attacks**	**Ships**	**BRT**	**Numbers**	**Tonnage**	**Numbers**
jan-mar	3070	289	8	3597	2	11131	94
apr-jun	2630	531	16	34778	12	39145	87
jul-sept	2312	450	11	12616	1	8998	39
oct-dec	1854	295	7	10037	6	22878	39
In total	9866	1565	42	61028	21	82152	259

Minelaying

1942	Mine-laying	Mines laid	Number sunk	Tonnage sunk	Damaged ships		A/C losses
Quarter	**Sorties**	**Numbers**	**Ships**	**BRT**	**Numbers**	**Tonnage**	**Numbers**
jan-mar	685	722	15	22535	2	62600	31
apr-jun	1316	2746	47	59129	8	22305	38
jul-sept	1329	2960	64	62459	13	34533	52
oct-dec	1577	3283	61	53482	9	14787	53
In total	4907	9711	187	197605	32	134225	174

Comparative results obtained by the Royal Air Force from Minelaying and from Direct Attack on Shipping at Sea 1942.

54 Stephen W. Roskill, *The War at Sea 1939–45*, vol. 1 (London: HMSO, 1954), Chapter VI Coastal Warfare 1942, Tables 12, 14, 18 & 20

55 Poul Bech, *Søkrig i danske farvande under Anden Verdenskrig 1939–1942* (Schønberg: 2008), pp.81–82

56 'Monthly overview of mine swept and detonated British bottom mines, Jan-Jun 1942.' Danish Naval Armoury, Holmen. A total of 99 Danish, 42 German and 14 ships from other countries were hit by mines in Danish waters in 1942.

Chapter 9

9.1 The Mine War – the Technological Race

As clearly demonstrated in May 1942, the German minesweeper organisation in Denmark had gradually developed some effective sweeping methods, aided by *Orlogskaptajn* Bahnsen and the Danish Navy. Therefore, the British Admiralty developed new types of bottom mines during 1942: an improved magnetic mine, a new acoustic mine and combination mines. The first magnetic mines had a built-in delay mechanism so that the mine did not detonate at the first noticeable change in the magnetic field, risking premature detonation. Only when the impact was 50 milligauss (mg) or more would the mine detonate. This uncertainty was avoided in 1942 by utilising the fact that a ship's magnetic field when passing a mine affected the mine's magnetic field from negative to positive and then back to negative. A newly developed circuit relay required first an influence in one direction and then an influence in the other direction before the current from the battery was sent to the detonator. In addition, the mine was now independent of the strength of the field. This also affected ships with demagnetisation systems that had reduced the ship's magnetic field to below 50mg. This meant optimal use of the mine, and at the same time it was harder to sweep or defuse.[1]

In England, various intelligence sources, including the Danish (illegal) intelligence service in Sweden and agents in Denmark from the British Special Operations Executive (SOE) and Secret Intelligence Service (SIS – now MI6), revealed that minesweeping in Danish waters in particular became more effective during 1942. The explanation, Bahnsen's efforts and the new technical inventions. was not realised until two Danish naval officers managed to make the trip in a fishing boat from the west coast of Jutland to the United Kingdom in January 1943. The British Admiralty took up the issue of Danish minesweeping, investigating the possibilities of sabotaging the effective floating magnets. They did not want to attack the minesweepers, but to destroy the floating magnets in the harbours and at Elsinore Shipyard.

In the British archives, the case can be followed from department to department, but in the end, the Admiralty closed the case with the remark that, '... the Danes are merely doing their own house-cleaning'.[2] It seems that a message from *Orlogskaptajn* Bahnsen to London, via SOE's leader in Denmark, Major Flemming B. Muus, contributed to this decision. In it, Bahnsen gave an account of the naval arrangement between the Danish and German naval authorities in 1940. To reiterate, the *Kriegsmarine* was responsible for the north-south

1 J. S. Cowie, *Mines, Minelayers and Minelaying* (Oxford: OUP, 1949), p.153.
2 Palle Roslyng-Jensen, Palle, *Værnenes politik – politikernes værn* (Gyldendal: 1980), p.39.

routes, while the Danish Navy took care of the east–west routes, which were typically the domestic ferry routes. As mentioned earlier, the Danish naval leadership gradually took on a certain amount of sweeping in the north-south waters, for the sake of ferry traffic and domestic Danish shipping. They were also interested in building up a well-functioning minesweeper service, which would certainly be needed when the war eventually ended.[3]

Until the navy's new minesweeping system became widespread, and later as a supplement to the new floating magnets, the *Kriegsmarine* deployed the reasonably effective *sperrbrechere*,[4] which would deliberately detonate the mines. These ships, as mentioned above, were equipped with a very powerful magnetic and noise field created by a large electromagnet and a type of noise transmitter, a motorised hammer, under the ship. The mines would therefore detonate in front of the ship – if everything went according to plan. As the RAF's mine tonnage consisted mainly of bottom mines, the Air Ministry decided to launch an offensive targeted at the German *Sperrbrechere*. Bomber Command's minelayers therefore carried a few mines in their load that were specially designed for this type of minesweeper. Some of these mines were detonated only by the very strong magnetic effects that the *sperrbrechere* were surrounded by. The plan succeeded. Within a few months, the *Kriegsmarine* lost so many *sperrbrechere* in the English Channel that they were eventually withdrawn from the area and not used there for the rest of the war.[5]

9.2 Mausi

In early 1940, when German minesweepers had succeeded in having an undamaged British bottom mine brought to Kiel for closer examination by the *Sperr-versuchskommando der Kriegsmarine*, they sent for Theodor Benecke, who was responsible for *Abwurfwaffen See*.

The investigation showed that the British mine was equipped with an induction ignition, which Benecke happened to know about through his PhD work on solenoids and homogeneous vertical magnetic fields. On this basis, he prepared a report recommending the sweeping of the British magnetic mines using an artificial magnetic field created by an aeroplane. On 3 May 1940, *Generaloberst* Udet, the head of the Ministry of Aviation, made two Ju 52s available for experiments with minesweeping aircraft. Together with physics professor Gerlach from the Technische Universität München, Benecke developed a ring coil with a diameter of 15 metres by August, which could be hung under an aircraft and created a strong magnetic field via the current from a searchlight generator on board.

The test of a converted Ju 52 took place on 7 September 1940 from Dessau airfield, where, using a trigger from an original British mine, it was found that up to an altitude of 70 metres the aircraft's magnetic coil could trigger the ignition.[6]

3 Jørgen Møller, 'Mytteriet på Søridderen' in *Marinehistorisk Tidsskrift*, 1989, no. 1, pp.3–5; Palle Roslyng-Jensen, *Værnenes politik – politikernes værn* (Gyldendal: 1980), p.40.

4 *Sperrbrecher* literally translates into English as 'mine destruction ship', but as this is a little clunky, I have continued to use the German term.

5 Friedrich Ruge, *Im Küstenvorfeld* (Munich: 1974), p.120.

6 Friedrich Ruge, *Im Küstenvorfeld* (Munich: 1974), p.61; Menensuchgruppe Mausi, <http://de.academic.ru/dic.nsf/dewiki/960979#Hintergrund>.

Ju 52 MS 'Mausi'.

In the following days, the minesweeping tactics were developed. A Ju 52 MS (MS = magnetic coil) was to fly at a speed of 120km/h at a height of 30 metres above the water surface in the area where mines were to be swept. From studies of British mines, it was known that there was a 6-second delay after the first magnetic impulse was registered so that the mine would not detonate too far ahead of a ship target. The explosion created a pressure wave in the form of a gas bubble that raised a column of water 100–110 metres high. The tail gunner, who sat in a semi-open and rear-facing position on the aircraft, was tasked with photographing the water column to record the mine sweep.

To avoid collision with the water surface, the aircraft was equipped with a towing cable on the underside. At a height of less than 10 metres, the cable touched the water surface, which could then be registered on the pilot's instrument panel. The ideal tow height was thus between 10 and 30 metres.

On 19 September 1940, *9 Fliegerivision* with a Ju 52 MS succeeded in detonating two British mines. By 21 November 1940, *Sonderkommando Mausi* already had six Ju 52 MS. At the end of 1941, the *Luftwaffe* sweeping force was renamed *Minesuchgruppe 1*, which during the war had almost 150 Ju 52 MS, divided into different areas of operation. The distribution in 1942 was:

1. Squadron: Denmark and Oslo harbour area
2. Squadron: German Bight and English Channel coast
3. Squadron: France – the Atlantic coast from Brest to Biarritz
4. Squadron: Italy – Adriatic Sea, Mediterranean Sea, North Africa
5. Squadron: Romania, Crimea, Danube Delta
6. Squadron: The entire Baltic Sea coast from the Kaiser Wilhelm Canal to the Eastern Baltic Sea[7]

To counter the German Mausi aircraft, the British Admiralty developed a type of mine that responded to the slightest magnetic influence, from the normal 60 micro-amps to 15, 5

7 Heinz Nowarra: *Minensuchgruppe Mausi. Mit der Tante Ju im Kampfeinsatz* (Illertissen: Flugzeug Publikations GmbH, 1995), p.90.

and in special cases as low as 3 microamps. In relatively shallow water, they were detonated just before the Mausi aircraft passed, and the 50–80 metre water column caused by the explosion was planned to hit the aircraft![8]

Photo taken from the rear gunner's seat on a Ju 52 MS 'Mausi'. Behind the rudder, the water column from the mine detonation can be seen rising 70–100 metres in the air.

9.3 Technological Chess – Moves and Countermoves

The RAF also began to combine the magnetic ignition rates of the different types of mines with clocks and countdown timers. For example, the mines could be set to activate after 36 hours or up to 45 days. In addition, for each passage from 1–14, a countdown timer could ensure that the mine did not detonate until, for example, the 8th ship passed over. This proposal made it almost impossible for the Germans to clear Danish waters to the same extent as previous.

While the *Kriegsmarine* adjusted the setting of their mines according to how much traffic and what size of ship was expected in the minefield, the British Admiralty often made up their mine types by drawing lots from a hat! By leaving it to chance, it was impossible for the German minesweepers to work out which types of mines to expect. By simultaneously shifting minelaying efforts from area to area, and each time with little unpleasant surprises, Bomber Command stressed the German minesweeping organisation in a way that could not have been done if all target areas were mined continuously. At the same time, the sensitivity of the mines used was set to either high, medium or low. The setting of each mine was also, from time to time, decided by literally drawing lots from a hat, which created an element of randomness in the composition of settings that was impossible to predict and thus impossible to counteract by the Germans.[9]

In August 1942, the British Admiralty had a newly developed type of mine ready: the acoustic mine. The *Kriegsmarine* had been using this type of mine since 1940, usually in a combined magnetic and acoustic ignition mechanism. The British naval command discussed whether it would be too easy for the German minesweepers to neutralise a purely

8 J. S. Cowie, *Mines, Minelayers and Minelaying* (Oxford: OUP, 1949), p.153.
9 Air 14/2064, sheet 61A 'Magnetic mining offensive against U-boats'.

acoustic mine. The Admiralty's mine laying staff insisted that the element of surprise had to be fully utilised, and so for two consecutive nights, a total of 500 acoustic mines were dropped, spread over as many target areas as possible.

As expected, success was short-lived, with shipping traffic in the selected areas suffering heavy losses. By the time the German minesweeper organisation realised the connection and began to use automatic hammers on ship hulls, noise machines in tow and small depth charges, the British Admiralty had meanwhile started developing and manufacturing combined magnetic-acoustic mines. They were equipped with an additional detail: the magnetic measuring system had a triggering device that, upon the first magnetic impact, started a clockwork mechanism and simultaneously set the detonator in the safe position. If, within a period of 6 to 16 seconds, there was another magnetic impact, the mine detonated. If not, the detonator went back to the safe position and the clock stopped. This trigger made it almost impossible for surface vessels to sweep the mine, and completely impossible for Mausi aircraft. In combination with the acoustic mechanism, the new mines were thus highly effective.[10]

From early 1943 until the end of the war, the technological battle between minelayers and minesweepers escalated. The British Admiralty had recognised that something had to be done to develop and produce new types of mines at a faster pace. Intelligence on German minesweeping techniques and equipment had to be utilised immediately to develop countermeasures. The normal process of designing and mass-producing new types of mines, even with much of the industry converted to weapons production, was far too slow. By the time the new mines could be used in practice, the enemy's anti-mine techniques and equipment might already have been modified or improved. Therefore, a special organisation called MX was set up in January to 'customise' special types of mines quickly and in small quantities. The organisation was based in Portsmouth, where a team of naval officers and designers produced drawings and descriptions of each mine's ignition mechanism, which were then manufactured locally and installed in standard mines. MX could produce an average of 50 specialised mines per week, which were distributed to the respective airfields that would lay the mines in the selected target areas. Each of these mines had a short-term effect on German mine sweeps, and individual types that proved particularly effective were then incorporated into the design of the large production runs of standard mines.

The aforementioned triggering mechanism in the first British magnetic-acoustic mine was the result of intelligence on German minesweeper methods. From reconnaissance photos, it could be seen that U-boats and other important naval vessels always had a minesweeper sailing ahead of them at a certain distance. With intelligence on the speed of the vessels over the seabed, the interval between the first magnetic impact and the next could be set to an appropriate number of seconds, corresponding to the normal distance between a ship and its escort. The German minesweeper organisation's counter-move was then to put two minesweepers in front of the ships they were escorting. The MX detachment responded with a trigger that allowed two ships to pass before the mine was triggered by the third. The German countermeasure was to put three minesweepers in front, and the British Admiralty

10 J. S. Cowie, *Mines, Minelayers and Minelaying* (Oxford: OUP, 1949), p.154.

Three Ju 52 MS 'Mausi' in minesweeper formation.

began to visualise the dream scenario: the last German U-boat was escorted by the entire mine sweeper force.[11]

When the first British acoustic mines appeared at the end of 1942, the *Luftwaffe*'s *Minensuchgruppe 1* equipped a Ju 52 with a *Knallkörper-gerät*. This was a box containing 30 small explosive charges that were dropped into mined areas every few seconds. The normal procedure was for three Ju 52 MS to fly in close formation and sweep the magnetic mines, while the Ju 52 KK flew some distance behind them and swept the acoustic mines. The normal flying speed was approximately 175km/h.[12]

In both Germany and Britain, naval commanders had developed a third type of mine – the pressure mine – which was triggered by the pressure of the water displaced by a ship while travelling. The British Admiralty had already developed a pressure mine before the outbreak of war in 1939, while the German pressure mine was only developed in 1943. However, neither side dared to use this type of mine for fear that the enemy had developed a way to counter it.

Because they did not have many themselves, Hitler had forbidden the use of the 400 mines they had ready until a very special opportunity presented itself. It did not come until the Allied landings in Normandy on 6 June 1944. Throughout the spring of 1944, the Germans had laid contact, magnetic and acoustic mines along the French coast. The Allied invasion was expected in May and the mines were therefore set to become ineffective after 1 June. Six days before the invasion, thousands of German mines were rendered ineffective. German E-boats hastily laid fresh minefields in the following days, but on a much smaller scale. On 7 June, Hitler ordered the new pressure mines to be laid and on 15 June, the first were laid by the *Luftwaffe* in an attempt to stop the steady flow of troops and supplies from the United Kingdom to the landing zone.[13]

---

11 J. S. Cowie, *Mines, Minelayers and Minelaying* (Oxford: OUP, 1949), pp.155–156.

12 Carsten Petersen, *Luftkrig over Danmark*, vol. IV (Ringkøbing: 1989), p.45.

13 J. S. Cowie, *Mines, Minelayers and Minelaying* (Oxford: OUP, 1949), pp.158–159. A list from the *Minestrygertjeneste* in 1948 shows that at that time there were 2,301 magnetic mines, 107 magnetic-

The day before, allied interception of German military communications had intercepted a message sent using 'Enigma', that an unidentified type of mine would be laid the following day in the landing area. Five days later, the British Navy managed to get hold of two of the new pressure mines, which had been dropped on dry land on a stretch of beach under British control. They codenamed the new mine 'Oyster'.

Over the next 24 hours, the mines were brought in for examination by the mine engineers, and by 22 June, they had unravelled its secrets and found several ways to protect themselves from it. By reducing speed over the minefield, a ship could significantly reduce the water pressure. In water depths of between 20 and 30 metres, the maximum speed for ships over 15,000 gross tons was 6 knots, for destroyers 12 knots, while there were no restrictions for smaller vessels.[14] They had also experimented with groups of ships at high speed and with large decommissioned ships that could be sent into an expected minefield. At the same time, the violent storms on the Channel coast in June affected the waters to such an extent that the mines did not work. Their effectiveness was therefore somewhat reduced, but the Allies still suffered significant losses due to the new type of mine.[15]

9.4 English Bottom Mine Types[16]

There were many subtleties in the development of new types of mines, and it would be pointless to go into all the technical inventions that were built into sea mines during World War II. The Germans found that the British had at least 68 different types in use during the six years of the war.[17] This is a brief overview of the 9 basic British Mk.I-IX types and their possible combinations.

Length in mm.	Diameter in mm.	explosives in pounds	weight in pounds
A Mk. I-IV 2.920	450	750	1.500

Mk I – Mk IV actually denoted 4 types that only differed from each other in detail, see below. They consisted of a explosive compartment and a mechanism compartment which were bolted together. The explosive compartment was bevelled at the lower end and was equipped with an eye bolt where a wooden filler piece could be clamped. This served to stabilise the mine during its flight through the air and was released on impact with the

acoustic mines and 30 special mines active in Danish waters! (Material from Poul Adam Mørch via Birger Hansen.) As head of the naval staff's intelligence section from 1935, Mørch communicated naval intelligence to the United Kingdom via Stockholm during the Danish occupation. From November 1943, together with Einar M. Nordentoft, he headed the Danish Intelligence Service's office in Stockholm and acted as a link to Allied agencies. After the war, Mørch continued to work in the Danish Defence Intelligence Service until his retirement as a *Kommandør* in 1960.

14 Howard S. Levie, *Mine Warfare at Sea* (Leiden: Brill, 1992), pp.81–82 & pp.109–110.

15 Brian Johnson, *The Secret War* (Barnsley: Pen & Sword, 2004), p.252.

16 Transcript after description in letter folders ii-e p.17–19 incl., *Søværnets Våbenskole* 'Aircraft-launched Mines.' www.navweaps.com/Weapons/WAMBR_Mines.htm

17 J. S. Cowie, *Mines, Minelayers and Minelaying* (Oxford: OUP, 1949), p.159.

A Mk I Mine being prepared for loading into a Hampden.

water surface. Within the bevelled end was a void extending to a vaulted bottom; this space was filled with water after the throw to ensure the mine sank properly.

In the explosive compartment was the explosive charge, which could consist of trotyl (TNT), Amatol (trotyl and ammonium nitrate in a 50/50 ratio to save on trotyl) or Minol, which was Amatol with 20 percent aluminium added to increase the blasting power.

The mechanism compartment was enclosed at one end by a slightly recessed vaulted end floor, which provided space for the packed main and auxiliary parachute. The mine could be equipped with the following ignition systems:

1. Relay that delayed the ignition of the cartridge for 7 seconds.
2. 45-day clockwork.
3. Passage counter up to 14 passages, with approximately 4 minutes between each.
4. Immobiliser that short-circuited the battery after a certain period of time.
5. Timed contact mechanism that made minesweeping difficult.

Some mine types had an impact switch, namely the B234 and D416, and were used when mines were dropped in shipping lanes near land. If the mine fell on land or shallow water, the impact switch caused the mine to detonate after 6 seconds. If the mine was dropped at a depth of more than 3 metres, it would sink to this depth before the 6 seconds had elapsed, causing the impact switch to be disconnected and the water pressure switch to work. If the mine was lifted up again, the water pressure switch would be switched off and the impact switch would work again, detonating the mine after 6 seconds.

Mines with the F602 and F608 ignition system were fitted with a larger charge than usual. The nose was therefore dome-shaped.

As Hampdens were replaced by Wellingtons, Whitleys, Manchesters, Stirlings and Lancasters, from 1 to 6 mines could be carried per aircraft. The mines were initially dropped from a low altitude, about 300 to 500 feet, but from early 1944 high level minelaying started at 12,000ft (3,658m) but before long the cleared height was up to 15,000ft (4,572m) which became the standard height, with a maximum drop speed of about 250 feet per second.[18] The parachute had a diameter of approximately 6 feet and had no significant load-bearing capacity, but served mainly to stabilise the mine during its speed through the air. The parachute was released when the mine hit the surface of the water. As the mine's weight and density caused it to drift downwards, it went to the bottom where the slope at one end ensured that it remained in a horizontal position on the seabed. Once the fuse in the water pressure switch was dissolved, the piston would be moved in by the water pressure, thereby arming the mine. This required a minimum water pressure corresponding to a water depth of two metres.

The mines were painted black or dark green and the ignition system was labelled with a letter and a number. The letter meaning:

- A: Simple magnetic influence.
- B: Double magnetic impact. Two impacts of opposite polarity. The type B234 was also equipped with an impact switch.
- C: Double magnetic impact. Two influences of the same or opposite polarity with a specific time interval.
- D: Acoustic impact. The D416 type also had an impact switch.
- E: Detonation after expiration of clockwork set time. Type E502 was equipped with a hydrostatic switch that started a clockwork and detonated the mine after the set time had expired.
- F: Types numbered up to and including F 614 were used as a bomb, for example F612 was used as a timed underwater bomb. Types numbered F616 and above were specialised mines.
- G: Combined magnetic and acoustic impact.
- H: Specialised mines.
- I: Specialised mines.
- K: Acoustic impact.

Ignition systems:

1. Magnetic ignition system [A Mk. III and IV, ASY, A100 and A101].
2. Magnetic-Acoustic Ignition System [A Mk. III and IV, ASY, G708 and G709].

18 Aviation History Research Centre, <https://www.facebook.com/Navman239>.

3. Acoustic-Acoustic [ASY and K1002]. Ignition occurred 5–10 or 14–19 seconds after the first component's impact (at approx 200 Hz) when there was simultaneous noise with very low frequencies, deep tone approx 20 Hz. The specified time intervals in which ignition could occur differed from mine to mine and could be changed within 26 seconds by replacing a cam disc. The purpose of this change was to make it more difficult to strike the mine with noise equipment.
4. Water pressure switch was used in A Mk III and Mk IV as well as Mk VIII and Mk IX.

The above-mentioned ignition systems worked when the following units were activated:

a: Induction coil.
b: Shake contact.
c: Moving coil relay.
d: Double contact relay.
e: Vibrators for normal and deep tone.
f: Reinforcement delay movement = 45-day clockwork which was started by water pressure switch.
g: Ignition delay mechanism, used in mines with ignition system 'A', 5–7 second delay.
h: Crossing switch, setting from 1–14 crossings.
i: Time condition switch, conditioned a specific time interval for the impacts that would cause the mine to detonate.
j: Immobilisation devices: a) Resistive discharge device; b) Electrolytic device or 45-day clockwork or 26-week clockwork.

Examples of later mines:

Length in mm. (parachute = + 300)		**Diameter**	**Explosives in kilograms**	**Weight in total in kilograms**
A Mk. V	2.050 – aug. 1940	400	318	490
A Mk. VI	2.600 – 1944	450	454 a / 499 b	907-952
A Mk. VII	2.000 – 1944	400	252 a / 277 b	499-424
A Mk. VIII	1.400 – 1944 rivermine	330	82 a / 91 b	227-236
A Mk. IX	2.840 – 1944	470	474 minol	837

* Explosives: a = Amatol og b = Minol

Sea mines wait to be loaded aboard a Halifax V Series IA of 77 Squadron, probably at Full Sutton in Yorkshire, shortly after the airfield was opened in May 1944.

Chapter 10

10.1 Mine Laying 1943 - 1944

During the winter months, the weather was often so bad that many bombing missions had to be cancelled. Even the minelayers, who were often on missions when the bombers could not fly, were all too often prevented by rain and fog over England. If fog was expected over the airfields on their return, the mission was also often cancelled. The plan was to try to overcome this problem by having the mine planes take off late in the day so that they would be over the target area shortly before nightfall. This way, the planes would return in the middle of the night before the morning fog rolled in over the country.[1]

On the day, 6 January 1943, that this directive was issued in England, the senior command of the *Kriesmarine* gathered for a meeting with Hitler. The commander of the fleet, *Grossadmiral* Raeder, had to answer to the Fuhrer. Hitler believed that the large warships were doing too little and that they had obviously outplayed their role. They would either be scrapped or used as barracks ships if Raeder could not show significant results within the next six months.[2] Faced with this ultimatum, Raeder immediately decided to send a large naval force to Norway to attack the Allied convoys in the Atlantic. The force would consist of the battleship Scharnhorst, the cruiser *Prinz Eugen*, and three destroyers: *Friedrich Ihn*, *Paul Jacobi* and *Z 24*.[3] The ships were based in Gotenhafen (Gdynia) and had to pass either the Øresund or the Great Belt to reach further north to Norway. The Admiralty in London was quickly informed of the German plans. Once again, the minelayers would try to stop a large German naval force in Danish waters. Eight Lancasters from 44 Squadron 5 Group and six Lancasters from 9 Squadron 3 Group were ordered to lay mines in 'Daffodil' near Copenhagen and 'Quince' in the Langeland Belt.[4]

From German reports, we know that another dozen aircraft participated in the mine laying on 8–9 January. For various reasons, two aircraft from each of these squadrons did not take part, thus, only ten aircraft took off on the afternoon of 8 January. Of the four aircraft that were to lay mines in the Langeland Belt, two of the pilots had great difficulty locating the target area. They therefore brought the mines back home. The others dropped the mines according to plan. The six aircraft from 44 Squadron had the same problem

1 Air 14/2064. Bomber Command 'Gardening'. HQ BC to 1, 3-6 Gr. 6/1–43.
2 P. K. Kemp, *Victory at Sea, 1939–1945* (London: White Lion, 1958), p.100.
3 Hans H. Hildebrand, *Die deutschen Kriegsschiffe. Biographien – ein Spiegel der Marinegeschichte von 1815 bis zur Gegenwart*, (Herford: Koehlers, 1982), vol. 5, p.100.
4 Air 28/880. Waddington ORB, 8–9.1.1943.

due to the dense cloud cover over the waters. Three of the pilots chose to turn back, and only one aircraft reached 'Daffodil', where the mines were dropped. The aircraft had to withdraw quickly due to the very powerful flak from batteries in the Copenhagen area. During the flight, the aircraft travelled so far south that a light flak position at Stenodde on Tåsinge caused a few direct hits on the rear gunner's turret. However, none of the Lancaster's crew members were hit. The aircraft suffered a few scratches, but was able to continue the journey home.

The last two aircraft were not so lucky. One was shot down by a German night fighter close to Søst Skov, 4km west of Åbenrå.[5] The other must have crashed into the sea, because no other aircraft crashed in Denmark that night apart from the one mentioned. Perhaps it was a night fighter over Rømø that hit it. A German report states that a Stirling, which was fired upon by a German fighter, crashed about 20 kilometres west of Rømø. Although the tails of the two aircraft types were very different, both were four-engine aircraft. It can also be seen that not all the German air reporting posts had studied the remote signalling book carefully. Time and time again, there are completely incorrect type designations in the German reports. So it is likely that it was the Lancaster that met its fate over Rømø after all.[6]

On the morning of 9 January, the German naval force left Gotenhafen. During the day, it reached the Great Belt, which it passed without incident. However, in the northern part of the Kattegat, the German ships were observed by British aircraft. Fearing a major air attack before the ships could reach a safe harbour, *Admiral* Schniewind on *Scharnhorst* decided to turn back.[7] The *Luftwaffe* had provided fighter protection during the evening. For the same reason, a no-fire order had been issued to all German flak units in North Jutland, as a large number of fighters would be operating in the area around Frederikshavn and Skagen. Only if the flak positions were 100 percent certain that it was an enemy aircraft could they open fire in exceptional circumstances.[8] This order proved to be of great benefit to the British.

At night, a large minelaying force was dispatched to Danish waters. A total of 121 planes participated, 97 of which laid their mines.[9] A single aircraft was shot down at Brøndum, near Esbjerg Airfield. It was a Halifax from 158 Squadron, which was the only victim over Denmark that night. Unfortunately, three more aircraft of the same type did not return.[10]

However, the German ships made it back safely to Gotenhafen again. In the following days, Bomber Command laid several mines in Danish waters. The Admiralty was pretty sure that Schniewind had received strict orders from Raeder that, on the one hand, the ships must not be put out of action on their way to Norway, while on the other hand it

5 Air 27/450. 44 Squadron. ORB, 8.1.1943; Anders Bjørnvad, *Faldne allierede flyvere 1939–1945* (Odense: 1978), p.161; Adm. Danish, 8.1.1943; Frank Weber, 'En sønderjysk hilsen til engelske flyvere' *Jydske Tidende* 30.8.1985.

6 Adm. Danish, 8.1.1943.

7 Hans H. Hildebrand, *Die deutschen Kriegsschiffe. Biographien – ein Spiegel der Marinegeschichte von 1815 bis zur Gegenwart* (Herford: Koehlers, 1982), vol.5, pp.69 and 100.

8 Adm. Danish 9.1.1943.

9 SCL, 9-10.1.1943; Martin Middlebrook & Chris Everitt, *The Bomber Command War Diaries: An Operational Reference Book 1939–1945* (Bungay: Viking, 1985), p.342

10 Anders Bjørnvad, *Faldne allierede flyvere 1939–1945* (Odense: 1978), p.84.

was important to demonstrate the ships' effectiveness. Another breakout attempt could therefore be expected in the near future. Meanwhile, shipping in Denmark was almost paralysed for a week. A dozen ships sank after mine explosions, causing many captains to wait and see.[11]

On 25 January, the expected breakout came. This time, two more destroyers joined the naval force.[12] The action repeated itself. The German ships passed the Great Belt unhindered and had reached the Skagerrak when they were again observed by British aircraft. The force turned 180 degrees and sailed the same way back to Gotenhafen, from where it had come. It reached port on the morning of 27 January. *Grossadmiral* Raeder now realised that he would not be able to argue for the continued maintenance of the large warships' efforts. If he couldn't even get such a large naval force moved from the Baltic to the Skagerrak, let alone to Norway, what would happen if the ships were to be sent into battle in earnest? He therefore decided to resign as Commander-in-Chief of the German Navy. Four days later, his place was taken by *Grossadmiral* Dönitz. By order of Hitler, the *Prinz Eugen* was then converted into a training ship for sea cadets. In March, *Scharnhorst* finally managed to get safely to Trondhjem.[13]

So it was not the mines that ultimately took *Prinz Eugen* out of active combat, but some British reconnaissance planes over the Skagerrak that very luckily happened to be there at the right time. Or was it luck? There are indications that Danish intelligence had a hand in it. On 2 February, this message was sent from London to Ebbe Munck in Stockholm:

> Our naval expert also sends you the following message: We are most grateful for the report of *Scharnhorst* passing through Great Belt and returning again. She went well into the Skagerrak, but turned around before our aircraft were able to attack.[14]

On the night of 28 April 1943, Bomber Command laid the new acoustic mines together with magnetic mines for the first time. A total of 459 mines were distributed from the Bay of Biscay to the North German coasts. The following night, another 586 mines were laid, mainly in Danish waters. On 2 May, the troop transport ship *Gneisenau*, carrying troops from Germany to the Russian front, was hit by a British mine. After the mine explosion, the wreck protruded so far out of the water that the Germans used it as an air observation

---

11 *Flyvehistorisk Tidsskrift*, 1965, no. 4, p.2.

12 Hans H. Hildebrand, *Die deutschen Kriegsschiffe. Biographien – ein Spiegel der Marinegeschichte von 1815 bis zur Gegenwart* (Herford: Koehlers, 1982), vol. 5, p.69.

13 Hans H. Hildebrand, *Die deutschen Kriegsschiffe. Biographien – ein Spiegel der Marinegeschichte von 1815 bis zur Gegenwart*, vols 1–7 (Herford: Koehlers, 1982), vol.5, pp.69 and 100; Walther Hubatsch, *Kriegswende 1943* (Darmstadt: 1966), pp.106–107. Erich Raeder became *Grossadmiral* and Commander-in-Chief of the *Kriegsmarine* in 1939. He had led the naval build-up from 1935–1943 and was the originator of Operation Weserübung, the invasion of Denmark and Norway in April 1940. Raeder was in favour of a navy with large battleships. Hitler did not agree as he feared that the loss of battleships would damage the morale of the population. On the other hand, Hitler was fascinated by Dönitz's U-boat tactics. It was cheaper and losses were easier to hide from the population. Nevertheless, Raeder was given a chance to prove his battleships' worth, but as it turns out, he failed to fulfil expectations. This led Hitler to focus on U-boats, and he replaced Raeder with Dönitz as Commander-in-Chief of the *Kriegsmarine* on 31 January 1943.

14 Ebbe Muncks supplement sheet, pk. 2–3.

post until the end of the war.[15] In the days that followed, a number of merchant ships, minesweepers and auxiliary vessels were sunk, including 3 in Danish waters.

10.2 Operation 'Distil'

The era of the large German warships was coming to an end. But the traffic of troop and supply ships between Germany and Norway continued unabated through Danish waters. The RAF had realised that there was little point in laying a lot of mines in enemy waters if the enemy's minesweepers could quickly and effectively neutralise them. An offensive against the German minesweepers had therefore been launched during 1943.

As already noted, the German Mausi aircraft were sometimes effective at sweeping magnetic and acoustic mines. A Mausi formation often consisted of four aircraft; one aircraft had a wire hanging down into the water, at the end of which was a device that made loud bangs underwater. This was to activate acoustic mines. The other three aircraft were equipped with their large, round electromagnet under the fuselage. These aircraft had to fly at very low level. Otherwise, the magnetic field would not be able to activate the magnetic mines. For all four aircraft, it was crucial to fly at the lowest possible speed.

As mentioned above, Bomber Command also dropped mines specifically targeting the Mausi aircraft. The mines were equipped with an extremely high sensitivity, so they detonated at the slightest sound or change in the magnetic field. They therefore detonated early enough for the water column created by the explosion to hit the Mausi aircraft. However, there are no reports of this happening in Danish waters.[16]

The RAF now launched special fighter raids against the Mausi aircraft. The slow German Ju 52s were easy targets for the British fighters of Fighter Command. This operation against the Mausis was codenamed 'Operation Distil'. On 16 September 1943, not a single Mausi aircraft had yet been shot down, as was stated in a memorandum to 16 Group, Coastal Command. In this memorandum, Fighter Command proposed cooperation in the fight against the German minesweepers.[17] Beaufighters from Coastal Command would attack the German *Sperrbrechere* and the other minesweepers, while Fighter Command would take care of the Mausis. The proposal was adopted and the hunt for the minesweepers began in earnest. On 4 October 1943, eight P–51 Mustangs from 309 (Polish) Squadron took off to perform a 'Distil' off the Danish coast. [18]

15 Stephen W. Roskill, *The War at Sea 1939–45*, vol. 2 (London: HMSO, 1956), p.393; <http://www.vragguiden.dk/wreck.asp?wreckid=380>. The wreck of the *Gneisenau* was blown up several times, most recently in the late 1950s. The remains can still be seen on the bottom in the waters between the German coast and Falster.

16 Friedrich Ruge, *Im Küstenvorfeld* (Munich: 1974), p.68.

17 Air 15/541. HQ 12 Group, Fighter Command to HQ 16 Group, Coastal Command, 16.9.1943. 'Operation Distil'.

18 M. J. F. Bowyer, *Action Stations: Wartime Military Airfields of East Anglia* (Cambridge: Paytrick Stephens Ltd, 1979), p.183.

RAF 309 Polish Squadron Mustangs.

It does not appear that they were successful, but it was the first example of British fighters specifically trying to hit Mausi aircraft over Danish territory. Later in the war, however, British fighters were able to successfully attack several German minesweepers in Denmark.[19]

The Danish minesweepers and their support vessels were busy in the spring of 1943. They continued to sweep mines to keep the Danish ferry routes clear, but they also searched the waters travelled by domestic shipping. These included the Småland Sea, the Isefjord, Svendborg Sound and the entrances to Nakskov and Odense. On board the Danish vessels, there was growing dissatisfaction with minesweeping, which was perceived as being of greatest benefit to the occupying power – Germany.

As mentioned, Raeder was replaced by Dönitz as Supreme Commander of the German Navy on 31 January 1943. This also had consequences in Denmark and did not improve relations between the German and Danish navies.

Since the occupation in April 1940, the *Kriegsmarine* in Denmark had been led by *Admiral* Raul Mewis with the title *Marinebefehlshaber Dänemark*. But when Dönitz became the commander of the *Kriegsmarine* in January 1943, Mewis was replaced by *Vizeadmiral* Hans-Heinrich Wurmbach, who came from a position as senior *Admiral* of the Navy in the Black Sea and had previously been Chief of Staff of Naval Station Ostsee. Wurmbach had experience of operational service in wartime: during the First World War as a submarine commander and from 1938 until the outbreak of war as commander of the pocket battleship *Admiral Scheer*. Therefore, it was a highly experienced and battle-hardened Vice Admiral who entered his new headquarters at Hotel *Phønix* in Copenhagen on 19 March, even with a new title as *Admiral Dänemark*.

By this time, relations between the Danish Navy and the *Kriegsmarine* had become more tense. Mewis had planned a farewell visit to Crown Prince Frederik to emphasise the high level of cooperation with the Danish Navy, but Hitler cancelled this on the recommendation of the Danish Army Chief of Staff, von Hanneken. *Admiral* Wurmbach was not prepared to

19 For example, Kipp and Caine's raid of 14 April 1944 where they intercepted a Mausi aircraft. Carsten Petersen, *Luftkrig over Danmark* (Ringkøbing: 1989), vol. IV. pp.44–46.

The shooting down of a Junkers Ju 52/3mg6e minesweeping aircraft of the *Minensuchgruppe*, 1944.

cooperate with the Danish naval command in the same way as his predecessor, but on the contrary, he worked from day one to expand his powers and to take control of the Danish Navy to minimise risk without weakening the help that the *Kriegsmarine* received from the Danes.[20]

10.3 29 August 1943

As early as 1942, the German Army command in Denmark began to expect a British invasion in Denmark, specifically in West Jutland. The Danish Army was therefore not allowed to be present in Jutland from October 1942 onwards, and no Danish warships, except those engaged in mine sweeping, were allowed to approach Jutland.

At the turn of the year, a clear tightening of the situation could be seen, partly due to the change in the German naval leadership in January 1943 and German Army Chief von Hanneken's increasingly harsh rhetoric towards the Danish military defences. Therefore, on 30 May 1943, the Danish naval command issued a secret order to all operational ship

20 Poul Bech, *Søkrig i danske farvande under Anden Verdenskrig 1939–1942* (Schønberg: 2008), pp.41–43.

commanders on how they should act in the event of a German takeover attempt. They were to try to escape with the ship to Sweden, and if that failed, the crew was to sink the ship. To this end, the Danish Navy's naval mining service discreetly produced a number of specially designed bombs, which were distributed to the ships during the summer.

Faced with a decision by Hitler, the German High Command in Berlin and Von Hanneken that peace and order in Denmark could only be created by quickly disarming the Danish Army and navy, an operation codenamed 'Operation Safari', the German *Admiral* Dänemark had a vague desire to wait and see. The usefulness of the Danish Fleet was greater than the problems it created for the Germans. But the total German military takeover was already planned. On 26 August, *Admiral* Dänemark had a plan ready for the takeover of the Danish Fleet.[21]

By a twist of fate, the Danish naval commander *Viceadmiral* Vedel managed to issue the order to sink the ships on the morning of 29 August at 04:07, in time for 27 of the 28 ships in Copenhagen's naval harbour of Holmen to be sunk by their crews within half an hour. Around the country's harbours, Danish warships were not so lucky. Despite bold and brave attempts to escape, several ships were taken over by the Germans. In a few cases, the crews managed to sink their ships, but a total of 13 warships were able to escape to Sweden.

With the action on 29 August 1943, the *Kriegsmarine* had lost a large part of its total minesweeper capacity. 65 Danish warships had until then guarded coastlines, searched 34 forced routes with a total length of 550 nautical miles, and defused more than 100 mines. The *Kriegsmarine* now had to handle this effort on its own.

At the same time, Sweden had put an end to German transit traffic through Swedish territorial waters, forcing German transports to navigate some of the riskiest waters in Europe. The *Kriegsmarine* in Denmark had only a dozen mine sweepers and 35 pseudo-minesweepers[22] at its disposal. This force was in no way equal to the task.

On 1 December 1943, *Admiral* Dänemark had a total manpower of 12,110 sailors, including 2,174 officers, 163 service men and 612 administrative staff. In the strategically most important harbours: Skagen, Frederikshavn, Hals, Aalborg, Fredericia, Esbjerg, Nyborg, Helsingør and Copenhagen, harbour protection flotillas were established from the start in 1940. They were responsible for protecting the harbours, entrances and the nearby sea area, and primarily consisted of up to 40 small vessels, mainly cutters, tugs and guard ships. The coasts were guarded by the Danish police and, on certain stretches of coastline on Zealand, by Danish naval vessels until August 1943. In addition to the harbour protection flotillas, so-called security flotillas were stationed in several major ports to monitor Danish waters. They were responsible for guarding minefields and net blockades, checking and minesweeping the shipping lanes – and not least protecting convoys to and from Norway. These flotillas were all under the command of the BSO. The security flotillas consisted of outpost boats, submarine chasers, barrage breakers and minesweepers, often with 12–15 boats in each flotilla.[23]

21 Poul Bech, *Søkrig i danske farvande under Anden Verdenskrig 1939–1942* (Schønberg: 2008), pp.87–89.

22 These were rebuilt and adapted fishing boats, and similar vessels.

23 Poul Bech, *Søkrig i danske farvande under Anden Verdenskrig 1939–1942* (Schønberg: 2008), p.42.

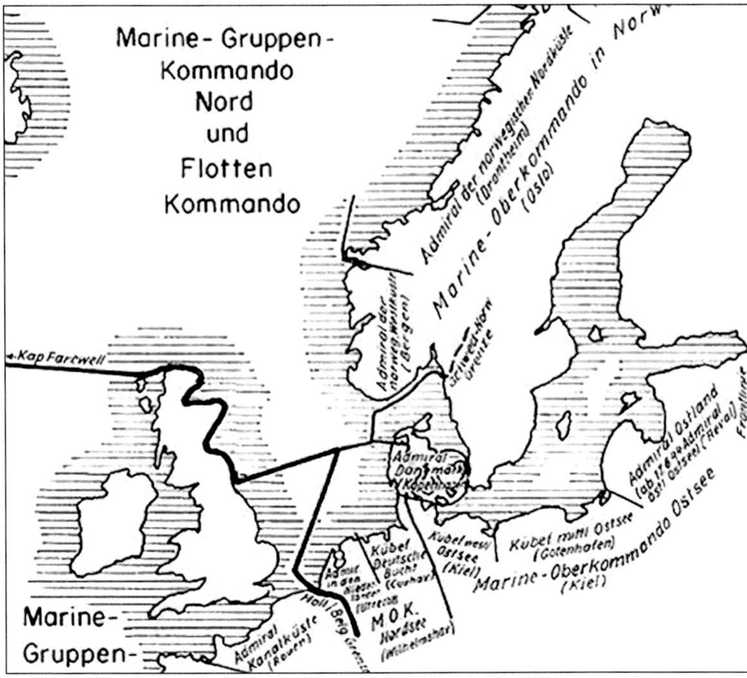

Command boundaries of the *Kriegsmarine* on 1 December 1943.

The complicated power structure in the navy, the cumbersome chain of command and the problems of utilising the still very limited resources for mine sweeping and convoy protection made it necessary to reorganise. In April 1944, *Admiral* Wurmbach, *Admiral Dänemark*, finally realised his wish to be granted greater powers. From 15 April, he was appointed *Admiral Skagerrak*, with command of all security ships in the inner Danish waters and most of the Skagerrak.[24]

All existing security flotillas and harbour protection flotillas were now reorganised into a number of new security flotillas in largely the same ports. 4. Security Flotilla in Fredericia, 5. in Korsør, 12. in Nyborg, 8. in Copenhagen, 9. in Aalborg, 10. in Aarhus, 15. in Esbjerg and 16. in Thyborøn. Three other flotillas that operated in minesweeping and patrolling kept their names, namely *MS-flotille Nr 29* and *Sperrbrecherflottille Nr 3*, both based in Aarhus, and *Vorposten-flotille Nr 16* in Frederikshavn. In addition, 5. Artillery Carrier Flotilla was located in Esbjerg with large ferry barges that were used to reinforce coastal defences as they were equipped with artillery and anti-aircraft guns.

In the final years of the war, more flotillas were sent to the west coast and northern Denmark as Germany was pushed back in both east and west. *Admiral Skagerrak*'s area of power included the Sound, the two belts, the Kattegat and Skagerrak, the west coast and not least the total coastal defence of Denmark. The BSO was withdrawn completely from Danish waters with a permanent base in Swinemünde.

24 Walther Lohmann and H. H. Hildebrand, *Die Deutsche Kriegsmarine 1939–1945*, vol. 1 (Bad Nauheim: 1956), Chapter 3, p.1.

Admiral Skagerrak was still under the command of *MOK Ostsee* in Kiel, but had complete freedom of action with regard to his own ships. The home base for *Admiral Skagerrak* was not particularly ideal, however. Copenhagen was actually at the far end of the operational area, but then, as now, it was difficult to see it from the centre. From 15 April 1944, the daily management of the new interceptor flotillas was assigned to a newly created *Sicherungs-Division Nr 8* with Max Klein as commander. At the end of May, the division moved permanently to a newly built bunker facility in Havreballe Forest near Marselisborg in Aarhus to be closer to the theatre of operations.

By the end of 1943, the German Army Commander in Denmark, von Hanneken, had moved from his headquarters at Nyboder Skole at Østerport Station in Copenhagen to Silkeborg Bad in Central Jutland. On 21 October, *Admiral Skagerrak* also moved to Aarhus. So in the last days of the war, Aarhus became a truly powerful naval base with two command staffs, *Sikringsflotille Nr 10*, *Sperrbrecherflottille Nr 3* and *MS-Flotille Nr 29*, and there was a lively traffic of troop transport ships between Aarhus and Norway. While *Admiral Skagerrak* now had full responsibility for clearing mines and securing convoys, the responsibility for troop transports lay with other organisations.

The decision to move troops by sea always came from the Army High Command in Berlin. The order was passed on to the Navy High Command, which also resided in Berlin. If the ships were to depart from Aarhus, the navy's service centre in Aarhus was tasked with selecting the supply ships to be used for the task. The next step was *MOK Ost* in Kiel, which had overall responsibility for all sea transport in the Kattegat and Skagerrak. From spring 1944, orders went out from here to the 8 Security Division under *Admiral Skagerrak* to provide the necessary number of security vessels. Finally, the harbour commander in Aarhus was ordered to take care of the practicalities of accommodation et cetera.[25]

10.4 Increased Flak and a New Method of Laying Mines

During 1943, German anti-aircraft ships were equipped with radar systems and better sighting equipment, which contributed to much better fire control than before. At the same time, light anti-aircraft batteries had already begun to be set up in 1941 at inland locations that the Germans knew from experience would be flown over by British minelaying aircraft on their way to the mined areas. At the last minute, the *Kriegsmarine* had also received a lot of additional flak material. A large consignment of 15mm and 20mm flak was to have been used to protect various airfields. However, the German armaments inspector had these weapons transferred to the flak and minesweeper ships, an action that should probably be seen in light of the inspector's past in the German Navy.[26]

As the tide of the war turned and the Germans were forced into the defensive, the performance of the flak defence and the German night fighters was further improved. The low-flying and slow-flying British minelaying aircraft, which had necessarily to descend to an altitude of 650 to 1,200 feet, were already easy targets for the German flak. During 1943,

25 Poul Bech, *Søkrig i danske farvande under Anden Verdenskrig 1939–1942* (Schønberg: 2008), pp.159–160; KTB Marine High Command East, 1944; KTB Admiral Denmark, 1944.

26 Friedrich Ruge, *Im Küstenvorfeld* (Munich: 1974), pp.70 & 108.

The wreck of the German troopship *Gneisenau*, sunk by a mine 2 May 1943.

these aircraft were being shot down in ever-increasing numbers. For example, on the night of 29 April, a total of 208 minelaying aircraft were to drop their loads in Danish waters and the southern Baltic Sea. Approximately 550 mines were dropped, making it the largest minelaying operation of the war, but it was also the raid with the highest losses of minelaying aircraft. A total of 22 aircraft did not return – a loss rate of more than 10 percent. 11 of the 22 aircraft crashed on Danish soil, and several of the others in the waters around Denmark. In the following week a dozen ships were blown up in the mined areas, including the large German troop transport ship *Gneisenau* on 2 May.[27]

Bomber Command's response was, in March 1943, to experiment with a new minelaying method called 'high-level minelaying'. The new navigation and radar aids, especially H2S, enabled aircraft to find the target from an altitude of 3,000 feet, despite dense cloud cover, and by the end of the year the altitude was experimentally increased to between 12,000 and 15,000 feet.[28] At these high altitudes, the aircraft were reasonably safe from light and medium flak. The mines had to be dropped from this height, and a parachute still ensured that the mines did not come down too fast and risk being crushed when they hit the water surface. At the end of September 1943, the high-level method was included in the general mine laying policy §4a where aircraft were allowed to go up to 6000 feet (Mk V-VII) and 15,000 feet (MK I-IV) respectively.[29] The fact that things did not go according to plan at first became obvious when 20 Stirlings were sent on a minelaying mission to the Kattegat and the waters off Aalborg on the night of 5 November 1943. Four of these aircraft were shot down by German night fighters,

---

27 Carsten Petersen, Petersen, Carsten, *Luftkrig over Danmark* (Ringkøbing: 1990), vol. V, pp.35–43. Minelaying on the night of 28/29 April 1943, <http://www.flensted.eu.com/19430042.shtml>. Image source: <https://www.vragguiden.dk/wreck.asp?wreckid=380>.

28 Frank Weber et al, *Vestallierede luftangreb i Danmark under 2. Verdenskrig* vol. 1 (Viborg: Aarhus Universitetsforlag, 1988), chap. XI. pp.287–292.

29 Air 14/705 83708 Bomber Command 20.12.1943.

while British intelligence was able to follow the drama by intercepting the fighters' radio communications with the fighter control centre in Karup.[30]

The new method was officially tested operationally for the first time on 4 January 1944, when six Halifaxes laid mines off Brest.[31] However, the crews lacked the necessary training to calculate when to drop the mines. With the new method, the mine hovered somewhat longer in the air, so suddenly even more consideration had to be given to the direction and strength of the wind. This problem became obvious when some mines did not fall into the Sound as planned, but instead drifted over the Swedish coast and landed 56 kilometres from the target area. The RAF took the consequences of this unfortunate event and intensified the crews' training in calculating the drift under the given weather conditions.[32]

The laying of mines on the night of 25 February 1944 should have been carried out in the 'old' way. The laying of mines was also a diversion for a major bombing raid on Schweinfurt's ball bearing factories with 734 bombers. It was the first but would not the last time Bomber Command attacked the town. 94 out of 115 minelaying aircraft laid mines in Danish waters, where troop transports between Germany and Norway were the main target. A large proportion of the planes would therefore lay mines in the southern end of Kattegat, but as Aarhus was taking over the role of shipping point for this traffic, nine mines were laid off Aarhus that night for the first time during the occupation. A total of 45 aircraft were to have laid mines in Kieler Bay, but in the afternoon the units involved were informed that the target was instead the northern part of Øresund. It was 34 Halifaxes from 4. Group were tasked with the job, and the mines were to be dropped using the new high-level method.

However, the mission did not go so well. The combined force followed the planned route over the North Sea and passed the west coast just south of Esbjerg. There the three groups separated in the direction of Aarhus, Kattegat and Øresund. In Eastern Denmark, there was dense cloud cover at an altitude of 8,000 feet, and since the minelaying was to take place from an altitude of 15,000 feet, three special pathfinder aircraft equipped with H2S radar had to locate the target area and drop flares just above the cloud cover at five-minute intervals. A few of the aircraft had to turn back before reaching the target area due to technical problems, but 24 of the 32 aircraft managed to set their mines in what they believed to be the right place. The crews of the last eight aircraft arrived at the target area so late that the last flares had burnt out, so seven of the pilots chose to take the mines back to base and the last aircraft dropped the payload in deep water in the North Sea. Overall, the evening raid was considered a success.[33]

Three days later, the Admiralty informed Bomber Command's leaders that the British naval attaché at the embassy in Stockholm had reported that eight of the mines had landed in Sweden 25–50 kilometres east-southeast of the target area.[34] The routine debriefing of the crews after the raid had not revealed any irregularities in relation to the plan, and the raid

30 Carsten Petersen, *Luftkrig over Danmark*, (Ringkøbing: 1989), vol. 1V, pp.7–12.
31 Denis Richards & Hilary St George Saunders, *Royal Air Force, 1939–1945*, vol. 3 (London: HMSO, 1954), pp.17–18.
32 Stephen W. Roskill, *The War at Sea 1939–45*, vol. 3 1 (London: HMSO, 1960), p.288.
33 Air 24/206. Bomber Command ORB, 24–25 February 1944.
34 Air 14/705 'M' mine: Plan WA15 for operations against enemy shipping: From Naval Staff Officer to SASO HQ Bomber Command 28.2.1944.

had therefore been labelled a success. Now all crew members were debriefed again and their information was analysed together with the other information that could be collected. The conclusion was that:

a) A high pressure had been stable over the North Sea, creating large differences in wind strength and wind directions around it. As a result, most aircraft reached the Danish coast faster and further south than expected.
b) As a result, several of the aircraft did not reach the correct area on the west coast, from where the planes had to change direction. They were unable to correct this because only two of the three flares placed to mark the spot worked as intended and only stayed alight for about 6–10 minutes.
c) The three pathfinder aircraft that were to place the flare markers en route had no previous experience with this, as it was the first time Bomber Command had used crews from the participating units instead of crews from the regular pathfinder force.
d) Each of the pathfinder aircraft carried only two flares.
e) The first flare over the target area failed, and another 6 minutes passed before the next two flares were dropped. They were only alight for 7 minutes of the expected 13 minutes. Since several of the planes had arrived faster than expected and were on a course that took them south-southeast of the target area, only the rear flight crews saw the last two flares and could therefore correct the error.
f) About half of the participating flight crews were relatively inexperienced.
g) It was not possible to identify the four aircraft that dropped the mines over Swedish territory with certainty.

Against this background, on 10 March it was recommended that pathfinder aircraft should carry plenty of flares to ensure that the markings were carried out. At the same time, the flight crews should be instructed and better trained to take into account wind and weather conditions along the way, and to follow the instructions carefully, including using the markings as a guide.[35]

The increased minelaying activity in Danish waters as a result of the high-level method prompted the *Kriegsmarine* to react. The *Luftwaffe* and the *Kriegsmarine* organised a large-scale wargame in February 1944. The game was organised in *Gruppe Nord* under the code name 'Leuthen'; The German military staff often used wargames during planning.[36] The liaison officer between the two services, *Kapitän zur See* Wilhelm Mössel, concluded from this that the enemy would obviously disrupt, if not completely destroy, the important traffic of supply ships to Norway. The main weapon was mines dropped by the RAF. It should therefore be considered whether the night fighter force in Jutland could be reinforced. Under strong pressure from the *Kriegsmarine*, fighter reinforcements were sent to Jutland. However, in April Mössel reported that further precautions had to be taken against the British minelaying

35 'M' mine: Plan WA15 for operations against enemy shipping: Report on Minelaying Operations carried out by 42 Base – on the night of the 24/25 February 1944.

36 Michael Salewski, *Die Deutsche Seekriegsleitung 1935–1945*, vol. 2 (Frankfurt am Main: 1975), p.477.

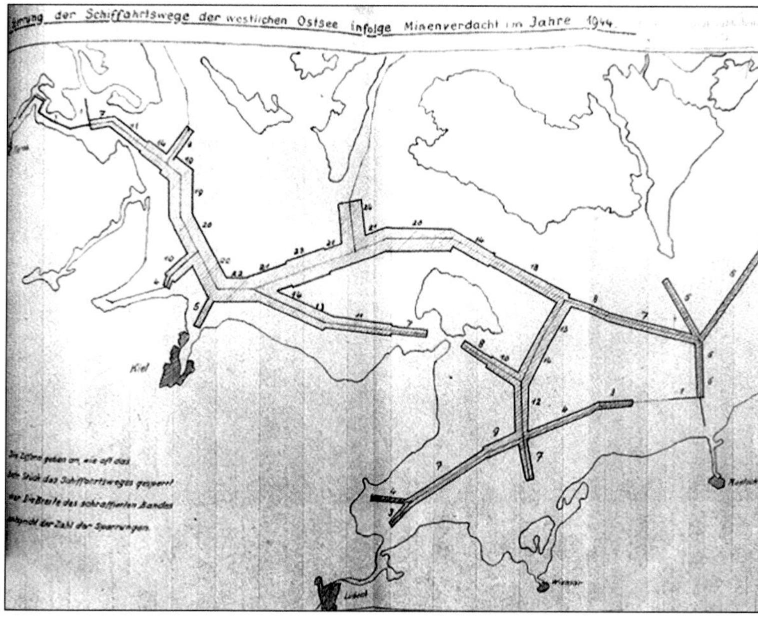

Closure of the shipping routes of the Western Baltic Sea due to suspected mines in 1944. German map from the end of 1944. Digits indicating time closed from 1 to 28 days.

planes. Otherwise, they could not be stopped effectively. Now that the British aircraft were out of range of the flak batteries, the only effective weapon was the night fighters.[37]

In April 1944, minelaying operations were concentrated around the Bay of Biscay in preparation for the impending Normandy invasion. Danish waters were among the few areas in Europe where mines were still being laid on the same scale as before, for example on 9 April, 12 April and 18 April. On 23 April, minelayer planes were again flying over Danish waters and down the Atlantic coast.[38] This minelaying was supposedly the last mission of this type before the Normandy landings six weeks later. In the meantime, all Bomber Command resources were to be deployed in support of the invasion preparations.[39]

On 23 April, 63 Halifaxes, 26 Stirlings and 13 Lancasters were sent on mine laying missions to Danish waters. Despite an intense German night fighter effort, only six aircraft were shot down.[40] The laying of mines on 23 April was perhaps the last in the rest of Western Europe before 6 June, but not the last in Danish waters. Both German and British sources indicate that nine more minelaying missions were launched there: mines were laid on 24 April, 16 May, 21 May, 23 May, 24 May, 27 May, 1 June and 2 June. On the night of 21/22 May the force was 23 aircraft, while the other raids were carried out by 5 to 10 aircraft.[41] The

37 Denis Richards & Hilary St George Saunders, *Royal Air Force, 1939–1945*, vol. 3 (London: HMSO, 1954), p.17.

38 Geoffry P Jones, *Night Flight. Halifax Squadrons at War* (London: Harper Collins, 1981), pp.160–168; Anders Bjørnvad, *Faldne allierede flyvere 1939–1945* (Odense: 1978), p.14.

39 Geoffry P Jones, *Night Flight. Halifax Squadrons at War* (London: Harper Collins, 1981), pp.158–160.

40 Carsten Petersen, *Luftkrig over Danmark* (Ringkøbing: 1989), vol. 14, pp.13–19.

41 Adm. Dän., 8 Security Division, 34/405-407; Martin Middlebrook & Chris Everitt, *The Bomber Command War Diaries: An Operational Reference Book 1939–1945* (Bungay: Viking, 1985), pp.498, 511, 513–14, 518.

large effort can be taken as an indication of how highly prioritised Danish waters were for Bomber Command.

The number of flights per month peaked in April 1944 to a total of 855 times that a bomber was sent out with mines in its load, and a total of 2,643 mines were laid. But despite 'only' 812 aircraft being sent out the following month, a total of 2,760 mines were laid; the highest number in a month during the whole war.[42] In May, two-thirds of the sorties were carried out using the high-level method,[43] which is reflected in the number of aircraft lost; in April: 20, in May: 10 and in June: 3. The high priority given to laying mines in Danish waters in April is reflected in the sad fact that 18 of the 20 aircraft lost were in connection with raids: 9/10 April (nine aircraft), 18/19 April (three aircraft) and 23/24 (six aircraft).[44]

The British aircrews could be satisfied with the effort, as evidenced by an issue of 1 Group's internal newsletter, where one of the regular columns was 'Mining'. The newsletter states that April 1944 really was 'the greatest ever for the horticultural enthusiasts'. Although the writer apparently used code names such as 'vegetables' for the rest of the text there was no doubt as to what it was about. The headline was, of course, a dead give-away!

That the British really did lay a lot of mines in Danish waters is reflected in the German minesweeping effort. For example, 38 of 84 Mausi aircraft available to Germany at the time were deployed in the waters around Denmark. The rest were spread across the English Channel, Biscay, the Mediterranean and the Black Sea.[45]

10.5 Crash at Gamtofte, 15–16 May 1944

Shortly after midnight on the night of 16 May, 40–50 minelayers reached the Danish coast.[46] Two Lancasters crashed over Denmark. One each came from 103 Squadron and 576 Squadron, were both stationed at Elsham Wolds and belonged to 1 Group.[47] During the approach, the Lancaster from 576 Squadron was shot down near the village of Gamtofte, five kilometres east of Assens on Funen. The village consisted of the church, four farms and six or seven houses. The entire settlement was centred around the church. The plane crashed into the vicarage garden, burning, and petrol and oil hit two of the farms, which immediately caught fire. The volunteer fire brigade arrived quickly, but were unable to do much against the fierce fire. The plane's load of four magnetic mines was thrown around when the plane hit the ground. Three mines were scattered in the surrounding fields, while the

42 Stephen W. Roskill, *The War at Sea 1939–45*, vol. 3 1 (London: HMSO, 1960), p.289, 'Jan.-May 1944'.

43 Stephen W. Roskill, *The War at Sea 1939–45*, vol. 3 1 (London: HMSO, 1960), p.288.

44 Stephen W. Roskill, *The War at Sea 1939–45*, vol. 3 1 (London: HMSO, 1960), p.289. Stephen W. Roskill, *The War at Sea 1939–45*, vol. 3 2 (London: HMSO, 1962), p.142

45 Franz Kurowski, *Seekrieg aus der luft* (Herfords: 1979), p.305. Inventory on 31.3.44.

46 Adm. Dän. 21/260 and 34/407. Five mine swept routes were heavily mined, approximately 660 mines were laid in May 1944, of which 33 were swept during the following two days. 'Monthly Summary of Mines Laid by Bomber Command by Areas, May 1944'.

47 Anders Bjørnvad, *Faldne allierede flyvere 1939–1945* (Odense: 1978), pp.73 & 103; James J. Halley, *The Squadrons of the Royal Air Force* (Tonbridge: Air Britain Historians Ltd, 1980), pp.139–140 & 319; Philip J. R. Moyes, *Bomber Squadrons of the R.A.F. and Their Aircraft* (London: MacDonald, 1964), p.306.

Example of the mention of mine laying in Bomber Command 1 Group ORB, May 1944.

Page No. 6.
May, 1944.
SECRET.

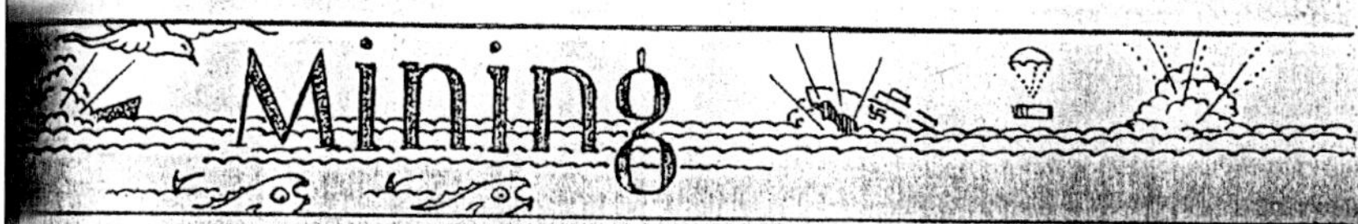

1. Last month was the greatest ever for the horticultural enthusiasts. A grand total of 2760 vegetables were planted, a great percentage being devoted to the closing of the Baltic, to which this Group contributed all of their vegetable sowing sorties. The Group operated on 4 nights making 49 sorties, of which 43 were successful, and laid 253 vegetables. Many of the vegetables sown by the Command were of a new type. A larger mine than that hitherto used, and actuated by a diabolical and mysterious mechanism, they are expected to bring grief and disaster to Hun shipping. No. 8 Group assisted in the closing of the Baltic when Mosquitos carried out a low level mining sortie on the Kiel Canal.

2. Many reports have come in of the success of our recent offensive. The Swedish ship owners have declared that the waters of the Baltic, once peaceful and sheltered, are now as dangerous as the hazardous routes of the North Sea where shipping is open to the constant threat of bombers, torpedo boats and aircraft. To the plaintive cry of Neutral Sweden is joined the voice of the German's Finnish Allies. Finnish ship owners are reported to be laying up their ships on the pretext of repairs, and pressure by the Hun to force their sailing has been largely unavailing. Further good news comes from a U.S. Army Air Force Officer recently back from Denmark. He came back in a Dutch steamer in May and on passing Hals Point (1 Group went there on the 23/24th of last month) they saw the wreck of a troop transport. The Captain of the Dutch ship said that the transport had once had a notice on it stating that 7,000 troops of the great Herenvolk had lost their lives in it owing to the actions of the aggressor nations. The notice had since been removed, as one dark night the Danes rowed out to the wreck and painted HA! HA! underneath it. A further two wrecks were noticed a bit further North in the same area.

3. Cameras for photographing the H.2.S. screen were carried this month by several aircraft and the resultant photographs were of the greatest value in plotting the sticks of mines.

4. Now that 'D' day is with us, our role becomes increasingly important. The Germans now, more than ever, will want the sea lanes free in order to move up their guns and equipment, and our job is to see that they don't.

fourth remained in the burning aircraft. The impact and the intense heat caused the mine to detonate after a few minutes in a huge explosion.[48] The vicarage, church and the five nearest houses were heavily damaged. The aircraft and its crew were obliterated by the explosion.

The crash could be heard at Assens, five kilometres away, where the *Statens Civile Luftværn* immediately sent an orderly to find out what had happened. Meanwhile, residents in Gamtofte had discovered some round iron containers about 30cm long and 15–20cm in diameter, and rounded at both ends. A dozen of these containers were scattered around the fields. Rumours immediately arose that they were sawn-off bombs! Panic spread and even the orderly who had been dispatched lost his head. He completely forgot to report the crashed aircraft to Assens.

48 It is thus incorrect when Anders Bjørnvad (p.73) wrote that the entire load exploded.

Crater from the mine that detonated in the aircraft wreckage at Gamtofte. The vicarage can be seen in the background.

However, a few people had the good sense to set up a cordon around the presumed problem, and they were also wise enough to ensure that the three mines were contained within this cordon. Meanwhile, the *Statens Civile Luftværn* in Assens was a little worried about the whereabouts of their deployed employee. For safety's sake, an extinguishing train, an ambulance, a doctor and a police patrol were sent to Gamtofte. An air defence captain arrived, and he was immediately able to reassure the crowd that the 'causes' were just the crew's oxygen tanks. The mines, two of which were heavily damaged, were further sealed off until the German military forces could collect them.

Two farms, five houses and the church were heavily damaged, while another ten nearby properties escaped with minor damage. Despite the extensive material damage in Gamtofte, only two people were injured: a farmer and the farmer's wife, who were both hit by splinters from the windows. However, it should be mentioned that the vicar's wife was knocked over by the air pressure and 'bruised her face'.

The other aircraft laid their mines in the Great Belt, at Samsø and in South-West Kattegat. Finally, mines were laid in 'Kraut', the eastern exit from the Limfjord. German reports show that the attack took place between 01.10 and 01.48. The aircraft crashed in Gamtofte at 01.35, so it must have been in the leading part of the raid.[49] The flight altitude is reported to be

49 *Dansk Luftværns Blad*, 3rd year, 1944, no. 8, p.191, says that the aircraft crashed at approximately 00.35. Either this is a misprint, or it does not take into account the Danish summer time that was introduced on 3 April 1944. *Avisårbogen*, 1944, p.25.

Part of the fuselage of the Lancaster which crashed at Gamtofte on 16 May 1944. The aircraft was from Bomber Command's 576 Squadron.

Pieces of the wreckage from the Lancaster were found all over the village.

from approximately 13,500 feet to 15,000 feet, which shows that the high-level method was being used. Two more aircraft were shot down while minelaying that night. A Lancaster from 103 Squadron was presumably shot down by *Hauptmann* Franz Buschmann of *Stab IV. / NJG 3*. The bomber crashed into the sea between Lyø and Avernakø in the South Funen Archipelago, killing all on board. A Lancaster from 625 Squadron was probably also shot down by the same German pilot. It crashed in the North Sea 60 kilometres WNW of Westerland/Sylt and again the entire crew was killed. The night fighters that Mössel had asked to ne moved to Jutland had proved their worth.[50]

A week later, *Ritzaus Bureau* reported that a female crew member had been on board the crashed Lancaster in Gamtofte. She was said to have been dressed in regulation flight uniform and was allegedly a radio operator on board. The normal crew of a Lancaster was seven: pilot, flight engineer, navigator, radio operator, nose gunner, mid-upper gunner and tail gunner. In this case, there were eight on board, although we now know their identities, all men. There were two pilots, a navigator, a flight engineer, a bomb aimer and the three gunners, one of whom was also the radio operator.[51] As we have the names of the full crew, the claim must be dismissed as propaganda. British women did hold positions in the RAF as aircraft mechanics, radar and radio mechanics, electricians and transport pilots, but they did not take part in either bombing or mine raids, or as aircrew.[52]

10.6 Diversionary Manoeuvre, 21–22 May 1944

Late in the evening of 21 May, 717 aircraft were launched against German targets. The main force of 532 Lancasters was to bomb targets in Duisburg. Due to the extensive invasion preparations, there had been no raids of this magnitude for about three weeks. It was now an open secret that the invasion would come within the next few weeks, and the German air defence was thus on high alert. For the RAF, it was therefore important that the German fighters were dispersed so that the bombing force had a better chance of reaching the target. The aim was to create doubt in the German air defence command as to where the British main target was that night.[53]

The plan was to send aircraft from 4, 5 and 6 Group over Denmark and northern Germany as a diversion. The planes from 6 Group, 23 in total, were to lay mines in the waters north-east of Samsø. At the same time, 70 aircraft from 5 Group were to fly over Southern Jutland to 'Forget-me-not', the waters off Kiel. Here they would lay mines to prevent the German

50 Anders Bjørnvad, *Faldne allierede flyvere 1939–1945* (Odense: 1978), p.73; SCL, 16/17 May 1944; Adm. Dän. 34/407; *Avisårbogen*, 1944; *Dansk Luftværns Blad*, 3rd year, 1944, no.8, p.191. <http://www.flensted.eu.com/1944069.shtml>; <http://www.flensted.eu.com/1944067.shtml>.

51 <https://www.airmen.dk/p314.htm>. Anders Bjørnvad, *Faldne allierede flyvere 1939–1945* (Odense: 1978), p.73. Theories were also put forward that the eighth crew member might have been a journalist. *Aarhuus Stiftstidende*, Monday 22 May 1944.

52 Denis Richards & Hilary St George Saunders, *Royal Air Force, 1939–1945* , vol. 3 (London: HMSO, 1954), p.372.

53 The following sections are mainly based on: Air 24/273. Bomber Command ORB, app. 'Interceptions/Tactics no. 115/44', which mainly deals with the reactions of the German fighter forces during this raid.

U-boats from Kiel from entering the North Sea and English Channel, where they could have posed a major threat to the invasion fleet. For the same reason, the Kiel Canal was heavily mined during this period. Finally, 14 aircraft from 4 Group were to lay mines southwest of Sylt.[54]

The bombing force was to assemble approximately halfway across the English Channel and then head for Hamburg – at least that is what the Germans were led to believe. At Leeuwarden in The Netherlands, the force was to turn south-east, now heading towards Münster. Again, a deception. At Enschede, a force of 24 Mosquitos, which up to that point had followed the main force, was to split off and head for Hannover. While this was going on, the bomber force would finally fly directly towards the target, Duisburg. After the attack, the aircraft would take the shortest possible route home via Eindhoven.

The bombing force reached its target virtually unhindered. Along the way, it was only attacked by a single German night fighter, over Texel. Two of the bombers were hit by flak and crashed before reaching Duisburg. Over the Ruhr, on the other hand, the air was thick with fighters. The bombers had to turn for home swiftly after their bomb loads had been sent towards the target. The German fighters swarmed around them all the way to the coast and even well into the English Channel.

Normally, the fighters would have attacked the damaged bombers first, these were always some distance behind the main force. But in this case, the German fighter force was so strong that it immediately went after the main force, intending to deal with the stragglers later. The formation split, making it even easier for the German night fighters to finish off the British aircraft one by one. While only 2 bombers had been shot down during the approach, a total of 30 bombers fell prey to the fighters during the return flight.[55]

Nevertheless, the result was satisfactory for the RAF. A loss rate of 5.6 percent was within the acceptable range of losses. German aircraft communications had been intercepted, which revealed that the night fighter unit *NJ G 3* had not been authorised to take off before the large bombing force had crossed the Dutch coast. At the same time, the fighter force had been divided, as IV Group on Westerland was directed to the island of Pellworm at 00.13. From there, the German fighters would take care of the minelayers from 4 Group, while the rest of *NJG 3* was held back at Vechta and Stade airfields. However, the minelayers turned back over the North Sea, leaving IV Group unemployed for a short time. Twenty minutes later, I, II and III Groups were finally sent off towards the Ruhr, although it is doubtful if they arrived before the British force was too far away.

The waiting paid off for IV Group. Around 100 minelayer planes were heading towards the Danish coast. It was quite a substantial diversionary force that had been sent off with mines in their loads. The 23 Lancasters, which laid mines between Sjællands Rev and the coast of Djursland, met no enemy resistance. As mentioned, *IV/NJG 3* was sent to Pellworm

54 The division of tasks is not clearly set out in the material and is therefore based on the stated flight time for the two Groups.

55 Air 24/273. Bomber Command ORB, app. Bomber Command itself gave the total loss as 28 aircraft, but later the British newspapers corrected the figure to 30 aircraft; Keesing's Contemporary Archives, 1944, p.6457. From the German side, British losses were initially estimated at 41 aircraft, but this was later reduced to 33 aircraft. If we include the losses over Denmark, which the Germans must have done, the numbers match.

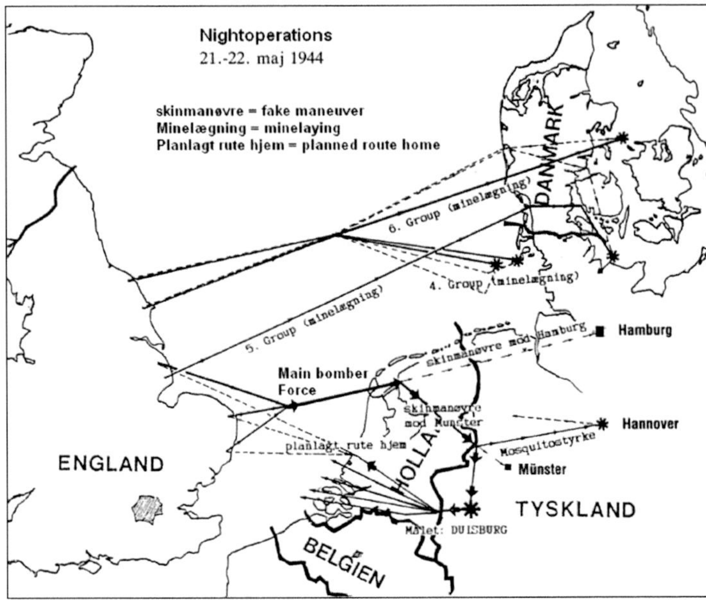

at 00.13. The aircraft from 6 Group passed Ringkøbing Fjord three minutes later. The night fighters therefore had no chance of reaching Pellworm before the British aircraft would be well on their way home.

In the end, it was probably also the large minelaying force of 65 aircraft that attracted the attention of the German air defence. After all, there was no way of knowing whether the cargo consisted of mines or bombs. If it was bombs, all the major cities in northern Germany could be potential targets. It was therefore a different kind of warm welcome that awaited 5 Group. The 65 aircraft reached the Danish coast at around 00.50. The coast was passed in the Esbjerg area, from where a heavy flak fire was sent towards the planes.

At the same time, some Ju 88s emerged from the darkness. They immediately attacked the British force, and the result was a Lancaster from 207 Squadron shot down and which crashed into the sea north of Mandø. Although the minelayers were then chased across the Jutland Peninsula, they suffered no further losses on their way to the target. Apparently, they were too successful. While the reports were initially labelled 'fighter attacks', they were later labelled 'air combat' as the planes headed south towards Kiel.

In the target area off Kiel, the British aircraft were met by several German night fighters. While the Ju 88s and Me 110s chased them, the remaining 64 aircraft dropped their mines in place. In fact, they set a 'world war record' in terms of mine laying. The 64 planes dropped a total load of 382 mines, which was the largest number of mines in a single target area, during one raid, during the entire War.[56] Although the crews did not have time to think in terms of records, for them, it was all about getting away in a hurry. They headed north. This manoeuvre seems to have saved them from suffering the same fate as the Duisburg bomber force. The German night fighters from *IV/NJG 3* had been sent to Pellworm to deal with the minelayers from 4 Group. However, they got no further than south-west of Sylt. When this 'ambush' failed, *NJG 3*'s leadership probably figured that the minelaying force at Kiel would take the shortest route home. This would bring it into the arms of IV Group. It was an unconventional but tactically smart manoeuvre that

56 Philip J. R. Moyes, *Bomber Squadrons of the R.A.F. and Their Aircraft* (London: MacDonald, 1964), p.328.

could easily cost the British dearly. Taking such a detour gave the German night fighters more time to get into position. Now, however, the British northward course home took the German fighter command by surprise. The night fighters therefore first caught up with the British aircraft over south-west Funen.

Near Assens, one of the aircraft from 57 Squadron was shot down, which was observed by a farmer in the village of Emtekær. Together with his family and the people on the farm, he stood in the courtyard to watch the scene in the air. The stricken aircraft crashed near the farm, and one of the men ran to see where it was. About 10 minutes later, a loud explosion was heard. When the man had not yet returned, the farm owner ran out after him, but he found him dead not far from the debris.[57]

Meanwhile, the other aircraft continued to Juelsminde, where they turned west towards Ringkøbing Fjord. From there, they would take the straight route home. However, one of the planes did not make it that far. Over Vejle, a Lancaster from 630 Squadron was attacked by a German night fighter. After a long chase, the British aircraft was set on fire over Thyregod, and it crashed near the railway line close to Vesterlund. All crew members were killed.[58]

The shooting down of this aircraft was immediately registered by the RAF. German radio traffic between the fighters and their base was intercepted, and at 02.13 hours the German pilot could be heard being congratulated on the shooting down of the Lancaster by fighter command at the airfield. Of the total mine force of 88 aircraft, only 3 were shot down. This can be characterised as a minimal loss. By carrying out the bombing raid and the mine-laying at roughly the same time, they had created the intended confusion in the German fighter defence.[59]

To avoid repetition, the following message was received on 22 May by *Admiral* Wurmbach, Commanding *Admiral Skagerrak*:

> The following message has been received from *Marineoberkommando Ost*: Increased night fighter forces have been deployed since May 22nd to combat night-time minelaying raids in the sea areas of the Frisian Islands, the German Bight, the Western Baltic Sea and Jutland. These night hunting units will also be held back during large-scale incursions into the Reich's territory exclusively for mine laying operations.

In addition, Wurmbach noted:

> This measure is very positive and will hopefully soon have a favourable effect on keeping the shipping lanes clear.[60]

57 *Aarhuus Stiftstidende*, 22.5.1944, front page and p.6; *Jyllandsposten*, 23.5.1944, front page. These newspapers and the SCL wrote, among other things, that the aircraft's cargo had been 5 high-explosive bombs, one of which had detonated. However, in fact, it had been a mine load. SCL Air sheet p.174.

58 *Aarhus Stiftstidende*, 22.5.1944, front page.

59 Air 24/273; Adm. Skagerrak, 21/260, 22.5.1944; *8. Sicherungsflottillie*, 34/405, 22.5.1944; Anders Bjørnvad, *Faldne allierede flyvere 1939–1945* (Odense: 1978), pp.73 & 92.

60 Air 24/273; Adm. Skagerrak, 21/260, 22.5.1944; *8. Sicherungsflottillie*, 34/405, 22.5.1944.

It seems strange that German night fighters were sent to Jutland with orders to attack only minelaying aircraft at a time when all eyes were on the west coast of France! Part of the answer can be found on another of the war fronts – Italy.

10.7 Minelaying off Aarhus, 1–2 June 1944

In the spring of 1944, German forces in Italy had managed to halt the Allied advance north from Sicily for a few months. For a brief period, the Allied forces were held in front of the German defence position of the Gustav Line, centred on the monastery at Monte Cassino. Repeated attacks on this line had been repulsed since mid-January. Even so, the Allies had expected to break through the defences relatively quickly. The 6 US Corps had therefore been landed at Anzio behind the German defensive line, only about 50 km from Rome. However, the breakthrough did not come as quickly as expected. The Germans deployed 14th Army against the American troops at Anzio, and for a while it looked like they would succeed in throwing 6 US Corps into the sea. The front was at a standstill for a month while the Allied air forces concentrated on bombing the German lines of communication behind the Gustav Line. The ancient monastery of Monte Cassino was one of the victims of the bombers during this period. In mid-May, the Allies attempted another breakthrough and the German defences began to falter.[61]

As a result of the fighting in Italy, there had been some reorganisation of the German forces in Denmark. On 29 April, the *Luftwaffe-Felddivision Nr 20* was taken from the coastal defence and replaced by the *Infanteridivision Nr 363*. The *Luftwaffe-Felddivision* was made ready as an OKW reserve in Aalborg. At the end of May, when the German forces in Italy were in high morale, it was sent to Rome, where, together with the *Panzerdivision 'Hermann Göring'*, it was to defend the Italian capital.[62] The transfer of the *Luftwaffe-Felddivision Nr 20* meant a noticeable weakening of the German forces in Denmark, which, by some officers in the German High Command, was still considered a weak point in case of an Allied invasion. The remnants of the *Panzerdivision Nr 25*, which had been sent from the Eastern Front to Norway on 3 May, were therefore to be sent on to Denmark. Here, the 8,000 men, together with the remnants of *Panzerdivision 'Norwegen'*, would replace the departing *Luftwaffe* Division.[63]

On 24 May, *Luftwaffe-Felddivision Nr 20* was sent south by rail. On 2 June, the *Daily Mail* reported that 40 German troop trains had been sent from Denmark to Italy during the night of 25 May. The source of this announcement was the Danish Press Service in Stockholm[64] It became necessary to procure transport ships for the *Panzerdivision Nr 25's* movement from Norway to Denmark. For the first few days, the warships on the Oslo-Århus route would take care of the transport. These were the former Larvik ferry *Peter Wessel* and the troop transport ship *Mar Del Plata*. The *Kriegsmarine Division* sent two empty transport ships

61 Politikens, *Anden Verdenskrig Hvornår-skete-det?* pp.347–364.

62 Helmuth Greiner, *Kriegstagebuch des Oberkommandos der Wehrmacht*, vol. 4 (Frankfurt am Main: 1962), p.58.

63 Helmuth Greiner, *Kriegstagebuch des Oberkommandos der Wehrmacht*, vol. 4 (Frankfurt am Main: 1962), p.925.

64 *The Daily Mail*, 2.6.44, back page

The troop transport ship *Mar Del Plata*.

to Oslo on 29 May. In addition, the *Wehrrnachtfiihrungsstab Heimatstab Übersee* sent the ship *Birkenau*. The transport was escorted by the coastal armoured ship *Adler*, a new name given to the Danish warship *Peder Skram* by the Germans.[65] In addition, two destroyers, *Z 30* and *Z 20 Karl Galster*, were to participate in the escort service. *Luftflotte 5* and *General der Luftwaffe* in Dänemark promised full air defence during the transport. Everything was ready and waiting.

On 26 May, the troop transport ship *Mar Del Plata*, escorted by *Adler*, carried the first shipment of troops and equipment to Aarhus. The two destroyers followed from Horten in Norway to Frederikshavn. On 1 June, the escort left the Danish port again and headed north. In the intervening days, British aircraft had flown over Skagen several times at night. From there they circled over Læsø Rende and the waters between Læsø and Anholt, after which they disappeared to the northwest again.[66] All indications were that they were conducting reconnaissance of shipping activity.

To stop the next, and probably the last, convoy of troops from Oslo to Aarhus, a rather special mine laying operation was ordered. It was now so close to D-Day that heavy aircraft could not be assigned to this task. It was therefore left to 692 Squadron which was equipped with Mosquito fighter-bombers. This type of aircraft had only been used as a mining aircraft once before, when the same squadron had successfully laid mines in the Kiel Canal two weeks earlier.[67] The mission to Denmark was therefore followed with great interest in the RAF.

65 Hans H. Hildebrand, *Die deutschen Kriegsschiffe. Biographien - ein Spiegel der Marinegeschichte von 1815 bis zur Gegenwart*, vols 1–7 (Herford: Koehlers, 1982), vol.7, p.53.

66 Adm. Skagerrak 21/260, 24 May to 1 June 1944, inclusive..

67 C Martin Sharp and Michael J F. Bowyer, *Mosquito* (London: Faber & Faber, 1967), pp.310–311.

Although bearing the squadron markings of 571 Squadron here, this aircraft, Mosquito Mk. XVI ML963, was first issued to 109 Squadron on 9 March 1944, going on to 692 Squadron on the 24th of the same month.

While five aircraft from 692 Squadron each laid a mine in the waters between Sletterhage and Samsø, six Mosquitos from 139 Squadron bombed potential shipping targets in Aarhus Harbour. They were also so-called 'Pathfinders', an elite unit in RAF Bomber Command that had to guide the other aircraft to ensure that the five mines were placed correctly. You might wonder why there was a need for five more mines off Aarhus Harbour. During April and May, 71 and 92 mines had already been laid in the waters between Sletterhage and Issehovedrev with the majority laid in the entrance to the Great Belt!

We are lucky enough to have a copy of the briefing the crews received before they set out.[68] According to this, the sequence of events was briefly as follows: The five Mosquitos were due to take off from their base, Graveley, shortly after 23:00 on 1 June. Via the lighthouse at Cromer, they were to head for the west coast of Denmark. A red and yellow marker flare would show where the approach would take place. This point was approximately 10 kilometres north of Blåvandshuk. The planes would continue on the same course. Then they would reach Randers Fjord at 01:12, where a green flare would be dropped. This was a sign for them to turn due south. After another three minutes of flying, they would be able to see another green flare. It would be over Skødshoved. The minelayer planes would turn to port,

68 Air 27/2217. 692 Squadron. ORB, app. Log Book, 1–2 June 1944.

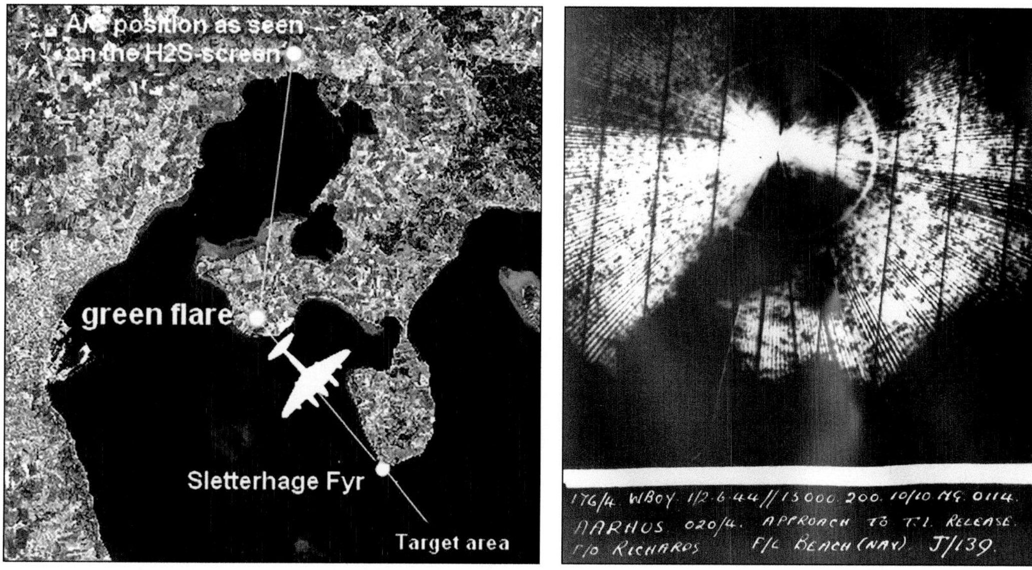

The flight path to the mine laying area. To the right a photo of the H2S radar as the aircraft from 139 Squadron with pilot Richards and navigator Beach was heading towards the green flare.

and shortly afterwards they should be able to see Sletterhage Lighthouse. Steady on course, they should release the mines 20 seconds later. Then the planes were to head west towards Ringkøbing Fjord, from where they would fly directly home. The mission went pretty much as described. After seeing the markings at Randers Fjord, the minelaying crews found their way to Sletterhage, partly with the help of the H2S radar, and from there to the target area. They encountered no enemy resistance at all during the flight.

Unfortunately, the German troop transport was not affected by the night's raid either. It entered Frederikshavn in North Jutland, where the British minefield at the entrance had not been mined since September 1942 and only with a total of 16 mines!

In comparison, the minefield in the entrance to Aalborg, 'Kraut', had been heavily mined right up until May 1944 with a total of 114 mines. The Admiralty quickly realised this regrettable oversight, and between August 1944 and February 1945, a total of 447 mines were laid in 'Yewtree' off Frederikshavn. Nevertheless, the German minesweepers managed to keep a channel clear until April 1945, at which time it was the only open connection to Norway.[69]

In June 1944, the entire British mining effort was put onto the Bay of Biscay. The laying of mines here was part of 'Operation Neptune', the maritime part during the early stages of the invasion. By July, the Normandy beachhead had been secured to such an extent that the main emphasis of mine operations could again shift northwards to the Dutch, North German and Danish coasts.[70]

69 Air 27/2217. 692 Sqdn. ORB, app. Log Book, 1–2. June 1944. Air 25/153. 8 Group ORB, 1–2 June 1944. Air 27/2216. 692 Sqdn. ORB, 1–2.6.1944. Air 28/325 Graveley ORB, 1–2.6.1944.

70 Stephen W. Roskill, *The War at Sea 1939–45*, vol. 3 2 (London: HMSO, 1962), p.140. Information from Birger Hansen in letter dated 19.09.1984.

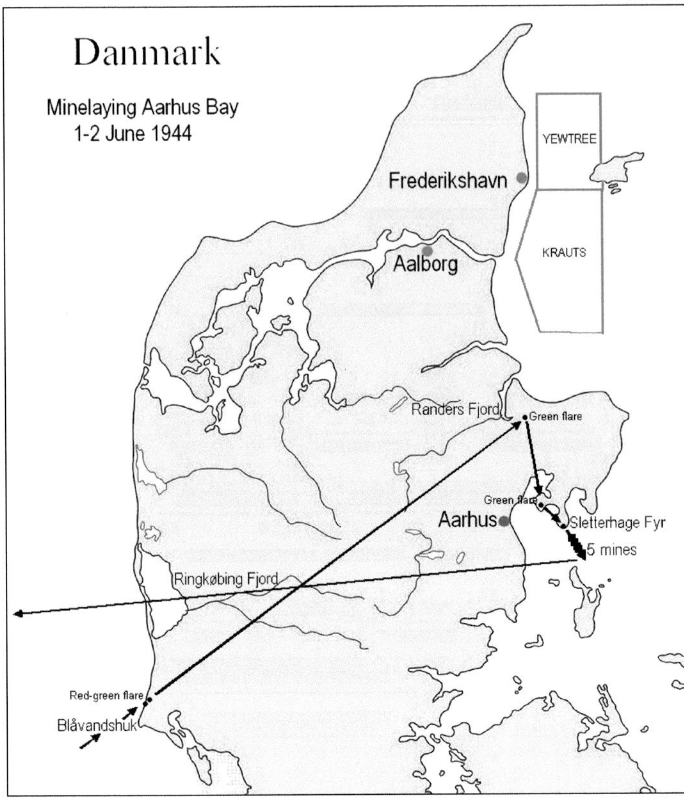

It does not appear that there were any further pin-point minings, such as the one mentioned above at Aarhus. The high-level method was more common, and it was now rare for minelayers to use the 'old' low-level method. Even though aircrews now received better training in the high-level method based on previous experience, it was inevitable that a large number of mines still drifted in over land and shallow water areas. The German mine experts were therefore able to get hold of them far more quickly than earlier and to understand the latest British developments regarding the mine mechanisms.

In the last 4 to 5 months of 1944, the minelayers were mainly deployed in the Baltic Sea, Kattegat and Oslo Fjord. The nights became longer again and they could therefore operate for longer periods over the target areas. The intensive British laying of mines in the Baltic Sea caused Swedish insurance companies to deny compensation to ships calling at North German ports on 18 August. *Kapitän zur See* Mössel, the liaison officer between the *Luftwaffe* and the *Kriegsmarine*, had to conclude in September that Germany no longer controlled the sea routes within the German sphere of influence. The sea routes in the Baltic Sea were repeatedly blocked for days or even weeks.[71]

There were also fewer and fewer safe harbours for repairs. Finland signed an armistice with the Russians on 4 September and 18 days later Tallinn, the Capital of Estonia, fell.[72] This closed the Gulf of Bothnia. On 27 September, Swedish ports were closed to German ships, and on 1 January 1945 a real embargo was imposed on deliveries to Germany. During October 1944, Russian forces entered East Prussia. The German U-boat and naval harbours in the Baltic Sea were in danger. A large number of German ships therefore headed out into

71 Denis Richards & Hilary St George Saunders, *Royal Air Force, 1939–1945*, vol. 3 (London: HMSO, 1954), p.17.

72 The ceasefire was not signed until 10 September 1944, but came into effect six days earlier, after oral negotiations.

Mine selection – No.1 group mining cartoon, ORB 1944.

the open sea. To prevent this traffic, Bomber Command laid even more mines. Although September 1944 is described in Bomber Command reports as a month of limited action, a total of 748 mines were laid. At the same time, Bomber Command had now filled up its mine stockpiles with several variants, so aircrews could look forward to a major offensive where 'our old plots' could be revisited.[73]

'C' for Charlie

On 4 October, 47 Lancasters and 31 Halifaxs were sent to Kattegat and Oslo Fjord loaded with mines. Of the Lancasters 17 came from 5 Group and were to lay mines in 'Silverthorn' in Kattegat. Two Lancasters and one Halifax were shot down. One of these aircraft, with the call signs KM-C, 'C' for Charlie, from 44 Squadron, was flown by Flying Officer Norman Joseph Evans with his six-man crew. They had been relocated a few days earlier from their original base to Spilsby, north of Boston. Because of the move, the crew had not participated in minelaying missions for more than a month. Some of the routine was gone, and that could prove fatal. The long journey across the North Sea, with no landfall along the way, placed great demands on the pilot and the navigator.

Despite the great improvements that had been made in aircraft navigation, there was still room for error. We do not know whether it was the weather, the navigation or the aircraft's instruments that caused the error, but at 19.56 the aircraft was detected by the German radar in Hanstholm, and an anti-aircraft alert was sounded. In the starry weather, there was good visibility for the anti-aircraft guns in this north-west Jutland fortress. Lancaster 'C'

73 Air 25/14, no. 1 Group, 'Mining' September 1944 (includes the drawing shown here).

therefore had little chance when the aircraft passed just north of Hanstholm three minutes later. A series of shells peppered the aircraft as Evans tried his best to evade the fire. A 10.5cm shell hit the aircraft, which had now turned round and was heading south-east. From the flak batteries in Hanstholm it could be seen that the aircraft lost altitude as it continued over Thy and Mors. A few minutes later, it crashed in Risgaarde Bredning in the Limfjord off Grættrup. Five crew members were killed in the crash, while the two survivors were captured by the German. With usual German thoroughness, the fire was recorded: 106 rounds with a 2cm AA gun, 47 rounds with a 3.7cm AA gun and 227 rounds with a 10.5cm AA gun.

While this was going on, the other 15 aircraft from 5 Group laid their 89 mines in the Kattegat. The *Kriegsmarine* was therefore forced to close nine of the forced routes in the Kattegat, as well as five anchorages on the east coast of Jutland, until the minesweepers had cleared the way again. In the *Kriegsmarine*'s war diary for 4 October, the commander, *Admiral* Wurmbach, noted:

> Unfortunately, these enemy minelayers were again carried out without our own effective night fighter defence.

This was not entirely correct. A German night fighter JU 88 flown by *Oberleutnant* August Györy from *5/NJG 3* had taken off from Fliegerhorst Aalborg West when the radar message was received. He headed west and passed the west coast near Lemvig. He spotted the Lancaster and followed it until it approached Hanstholm. He attacked the British bomber, which burst into flames. As mentioned, it continued south-eastwards over Mors and Salling until, in a dive, it hit the water in Risgaarde Bank and exploded. The German pilot could see five parachutes leaving the aircraft, but three were engulfed in flames. The pilot and the AA battery shared the credit for the shooting down.

Vizeadmiral Wurmbach salutes the guard in front of Hotel Royal in Nyborg.

The laying of mines that night was nevertheless 'the straw that broke the camel's back.' Wurmbach demanded a sufficiently large night fighter force from the *Luftwaffe* to prevent the British minelayers from reaching their target areas in Danish waters. His demands were met. During the following week, 120 night fighters were assigned to this task. However, there were

1943	Direct Attack		sunk	Tonnage sunk	Damaged ships		A/C losses	
quarter	Sorties	attacks	ships	BRT	numbers	tonnage	A/C	%
jan-mar	2190	158	3	5258	0	0	29	1,3
apr-jun	5851	858	27	63048	3	9221	101	1,7
jul-sept	4664	579	15	8818	3	9779	48	1,0
okt-dec	4158	398	9	19519	4	*25194	51	1,2
In total	16883	1993	54	96643	10	44194	229	1,4

1943	Minelaying		sunk	Tonnage sunk	Damaged ships		A/C losses	
quarter	Sorties	laid	ships	BRT	numbers	tonnage	A/C	%
jan-mar	1687	3602	40	27286	4	8309	61	3,6
apr-jun	1888	5305	62	70625	8	20354	56	3,0
jul-sept	1210	3218	33	1438	8	*24967	23	1,9
okt-dec	975	2852	22	6868	4	6988	22	2,3
In total	5760	14977	157	106217	24	60618	162	2,8

Comparative results obtained by the Royal Air Force from Minelaying and from Direct Attacks on Enemy Shipping at sea 1943. Includes air attack on 20 October 1943 on the 17,000 GRT hospital ship MS *Strassburg* (former Dutch passenger ship MS *Baloeran*) which hit a mine on 1 September 1943 en route from Rotterdam to Hamburg and therefore grounded. British torpedo boats fired on the ship on 19 September. According to several sources, the hospital ship was equipped with anti-aircraft guns.

1944								
	Direct Attack		sunk	Tonnage sunk	Damaged ships		A/C losses	
quarter	Sorties	attacks	ships	BRT	numbers	tonnage	A/C	%
jan-mar	2882	440	18	34617	4	20665	34	1,2
apr-jun	5382	923	34	28862	7	20978	44	0,8
jul-sept	5440	1648	75	79381	6	12562	77	1,4
okt-dec	3751	725	37	48003	23	74639	44	1,2
In total	17455	3736	164	190863	40	128844	199	1,1

1944	Minelaying							
	Minelaying		sunk	Tonnage sunk	Damaged ships		A/C losses	
quarter	Sorties	Laid	ships	BRT	numbers	tonnage	A/C	%
jan-mar	1554	4234	41	35294	10	14720	18	1,2
apr-jun	2130	7181	68	35910	10	32825	33	1,5
jul-sept	761	3042	53	28937	27	41325	20	2,6
okt-dec	686	3043	41	35945	34	40179	13	1,9
In total	5131	17500	203	136086	81	129049	84	1,6

Comparative results obtained by the Royal Air Force from Minelaying and from Direct Attacks on Enemy Shipping, 1944.

only trained pilots for about half of the planes, and there was a severe rationing of aviation fuel. This all prompted *Admiral* Wurmbach to note the following in his war diary on 9 October: 'Unfortunately, this means that an effective defence against enemy minelaying aircraft still cannot be expected.' And he was right.[74] Looking again at the RAF's activities against enemy ships throughout Europe in 1943–1944, the ratio of direct air strikes to mine laying was virtually unchanged.[75]

The advantages of minelaying over direct air strikes on ships were still clear. In 1943, it took 313 aircraft to sink an enemy ship using direct air strikes, in comparison it only took 37 mine laying aircraft. Looking at the total tonnage, an average of 6 GRT was still sunk per aircraft that carried out air strikes, while minelayers had sunk an average of 18 GRT per aircraft. So from a military point of view, the mine laying was still a great success. The aircrews were perhaps most interested in the loss rate, which was not so good for the 'gardeners'. It was actually twice as high, but with a loss rate of 2.8 percent, it was still considered an acceptable level in the RAF. During 1944, the loss rate came down to 1.6 percent, thereby approaching the figure for direct air attack losses, which went from 1.4 to 1.1. Now only 106 aircraft were needed to sink a ship via air strikes, while 25 minelaying aircraft could achieve the same. Air strikes sank 11 GRT per aircraft, while minelaying aircraft sank 27 GRT per aircraft.

10.8 Sweden's Situation 1941–1944

During 1940, the Swedish Government negotiated an agreement with the warring parties on free shipping to and from the Atlantic. The number of voyages was limited and the cargo ships involved in this traffic had to follow very specific forced routes. In 1941, international traffic accounted for 12 percent of the country's imports, rising to 20 percent in 1942. Most of the supply of hides and leather, wool and cotton, vegetable and mineral oils, concentrated feed, coffee, tobacco and grain were imported in this way. During these years, most of the traffic went to the US and back. When the US was drawn into the war in December 1942, Argentina became the primary destination for the ships instead.

British magnetic mines in the southern Kattegat sank seven Swedish merchant ships in 1942, and when British minelaying in the waters south of Denmark intensified in 1943, three more Swedish merchant ships were hit by mine explosions. In the spring, a shipping office was set up in the most important Swedish harbours, where ship masters could obtain sailing directions through the mine-strewn routes at any time.[76] Nevertheless, five merchant ships were sunk by British mines during 1944. In the summer of 1944, the mine danger and

74 Airwar over Denmark, <http://www.flensted.eu.com/1944137.shtml>. Letter from Frank Weber to Mr Sieg, 3 May 1990. <http://www.airmen.dk/p378t.htm>.

75 Source <http://www.derbysulzers.com/shipbaloeran.html>. Roskill incorrectly calls the ship *Balderan* in table 3, p.94. 1943: Stephen W. Roskill, *The War at Sea 1939–45*, vol. 2 (London: HMSO, 1956), Table 34 p.392 and table 35 p.394; *Ibid.*, vol. 3 1 (London: HMSO, 1960), Table 3 p.94 and table 5 p.96; *Ibid.*, vol. 3 1 (London: HMSO, 1960), Table 17 p.288, table 18 p.289; *Ibid.*, vol. 3 2 (London: HMSO, 1962), Table 29 p.139, table 30 p.142.

76 Rolf Vallerö, *Svenska handelsflottans krigsförluster under det andra världskriget* (Stockholm: 1963), p.18.

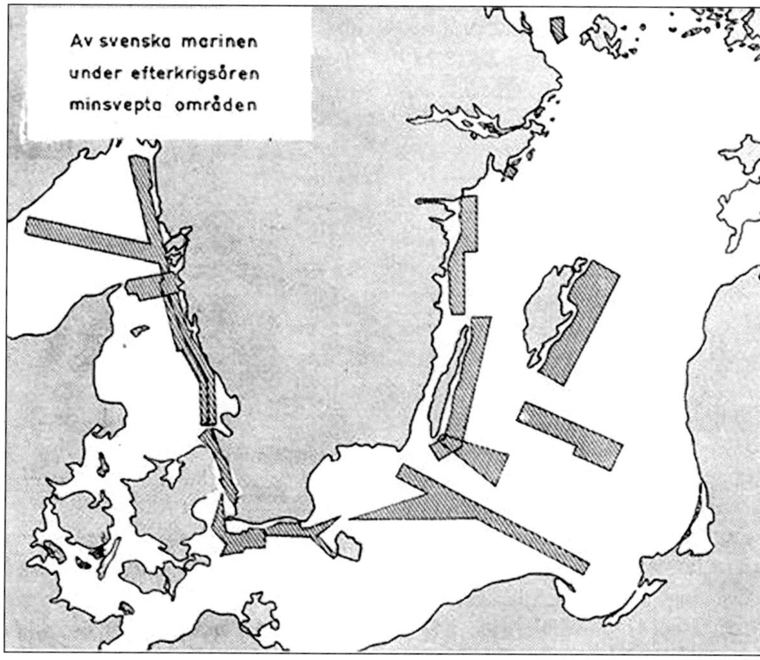

Areas that Swedish minesweepers surveyed for mines after 1945.

repeated air attacks on shipping traffic carrying iron ore to Germany and coke back along the Danish west coast led to a halt in the possibility of taking out Swedish war insurance on the route. This brought traffic to an immediate halt.[77]

By 5 August 1943, the transit route between Germany and Norway had been definitively blocked. The tide of war had turned against Germany's favour and Sweden no longer felt compelled to allow these transports into occupied Norway. This was part of the reason for a reversal of Swedish foreign policy in favour of the Allies.

Between 1939 and 1945, new naval vessels were built for the Swedish Navy, including 38 new minesweepers. They were supplemented by a total of 69 auxiliary minesweepers, mostly consisting of converted fishing boats. During the war, these vessels neutralised a total of 3,775 sea mines and escorted more than 17,000 merchant ships.[78] This probably explains the relatively low loss figures due to mines. It is also worth noting that the average gross tonnage sunk inside the cordon was significantly lower than that sunk outside.

Sinking Swedish merchant ships inside and outside the German Skagerrak Barrier

The overview below includes all ships sunk that were used to transport passengers, mail or cargo in the period 8 April 1940 – 8 May 1945, broken down by position and cause.[79]

77 Rolf Vallerö, *Svenska handelsflottans krigsförluster under det andra världskriget* (Stockholm: 1963), p.20.

78 Commander's Book 2003, www.flottansman.se/uploads/angelholm/orlogsbok03.pdf

79 Rolf Vallerö, *Svenska handelsflottans krigsförluster under det andra världskriget* (Stockholm: 1963), p.51, table 12.

Reason	Inside the cordon		Outside the cordon	
	Number of ships	GRT	Number of ships	GRT
Mined	36	60.863	10	40.944
Mined or torpedoed	1	1.046	1	1.972

In Finland, during July 1944, Russian troops were pushing the German troops back so far that they were likely to be withdrawn to the southern end of the Baltic Sea. In this situation, the British Prime Minister, Winston Churchill, offered in a telegram to Stalin on 4 August to send six submarines across the Channel from the White Sea to the northern end of the Baltic Sea. They could help to cut off the withdrawal of German troops. Stalin replied the next day that unfortunately the canal was so badly damaged by the Germans that it would not be opened until spring. He therefore suggested that the six submarines be sent in through Danish waters to the Baltic Sea, as had been done during World War I. A week later, on 12 August, Churchill regretfully informed Stalin that the possibility of sending submarines into the Baltic Sea through the Skagerrak and Kattegat had now been investigated, but that this was not possible due to not only both the German minefields and net blockades, but also the extensive British minefields.[80]

The German Navy in Denmark experienced its most difficult period in the autumn of 1944 and around the turn of the year. It had to do without many ships that were sabotaged while under repair in shipyards and harbours. The laying of mines continued with renewed vigour after the invasion of France. Then, in the final months of the year, a new threat emerged – British aircraft consistently attacking shipping targets in the Skagerrak and Kattegat.

Aircraft from 489 Squadron attack an armed trawler shortly after D-Day.

80 Winston S. Churchill, *Krigskorrespondance mellem Churchill og Stalin, 1941–1945* (Förlaget Rosenkilde 2nd edition 2010), pp.297–301.

Chapter 11

11.1 1945 – The Endgame in Danish Waters

The RAF continually mined the Danish waters, which by the turn of 1944–1945 were heavily trafficked. As the Russians took the harbours on the Baltic one by one, a large number of German ships headed out into the open sea. But the RAF's targeted efforts against the German minesweepers were beginning to pay off. Time and time again, German ships had to sail through mined fields without minesweeper assistance. The countless air strikes put the German minesweepers under severe mental and physical pressure. Several were damaged by anti-minesweeper mines and sought out the North German harbours for repairs, but the systematic air attacks on these harbours made the work impossible. A large number of minesweepers were also sunk or otherwise neutralised in the ports by Allied air raids, and in Denmark by saboteurs, including British-trained SOE operatives. The number of German minesweepers was therefore significantly reduced by the winter of 1944–1945.

The invasion of Normandy had cost the German U-boat fleet heavy losses. A large part had then travelled to Norway to regroup and repair any damage. For the British, it was obvious that as soon as the German U-boats had regained their strength, they would resume attacks on the Allied shipping convoys in the Atlantic. On 2 September 1944, almost three months after the Normandy invasion, the German naval command had ordered the expansion of the U-boat bases in Norway on the grounds that the future U-boat war would be fought from here. In fact, this was the only option available after the loss of the French Atlantic coast.

Since the beginning of the war, the Baltic Sea had been a training area for the German U-boat crews. One of the best places for the British to strike the U-boats was therefore the waters of the Baltic Sea to Norway – the Danish waters – when the U-boats had to be transferred from their training bases to their operational bases. Finally, shipping between Norway and Germany was the last important source of raw materials for German war production, especially after Sweden closed its harbours to trade with Germany in September 1944. However, it was the U-boats that initially caught the attention of the British, and it was Coastal Command that was tasked with hunting them down.

11.2 British Anti-Ship Units

In late August to mid-September 1944, 58 and 502 Squadrons from 18 Group were transferred to Stornoway in the Hebrides to carry out anti-submarine patrols, both day and night.[1] Both squadrons flew Halifax bombers equipped with radar, and were thus able to detect enemy vessels without visual contact. On 4 October 1944, the two Halifax squadrons were informed that in future they would mainly conduct nighttime anti-ship patrols. The area of operation was along the Norwegian coast and the Skagerrak and Kattegat, but they were to concentrate primarily on the shipping routes between Oslo, Kristiansand and the Danish harbours.[2] The target was the German ship transport of iron ore and other raw materials from the Norwegian harbours, materials that were very much-needed for German war production. [3]

Additional units in 18 Group were assembled in the so-called 'strike wings'. These were units that were specially equipped for daytime attacks on ships, and were now also tasked with attacking shipping along the Norwegian coast. These units were equipped with rockets and 20mm cannon with armour-piercing rounds. The latter were normally used against enemy flak, while the rockets were used to sink or damage ships. At Banff Air Station in north-eastern Scotland, 248, 235 and 143 Squadrons were stationed, all flying Mosquitos. These squadrons made up the Banff Strike Wing. Banff also had a section from 333 Squadron, which was a Norwegian unit. This squadron, also equipped with Mosquitos, flew reconnaissance flights for the Banff Strike Wing. The pilots and navigators of the 333 Squadron were, of course, specially qualified to find German ships in the many Norwegian fjords. Later, it became the practice to send two Mosquitos from 333 Squadron as reconnaissance aircraft ahead of the main force.[4]

The escalation of British minelaying operations in Danish waters in the autumn of 1944 had worried the Commander-in-Chief of the *Kriegsmarine* in Denmark, *Admiral* Wurmbach (from December 1944 titled *Admiral Skagerrak*). In his judgement, the only effective remedy against the minelaying was an increase in the night fighter force. Therefore, as mentioned above, at the end of September he asked the naval warfare command for more night fighters. On 30 September 1944 he received the answer that *Luftflotte Reich* had just built up a night fighter centre of gravity in the Jutland-Slesvig-Holsten area, namely two groups in Grove, one group in Westerland, one group in Schleswig and one group in Lübeck. *Luftflotte Reich* was also preparing to transfer a night fighter unit to Lister in Norway. While Coastal Command intensified anti-ship patrols in the Skagerrak and Kattegat, and Bomber Command increased the number of mines laid, the Germans were busy building a stronger night fighter defence in Denmark.

The British Admiralty had a very precise insight into the shipping traffic between Norway and Denmark: which harbours the ships sailed from, when they departed, which warships made up the escort, why the ships were delayed, which routes they took, and so on. All this information came from various intelligence sources. One source was the interception of

1 K.A. Merrick, *Halifax : An Illustrated History of a Classic World War Two Bomber* (London: Ian Allan, 1980), p.131; Air 27/545. 58 Squadron. ORB – Administration September 1944; Air 27/1960. 502 Sqdn. ORB, dd. 8–14.9.44.

2 K.A. Merrick, Halifax : An Illustrated History of a Classic World War Two Bomber (London: Ian Allan, 1980), p.131; Air 27/545. 58 Squadron. ORB – operations October 1944.

3 Air 15/391. Note on the employment of the anti-shipping squadrons and 18 Group, dd. 19.4.45 (retrospective).

4 Frank Weber et al, *Bomber over Denmark* (Nyt Nordisk Forlag, 2012), p.686.

German radio communications between the ships and the various bases, which the British had been able to monitor since 1941 after breaking the Enigma codes. The British were particularly interested in troop transports, and all messages relating to these were studied so closely that they could be mapped and followed in detail, and sometimes even predicted. This radio intelligence reached its peak in the last months of 1944 and early 1945, when the Germans were transporting large amounts of equipment and troops from Norway. If there was a gap in the information, for example a missing departure and arrival time for a convoy, the missing information could often be obtained via reports from agents. This information was very reliable and one of the Admiralty's important sources was, as mentioned, the British naval attaché in Stockholm. There can be little doubt that one of the attaché's important sources was the Danish intelligence service. All relevant information naturally flowed to Coastal Command, Bomber Command and Fighter Command, so when the campaign against German shipping around Norway and Denmark began, it was possible to coordinate operations. [5]

11.3 The First Airstrikes

From October 1944 until February 1945, the British Admiralty's prioritisation of ship targets was:

1. Enemy naval units of all sizes.
2. Military support vessels.
3. Cargo ships.[6]

The consequence of this prioritisation was that if Coastal Command patrols found an enemy convoy, the attack should primarily be directed against ships of the type that had the highest priority. In many cases, however, the target was just a few cargo ships, which were then attacked without hesitation.

In Danish waters, German naval vessels mostly comprised smaller units up to the destroyer class, if we disregard the light cruiser *Nürnberg*. In addition, there were motor torpedo boats, minesweepers, barrage destroyers, and flak ships. The last type, 'flak ships' or 'anti-aircraft ships', was an English term that covered several types of ships. These included German outpost boats and U-boat destroyers. These boats were originally built as fishing trawlers and converted for various naval purposes. As the name suggests, the ships were equipped with extra anti-aircraft guns. Air strikes on these targets should therefore be seen as part of an overall offensive against German traffic in Danish waters. By keeping minesweepers as a high priority target, support could be provided to Bomber Command's extensive minelaying campaign. Preventing the German Navy from clearing the mines effectively would result in casualties, or at the very least create major delays in shipping traffic.

5 Frank Weber et al, *Bomber over Denmark* (Nyt Nordisk Forlag, 2012), pp.686–687; ADM 1117490. Coordination of air attack on enemy shipping within range of shore-based aircraft, dd. 11.11.1944.

6 Christina J. M. Goulter, *A Forgotten Offensive: Royal Air Force Coastal Command's Anti-Shipping Campaign 1940–1945* (London: Routledge, 1995), p.255.

October 1944 was a busy month for 58 Squadron and 502 Squadron They carried out a total of 27 attacks, but in night raids the results were often difficult to ascertain. Only in one case did they succeed in setting fire to a merchant ship and its escort with certainty. The fact that aircrews could not positively determine the outcome of their attacks did not necessarily mean that their mission had been unsuccessful.

Pilot Officer Crick of 58 Squadron spotted the German freighter *Braunau* on the night of 16 October. The ship was observed north of Skagen on its way from Oslo to Danzig with 900 tonnes of water in ballast. The aircraft attacked at 01:05 and dropped five 500-pound bombs, but due to the German flak, Crick had to make evasive manoeuvres and therefore the crew could not observe the result, but the bombs fell so close to the ship that they punched holes in the hull. However, these were not too large to be plugged, and *Braunau* then headed for Copenhagen to be repaired. But, the ship only made it as far as the northern Kattegat, where it ran into a mine on 17 October. A distress signal was sent out and a tugboat towed the cargo ship to Copenhagen. There were no docks available, and after a month the ship was towed to Nakskov, where it was still docked when the war ended.

Coastal Command was well aware that the ship had been decommissioned. This was known through photo reconnaissance aircraft that constantly took pictures of the Danish harbours. It is not possible in this book to describe all the air raids that took place in Danish waters in the last six months of the war, but only to look at their impact on shipping between Norway and Denmark, especially the troop transports and their escorts. However, the attack on the *Braunau* illustrates the pressure that the British wanted to put on German shipping through both minelaying and air raids.[7]

Coastal Command's increased efforts in the Skagerrak and Kattegat were the direct reason why *Admiral* Wurmbach strongly favoured forced convoy sailing between Norway and Denmark. Ships were to gather at specific anchorages to form a convoy and would be accompanied by flak ships and minesweepers. However, Wurmbach did not believe it was possible to provide sufficient protection without additional escort ships, which he reported to the *Kriegmarine's Oberkommando Ost* on 16 October. The same day, he was told that the increasing ship losses naturally forced the navy to increase the security of the convoys. If it was not possible to muster the required number of escort ships, the convoys would have to be held back until the desired strength was reached. The answer ended with a reminder that safety came before speed. Escort vessels remained Wurmbach's big problem, and he realised that compulsory convoy sailing could not be introduced until more escort vessels were available. Therefore, the ships still had to sail without adequate protection. To shorten the voyage, ships travelling to Oslo were allowed to sail to Horten, about 100km south of Oslo. Wurmbach also called in vain for continuous fighter protection from Aalborg West. However, only a training unit was available here, which had not yet been trained for operational deployment. The *General der Luftwaffe* in Denmark had no other fighter aircraft available to him.[8]

7 Frank Weber et al, *Bomber over Denmark* (Nyt Nordisk Forlag, 2012), p.687.

8 Frank Weber et al, *Bomber over Denmark* (Nyt Nordisk Forlag, 2012), p.688. Adm. Skagerrak, 22/261. October 1944.

At the end of October, four large troop carriers were transferred to the Baltic Sea. They were the *Mar Del Plata, Isar, Donau* and *Wolta*. This created an acute need for transport ships on the route from Norway to Denmark.[9]

11.4 German Problems With Troop Transfer

Although Coastal Command could not show great results in either October or November, their increased presence still caused Wurmbach great concern. Of course, his concern was not diminished by the fact that two *sperrbrechere* were damaged by mines in early November. This left only one operational *sperrbrecher* in Danish waters, and there was no prospect of reinforcements. The Danish shipyards were so overloaded that there was a long wait for repairs. However, one *sperrbrecher* was under repair, and it became operational again shortly afterwards.[10]

In mid-November 1944, 26,000 soldiers from *Volksgrenadierdivision* Nr 560 in Oslo were waiting to be transferred to Denmark. The two large troop transport ships *Kniprode* and *Moltkefels*, of 10,123 GRT and 7,862 GRT respectively, were available. In addition, three smaller transport ships were deployed in a so-called fast route, namely *Jupiter, Mars* and *Bretagne* of 560 GRT, 2,469 GRT and 3,295 GRT. From 21 November, the *Gijon* of 3,353 GRT was also to be deployed on this express route. To provide the transport ships with sufficient protection, a total of 25 escort vessels were needed. However, only two destroyers, the *Galste* and *Riedel*, four minesweepers, three torpedo boats, the two *sperrbrechere* and two unspecified escort ships were available. The navy was therefore still short of one *sperrbrechere* and 11 other escort ships. However, reinforcements were on the way. The torpedo boats *T17* and *T20* arrived in Aarhus on 19 November and the *T33*, which had been in the shipyard, was ready again on 25 November. On 17 and 26 November, *Marineoberkommando Ost* had also promised *Admiral* Wurmbach two more minesweepers and the torpedo boats *T13, T16, T19* and *T21*.[11]

The escort vessels were in place, but additional transport capacity was needed. Some of the ships that had been transferred to the Baltic Sea at the end of October were now sent back to the Skagerrak and Kattegat. These were the two large transport vessels *Dona* and *Isar*, of 9,035 GRT and 9,026 GRT, as well as the smaller 1,923 GRT *Hansa 1*, the 1,454 GRT *Süderau* and *Rolandsbeck* of 1,845 GRT.[12]

At this time, the Commander-in-Chief of the *Kriegsmarine*, Karl Dönitz, was optimistic about the transport of troops from Norway to Denmark. The desired ship tonnage was available, both for troop transport and protection. At the same time, the Norwegian railway from north to south, along which the troops were transported to southern Norway, could easily handle the capacity. Therefore, the transports had to be able to proceed at the desired pace. The transport could now only be delayed by bad weather, air raids and a possible lack of escort vessels. Hitler was less calm, and during a meeting with Dönitz on 30 November 1944,

9 ADM 223/43. P.1. Oslofjord – Denmark Troop Convoys. November 1944.

10 Frank Weber et al, *Bomber over Denmark* (Nyt Nordisk Forlag, 2012), p.689.

11 Adm. Skagerrak, 22/261. November 1944; Adm. Skagerrak, 4/97. November 1944. Baltic Sea situation overview.

12 ADM 223/43. S.1 Oslofjord – Denmark Troop Convoys. 28.11.44.

he pointed out how important it was that the *SS Gebirgsdivision Nr 6* and *Gebirgsdivision Nr 2* – a total of 36,000 men – were transferred from Norway to Denmark as soon as possible.[13]

Coastal Command was aware of German plans to move troops from Norway southwards to the troubled fronts in Eastern and Western Europe, so Air Chief Marshal Sir W. Sholto Douglas wanted the German shipping convoys to be attacked during the day by all units available. There was a problem, however, as the two strike wings did not have the necessary range. It was not possible to increase the Beaufighter's range any further, but it was possible with the Mosquito. Therefore, Sholto Douglas wanted the three squadrons equipped with Mosquitos, i.e. 143, 235 and 248 Squadrons to be fitted with 450 litre drop tanks.

The German night fighter threat was now also a factor that had to be taken seriously. Both Coastal Command and Bomber Command had realised that aircraft operating south of Anholt were particularly vulnerable to night fighter attacks. It was therefore decided that 18 Group should not operate south of Anholt unless there were particularly attractive targets there, but instead concentrate on the area between Oslo and Anholt.

The primary task of 58 Squadron and 502 Squadron continued to be to patrol between Norway and Denmark. Despite the bad weather, it was still possible to find and attack several ships in December. However, this did not seem to significantly hamper the transports. It was not until the night of 28/29 December 1944 that they finally managed to damage a ship travelling in convoy. It was the tanker *Orion* with 6,000 tonnes of oil on board, which together with *Jupiter* was escorted by the torpedo boat *T20*. The ships were on their way from Frederikshavn to Oslo Fjord.

11.5 Changed German Tactics

The attack on *Orion* gave *Admiral* Wurmbach cause for new considerations, and already on 29 December 1944 he had suggested to *Marineoberkommando Ost* that they should try alternating sailing during the day and at night, as approaches to the Skagerrak area were extremely rare during the day and during periods with a full moon. The intention was to reduce the risk of attack and utilise the time when there were no approaches.

Marineoberkommando Ost agreed to the experiment, but did not want daylight sailing to become the rule rather than the exception, as all experience had shown that as soon as the British discovered an important target, reinforcements arrived very quickly. This had cost the *Kriegsmarine* significant losses, and there was particular concern about letting the troop transports sail during the day. As early as 30 December, the convoys began to sail by day without being attacked by British aircraft. This alternation between day and night sailing remained a rule until March 1945. The British Admiralty was quick to notice that the German convoys were now also travelling by day, but it was believed that the departure times were determined more by the mine situation and the number of escort vessels available than by the need for a safer crossing. Coastal Command's 18 Group could do nothing to exploit the change in German tactics until the Banff Strike Wing increased its radius

13 Gerhard Wagner, *Lagevorträge des Oberbefehlshabers der Kriegsmarine 1939–1945* (Munich: 1972), pp.618–619.

of action with the extra tanks. Therefore, at *Admiral* Wurmbach's suggestion, the convoys were given some extra sailing hours where the risk of air attack was very low.

The large accumulation of troops in Norway, waiting for a ship to Denmark, made it necessary to add more transport ships to the area, and on 12 December, the High Command of the Norwegian Navy announced plans to reinforce the Oslo-Aarhus voyage with the troop transport ships *Neidenfels* of 7,838 GRT, *Ulanga* of 6,859 GRT, *Darss* of 7,000 GRT, and the *Angamos* of 3,540 GRT. Around 23 December, all the ships except the *Angamos* had arrived, bringing the total tonnage up to 72,632 GRT.[14]

As of 1 January 1945, Bomber Command concentrated its minelaying efforts exclusively on the waters between Norway and Denmark, Danish waters and the Western Baltic Sea. No more mines were laid west of the Weser River and east of Swinemünde.[15]

Bomber Command had thus intensified the laying of mines throughout the 'Silverthorn' in Kattegat, but especially along the Swedish coast. Ship traffic was more focussed on the Swedish territorial waters as the mines accumulated in the Kattegat. In order not to risk too many cases of mines drifting into Swedish territory after the high-level method became the norm, Bomber Command had emphasised the necessary precautions, including avoiding getting too close to Swedish waters. But now, as the intervals between encounters with German night fighters increased, the British minelaying aircraft occasionally carried out operations using the 'old' and more accurate low-level method.[16]

German troops were now in retreat right across Europe. The Eastern Front was advancing westwards at a rapid pace, and in January the German defence lines collapsed and Russian forces reached the German territories on the Baltic Sea. The *Kriegsmarine* began a large-scale evacuation of fleeing civilians and wounded soldiers. The initial plan was to simply move them further west in Germany, but the German Baltic Sea harbours were unable to cope with the large numbers. Therefore, on 4 February Hitler issued an order that the ships should sail to Denmark to relieve the transport situation in Germany. *Admiral* Wurmbach directed the ships to Copenhagen and Aarhus. The first ship arrived in Copenhagen on 11 February with 2,500 wounded and 200 refugees from Königsberg on board.[17]

Under pressure from the head of Coastal Command, Air Chief Marshal Sir Sholto Douglas, the attack list was changed in February 1945. The new prioritisation list read:

1. Submerged U-boats.
2. Pocket battleships.
3. Cruisers and large minelayers.
4. Tankers.
5. Troop transports.
6. Merchant ships.
7. Other naval vessels.[18]

14 Frank Weber et al, *Bomber over Denmark* (Nyt Nordisk Forlag, 2012), pp.690–692.

15 Air Ministry. Air Historical Branch, *The RAF in Maritime War*, vol. 5 *Atlantic & Home Waters – The Victorious Phase May 1944-May 1945* (London: Air Historical Branch, 2012). p.145.

16 Poul Bech, *Søkrig i danske farvande under Anden Verdenskrig 1939–1942* (Schønberg: 2008), p.177.

17 Poul Bech, *Søkrig i danske farvande under Anden Verdenskrig 1939–1942* (Schønberg: 2008), pp.198–199.

18 Christina J.M. Goulter, *A Forgotten Offensive: Royal Air Force Coastal Command's Anti-Shipping Campaign 1940–1945* (London: Routledge, 1995), p.255.

However, this new prioritisation had no significant impact on the situation in Danish waters, and there were several reasons for this. As there were no pocket battleships and only the occasional light cruiser in Danish waters, only U-boats had higher priority than cargo ships. However, attacks on U-boats were rare in Danish waters until March 1945. There were not many tankers left in Danish waters, so the troop ships, which now regularly travelled through Danish waters between Norway and Denmark, had the highest priority. Even though the Allies prioritised attacking the troop transports, this did not mean that they were the only targets. On the patrols, the planes attacked virtually every ship target that there was available. It was very important for the Allies to try to prevent, or at least delay, the transports. The goal of the operations was therefore now more tactical in nature, whereas earlier in the war it had been based on strategic objectives, especially the traffic of raw materials from Sweden southwards and coal from Germany northwards. Previously the goal had been to hit the German war economy at several points, it was now to provide direct and indirect support to the Allied Armies.

In January, there had been storm warnings for 17 days. However, this did not prevent the Germans from transferring more troops from Norway to Denmark than in December 1944. Hitler had even told Dönitz several times during January that things were moving too slowly. Each time, Dönitz had to explain that the severe weather and especially the British mines made the situation difficult. The minesweepers and escort ships could not cope with the stormy weather, and there were far too few of them. However, Dönitz reassured Hitler that at the end of January, a *sperrbrecher* was transferred to alleviate the situation, and another *sperrbrecher*, which was in the shipyard for repairs, would soon follow. Supplemented by two more transport ships, there was hope for the future.[19]

However, February was as bad as January in terms of weather. The RAF could not carry out patrols for more than 11 nights that month, and these operations were hampered in the latter part of the month by the increased night fighter activity due to the full moon.[20] On the Eastern Front, the German Armies were being pushed further and further back, and Hitler wanted the shipping between the evacuation harbours in the east and Germany to be reinforced. At a meeting with Hitler on 17 February 1945, Dönitz explained that all options for increasing this shipping had been exhausted unless the transports between Norway and Denmark were weakened, which he would not recommend. Dönitz hoped that it would be possible to transfer *Infanteriedivision Nr 169* to Denmark within the next two weeks. However, he was unsuccessful.

The ships *Mars* and *Jupiter* were transferred to the Baltic Sea on 22 February. *Kniprode*, which had been in the shipyard in Aarhus since January, followed the same day and was deployed as a hospital ship. Five days later it was the turn of *Moltkefels* and on 27 February the ship also set sail for the Baltic Sea. This departure of ships did not concern *Admiral* Wurmbach, however, as the transport of troops to southern Norway did not happen any faster and the remaining tonnage of just over 45,000 GRT, across 8 ships, was sufficient to keep up.[21]

19 Adm. Skagerrak, 22/262. on 7.2.45; Gerhard Wagner, *Lagevorträge des Oberbefehlshabers der Kriegsmarine 1939–1945* (Munich: 1972), pp.631–632, 639 & 642.

20 Frank Weber et al, *Bomber over Denmark* (Nyt Nordisk Forlag, 2012), p.696.

21 Adm. Skagerrak, 22/262. on 27.2.45; Adm. Skagerrak, 4/97.1. on 15.2.45; Gerhard Wagner, *Lagevorträge des Oberbefehlshabers der Kriegsmarine 1939–1945* (Munich: 1972), pp.654–655.

In Bomber Command, Harris was well aware that victory was within sight, but he did not fully share the Admiralty's new policy of cancelling all mines in Danish waters to a life of only 52 days. In a letter to the Air Ministry on 7 February, he complained about the decision. In his judgement, it would be more than 52 days before it would be necessary for the Allied forces to pass through the Danish Straits and Belts. Thus, Bomber Command aircrews were forced to continue to make unnecessary and dangerous sorties to maintain the minefields.[22]

The answer came promptly three days later. Not from the Air Ministry, but from the Allied Naval Commander Expeditionary Force. It stated that in light of the rapidly changing war situation, it had become necessary to review the lifetime of mines in Northern European waters. As a result, all mines in the Baltic Sea and Danish waters south of Skagen were given a 54-day life span. For mines in the South Norwegian fjords and in the North Sea off The Netherlands and Germany, the lifespan was set at 18 days. Harris agreed that it could take more than 54 days before it became necessary for the Western Allied naval forces to pass through Danish waters. However, in order not to create complications with the Soviet Union's unknown intentions, they considered further reducing the mine life to just 28 days! After confirming whether this was SHAEF policy, the Allied Naval Commander Expeditionary Force would notify the Admiralty.[23] The Air Ministry, after expressing great understanding of Harris' views, and after obtaining the Admirality's views on the proposal from SHAEF, which was negative, chose to maintain the agreed mine life of 54 days. At the same time, they understood that Bomber Command could not compensate for the shorter mine life by increasing mine laying activity.[24]

In March 1945, the German minesweeper organisation completely collapsed. In one month, the number of German ships sunk by mines rose to 26, while 11 more were damaged. In April, these numbers dropped to 16 and 7 respectively. However, this must be seen in the context of the greatly reduced shipping traffic at this time.[25] British air attacks on shipping increased and they could now operate more or less unhindered. Only three times in March were German night fighters observed, but none of them attacked. The lack of aviation fuel for the *Luftwaffe* had become seriously noticeable.

Hitler was now interested in transferring the *Infantriedivision Nr 169* as quickly as possible, which he told Dönitz on 15 March. The *Grossadmiral* expected this to happen within a short time, especially since four-fifths of the division was already in Denmark at the time. But just two days later he had to inform Hitler that two more ships had been damaged, this time by mines. Three other ships would be deployed instead. But before these ships could be deployed, on 19 March another transport ship, the *Mar Del Plata*, struck a mine west of Sjællands Odde on its way from Aarhus to Oslo with 600 soldiers aboard. The ship was so badly damaged that it had to return to Aarhus with the assistance of tugboats, where it remained for the rest of the war. Dönitz was able to deliver

22 Air 14/705 From Harris to the Under Secretary of State, Air Ministry, 9.2.1945.

23 Air 14/705 From Supreme Headquarters Allied Expeditionary Force (SHAEF) to Air Staff, Bomber Command 12.2.1945.

24 Air 14/705 From the Under Secretary of State, Air Ministry to AOC-in-C Bomber Command, 21.2.1945.

25 Stephen W. Roskill, *The War at Sea 1939–45*, vol. 3 2 (London: HMSO, 1962), p.274.

this news to Hitler on 23 March, but at the same time he assured him that four more ships would be deployed on the route between Norway and Denmark.[26] The reinforcements did not arrive until a week later.

On 4 April, 153 Squadron of 1 Group in Bomber Command was ordered to participate with 5 Lancasters in a total force of 30 aircraft to lay mines in Oslo Fjord and in the Samsø Belt in the southern Kattegat. Although the minelaying had now been recognised as highly effective, the aircrews were concerned about the relatively high loss rate that still existed on these raids. The few German night fighters that could be kept flying despite the fuel shortage were manned by the most experienced and efficient pilots. Bomber Command realised that with the expanded radar system in Denmark, including Læsø and Anholt, combined with effective night fighter control in Grove, it was still a very dangerous task.

The crews laying mines in the Kattegat felt they were being attacked by German night fighters coming out of the darkness from the west and could see the British aircraft as clear silhouettes with the light from undarkened Sweden as a background. Morale in 153 Squadron was therefore at the lowest point since its creation in October 1944 and the squadron commander, Wing Commander Francis Powley, put himself on the list of pilots for the upcoming raid. He was normally exempt from operational flying, but he wanted to set a good example and show that he was ready to take his turn. So he was there when the five Lancasters took off from Scampton at 19.07.

The long journey across the dark North Sea alone made many crew members shudder at the minimal chances of survival if the aircraft was forced to make an emergency landing in the cold water. During the winter period, the most you could survive in the North Sea was two minutes. Of the force that was to lay mines in the Samsø Belt, two Lancasters from 153 Squadron were attacked by a German JU88 night fighter. The attacker happened to be one of the most experienced night fighter pilots, *Major* Werner Husemann, Group Commander of *I/Nacht-jagdgeschwader 3*. On patrol over the target area, he first attacked Wing Commander Powley's aircraft and then Flight Lieutenant Winder's, which were both shot down over Kattegat.[27]

The night raid, which had cost the squadron commander and two crews their lives, was the last minelaying raid for this unit, and it was probably just as well for morale. Since the squadron's formation, 34 aircraft had carried out minelaying missions and laid 203 mines, but at the cost of four aircraft lost, two heavily damaged aircraft and the deaths of 27 of the most experienced crew members.[28]

A history of 153 Squadron, written by John A. Johns, describes what it was like to fly minelaying missions in general and especially the last months before the war ended:

26 Air 15/474. Survey of damaged shipping; ADM 223/43. SJ.Oslofjord – Denmark Troop Convoys. 18.3 and 24.3.45; Gerhard Wagner, *Lagevorträge des Oberbefehlshabers der Kriegsmarine 1939–1945* (Munich: 1972), pp.676, 678 and 684.

27 <https://www.wartimememoriesproject.com/ww2/view.php?uid=110432>. Husemann was awarded the Knight's Cross of the Iron Cross on 30 September 1944 after having his 30th kill recognised. That night, he added two more and ended the war with a total of 34 victories in over 250 night fighter missions. He died aged 94 in 2014. <https://en.wikipedia.org/wiki/Werner_Husemann>.

28 Air 27/1029 No 153 Squadron: Operations Record Book, 1944 Jan–1945 Sept.

Left to right: P/O Bob Purves the usual pilot of V – Victor (above) of B Flight 153 Squadron at RAF Scampton; S/L McClauchlan; W/C Powley, O/C 153 Squadron; S/L John Gee and F/L Art Winder. S/L Gee's crew were lost with W/C Powley on a minelaying sortie in the Kattegat on 4/5 April 1945. F/L Winder and his crew were also lost on the same operation.

It was also the practice of Bomber Command to rotate Gardening Ops around their squadrons – 153 Squadron was first given this task on 4 February 1945. The Squadron quickly found that certain aspects remained constant. Each Gardening operation required the squadron to provide five aircraft – never more, never less – each carrying six airborne magnetic/acoustic mines; each mine was 10 feet in length with a diameter of 18 inches and weighed around 1,500lbs (including an explosive charge of 740lbs). Take off was usually around dusk and return journey times were about 6 to 6½ hours duration. To avoid detection by enemy radar, the outward route was Base, Scarborough and (staying below 1,000 feet) out over the North Sea. With the exception of Heligoland Bight, on reaching longitude 6E and latitude 58N off the southern tip of Norway (a leg of 384 miles that took a little over two hours flying time), aircraft then climbed towards a point in the Skagerrak, south of the Oslo Fiord and north of the tip of Denmark, before reaching which they had levelled off at their predetermined dropping height of 11,000 feet. Having verified their position, they then set course for their designated area in the Kattegat or further into the Baltic Sea. From this point real problems arose. In the Kattegat there are very few deep-water channels suited to larger vessels, and these were well known to both contestants. Knowing just where the mines had to be dropped, enabled the Germans to vector their night fighters to best effect. The islands of Læsø and Anholt housed air defence controllers and radar stations. Neutral Sweden, with no need to operate a blackout, lay to the east of the bombers' route; German's fighters came up, hidden by the darkened background of occupied Denmark, to seek out the bombers which were silhouetted against the lights of Swedish towns. Clearly the advantages lay with the defenders. When turning south into the Kattegat, crews had to switch on H2S (the airborne radar which showed an image of the area being overflown) presenting them with excellent pictures of the coastlines of Denmark and Sweden, thus assisting them to fly an accurate track past Læsø and Anholt to the drop zone and allowing navigators to verify the wind speed and direction. Unfortunately, the H2S emissions could be picked up by the night fighters, who would 'home in' on the transmitting aircraft, whose only defence was to throw out 'Window' (flares) non-stop in the hope that it would confuse the attackers' homing devices. To reach the actual dropping zone, it was frequently necessary first to accurately determine the aircraft's position from an established location, and then fly directly to the release point, where the bomb doors were opened. Then followed what many crews have subsequently described as the longest minute of their lives – the release of mine number one, followed by a succession of 10 second intervals before dropping numbers two, three, four, five and six. All this at a constant speed, height and direction, thereby inviting attack from the lurking fighters. Mercifully there was no requirement to continue while the customary confirming aerial photograph of the target was taken – the evidence was recorded by photographing the H2S readings. Unlike the saturation raids flown against the German cities, where sheer weight of numbers provided a measure of protection, Gardening drops were conducted by individual attacks – albeit conforming to an overall design – so that crews felt themselves cruelly exposed to any enemy action. The German defences were often augmented by the addition of naval and other gunships, which, with ability to fire predicted flak at these individual targets, proved to be very accurate. Given their mobility they could be encountered almost anywhere along the bombers' route. From the foregoing, it will be apparent that Gardening operations were not welcomed by aircrew, who stoically accepted that they were more hazardous than other operations. Many particularly dreaded the fact that flights were made almost entirely over water, and invariably in total darkness. Should the aircraft be shot down or seriously crippled, the chances of survival were so negligible as to be nonexistent. To carry out a successful 'ditching' at night would require phenomenal luck for even the most highly skilled pilot, and the prospect of a subsequent launching of the dinghy in total darkness into a hostile sea, heavily encumbered by full flying kit, did not bear thinking about. Over land, crews could take their chances with a parachute jump; over water, even if successful, this would result in certain death from exposure. As found by sailors on Russian convoy duties, the survival time in northern waters during the winter months was unlikely to exceed two minutes. Lacking a satisfactory degree of heating – particularly to the aircraft's gun turrets – a substantial amount of clothing was normally donned before undertaking operational and/or high-level flying. Suspended from a thong round the neck were hung identity discs or 'dog-tags', giving name, service number and religious persuasion ... In many squadrons, these operations were regarded as useful introductory exercises for the harder tasks ahead; but this was not the case in 153 Squadron where generally the most experienced crews appeared on the Battle Order. Altogether, the squadron mounted 35 Gardening sorties, the task being shared unevenly by 18 of the 24 experienced crews.[29]

11.6 The Allies Take Stock Before The Final Act

All significant changes in German transports were recorded by British intelligence. Against this background, SHAEF issued a memorandum on 4 April 1945 stating that there had been a reduction in troop movements despite the fact that the enemy was anxious to continue the withdrawal of troops from Norway as quickly as possible. SHAEF's conclusion was that as a result of Bomber Command's minelaying and Coastal and Fighter Commands' air attacks in the area between Norway and Denmark, and intensive and continuous railway sabotage in both countries during the past three months, German transport had been seriously disrupted.

In Norway, there were still seven divisions that could be transferred and were badly needed by the German military command. Even if these troops could not reach the front lines and make a significant impact, they could still pose a potential threat if they fortified the Northern European harbours – this was probably mainly the North German harbours. The main conclusion of the memorandum was that the anti-ship campaign should continue despite the Allies' progress on all fronts.[30]

The aim was not only to prevent the transfer of troops and materiel from Norway to Germany, but also to prevent communication between the fortified harbours in Norway and Germany. By cutting off troops and supplies from reaching Norway, from where a U-boat war could continue after the fall of Germany, SHAEF hoped that Coastal Command could prevent an extension of the war.[31]

April 1945 was also the month in which the shipping in the Baltic Sea and Skagerrak-Kattegat suffered the greatest losses to date. A total of 14 Strike Wing operations were carried out in April, all with strong fighter escort. Mosquitos carried out repeated attacks on anchored ships in Oslo Fjord and on ships in the Skagerrak and Kattegat, while two Halifax squadrons ensured that German transports were not safe at night.[32]

29 John A. Johns. 'The History of 135. Squadron, Oct 44-Sept 45, Bomber Command, RAF (Salisbury: J.A.Johns, 1998) page 82–88.
30 Air 15/391. Memorandum from SHAEF dated 4.4.45. Subject: Movement of German Troops from Norway.
31 Air 15/391. Note on the employment of the Anti-shipping Squadrons of 18 Group, 8.4.45. Dated 9.4.45.
32 Stephen W. Roskill, *The War at Sea 1939–45*, vol. 3 2 (London: HMSO, 1962), p.281.

However, when troop transports from Norway to Denmark came to a virtual standstill at the end of April, it was not due to a lack of shipping tonnage, but because of a lack of troops in the ports of embarkation. Despite the many ship losses, as late as 17 April 1945, the *Kriegsmarine* considered the transports from Norway to be on schedule. But on 23 April, the tone was completely different: 'Attacks against the transports in the Baltic Sea, Skagerrak and off the coast of Norway are increasing. Own ship losses increasing.'[33]

By the end of April 1945, it was clear to the Allies that Germany's shipping was disintegrating. There was no longer such strong traffic around Norway or in the southern North Sea. The focal point was in the western part of the Baltic Sea, where a constant flow of ships carried refugees and troops from east to west. However, Dönitz had by no means given up the fight, and as late as 25 April, he did not want to hear talk of surrender in the North.[34]

As Norway was destined to be the centre of a future U-boat war, it is understandable that Dönitz was against a capitulation in the north. The first modern U-boat of the XXI type to sail on an operational mission did so from Bergen on 30 April, but before it saw combat, the war was over.[35]

In the last week of the war, German troops in northern Germany attempted to carry out a large-scale evacuation by ship from northern German harbours. These were the targets of extensive air raids in the days between 2 and 4 May.[36] The RAF's activities over the western part of the Baltic Sea and Danish waters were very hectic in this final phase, and it has not been possible to determine with certainty in all cases which units attacked which ship targets.

However, it was not only German troops that were evacuated. Thousands of German refugees and in some cases liberated concentration camp prisoners were on board some of the ships. There were therefore some incidents where refugee ships were attacked.[37] This was obviously not the intention of the RAF. But for the aircrews involved, it was often impossible to distinguish between a transport ship carrying troops and one carrying refugees. Of course, the situation was further complicated by the fact that several of the refugee ships were regular merchant vessels. These ships had been identified in Allied intelligence reports as participating in troop transports between Denmark, Norway and Germany.[38]

11.7 The Last Mines are 'Planted'

Bomber Command continuously laid mines in Danish waters and the western part of the Baltic Sea until 21–22 April, when 20 Lancasters from 6 Group laid the last mines in the Kattegat.[39]

33 Daily file: Seelage for April 1945.
34 Michael Salewski, *Die Deutsche Seekriegsleitung 1935–1945*, vol. 2 (Frankfurt am Main: 1975), p.544.
35 Alfred Price, *Aircraft versus Submarine* (London: Harper Collins, 1973), p.226.
36 Frank Weber et al, *Bomber over Denmark* (Nyt Nordisk Forlag, 2012), p.641.
37 Danish Maritime Accident Statistics (DSS) 1945. p.55; Air 15/474, A Survey of Damage Shipping in N. Germany and Denmark No. 20.
38 Danish Maritime Accident Statistics (DSS) 1945. p.55.
39 Martin Middlebrook & Chris Everitt, *The Bomber Command War Diaries: An Operational Reference Book 1939–1945* (Bungay: Viking, 1985), p.698. The only minelaying thereafter, the last of the war,

In 1945, almost 37 percent of all Bomber Command mines were laid in Danish waters. Air strikes on enemy ships were also primarily conducted in the northern latitudes, mainly in the North Sea, Danish and Norwegian waters and the western part of the Baltic Sea.

1945	Direct Attack						
	Direct Attack		sunk	Tonnage sunk	Damaged ships		A/C losses
quarter	Sorties	attacks	ships	BRT	numbers	tonnage	A/C
jan-mar	3075	1117	62	52396	18	49381	72
apr-maj*	3765	1759	67	116955	23	117929	59
In total	6840	2876	129	169351	41	167310	131

1945	Minelaying						
	Minelaying		sunk	Tonnage sunk	Damaged ships		A/C losses
quarter	Sorties	laid	ships	BRT	numbers	tonnage	A/C
jan-mar	720	3220	67	137764	32	101224	20
apr-maj*	271	1362	19	26566	7	16727	3
In total	991	4582	86	164330	39	117951	23

Comparative results obtained by the Royal Air Force from Minelaying and from Direct Attacks on Enemy Shipping at sea 1945. *Air attacks 1–4 May, there was no minelaying in May 1945.

The trend in the comparison between the effect of direct air strikes on ship targets and minelaying in the British Home Theatre, which was now limited to Northwest Europe, was similar to previous years. Sinking a ship via direct air attack cost 52 flights while 12 minelaying aircraft could do it. A total of 25 GRT per aircraft by direct attack, while 166 GRT were sunk for every minelaying aircraft that was dispatched. The loss rate continued to be higher for the minelayer planes, although they approached the level of direct air strikes.[40]

On 3 May 1945 at around 20:00, aircraft from 144 Squadron attacked the three ships at Slotø in Nakskov Fjord. The ships were fired upon with both rockets and 20mm cannon shells and the *Java*, which was in the centre, was so badly damaged that it sank.

Ironically, the pilot who led the air strike was Jørgen Kjeldbæk, a former employee at the ØK shipping company which owned the three ships! He came to the United Kingdom via Singapore and joined the RAF in 1942 and had now advanced to Wing Commander. However, all three ships were repaired and sailed for several years after the war. *Jutlandia* later became famous for her participation as a hospital ship in the Korean War – but that is a whole other story.[41]

was on the night of 26 April when 14 Lancasters laid mines in Oslo Fjord. p.701.

40 Stephen W. Roskill, *The War at Sea 1939–45*, vol. 3 2 (London: HMSO, 1962), p.275, Table 34 and p.282, Table 36.

41 SCL on 3–4 May 1945; Lolland-Falster Social Democrat on 4 May 1945 <https://nakskovlokalarkiv.dk/jutlandia-fra-nakskov>.

Photo from the air raid on 3 May 1945 on the East Asia Company cargo ships *Java*, *Falstria* and *Jutlandia*.

Chapter 12

12.1 Concluding Considerations

In 1945, the number of German ships sunk/damaged by direct air strikes exceeded the number sunk by mines. But looking at the entire period 1940–1945, there is no doubt that Bomber Command's minelaying operations were by far the most successful. In fact, Bomber Command's efforts in this area were one of the most effective and successful of all operations according to the RAF's post-war conclusions. For example, 289 German merchant ships were sunk by air attack, while 604 ships were sunk by mines.[1]

12.2 Operation Gardening, 1940–1945, and Its Consequences

The overall statistics of the minelaying programme are: 48,148 mines laid in Western European waters.[2] A total of 762 German merchant ships and warships sunk, and 196 more were damaged. Mines sank 17 U-boats and damaged just as many. The switch to the larger aircraft types from 1942 is clearly visible in the number of mines laid.[3]

Out of 19,600 flights, only 533 aircraft were shot down, or just under 3 percent.[4] Of the 48,148 mines laid by the RAF, Bomber Command laid 47,222 – over 98 percent. It is widely agreed that laying mines was Bomber Command's greatest contribution to the victory over

1 Stephen W. Roskill, *The War at Sea 1939–45*, vol. 3 2 (London: HMSO, 1962), pp.282–83. Harris himself states that from February 1942 to May 1945 alone, Bomber Command's minelaying efforts sank 491 ships and damaged 410 more. Arthur T. Harris (Sebastian Cox Ed.), *Despatch on War Operations: 23rd February 1942 to 8th May 1945* (London: Routledge, 1995), p.171.

2 'Western European waters' here covers the same as the British Home Theatre, that is, from Arkhangelsk in the north to Gibraltar in the south, and out to 350 miles (approx. 560km) west of the European coastline and including the western part of the Baltic Sea, but not the Mediterranean. Stephen W. Roskill, *The War at Sea 1939–45*, vol. 3 2 (London: HMSO, 1962), p.275.

3 The information in the chart comes from the authoritative work: 'The War at Sea, 1939–1945'. By S. W. Roskill. The following tables are used:
Vol. 1: Table 10 'Jun 40-Mar 41', p.336; Table 17 'Apr 41-Dec 41', p.511.
Vol. 2: Table 14 'Jan 42–1ul 42', p.167; Table 20 'Aug 42-Dec 42', p.264; Table 35 'Jan 43-May 43', p.394.
Vol. 3 1: Table 5 'Jun 43-Dec 43', p.96; Table 18 'Jan 44-May 44', p.289.
Vol. 3 2: Table 30 'Jun 44-Dec 44', p.142; Table 34 'Jan 45-May 45', p.275.
The figures from April and May 1940 are discussed in vol. 1, p.336. All figures refer to the British 'Home Theatre'.

4 Stephen W. Roskill, *The War at Sea 1939–45*, vol. 3 (London: HMSO, 1962), p.275

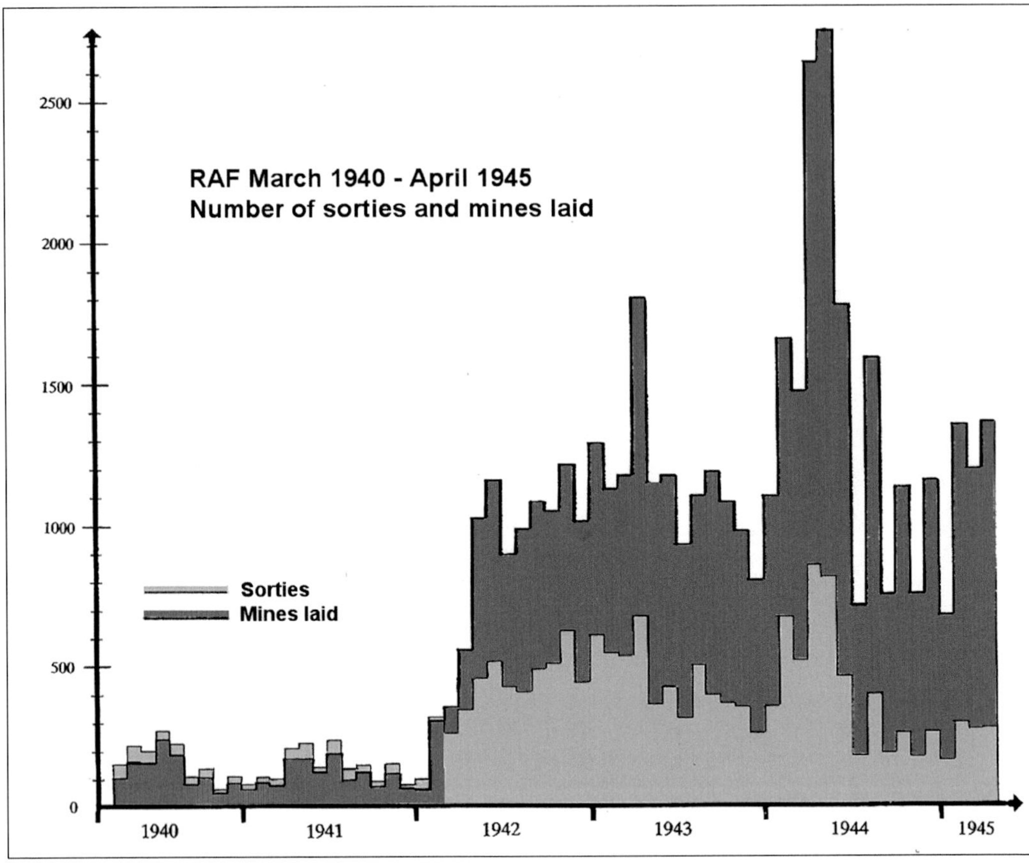

Number of RAF sorties, and mines laid in the European Theatre, March 1940–April 1945.

the German and Italian naval forces. Of the 47,222 mines laid by Bomber Command, 7,819 or 16.6 percent were laid in Danish waters. Of these, the Germans managed to neutralise only 1,038.[5] But it was not until the end of the war that the effectiveness of minelaying as a weapon could really be confirmed.

In this Chapter, I will try to answer the following questions:

a) Did the mine war in Danish waters follow the overall development of the war in Europe?
b) What were the consequences of Operation Gardening in Danish waters in terms of sunken ships, damaged ships and delays?
c) What were the side effects?
d) How many British mines would be left after the mine sweeps from 1945–1972 to the present day?

5 *Strygetidende*, no. 6, 1946, pp.59 and 63.

I will first look at the military tactical development that the RAF's minelaying efforts went through during the war and see if it was reflected in Danish waters. I have chosen to divide the entire period into four periods, by combining Arthur T. Harris' own division in his 'Despatch on War Operations' with the periodisation of the German occupation of Denmark 1940-1945:[6]

12.3 First period: April 1940 – March 1942

Mines laid 1940	
Kattegat	29
Øresund	91
Storebælt	113
Lillebælt	25
Østersøen	42
Nordsøen	0
total in DK	300
total in Eur	765
DK in %	39,2

Mines laid by Bomber Command in Danish Waters and in Europe Waters in 1940.

The start of the period was characterised by relatively few flights and even fewer mines. This was due to the low prioritisation of minelaying and the use of aircraft types such as Hampdens and Wellingtons, with a relatively low load capacity of only 1 and 2 mines per aircraft respectively. Despite the obvious benefits as a result of the first laying of mines by Bomber Command in Danish waters in April-June 1940, the German advances in Western Europe in May–June and the resulting direct threat to the United Kingdom meant that Bomber Command's efforts were directed towards invasion defence from July through October 1940. The coastal waters of The Netherlands, Belgium and France were thus mined during July-August. However, a single Hampden squadron continued to maintain the minefields in the Baltic Sea, and from 4 July two more squadrons joined this effort. But from October onwards, Bomber Command's main objective was to bomb targets in Germany, and minelaying was clearly secondary.

But from their own bitter experience, the British had learnt how effective the mine was, especially the new magnetic mines dropped from aircraft. During August 1940, the British Admiralty ramped up production of these mines, while the RAF intensified the training of aircrews in this specialised form of warfare.[7]

Danish waters were thus where the British magnetic bottom mine would be put to its first test, and just over 39 percent of all mines laid by Bomber Command in 1940 were laid here. As the table shows, proportionally more mines were laid in the Øresund and Great Belt, which were the busiest waterways.[8]

In November, the Admiralty took stock of the RAF's minelaying activities, categorised the minefields into three priority categories, and asked the Air Ministry to provide aircraft capacity to lay mines in the most important fields at least once a week. Mines were plentiful at this point, but it was difficult to find enough aircraft. Five squadrons from 5 Group was set as a minimum, but naval escort and anti-submarine warfare increasingly monopolised

6 Arthur T. Harris (Sebastian Cox Ed.), *Despatch on War Operations: 23rd February 1942 to 8th May 1945* (London: Routledge, 1995), p.171.

7 Stephen W. Roskill, *The War at Sea 1939–45*, vol. 1 (London: HMSO, 1954), p.335.

8 Bomber Command and Admiralty Mining Department Records and Air Historical Branch.

the long-range bombers. In the last three months of 1940, a total of only 143 mines were laid, 11 of them in Danish waters. In return, the Admiralty received a promise from the Air Ministry to get the first squadrons to be equipped with the new Stirling and Manchester aircraft for use in laying mines.[9] Eventually, 64 minefields, or 'Gardens', had been designated throughout Western Europe, specifically what the British called the 'Home Theatre.' Nineteen minefields covered the Danish waters.

Kattegat	Silverthorn 1-7 - Kattegat Area
	Krauts – Lim Fjord
	Undergrowth - Kattegat
	Yewtree – Kattegat
Øresund	Daffodil - The Sound
	Nasturtiums - The Sound
	Verbena - Copenhagen Approaches
Storebælt	Asparagus - Great Belt
	Broccoli - Great Belt
	Pumpkins - Great Belt
	Quinces - Great Belt / Kiel Bay
Lillebælt	Carrots - Little Belt
	Endives - Little Belt
Østersøen	Pollock – Bornholm-area
	Radishes - Kiel Bay
	Sweet Peas - Rostock and Arcone Light
	Wallflowers - Kiel Bay
	Willows - Arcona to River Dievenow
Nordsøen	Hawthorn - Esbjerg Approaches

The 19 'gardens' in the six Danish Waters 1940–1945.

During 1941, new types of aircraft were introduced: the Manchester, the Stirling and the Halifax, which could load 2, 4 and 2 mines respectively.[10] The Bomber Command leadership was not in favour of increasing the number of minelaying squadrons, so for the first three months of the year it was mainly Coastal Command that laid mines. Of a total of 235 mines laid, only 3 were assigned to Danish waters during that period! The Coastal Command leadership requested either a squadron of long-range minelaying aircraft or that Bomber Command resume laying mines themselves. Both requests were refused.[11]

As minelaying was organised, it was the Admiralty that decided where the mines were to be planted, what types of mines were used and in what numbers. It was Coastal Command's job to carry out these orders, and in cases where the target areas were beyond Coastal Command's reach, Bomber Command had to be asked for help. Bomber Command's leadership decided in March 1941 that minelaying was to be prioritised in line with training flights but always secondary to bombing raids over Germany.[12]

9 Stephen W. Roskill, *The War at Sea 1939–45*, vol. 1 (London: HMSO, 1954), pp.335–336; Mine blasts in Danish waters April 1940–July 1943, May–June 1945, Danish Navy Weapons school, archive folder 3.

10 A Stirling could carry 6 mines on board, but only 4 mines were taken to Danish waters because of the long distance involved.

11 Stephen W. Roskill, *The War at Sea 1939–45*, vol. 1 (London: HMSO, 1954), p.337.

12 Stephen W. Roskill, *The War at Sea 1939–45*, vol. 1 (London: HMSO, 1954), pp.509–510.

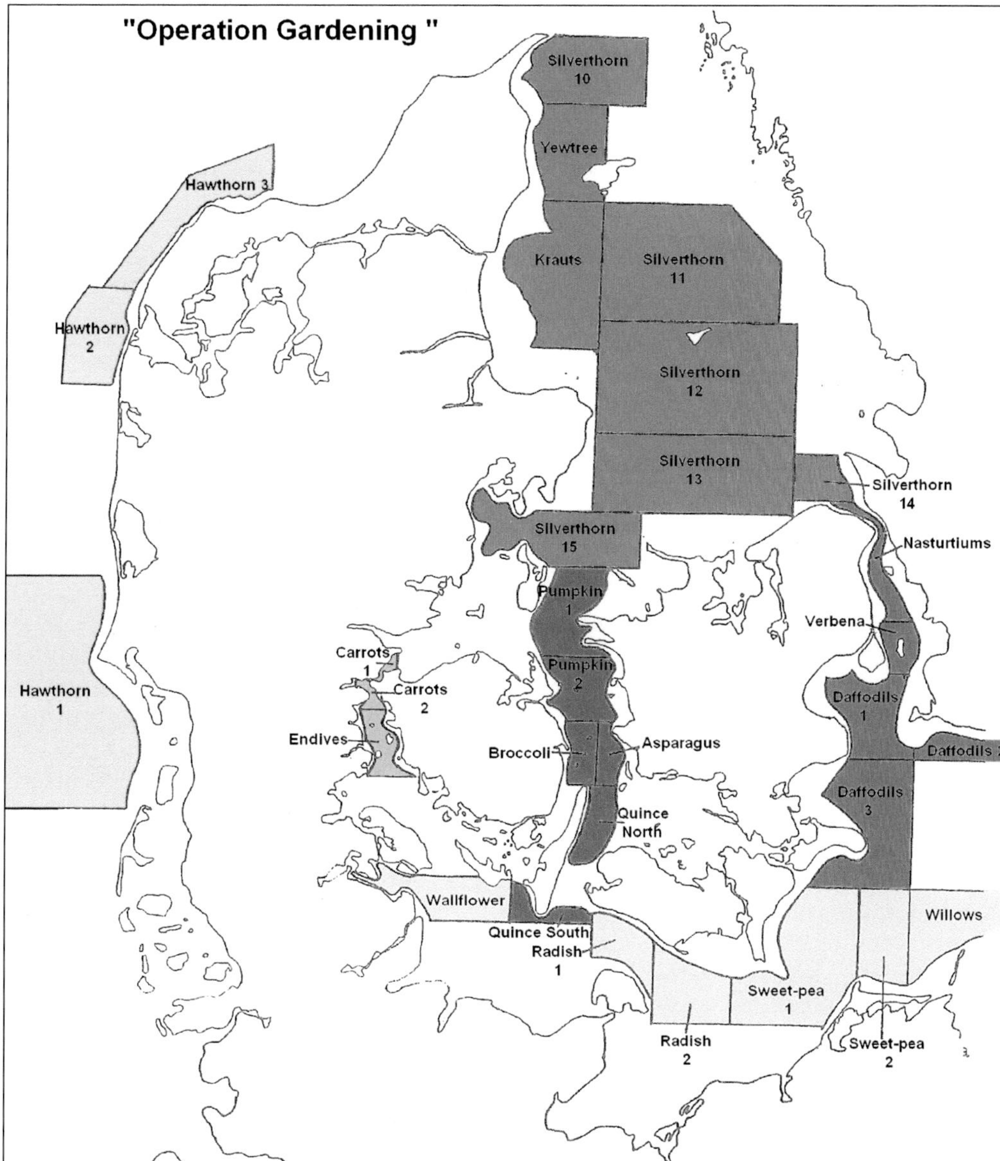

Map showing the 19 'gardens' placed in the six Danish Waters 1940–1945.

Arthur T. Harris, former head of 5 Group in Bomber Command, who had originally proposed the idea of minelaying aircraft, had worked hard for it in the early months of Operation Gardening and was DCAS between 25 November 1940 and 27 May 1941. His boss, Chief of the Air Staff Charles Portal, was very keen to realise the strategic bombing of Germany, while in 1940–1941 he had to fight not to hand over Coastal Command to the Royal Navy and at the same time slow down the army's attempt to create an independent air force. As a result, Operation Gardening took a back seat, despite both Harris and Portal agreeing on the important role of Bomber Command in it.[13]

Between April and September, only 62 mines were laid in Danish waters, bringing the total number since 1940 to a total of 365 magnetic mines laid by Bomber Command by 1 October 1941. Of these, 169 were detonated, or approximately 46 percent. This led to 95 ships sunk, while 74 mines were swept by German, Danish and Swedish minesweepers:[14]

British mines detonated or swept in Danish Waters	1940			1941			In total
	Apr-Jun	Jul-Sep	Oct-Dec	Jan-Mar	Apr-Jun	Jul-Sep	
Danish ships detonated	10	17	10	1	2	8	48
German ships detonated	18	10	2	3	1	1	35
Other ships detonated	5	1	2	1	2	1	12
German minesweeping	9	20	13	1	10	9	62
Danish minesweeping	0	2	2	0	1	0	5
Swedish minesweeping	0	0	6	0	1	0	7
In total	42	50	35	6	17	19	169

In the summer of 1941, the Admiralty changed its minelaying strategy. From the start of the operation in April 1940 until then, the strategy had been to stress the German minesweeper organisation to the limit by constantly creating new minefields in various locations. In this way, only a few mines were laid in each field, but with relatively little effort and relatively small losses, the enemy suffered heavy losses and almost daily delays. Mines were laid in all minefields in Danish waters.[15]

By now, however, the German minesweeper organisation was getting to grips with the situation, helped by the participation of the Danish Navy and improved sweeping equipment in the form of more *sperrbrechere* and Bahnsen's efficient floating sweeping magnets. Therefore, the Admiralty decided instead to lay more mines in the individual fields, one at a time, and in turn lay mines with widely varying settings in terms of sensitivity, counting mechanism and clockwork. Some mines were specifically aimed at the *sperrbrecher* and others just had to wait for up to 14 passages before they became active, and the last ones could be set for several days or weeks before they became active. It became more of a technological battle between British mine designers and German minesweeping technology.[16]

On 1 September 1941, the Air Ministry decided to divide the responsibility for laying mines so that Coastal Command would cover the waters from Terschelling in the north to St. Nazaire in the south, while Bomber Command would cover the areas south and north of

13 Dudley Saward, *'Bomber' Harris': The Story of the Marshal of the Royal Air Force Sir Arthur Harris* (London: Cassell Ltd, 1984), p.87.

14 Bomber Command and Admiralty Mining Department Records, Air Historical Branch. Mine explosions in Danish waters April 1940–July 1943 & May–June 1945, Søværnets Våbenskole, archive folder 3.

15 The 'Willow' and 'Silverthorn' minefields were not established until October 1941 and August 1942 respectively. Bomber Command and Admiralty Mining Dept. Records.

16 Stephen W. Roskill, *The War at Sea 1939–45*, vol. 1 (London: HMSO, 1954), p.510.

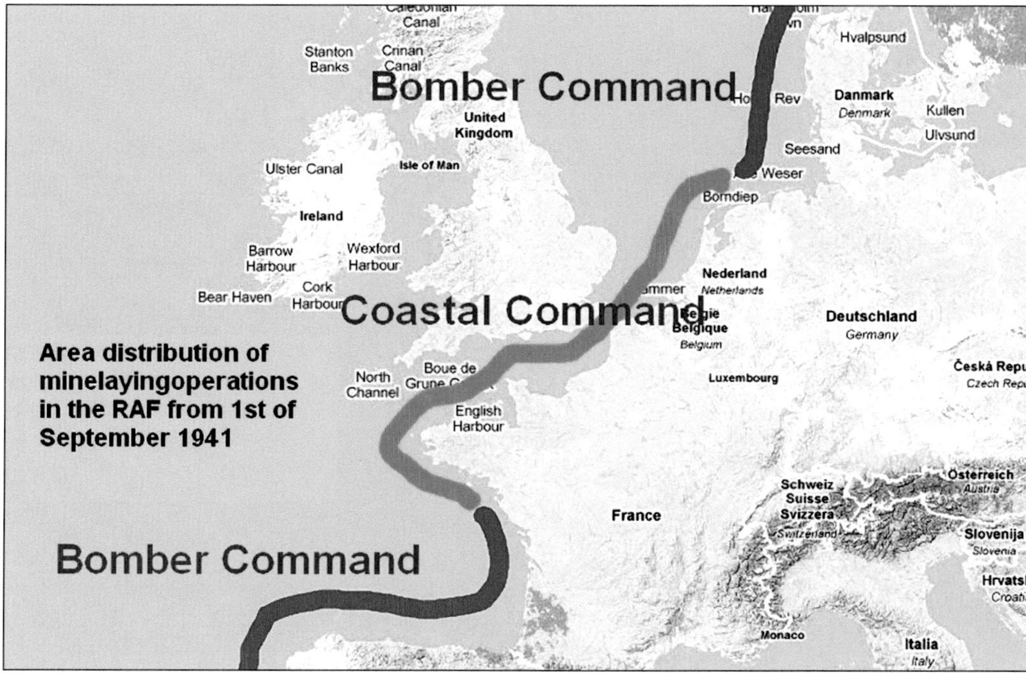

this stretch. Bomber Command laid 261 mines in the period October-December 1941, 41 of which were distributed over only 7 minefields in Danish waters.[17]

Navigation was improved with the use of the GEE system. It was a guidance system but with a relatively short range. However, it could ensure that the planes took off in the right direction and were also helped back home the last leg of the way across the North Sea. It was operationally tested by the end of 1941, and was put into service in earnest in the first months of 1942. It was similar to the German *Knickebein* system, which the *Luftwaffe* had used with great success from the start of the war.[18] However, Churchill's scientific adviser Professor Lindemann did not believe in the effectiveness of the German system since he did not believe that radio waves could be bent to follow the curvature of the Earth! Therefore, the development of the British system started very late. Nor was it helped by the fact that someone as centrally placed as DCAS Arthur T. Harris had a similar attitude. Harris stated in early 1941:

> We use no beams ourselves, but we bomb just as successfully as the Germans bomb … such aids are not indispensable to the successful prosecution of bombing expeditions. I would go further and say that they are not even useful … Long may the Boche beam upon us!'[19]

17 Bomber Command and Admiralty Mining Dept. Records. Stephen W. Roskill, *The War at Sea 1939–45*, vol. 1 (London: HMSO, 1954), p.510.

18 Frank Weber et al: 'Vestallierede luftangreb i Danmark under 2. Verdenskrig' Aarhus 1988 chap. XI 'British Air Navigation 1937–45' p.286–287.

19 R. V. Jones:' Navigation and War,' *The Journal of Navigation*, vol. 28, 1975, no. 1 p.14.

But it was still only 5 Group in Bomber Command that laid mines. Bomber Command had laid 765 magnetic mines in 1940, whereas a total of 1,055 mines were laid in 1941, including 105 in Danish waters. In the first three months of 1942 alone, Bomber Command laid 822 mines, of which only 6 were in Danish fields. But new times were coming … [20] The 47 magnetic mines in Danish waters in the last six months of the period caused another 7 explosions while 18 mines were swept. A full 53 percent of all planted mines were still waiting on the seabed.

British mines detonated or swept in Danish Waters	**1941**	**1942**
	Oct-Dec	**Jan-MaR**
Danish ships detonated	1	1
German ships detonated	3	0
Other ships detonated	2	0
German minesweeping	10	2
Danish minesweeping	3	1
Swedish minesweeping	1	1
In total	20	5

12.4 2nd period: April 1942-June 1943

After debating the role of Bomber Command since the outbreak of war in 1939, including whether greater support should be given to army and navy activities, the Air Ministry made a decision in March 1942 and issued a directive to both Coastal Command and Bomber Command. This stated that Bomber Command was to handle minelaying in the Home Theatre alone, i.e. most of Western Europe. This was on the condition that this job would only be carried out by new, inexperienced crews as part of their training or by experienced veterans who had completed their rotation and had been taken out of regular bombing missions. Bombing raids continued to be prioritised over minelaying.

As a consequence of this directive, 5 Group was now supplemented by 1 Group and 3 Group with their Wellingtons and Stirlings, and which were thus included in the mine-laying missions. This gradually meant more expeditions and significantly more mines. The Admiralty therefore increased the production of magnetic mines from 200 to 300 per week.[21] The laying of mines was prioritised for several reasons. One of them was the Butt Report of August 1941 – an investigation into the extent to which information from the debriefing of aircrews corresponded with the facts. Using 633 target photos taken during bombing raids, it compared the visible damage with the aircrews' own perception of the success of the raids. The conclusions were discouraging:

20 Bomber Command and Admiralty Mining Dept. Records. 1941 Air Historical Branch. Mines explosions in Danish waters April 1940–July 1943 & May–June 1945, *Søværnets Våbenskole*, archive folder 3.

21 Stephen W. Roskill, *The War at Sea 1939–45*, vol. 2 (London: HMSO, 1956), p.166–167.

a) Of the aircraft where crews believed they had hit the designated target, only one in three had hit within an eight kilometre radius of the target.
b) However, on a full moon, two out of five aircraft achieved this, while nights with a new moon meant that only one in 15 made it 5 miles or less from the target.

Post-war research has confirmed this analysis, showing that 49 percent of the bombs dropped by Bomber Command between May 1940 and May 1941 fell on open ground far from the target. Since not all aircraft even made it to the target area, it is estimated that only about 5 percent of a bomber force dropped their bomb load within a 5 mile radius of the target.[22]

The report had four immediate consequences for Bomber Command:

1. The bombing strategy was reassessed and changed, which was laid down in a directive on 14 February. Massive bombing forces were now to be deployed against strategic targets, including a breakdown in the morale of the German population.[23]
2. The new strategy required more and bigger bombers. In March 1942, Bomber Command had a total of 44 squadrons, but only 14 of them were equipped with large bombers: Stirling, Halifax, Manchester and only two squadrons had the new Lancasters, which were not yet operational. Apart from the Lancaster, the other types of aircraft were plagued by various types of malfunctions. Production was however increased and over the next six months, 200 Stirlings, 110 Lancasters and 65 Halifaxes were manufactured.[24]
3. Bomber Command was not at the force level that had been planned and anticipated. By giving up aircraft capacity, crews and ground personnel to the needs of the British Navy and operations in the Mediterranean, Bomber Command was far from being able to function optimally as a strategic bomber force. To rally and strengthen Bomber Command at this critical time in the war, the headstrong but strong personality Arthur Harris was chosen. So 8 days after the new Bomber Command directive was issued by the Air Ministry, Harris was appointed Commander-in-Chief Bomber Command.
4. Better means of navigation for the aircraft had to be developed as soon as possible.

The GEE radio guidance system was introduced in the autumn of 1941, but in addition, navigation was based on compass, stopwatch and sextant. When an aircraft reached the target area, it had two options. Either fly at a relatively low altitude so that it could establish the position via dead reckoning. This could be railway tracks, lakes and rivers, but cities

22 Dudley Saward, *'Bomber' Harris': The Story of the Marshal of the Royal Air Force Sir Arthur Harris* (London: Cassell Ltd, 1984), pp.110–112; AIR 14/1218 The Butt Report – transcribed as a public service by William Thomas in December 2014 from digital photographs of the original.

23 File 119A and B, 14 February 1942 – Air Min. ref. S.46368/111 D.C.A.S.

24 Sebastian Cox: 'Sir Arthur Harris and some Myths and Controversies of the Bomber Offensive' in *RAF Historical Society Journal*, no. 47, Witney: 2010, pp.7–9.

could also usually be located as the blackout was not always perfect. Or it could stay above cloud cover at a relatively safe altitude and carry out the bombing or minelaying mission at ETA (Estimated Time of Arrival), i.e. the estimated time of arrival based on heading, time and speed and thus the distance travelled. The many sources of error in ETA, such as compass misreading, inaccurate weather reports regarding wind speed, air pressure and wind direction, often meant that an aircraft was far from the target area. These errors ranged from a few miles to 100–200 miles.[25] On the other hand, the German air defence was confused by all the bombs dropped on farms, small towns, fields, lakes, forests and occasionally on a factory or a railway. The Germans tried in vain to figure out the strategy. For good reason, there was often not much flak in these scattered locations. New technical aids were therefore added: H2S, an early version of radar, OBOE for blind flying, MANDREL and WINDOWS that disrupted the German radar systems and MONICA and BOOZER that could warn bomber crews about German fighter planes. In addition, in the autumn of 1942, a pathfinder force was established, consisting of the best aircrews, including excellent navigators, who before a bombing raid dropped marker flares along the route and over the target to make it easier for the main force to find the correct target area.[26]

So what did all this mean for mine laying? The focus on strategic bombing with large forces was initially at the expense of minelaying, as this type of operation was still a lower priority. There was no change in this. But the general strengthening and reinforcement of Bomber Command, and with Harris as the new commander, who had been a strong advocate of mine laying right from the start, meant that all Bomber Groups were now involved in mine laying.

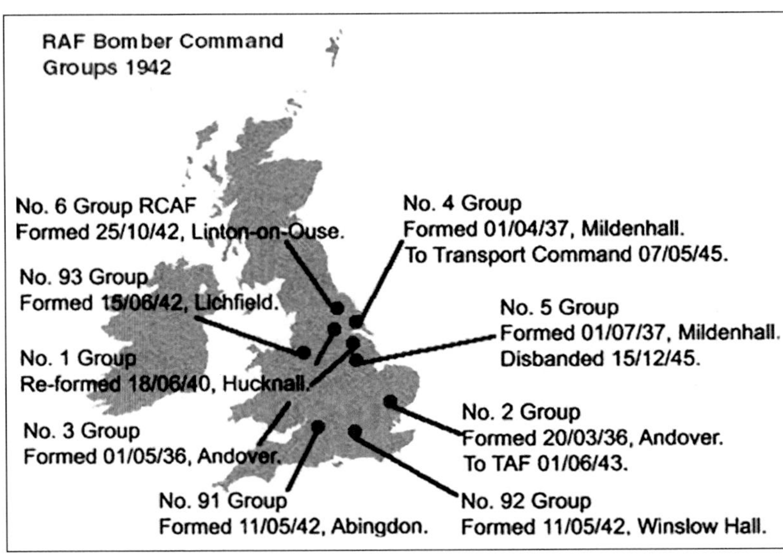

25 Frank Weber et al, *Vestallierede luftangreb i Danmark under 2. Verdenskrig* vol. 1 (Viborg: Aarhus Universitetsforlag, 1988), pp.273–285.

26 Frank Weber et al, *Vestallierede luftangreb i Danmark under 2. Verdenskrig* vol. 1 (Viborg: Aarhus Universitetsforlag, 1988), pp.285–292.

With an increasing number of new aircraft types that could carry more mines, including the newest type, the Lancaster, which carried 4 to 6 mines, 9,574 mines were laid in 1942 alone, including 1,566 in Danish waters.[27]

On 9 November 1942, mines are prepared for Lancaster W-4118 (ZN-L) of 106 Squadron. It was Wing Commander Guy Gibson's aircraft, *Admiral Prune*, and as commander of the squadron he decided that all its aircraft should have names beginning with 'Admiral' because their mine laying efforts were of great importance in the fight against the German fleet.[28]

Of the 2,357 new mines laid during the period, plus the 218 mines remaining from the first period, 693 were detonated or swept during the period, leaving 1,882 on the seabed.[29]

As mentioned, RAF minelaying increased during the period, and by September 1942, production had reached 1,600 mines per month to keep up with distribution, which had reached 1,000 mines per month. At the same time a satisfactory stockpile of the new acoustic mines had been built up so that they could be laid when the time was right. The temptation to lay them as they were produced had been overcome, so as not to lose the element of surprise and thus make the mistake the Germans had made with the same type of mine. By the end of September, 457 acoustic mines were laid together with the magnetic mines.[30]

27 ADM 234 British Minelaying campaign Sept. 39 – May 1945. Bomber Command and Admiralty Mining Dept. Records. 1942, 1945–1970.

28 <http://uamf.org.uk/viewtopic.php?t=1111 (23.02.2025)>.

29 Air 24/1(686) Air Historical Branch. Mine explosions in Danish waters April 1940–July 1943 & May–June 1945, Søværnets Våbenskole, archive folder 3.

30 Stephen W. Roskill, *The War at Sea 1939–45*, vol. 2 (London: HMSO, 1956), p.262–263.

		Hawthorne	Krauts	Silverthorns	Yewtree	Asparagus	Broccoli	Carrots	Daffodil	Endive	Nasturtium	Pumpkins	Verbena	Quinces	Radishes	Wallflowers	Pollock	Sweet Peas	Undergrowth	Willow	Total laid
1942	April	32	0	0	0	0	0	0	8	8	0	0	0	38	16	12	0	0	0	0	114
	May	79	0	0	10	34	14	21	57	19	14	36	5	64	48	4	0	29	0	25	459
	June	0	0	0	0	0	0	0	0	0	5	0	0	0	0	0	0	0	0	0	5
	July	14	0	0	0	18	9	0	0	0	9	0	0	8	0	0	0	0	0	0	58
	August	0	10	120	0	13	0	0	8	0	0	0	0	9	35	5	16	5	0	38	259
	September	17	12	87	0	4	4	2	30	6	10	6	12	10	13	7	22	20	0	17	279
	October	14	8	53	16	7	4	13	0	20	0	0	0	0	0	4	9	12	0	9	169
	November	2	0	8	0	2	4	7	0	7	0	0	0	0	0	6	6	0	0	0	42
	December	0	0	91	0	12	12	0	10	0	10	5	5	0	3	0	6	21	0	0	175
1943	January	0	0	72	0	6	0	0	3	0	0	12	0	0	0	3	0	46	0	0	142
	February	0	0	9	0	0	0	0	0	0	0	0	0	0	0	0	6	0	0	0	15
	March	0	0	104	0	0	0	4	0	6	0	0	0	0	0	0	15	12	0	3	144
	April	2	0	229	0	6	3	10	53	8	20	7	20	16	22	10	12	48	0	30	496
	May	0	0	0	0	0	0	0	0	0	0	0	0	0	0	0	0	0	0	0	0
	June	0	0	0	0	0	0	0	0	0	0	0	0	0	0	0	0	0	0	0	0
Total laid		160	30	773	26	102	50	57	169	74	68	66	42	145	137	51	92	193	0	122	2357

Mines laid in Danish waters by Bomber Command in the period April 1942–June 1943.

The table on the next page shows that the number of German ships damaged by mines tripled between July and September 1942, but then fell back to pre-July levels. The number of Danish ships damaged by mines also increased considerably until the end of the year, when it also fell back to pre-July levels. As the Germans were using acoustic mines themselves at this time, they had already developed sweeping equipment for these, and as there was a steady increase in the number of mines laid, the minesweeper organisation was expanded and also gained more experience.

In the first three months of 1943, Bomber Command laid 3,575 mines in Western Europe, including 301 mines in the Danish fields. But the laying of mines was still subject to the previous restrictions of bombing raids. However, RAF command had finally realised the effectiveness of mine laying in delaying and sinking enemy ships.

In March, the Air Ministry issued a new directive to Bomber Command that mines were to be laid on selected nights, in large formations and concentrated in selected waters. This coincided with the Admiralty having developed a new type of mine, a combined acoustic-magnetic mine, which was to be included in the armoury and distributed when a suitable quantity was in place. On the night of 27 April, 459 mines were planted. The following night, 568 mines, a mix of all three types, were laid off the German harbour towns in the Baltic Sea and in the Danish minefields, the largest minelaying in Danish waters during the war. Of the 226 bombers allocated to the mission, 207 took part, of which Bomber Command lost 23, a loss rate of 11 percent, the highest for minelaying during the war.[31]

31 Stephen W. Roskill, *The War at Sea 1939–45*, vol. 2 (London: HMSO, 1956), p.392–393; Carsten Petersen, *Luftkrig over Danmark* (Ringkøbing: 1990), vol. V, pp.35–43. A total of 11 of the 23 minelayer planes crashed on Danish soil, and several of the others in the surrounding waters. <http://www.flensted.eu.com/19430042.shtml>. Minelaying on the night of 28/29 April 1943. <https://218squadron.wordpress.com/report-no-136-bomber-command-report/>.

British mines detonated or swept in Danish Waters	1942			1943		In total
	Apr-Jun	Jul-Sep	Oct-Dec	Jan-Mar	Apr-Jun	
Danish ships detonated	24	38	36	22	22	142
German ships detonated	8	26	8	5	7	54
Other ships detonated	3	5	6	2	5	21
German minesweeping	64	59	64	68	80	335
Danish minesweeping	8	17	35	18	13	91
Swedish minesweeping	13	8	4	6	19	50
In total	120	153	153	121	146	693

Situation map from investigation report no. 136 at the end of May 1943 regarding the laying of mines on 28/29 April 1943.

Hardest hit was 3 Group, which participated with 33 aircrews, 8 of whom did not return home. Bomber Command immediately launched two independent investigations into what had gone so horribly wrong. The first investigation report was completed on 30 April and it attributed the primary responsibility for the fatal outcome to the planned flight routes. Incorrect and misleading weather forecasts had also caused problems for the navigators, causing all aircraft to fly a more southerly route than planned.

At the end of May, a more thoroughly prepared report, No.136, was submitted to Harris, and it rejected all the conclusions of the first report. It in turn attributed the high losses to the pilots' lack of experience in minelaying. However, a survey of pilots' general experience of flying night missions refutes this conclusion. Today, we can conclude that the pilots chose to go below cloud cover to get a visual landmark and 13 aircraft fell victim to light and medium levels of flak. The remaining bombers were shot down by five German night fighters from *NJG 3*, which together were directed towards their targets 30 times that night.[32]

Lancaster from 218. Squadron with mines loaded. 3 Group participated with eight aircraft of which three were shot down over Denmark.

32 <https://218squadron.wordpress.com/report-no-136-bomber-command-report/>.

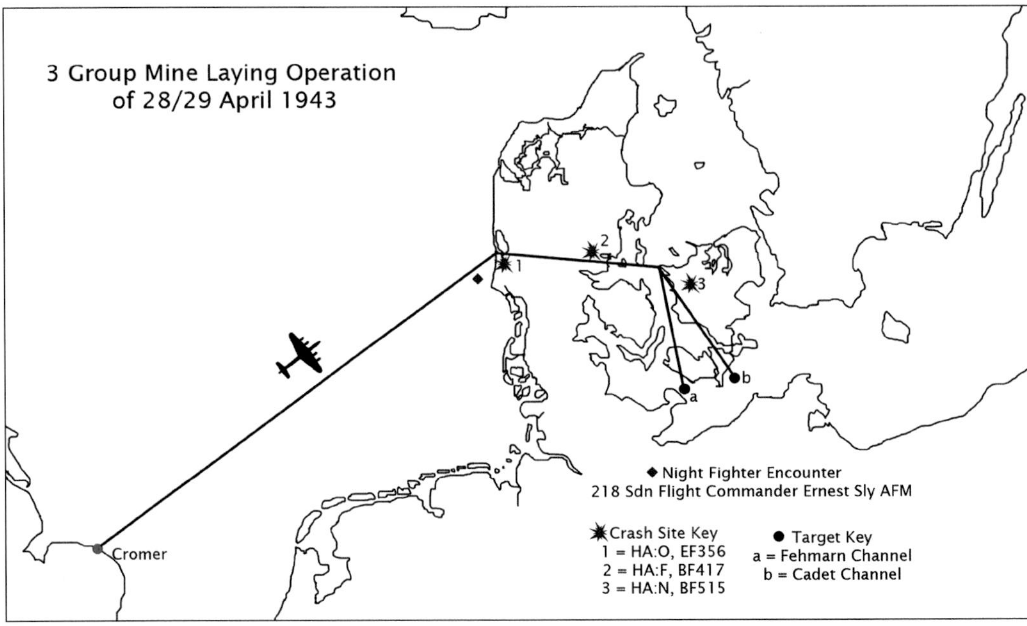
3 Group Mine Laying Operation
of 28/29 April 1943
Cromer
◆ Night Fighter Encounter
218 Sdn Flight Commander Ernest Sly AFM
Crash Site Key
1 = HA:O, EF356
2 = HA:F, BF417
3 = HA:N, BF515
● Target Key
a = Fehmarn Channel
b = Cadet Channel

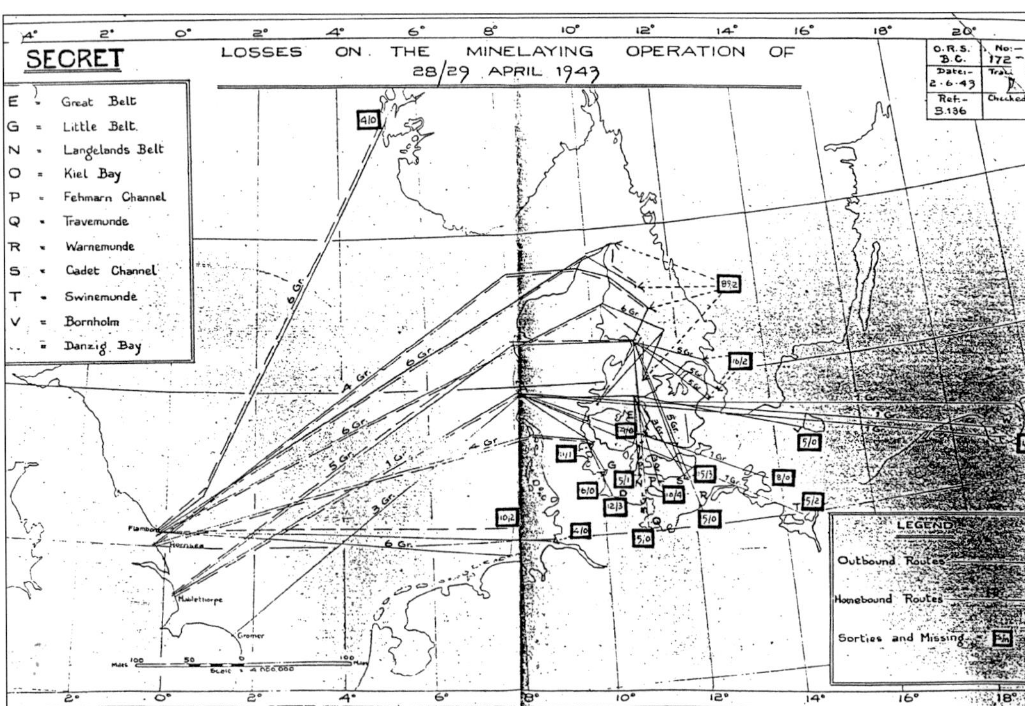
SECRET
LOSSES ON THE MINELAYING OPERATION OF 28/29 APRIL 1943
E - Great Belt
G = Little Belt
N - Langelands Belt
O = Kiel Bay
P - Fehmarn Channel
Q - Travemunde
R - Warnemunde
S - Cadet Channel
T - Swinemunde
V = Bornholm
Danzig Bay
LEGEND
Outbound Routes
Homebound Routes
Sorties and Missing
Cromer

12.5 3rd period: July 1943-June 1944

In the autumn of 1943, the RAF increased its minelaying activity. From October to December, 2,852 mines were dropped, of which 444 were distributed to Danish minefields, with 'Silverthorn' in Kattegat alone receiving 331. Several bombers were gradually equipped with the new H2S radar systems at the end of 1943, which made it possible to locate target areas more accurately at night and in dense cloud cover. The number of flights peaked and about three times as many mines were laid. In May–June 1944 alone, a total of 5,375 mines were laid – the reason was the impending invasion of Normandy.[33]

We can see that the directive to lay more mines in fewer selected fields was followed. The total of 1,484 mines laid in Danish waters were distributed across only 9 of the 19 fields, of which 'Silverthorn' in Kattegat received almost half.[34]

Bomber Command minelaying per month in Danish waters in the period July 1943 to June 1944

		Hawthorne	Krauts	Silverthorns	Yewtree	Asparagus	Broccoli	Carrots	Daffodil	Endive	Nasturtium	Pumpkins	Verbena	Quinces	Radishes	Wallflowers	Pollock	Sweet Peas	Undergrowth	Willow	Total laid
1943	July	0	0	0	0	0	0	0	0	0	0	0	0	0	0	0	0	0	0	0	0
	August	0	0	0	0	0	0	0	0	0	0	0	0	0	0	0	0	0	0	0	0
	September	0	9	69	0	0	0	0	0	0	0	0	0	0	0	0	0	0	0	0	78
	October	18	44	201	0	0	0	0	12	0	0	0	0	0	12	0	0	0	0	4	291
	November	0	5	29	0	0	0	0	0	0	0	0	0	0	0	0	0	0	0	0	34
	December	6	3	32	0	0	0	0	0	0	0	0	0	0	0	0	0	0	0	0	41
1944	January	51	0	21	0	0	0	0	0	0	0	0	0	0	0	0	0	0	0	0	72
	February	0	0	78	0	0	0	0	84	0	0	0	0	0	0	18	0	2	0	0	182
	March	2	0	0	0	0	0	0	0	0	0	0	0	0	65	0	0	0	0	0	67
	April	8	0	71	0	0	0	0	131	0	0	0	0	0	118	0	12	127	0	48	515
	May	0	104	92	0	0	0	0	0	0	0	0	0	0	0	0	0	0	0	0	196
	June	0	0	8	0	0	0	0	0	0	0	0	0	0	0	0	0	0	0	0	8
		85	165	601	0	0	0	0	227	0	0	0	0	0	195	18	12	129	0	52	1484

In addition to the general purpose of laying offensive mines in Danish waters, there were two particularly prioritised targets during this period because of the impending invasion of Normandy:

1. Troop movements from Norway southwards should be delayed and preferably prevented.
2. New U-boats from the bases in the Baltic Sea should also be delayed and preferably prevented from conducting practice sailing and then reaching the Danish waters or via the Kiel Canal to the North Sea.

33 ADM 234 British Minelaying campaign Sept. 39–May 1945. Bomber Command and Admiralty Mining Dept. Records.

34 Air 24/1(686), Air Historical Branch. Mine explosions in Danish waters April 1940–July 1943 & May–June 1945, Søværnets Våbenskole, archive folder 3.

Numbers of mines laid in Danish Waters in the period from July 1943 to June 1944

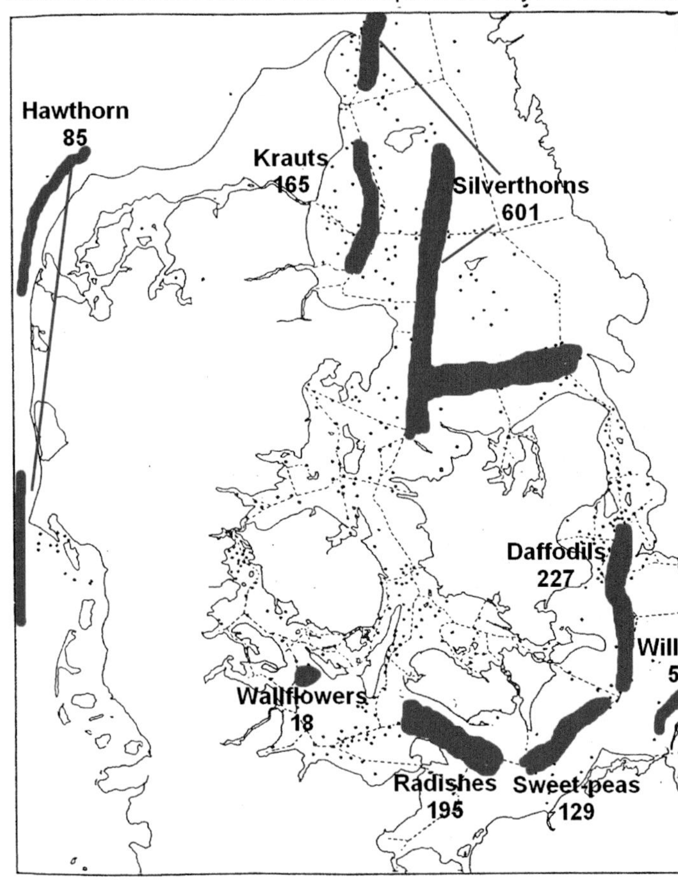

For the latter reason, the waters off the U-boat bases in Biskayen were also heavily mined during the period. As the table on the next page shows, Bomber Command still refrained from sending minelayers into Danish waters and the Baltic Sea during the three summer months when the nights were shortest.[35]

In the first months of 1944, the high-level minelaying technique was introduced, but only after some teething problems, with mines falling several kilometres inside Sweden and Swedish waters. Intensive training and practice flights improved the technique and by May, high-level raids accounted for two-thirds of all minelaying operations.[36]

At the end of March, the Admiralty in London expanded the area of operations to include the Gulf of Danzig (Gdansk), where a large part of the German U-boat fleet was prepared and carried out practice sailing. The 48 mines in the 'Willow' field in April 1944 should be seen in this context. German sources available since the War show that this mining interrupted the U-boat training programme for a month and caused major problems for coastal shipping. Only two U-boats were successfully sunk by the mines, but the delays and the tying up of many minesweeping units for long periods of time were of even greater significance. [37]

35 Stephen W. Roskill, *The War at Sea 1939–45*, vol. 3 1 (London: HMSO, 1960), pp.95–96 & 283.
36 Stephen W. Roskill, *The War at Sea 1939–45*, vol. 3 1 (London: HMSO, 1960), p.288
37 Stephen W. Roskill, *The War at Sea 1939–45*, vol. 3 1 (London: HMSO, 1960), p.288-289. U-854 hit a mine and sank on 4 February 1944 and U-803 did likewise on 27 April 1944.

1,484 mines were laid in Danish waters from July 1943 to June 1944. Together with the 1,882 mines from the previous period, there were a total of 3,366 bottom mines. But how many of these detonated is a little harder to quantify.

1943	Storebælt	Lillebælt	Østersøen	Nordsøen	Kattegat	Øresund
Juli	8		6	3	7	6
August	5	3	1	1	3	2
September	1	1	1	1	3	
Oktober			1	1		1
November				1	6	1
December					5	
1944						
Januar					6	1
Februar	2	1	1	3	6	
Marts	3		2		7	
April	1	2		2	2	
Maj	1		2	5	11	14
Juni	1		1	2	7	3

Danish Naval Weapons School, Overview of exploded influence mines in Danish waters July 1943 to June 1944.

At first glance, these figures look completely wrong. In the previous period, approximately 550 mines were swept in one year, and in this period it was apparently only 154. The Danish Naval Weapons School's 'Overview of blown distance mines in Danish waters 3/9 1939 – 5/5 1945' states for the entire occupation: 338 were swept, 439 exploded by ships and 214 exploded for other reasons, totalling 991. In the overview 'Minesprængninger i danske farvande 9 April 1940–July 1943' in the same binder, the total number of detonated mines is 799, but after a detailed count, the figure is 914.[38]

It is not clear where the navy got its information from in the period August 1943 to May 1945, when the Danish part of the minesweeping had ceased. I therefore lean more towards the German sources from this period, to the extent that records exist. The following example illustrates the difference between the Danish and German accounts.

From mid-April 1944 until the liberation in May 1945, the German *Sicherungsdivision Nr 8* was responsible for mine clearance and escort service in Danish waters and the western part of the Baltic Sea. For the period April to December 1944, the annual report states that 566 British mines were swept or exploded, whereas the Danish Naval Weapons School for the same period only counted 138 mines detonated!

38 Søværnets Våbenskole, 'Overview of exploded distance mines in Danish waters 3/9 1939 – 5/5 1945 and 'Minesprængninger i danske farvande 9 April 1940–Juli 1943', archive folder 3.

From the *Sicherungsdivision Nr 8* war diary (KTB) I have extracted information on how many of the British raids the Germans considered to be mine operations, the number of mine explosions as a result of bottom mines, and the mines swept. It also shows how many naval vessels were available for mine sweeping and escorting, as a large number were constantly in shipyards for repairs, some of them due to mine explosions.[39]

KriegsTageBuch 8. Sicherungsdivision, Spole A 6, Rigsarkivet (the 8th Security Division)				Ships being escorted				non-operative			
Period		Number of mine-laying events	mine explo-sions	War ships	Uboats	Transport ships	Number of mine-Sweepers in total	by mines	Air-attack etc.	Swept mines in total	See note nr.
15-04-1944	01-05-1944	3	2	6	14	102	238	2	65	8	1
01-05-1944	01-06-1944	6	4	4	55	255	237	5	52	76	2
01-06-1944	01-07-1944	3	5	15	48	218	246	4	60	42	
01-07-1944	01-08-1944	5	6	4	40	230	234	4	51	84	3
01-08-1944	01-09-1944	2	2	5	40	153	253	2	49	15	4
01-09-1944	01-10-1944	3	3	1	31	188	270	5	65	34	5
01-10-1944	01-11-1944	4	11	6	42	254	272	6	87	142	
01-11-1944	01-12-1944	5	7	2	25	200	275	8	77	39	
15-12-1944	01-01-1945	(6)	(9)	(4)	(24)	238)				(25)	
01-01-1945	01-02-1945	3	3	6	40	191	302	8	67	52	
Annual report 1944	15. April to 31. December	37 in total	49*	47	319	1838				517	

* 7 warships and 12 transport ships sunk, while 10 warships and 20 transport ships were damaged

Sicherungsdivision Nr 8 ORB.

Notes

1) Situational analysis:
   a) Protection of the Aarhus-Oslo convoy is extremely weak, mostly only by 2 boats, due to a lack of available vessels.
   b) The documents provided by tracking centres are extremely sparse and difficult to evaluate, as targets are usually lost quickly. In addition, tracking is only possible up to 8 km. As a result, an approaching enemy unit can only be detected at the last moment – and thus practically too late.
   c) The possibility of using minesweeping aircraft in the area as soon as possible is absolutely necessary. This is why clarification of this question is a priority.
   d) If enemy centres of gravity are formed regarding mine use in the Kattegat or the Baltic Sea approaches, it is not possible to control the situation with existing mineclearing vessels. In this case, mineclearing vessels must be requested immediately from other areas. If the centre of gravity is both in the Baltic Sea and the area of the *Sicherungsdivision Nr 8* arises, controlling the mine situation is extremely difficult even with the boats that must be called in from the schools and inspections.

39 *Sicherungsdivision Nr 8* KTB April 1944–Dec. 1944, Rigsarkivet.

2) On 22.5 'U-1164' at 55 degrees 59 minutes north, 11 degrees 1.8 minutes east was damaged by a mine hit.
3) Troop transfer under the code name 'Graf' Oslo/Aarhus started on 11 June and ended on 21 July. Close air cover requested was not provided due to lack of aircraft fuel.
4) Cooperation with the Air Force:
   Due to the general fuel situation, no air reconnaissance, close air cover or direct escort can be provided for the tasks of the *Sicherungsdivision Nr 8*.
5) Danish working method. Shipyards remain consistently sluggish and are exacerbated (consequently depressing) by strikes and threats of strikes. Docking opportunities in Germany and Denmark remain very difficult and inadequate. Of the six assigned M-boats M-517, M-572, M-575, M-581, M-582, M-584, only M-517 and M-584 were operational.

The crew aboard the German minesweepers were very aware of the dangerous task they were on. Hence their motto: 'Those who search for mines are closest to God.' The Danish Navy's minesweepers have a motto that is less dramatic: 'Wherever you sail, we have been!'

12.6 4th period: July 1944 – May 1945

While the main minelaying effort in June centred on supporting the invasion of Normandy and the Bay of Biscay, in July the focus moved further north to the Dutch and North German coasts. In August, the nights began to get long enough for Danish waters to be engaged. The German minesweepers and escort vessels worked at full speed and were able to minimise German ship losses with great skill. However, they themselves were increasingly exposed to air attacks and damage from mine detonations. At the same time, the North German shipyards were regularly bombed, making it difficult to get damaged vessels back into operational service.[40]

40 Stephen W. Roskill, *The War at Sea 1939–45*, vol. 3 2 (London: HMSO, 1961), p.140.

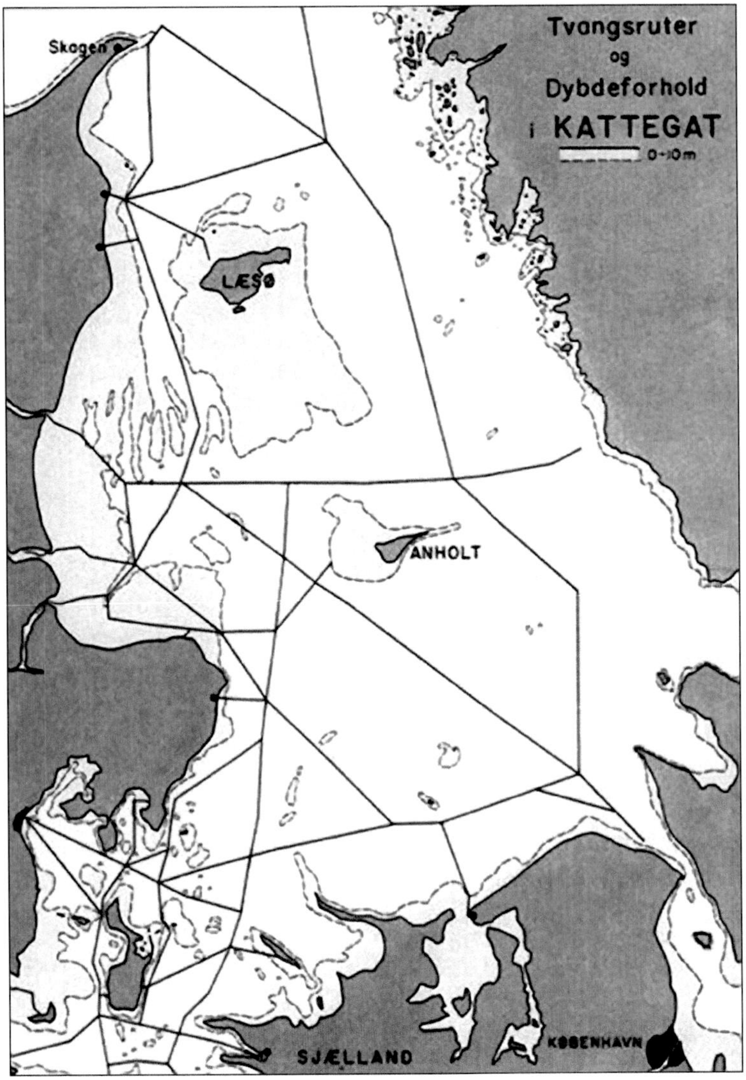

Secured routes and depth conditions in the Kattegat.

We can get a good insight into the difficulties of the minesweeper organisation via the *Sicherungsdivision Nr 8's* war diary for the period 15 April to the end of December 1944. As many as six flotillas of minesweepers and escort ships were positioned in Danish waters. One in each of the three passages from Kattegat to the Baltic Sea – Øresund, Storebælt and Lillebælt. One was located in the northern part of Øresund and one in the northern part of the Great Belt, while the last served the Kattegat. When enemy aircraft were detected approaching and it was suspected that was a minelaying operation, guard ships and air reporting posts were instructed to keep an eye out for possible minefields. All forced routes that could have been affected were then closed to traffic. Ships on the affected forced routes were to anchor immediately and await clearance. The responsible flotilla then began sweeping for mines. Typically, 3 or 4 vessels would pass through the closed routes between 3 and 6 times before the roads were cleared. It usually took a day or two. Due to a constant shortage of both minesweepers and minesweeping equipment, they had to concentrate on the main sealanes and traffic junctions, leaving the smaller byways for later.

In waters 40 metres deep or deeper, all important vessels were escorted by minesweepers equipped to neutralise magnetic, acoustic and combined magnetic and acoustic mines. As the table shows, the number of mines laid in the last period peaked in October with

808 mines, resulting in a total of 153 minesweeper operations.[41]

Sweeping the British mines, which were now laid in several different versions and combinations, became a very laborious affair. Different types of mines required different sweeping equipment and the British mine designers were winning the technological war. The mine type, which the Germans labelled ELM/JA 8, was a combined acoustic and magnetic mine with both a time setting from 4 to 14 days and a counting mechanism from 1–8 passes over, has 'become at that moment a serious danger to all ships, … All attempts to clear the ELM/JA 8 have so far been unsuccessful.' Another type, ELM/J Sp.V15, aimed at *sperrbrecher* is, the report says, 'very dangerous for all *sperrbrecher* due to its increasing sensitivity over time … '[42]

When the crew members of the German minesweepers had completed 100 days of active service at sea, they received the *Minensuchabzeichen* badge (Minesweeping badge).

Bomber Command's minelaying per month in Danish waters July 1944 to May 1945

		Hawthorne	Krauts	Silverthorns	Yewtree	Asparagus	Broccoli	Carrots	Daffodil	Endive	Nasturtium	Pumpkins	Verbena	Quinces	Radishes	Wallflowers	Pollock	Sweet Peas	Undergrowth	Willow	Total laid
1944	July	36	0	96	0	0	0	0	0	0	0	0	0	0	0	0	0	0	0	0	132
	August	0	0	0	0	0	0	0	0	0	0	0	0	0	0	0	0	73	0	0	73
	September	0	22	130	6	0	0	0	0	0	0	0	0	0	76	0	0	58	0	0	292
	October	0	98	651	59	0	0	0	0	0	0	0	0	0	0	0	0	0	0	0	808
	November	0	0	98	112	0	0	0	0	0	0	0	0	0	0	0	0	0	0	0	210
	December	0	40	354	115	0	0	0	0	0	0	0	0	0	0	0	0	54	0	0	563
1945	January	0	0	149	53	0	0	0	0	0	0	0	0	0	0	36	0	0	0	0	238
	February	0	0	173	102	0	0	0	0	0	0	0	0	0	0	0	0	2	0	71	348
	March	0	0	314	0	0	0	0	0	0	0	0	0	0	0	60	0	0	0	82	456
	April	0	0	238	0	0	0	44	0	0	0	5	0	1	0	159	0	0	0	0	447
	May	0	0	0	0	0	0	0	0	0	0	0	0	0	0	0	0	0	0	0	0
	Total laid	36	160	2203	447	0	0	44	0	0	0	5	0	1	76	255	0	187	0	153	3567

Despite the difficulties in sweeping certain types of mines, *Sicherungsdivision Nr 8* managed to escort 366 warships, including 319 U-boats and 1,838 merchant and troop transport ships, safely through Danish waters in the period from 15 April to

41 Bomber Command and Admiralty Mining Dept. Records. 8. Sicherungs Division KTB April 1944–Dec. 1944. Mine countermeasures, mine defence, mine clearance, vehicle positioning & ground mine control. , Rigsarkivet

42 *8 Sicherungs Division* KTB April 1944 – Dec. 1944, Rigsarkivet. Wegablaufen.

31 December 1944.[43] But the shortage of minesweepers, escort ships and especially the right mine sweeping equipment began to become noticeable in the autumn of 1944. Sweden, which had lost 51 ships of over 100,000 GRT due to air attacks, torpedoing and mines, refused to insure ships entering German ports from 18 August, and on 27 September all Swedish ports were closed to German ships.

Worse for the German Navy, large parts of the waters off Gdansk were now so heavily mined that test sailing with the new XXI and XXIII U-boats was disrupted and had to be repeatedly postponed. At the same time, Russian forces were advancing rapidly from the east, threatening the German U-boat bases in the eastern part of the Baltic Sea. Dönitz therefore upheld Hitler's decision that Kurland in western Latvia, the Gulf of Gdansk, Memel and East Prussia must be held at all costs. Russian forces surrounded the Kurland pocket, as it was called, and held 32 German divisions, with over 200,000 men, from October 1944 until May 1945, when the remnants of the German troops, some 135,000 survivors, had to surrender.[44]

When *Grossadmiral* Dönitz was asked after the war about the impact of British mine laying on U-boat operations in the Baltic Sea, he replied that the training voyages had not been affected. But he explained that they had simply moved the training and trials further east in the Baltic Sea, thereby confirming that they had indeed been affected by the laying of mines![45]

In the last four months of 1944, Bomber Command focussed almost exclusively on laying mines in Danish waters, particularly in the Kattegat and the Baltic Sea. However, Oslo Fjord was also visited during this period. Although not as many ships were sunk, the large number of mines were a huge burden on the German minesweeping organisation and on shipping as a whole. As an example, German U-boat U 877 left Kiel around midnight on 11 November 1944, heading for Horten in Norway. It was escorted by two minesweepers and two armed trawlers and all five vessels were, as had become standard, equipped with *Geräuschboje Turbine* as a defence against acoustic mines. After leaving Kiel, the weather deteriorated and for almost eight days, the force was forced to take shelter at Kalundborg and Frederikshavn. After five days, U 297 arrived and eventually there were also 10 to 15 merchant ships, all waiting for better weather. The reason was the weather, but an interrogation of the crew of U 877 later revealed that the route to Horten from Denmark was closed due to mine danger, as it could not be swept.[46] The *Sicherungsdivision Nr 8's* war diary of 16 January 1945 reveals the Germans' powerlessness:

> Even with the heaviest deployment of mine detection forces, no real mine safety can be achieved for about 2 months after an incursion; this does not include the

43 *8 Sicherungs Division* KTB April 1944 – Dec. 1944, Rigsarkivet. Escort service in the Skagerrak and Kattegat in the period 15 April – 31 December 1944

44 Stephen W. Roskill, *The War at Sea 1939–45*, vol. 3 2 (London: HMSO, 1961), pp.140–141; David L. Bashow, *None but the Brave: The Essential Contributions of RAF Bomber Command to Allied Victory during the Second World War* (Kingston, Ontario: Canadian Defence Academy Press, 2009), pp.144–145.

45 J. S. Cowie, *Mines, Minelayers and Minelaying* (Oxford: OUP, 1949), p.190.

46 Stephen W. Roskill, *The War at Sea 1939–45*, vol. 3 2 (London: HMSO, 1961), p.141; N.I.D 1/PW/REP/17 'Interrogation of Survivors,' www.uboatarchive.net/U-413INT.htm. On 27 December 1944, the U-boat was discovered by two Canadian Navy destroyers and forced to the surface by depth charges. The crew abandoned the boat in the dinghies and were taken prisoner.

> extreme difficulty of clearing VW-ZK special combinations. Against VW and ZK only the permanent escort of all ships is of any value.[47]

In March and April 1945, the minelaying continued, most of the aircraft now using the high-level method because the air defences on land and sea had been reinforced and were operated by highly experienced crews. This in turn meant that the German air defence, the night fighters, could have free rein. It was the night fighters that took down almost all of the 23 minelayers lost by Bomber Command in 1945. During the same period, the German minesweeper operation finally collapsed under the effect of numerous air raids by Coastal Command and the bombing of the shipyards. The remaining transport ships now often had to sail without adequate escort, and Bomber Command laid mines sank a total of 86 ships in 1945 and 39 more were damaged.[48]

The above chronological presentation of the British strategic and tactical measures regarding Bomber Command's minelaying as a result of the war shows that these were generally followed in Danish waters.

12.7 Bomber Command's Military Objectives with Operation Gardening

A. Anti-Submarine Operations

Throughout the war, the aim was to disrupt and interfere with the activities of German U-boats in the vicinity of their bases. In 1940–1943, U-boat bases on the French West Coast were a particular focus. At times they were mined intensively, including in November 1942, when it was important to neutralise the U-boats' freedom of movement, while large Allied convoys moved troops from the United Kingdom to Gibraltar, ahead of the invasion of North Africa. To supplement the efforts against the operational U-boats, Bomber Command laid mines in the U-boat training areas in the western part of the Baltic Sea.

After the war, military historians at the Air Historical Branch concluded that the mines in the German training areas in the Baltic Sea had the greatest impact of the two operations. The constant interruptions and cancellations of U-boat training due to the British mines greatly delayed the development and implementation of the new prefabricated U-boats of the XXI type. The Air Historical Branch estimates that approximately 20 of these new and more silent U-boats would have been operational in the winter of 1944–1945 if the mines had not delayed it. In the end, only a single U-boat XXI managed to get into operational service for a few days.[49]

B. Mines Targeting the Transport of Troops and Raw Materials

Merchant ships sailing for Germany were targeted by minelaying throughout the war. From 1942 onwards, there was a particular focus on iron ore transports from Sweden to

47 8. Sicherungs Division KTB April 1944 – Dec. 1944, The National Archives. *Besonders Vorkommnisse VW: Verzögerungswerk* – time setting from 4–14 days, ZK: Zählkontakt – turnstile 1–8.

48 Stephen W. Roskill, *The War at Sea 1939–45*, vol. 3 2 (London: HMSO, 1961), p.274.

49 Arthur T. Harris (Sebastian Cox Ed.), *Despatch on War Operations: 23rd February 1942 to 8th May 1945* (London: Routledge, 1995), p. XXXIII.

Germany and coal deliveries in the other direction. Ultimately, the risk of being blown up by mines was one of the main reasons why Swedish ship owners refused to sail for Germany in August 1944. Troop transports, as well as military equipment and weapons, to and from Norway, as well as from Germany and eastwards to the Russian front, were obvious targets. Securing these transports tied up large German resources in the form of minesweepers and escort ships.[50]

C. Laying Mines in Connection with the Normandy Invasion of 1944

Immediately prior to, and especially after, the Allied invasion of Normandy in June 1944, Bomber Command intensified mine laying in the Kattegat, 'Silverthorn' and 'Yewtree', and the waters of southern Norway to prevent German troop reinforcements from Norway from reaching the Western Front. They succeeded in delaying these German troops so much that they did not have a decisive impact on the fighting in France.[51]

D. Tactical Minelaying Targeting Larger German Naval Vessels

In all cases where larger German naval vessels were expected to pass through mineable waters, Bomber Command intensified mine laying on the possible routes. The most famous case is when the battleships *Scharnhorst* and *Gneisenau*, as well as the heavy cruiser *Prinz Eugen* sought passage through the English Channel from Brest to the German ports of Wilhelmshaven and Brunsbüttel. Although the *Scharnhorst* was hit by two mines and the *Gneisenau* by a single mine, all three warships reached harbour safely.[52] Similarly, Bomber Command attempted to hit *Prinz Eugen* on her journey from Trondhjem to Kiel for repairs, and her replacement, the heavy cruiser *Lützow* in May 1942. However, both escaped unharmed through the heavily mined Danish waters.

E. Harris and Operation Gardening

On 29 December 1943, Deputy Director of Operations Division (Mining) Captain J. S. Cowie sent a frustrated note to the Admiralty. He had found that since 1 October there had been only five minelaying expeditions to Danish waters and the western part of the Baltic Sea. Since, according to Cowie, this area was demonstrably one of the most profitable to mine, and it obviously could not be due to the RAF's lack of will, there had to be other reasons for the significantly low activity. On the one hand it could be bad weather, or perhaps it could be due to a lack of available bombers, due to many bombing missions or a reorganisation of Bomber Command squadrons. To the first, he had to deny that the weather had been *so* bad that mines could not be laid. To the second, he expressed confidence that AOC-in-C Bomber Command, Arthur Harris, was fully aware of the situation. Cowie therefore believed that it was doubtful whether an enquiry from the Admiralty to Harris would be necessary or desirable. However, he left it as an open question.[53]

50 Arthur T. Harris (Sebastian Cox Ed.), *Despatch on War Operations: 23rd February 1942 to 8th May 1945* (London: Routledge, 1995), 1995 pp.171–172.

51 Arthur T. Harris (Sebastian Cox Ed.), *Despatch on War Operations: 23rd February 1942 to 8th May 1945* (London: Routledge, 1995), p.172.

52 <https://en.wikipedia.org/wiki/Channel_Dash (24.02.2025)>.

53 ADM1/15466 Review – Offensive Minelaying D.D.O.D. (M) John Cowie 29.12.1943.

The Chief of Naval Intelligence (NID), Vice Admiral Edmund Rushbrooke, initially avoided responding to Cowie's enquiry about the Baltic, which he only acknowledged in his comment on 13 January.[54] Three days later, the head of the anti-submarine division replied that he agreed with Cowie that:

> this extremely important area is flagging ... [and] it is considered desirable to remind Bomber Command of the necessity for a continued effort in the area.

The next day, the Director of Plans announced that he was sure Cowie would make sure to remind Bomber Command about the mine laying, but that it was probably not wise to make an official approach at a time when Bomber Command was using much of its strength to fulfil the Point-Blank directive. This meant concentrated attacks on German aircraft factories and fighter bases to reduce German fighter defence before D-Day. The Director of Operations Division (Home) agreed when he sent his reply a few days later. He only hoped that Cowie would be able to announce in three months that the number of Bomber Command minelaying operations in the Baltic had increased significantly![55]

On 21 January Cowie concluded that the majority of respondents were of the opinion that nothing would be gained by an official approach to Bomber Command on this issue. But he believed that this situation clearly reflected the Admiralty's limited control over the management of British offensive minelaying activity. So that the Admiralty should be in no doubt about Cowie's position, he wrote, in the margin:

> The AOC-in-C Bomber Command must comply with the Air Ministry Directive which allows him to carry out minelaying when aircraft can be spared from other objectives.[56]

Director of Naval Intelligence Rushbrooke found a diplomatic way out a week later. With his knowledge of the consequences of minelaying for the *Kriegsmarine*, partly based on the Enigma decoding, he did not use the question of competence that Cowie had referred to, but rather the indirect results of minelaying. The mines affected German shipping traffic and tied up large resources in the form of minesweepers, observation posts, equipment and crews, which had to be counted in the result – it was not enough to just count damaged and sunk ships. He mentioned that the Ministry of Economic Warfare (M.E.W.) had pointed out early in 1943 that the overall result of activities directed against German shipping would require the building of replacement ships which in turn required extensive shipyard capacity for this and all repairs. This would inevitably be at the expense of other vital parts of the war industry, including the building and repair of U-boats and other warships. After considering three other factors, of which the minelaying in Danish waters and the Baltic was the only real weapon, he concluded with the following:

---

54 ADM1/15466 Comment by Director of Naval Intelligence, Rushbrooke, 13.1.1944.

55 ADM1/15466 Comments from Director of Anti-U-Boat Division, 16.1.1944, Director of Plans, 17.1.1944 and D.O.D. (Home) 19.1.1944.

56 ADM1/15466 Comments by D.D.O.D. (M) John Cowie 21.1.1944.

> To sum up, M.E.W.'s expectation that combined effect of our offensive action against Germany's merchant shipping would force her to divert effort from other forms of essential war production has received some valid confirmation. The Russian threat to Germany's Eastern Baltic shipbuilding and repair yards, the closing of the Swedish Transit Traffic, the importance which Germany clearly attaches to her activities in the Jutland Peninsula, and the increasing strain to which the manpower and industrial resources of Germany are progressively being put, emphasise the importance of maintaining our offensive action against German merchant shipping by all means at our disposal.

In manuscript, he had noted that steps had already been taken to persuade the Deputy Chief of Air Staff (Operations) to get Bomber Command to intensify mine laying in Danish waters and the Baltic Sea.[57]

In Chapter 8 I explained how Harris used the minelaying as a means to prevent further influence from the Admiralty on Bomber Command's operational dispositions. The above situation from the turn of 1943/1944 could indicate that Harris was more focussed on the large strategic bombing raids than the less spectacular minelaying operations. Perhaps a focus that changed from his time as C-in-C 5 Group, to his job as DCAS in the Air Ministry, to his responsibility for the entire Bomber Command in 1942!

In any case, he apparently had second thoughts at the end of the war. Harris's conclusion on the importance of minefields in 1945 was that all types of ship targets had been sunk or damaged by British mines laid by Bomber Command, including minesweepers. In addition, the minefields had caused major delays in German shipbuilding programmes, especially in the last two years of the war. The mining of the Kiel Canal and Heligoland Bight had caused major delays on the German-controlled waterways.

The effectiveness of the minelaying programmes in the western Baltic was documented by Harris by quoting extracts from a report sent to the German naval command by the *Kriegsmarine* liaison officer of the *Luftwaffe* Operational Division, *Kapitän zur See* Mössel in April 1943. In the report, Mössel drew attention to the lack of escort vessels, allowing escort of troop transports, tankers, hospital ships and warships only in the waters where the mine danger was greatest and where all ships required individual escort.

In February 1944, it happened again. Mössel concluded, based on a recent wargame, that the enemy clearly wanted to disrupt, if not completely destroy, the traffic of supply ships to and from Norway. The main weapon was mines dropped by the RAF. It should therefore be considered whether the night fighter force in Jutland could be reinforced. A few months later he announced that the night fighter force, which was indeed reinforced, might be able to disrupt the mine laying operations but not prevent them. Citing Bomber Command's use of pathfinders and several new types of mines, he concluded that increased activity of this kind in a larger area would prevent all German shipping in the Baltic. In September 1944, the situation was so hopeless that Mössel recorded:

57 ADM1/15466 Comments by D.D.O.D. (M) John Cowie 21.1.1944.

> Without training in the Baltic Sea, and safe escort through coastal waters and the routes to and from operations in the mid-Atlantic, there can be no submarine warfare. Without supplies by sea, it is impossible to hold the position in Norway. Without freedom of movement in the Baltic Sea, we cannot use the coastal German waters for transport ... but we no longer control the sea routes within our own sphere of influence, as evidenced by the daily and weekly blockades of shipping routes in the Baltic Sea area.[58]

When the war ended in Europe in 1945, the United Kingdom War Office asked all defence chiefs and their military commanders to prepare an account of their activities during the war. Many of these dispatches were published in *The London Gazette* after the intelligence services had scrutinised them for any security breaches. But one was missing from the series of publications. The Harris report was considered by the Air Ministry to be very one-sided, misleading and controversial. Most controversial was Harris' view of the bomber as the strategic weapon that would win the war by breaking the morale of the German population. The fierce bombing raids on German cities intensified during the last three years of the war and are still controversial to this day. Therefore, the Air Ministry did not allow Harris' 'Despatch on War Operations' to be published until 1995, and then only in an annotated edition in which various Air Ministry representatives supplemented and corrected most of Harris' chapters. But in the minelaying field, they agreed with Harris in both the explanation and the conclusion. Operation Gardening was clearly Bomber Command's success story.[59]

As many as two-thirds of the total German ship losses due to Bomber Command mines occurred in the Baltic Sea and Danish waters.[60] In a statement from the Danish Ministry of the Navy on 28 February 1948 to the Coastal Fleet and the Mine Ship Division, in response to an enquiry about how many ships were blown up by mines inside and outside the forced routes, it is stated that there were 36 ships sunk and 26 ships damaged in the routes and 202 ships sunk and 101 ships damaged outside the routes in the period April 1940 to 5 May 1945. A total of 365 mine explosions. In the period from the liberation until 15 February 1948, there were 6 ships wrecked and 3 accidents in the routes and 34 ships wrecked and 31 accidents outside the routes. However, the figures are stated with a great uncertainty.[61]

The RAF's, and thus Bomber Command's, first mine laying during World War II was carried out in Danish waters on 13–14 April 1940. The last order during the war to lay mines in European waters was sent to Bomber Command on 3 May 1945. The order read:

> Mission for heavies.
> Minelaying: Kattegat, Læsøo Rende, Aalborg.[62]

58 Arthur T. Harris (Sebastian Cox Ed.), *Despatch on War Operations: 23rd February 1942 to 8th May 1945* (London: Routledge, 1995) pp.173–174.

59 Arthur T. Harris (Sebastian Cox Ed.), *Despatch on War Operations: 23rd February 1942 to 8th May 1945* (London: Routledge, 1995), pp.1–22.

60 Stephen W. Roskill, *The War at Sea 1939–45*, vol. 2 (London: HMSO, 1956), p.392–393.

61 The Ministry of the Navy to the Coastal Fleet and Mineship Division, 28 February 1948, Danish Navy Weapons school, folder 3.

62 Air 14/3412. Operational Research Section, Final reports on operations. Bomber Command rep. on night ops 3/4 May 1945.

A total of 46 Lancasters, 12 from 3 Group and 34 from 6 Group, were to lay mines in the three mentioned waters during the night. However, shortly after the aircraft had left, they were called back,

> … for by that time it was plain that further obstruction of the coastal waters would only embarrass ourselves.[63]

The Danish waters were thus a focus from start to finish for the British Operation Gardening!

Quod erat demonstrandum! Or as the British might translate it, 'Which Was What We Wanted!'

63 Stephen W. Roskill, *The War at Sea 1939–45*, vol. 3 2 (London: HMSO, 1961), p.274.

Postscript

Demining from 1945 to Today – Are There Any Mines Left?

There is a fair degree of accuracy in terms of how many mines Bomber Command planted in Danish waters, and ideally you should be able to compare this figure with the number of mines laid and detonated. In the Chapter above, I tried to find out how many mines were left on 5 May 1945. Since when, British wartime mines have been and are still being destroyed.

As mentioned, the mine balance as of June 1943 was 1,882 mines. In addition, there were another 1,484 mines laid up to and including June 1944, and finally 3,567 mines laid up to May 1945. From this total of 6,933 mines must be deducted the mines detonated from July 1943 until the liberation. According to the Danish Navy's records from July 1943 to March 1944, 100 mines were laid or otherwise detonated. The *Sicherungsdivision Nr 8* states in its annual report for the period April to December 1944 that 566 British bottom mines were swept or detonated. That brings the figure down to 6,267 mines. It is very difficult to get an exact figure on how many mines were detonated in the periods from July 1943 to March 1944 and from January to April 1945. However, the difficulties in compiling an accurate mine account are not only applicable to Denmark, but are a general problem throughout Europe due to inadequate and varied German registration methods.

In *A forgotten Offensive*, the author describes how the German archive material regarding statistics and records of shipping traffic is very incomplete from September 1939 to 1 June 1942, when the Germans established a *Reichskommissariat für die Schiffahrt*. The problem until then was that many different services, units and administrations followed their own interests and only recorded information of importance to themselves.

Until 31 October 1941, no losses or damage to ships under 1,600 GRT were registered, and only after July 1941 were ships in the shipyards included in the statistics on idle ships. In some places, only the tonnage of the ships was recorded but not their number, and for others the other way round. Between May 1943 and November 1944, foreign ships were no longer counted in the statistics, after which the registration and documentation gradually disintegrated as the war drew to a close. The author concludes that only in the period from June 1942 to May 1943 are the figures valid and consistent with all other sources.[1]

Shortly after the liberation, mine sweeping of all the main traffic routes in Danish waters began. This was done with Danish, German and British vessels under British command. In

1 Christina J. M. Goulter, *A Forgotten Offensive: Royal Air Force Coastal Command's Anti-Shipping Campaign 1940–1945* (London: Routledge, 1995), pp.275–276.

October 1945, the Danish Mine Sweeping Division took over the management of this work, but now without British vessels. On 1 December, the Danish minesweeper fleet consisted of 38 minesweepers and a number of auxiliary vessels, cutters and the like, while the German division consisted of 2 mother ships, 6 *sperrbrechere*, 22 large and 22 small minesweepers and 10 auxiliary vessels. In the autumn of 1946, the Danish Navy had to allocate approximately half of the vessels to other tasks, while works on the smaller side and diagonal routes were swept.[2]

At an information meeting on 10 April 1946, organised by the Copenhagen motorboat clubs, *Kommandørkaptajn* E. M. Dahl from the minesweeper service gave a lecture on the mine danger in Danish waters. He did not have a concrete figure for how many mines were left, but said that it was expected that all magnetic mines would be inactive after three years and acoustic mines after only two years. All British mines should therefore be inactive by the end of 1947.[3] It was therefore natural to reduce minesweeping at that time, and in October 1947, the German units' efforts in Denmark ceased. In the autumn of 1948, the force was down to 6 or 8 minesweepers with some auxiliary vessels. New routes were now being swept between the existing forced routes from the war and the fishing grounds.[4]

The records from the Naval Weapons School show that in the years after the war, the navy became more than sceptical about the British claims. In connection with the investigation of the sinking of S/S *København* in 1948, an unnamed officer noted that a condition for excluding a British mine as the cause of the sinking required, 'that in the area in question ONLY the mines that have been confirmed by the British authorities to have been laid' were present (this last is unlikely).[5]

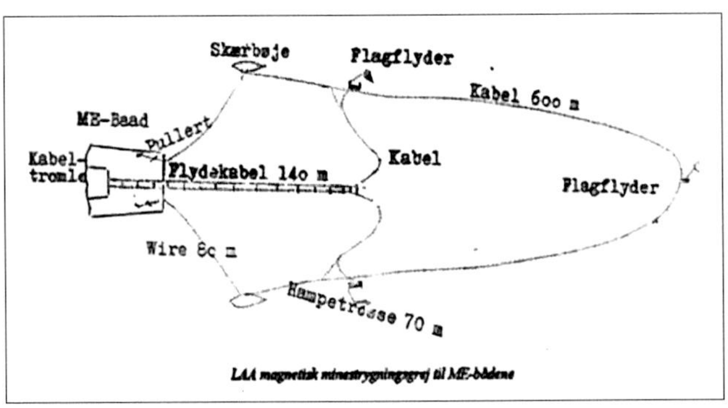

Post 1945 drawing showing how to sweep magnetic mines.

On 1 October 1948, *Kommandør* Poul Adam Mørch from the Danish Defence Intelligence Service compiled the following overview of remaining British mines in Danish waters.[6]

2 'Flåden i Korsør' in *Marinehistorisk Selskab*, nr. 3, 1998, pp.6–7 <https://www.marinehist.dk/FIKors/1998-3-FiKors.pdf> (25.02.2025).

3 Member magazine for *Sundby Sejlforening*, 1946, pp.4–5 &.8. However, it was soon discovered that the lifespan of the batteries in the mines was, for some, much longer than three years!

4 Member magazine for *Sundby Sejlforening*, 1946, pp.4–5 & pp.8–9.

5 'Considerations over which ignition systems in English 'A' Mark I-VI mines may have caused the sinking of S/S *Copenhagen* on 11 June 1948' item 4. *Søværnets Våbenskole*, Copenhagen.

6 Overview from Professor Birger U. Hansen, University of Copenhagen. Email 25 August 2015.

Minestrygningstjenesten Antal aktive miner pr. 1. oktober 1948	red Mark A	blue G700	green F622
Hawthorn 1 (Esbjerg)	151	1	5
Hawthorn 2 (Thyborøn)	24		
Hawthorn 3 (Hanstholm)	9	3	
Yewtree (Frederikshavn)	12		
Krauts (Limfjorden/Mariager/Randers)	93	20	
Silverthorn 10 (Skagen)	127	2	1
Silverthorn 11 (N Anholt)	122	5	
Silverthorn 12 (S Anholt)	321	9	5
Silverthorn 13 (N Sealand)	50	9	
Silverthorn 14 (N entrance of the Sound)	141	11	
Silverthorn 15 (Aarhus Bay)	94	5	2
Pumpkin 1 (N Samsoe Belt)	41		
Pumpkin 2 (S Samsoe Belt)	0		
Broccoli (Nyborg)	0		
Asparagus (Korsør)	114		
Quince N (NE Langeland)	53		
Quince S (S Langeland)	106		
Carrots 1 (Fredericia)	21		
Carrots 2 (Kolding/Middelfart)	21		
Endives (Haderslev/Assens)	32		
Wallflover (Flensborg)	52		
Nasturtium (Elsinore)	27		
Verbena (Copenhagen)	8		
Daffodil 1 (Koege bay)	211	5	10
Daffodil 2 (entrance Falsterbo-Sweden)	21		
Daffodil 3 (Fakse Bay)	41	7	1
Radish 1 (W Fehmern Belt)	215	12	6
Radish 2 (E Fehmern Belt)	6		
Sweet-pea 1	108	11	
Sweet-pea 2	4	6	
Willows			
Pollock (W Bornholm)	76	1	
Total	**2301**	**107**	**30**

Number of live mines in Danish Waters as of 1 October 1948.

According to the *Kommandør*, there should only be 2,438 mines left, but in a report in connection with a naval inquiry into a sinking, it is stated on 22 April 1949 that there were approximately 186 mines in 'Sweet Pea 2', and not just 2! On the other hand, it makes more sense that according to the list in 1948 there should be 113 mines in 'Krauts', when a report on 5 December 1950 calculates that there were approximately 110 active mines in this field. Nor can it be true that the mines in 'Daffodil 1' in a report dated 25 June 1951 are stated to be approximately 260 active mines, an increase of 50 mines! Whereas the 21 mines in 'Daffodil 2', which in a report dated 30 December 1953 have been reduced to approximately 11 active mines, is more accurate.[7]

Mine Counter Measures Denmark – MCM DNK – Divers badge.

The navy's mine clearance unit from Division 23 of 2nd Squadron (Mine Counter Measures Denmark – MCM DNK) is still hunting for British bottom mines in the fields from the war as an exercise during training. Often the Mine Counter Measures divers are called into action to examine the condition of the mines and set explosive charges. The mine rescue divers' motto is: 'Safety first, a mine diver never dies, he only smells like it'.[8]

Quotes from three newspaper articles in recent years reflect the uncertainty about the number of remaining bottom mines:

1. During the war, the British laid approximately 4,100 mines in our waters. These mines were bottom mines and mainly laid by aeroplanes.[9]
2. The mines, which date back to World War II, were dropped by British aircraft to close the passage to the Baltic Sea. It is estimated that the British dropped approximately 165,000 mines in the Baltic Sea, of which around 15,000 were in Danish waters.[10]
3. The British mines are bottom mines dropped by aeroplanes during World War II. The mines are distributed in the majority of Danish waters. There is no historical data indicating the positions of the mines, so they are difficult to locate. Because the technology for clearing mines on the seabed was not developed after World War II, a large number of mines still remain.[11]

In August and September 2015, I was in contact with the Royal Danish Navy's Mines Division with a purpose to obtaining information on the number of British bottom mines laid and otherwise detonated since May 1945. Despite a declared willingness to cooperate and a promise to forward the requested information, I have not received it. A tentative

7 'Minesprængte skibe,' map 1, *Søværnets Våbenskole* (Copenhagen).
8 'Flåden i Korsør' in *Marinehistorisk Selskab* nr. 3, 2000, p.19.
9 'Flåden i Korsør' in *Marinehistorisk Selskab* nr. 3, 2000, p.18.
10 <http://www.soefart.dk/?art=2576>. (March 2013)
11 <http://forsvaret.dk/2ESK/Nyt percent20og percent20Presse/Pages/2014-04-12-miner.aspx>.

reminder in May 2016 gave the same promise, but again without result. At the end of May, however, I received an apology for the lack of response and a short briefing from *Kaptajnløjtnant* Andreas Johansen, Operations Officer MCM Denmark. He wrote, among other things:

> Furthermore, it is very difficult for us to give a qualified answer to how many mines have been removed since 1945, as there is no comprehensive overview of this. There may be a few reports regarding efforts in some areas, but this is only a fraction of the amount that has been removed.
>
> In the time I have been involved in demining [since 2005], it is estimated that 150 mines have been found and blown up in Danish waters by the navy's mine clearers. The effort has not been coordinated overall but is based on the current need for training and education for the units. In 2013–2014 in particular, we made a major effort in the area around Yderflak (between Sjællands Odde and Samsø N) and found around 60 to 70 British bottom mines.
>
> In the same period, 5 to 10 mines were found in the Langeland Belt, both British bottom mines and German anchored mines (previously mechanically swept).[12]

As stated above, there were almost certainly 6,267 British bottom mines left, from which must be subtracted the result of 12 months of German demining in the period 1943–1945, as well as the demolitions after May 1945. How many are left must therefore still be an unresolved question …

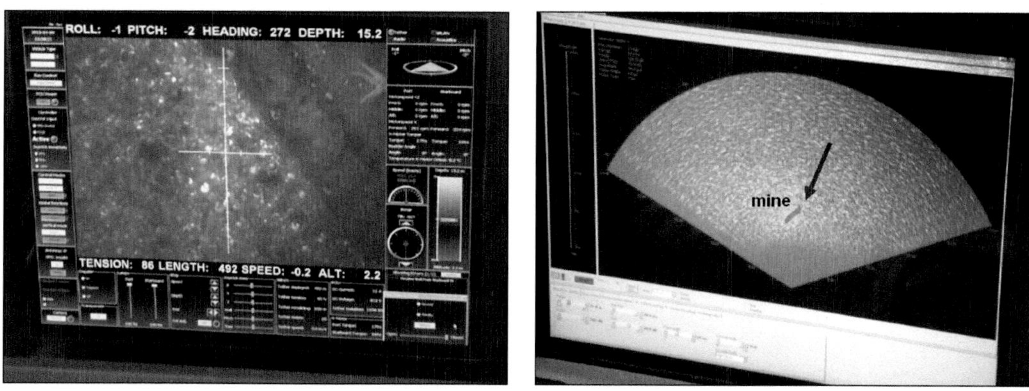

Left: The mine is localised with sonar and an underwater robot is sent down to take a closer look. Right: A 10–20kg explosive charge is placed using the robot. At a safe distance, the explosive charge is detonated and with it the contents of the mine.[13]

12 Email to Frank Weber from *Kaptajnløjtnant* Andreas Johansen, Operations Officer, Mine Counter Measures Denmark (MCM DNK) at the end of May 2016.

13 Navy <http://forsvaret.dk/2ESK/Nyt percent20og percent20Presse/Pages/S percentC3 percentB8v percentC3 percentA6rnetsMinerydningsenhederbortspringerminer.aspx>.

British bottom mine found in April 2010 at Sejerø. It had to be moved before it could be destroyed as it was too close to underwater cables where it was found.

Appendix I

Bomber Command Minelaying Area Codes 1940 - 1945

Anemones - Le Havre	**Melon - Kiel Canal**
Artichokes - Lorient	Mullet - Spezia
Asparagus - Great Belt	Mussels - Terschilling Gat
Barnacle - Zeebrugge	**Nasturtiums - The Sound**
Beech - St Nazaire	Nectarines - Friesan Islands
Bottle - Haugesund	Newt - Maas and Scheldt
Broccoli - Great Belt	Onions - Oslo
Carrots - Little Belt	Oysters - Rotterdam
Cinnamon - La Rochelle	**Pollock – Bornholm-area**
Cypress - Dunkirk	Prawns - Calais
Daffodil - The Sound	Privet - Danzig
Deodar - Bordeaux	**Pumpkins - Great Belt**
Dewberry - Bologne	**Quinces - Great Belt / Kiel Bay**
Eglantine - Heligoland Approaches	**Radishes - Kiel Bay**
Elderberry - Bayonne	Rosemary - Heligoland
Endives - Little Belt	Scallops - Rouen
Flounder - Maas and Scheldt	**Silverthorn 1-7 - Kattegat Area** (25/7-42 ff)
Forget-me-Nots - Kiel Canal	**Sweet Peas - Rostock and Arcone Light**
Furze - St. Jean du Luz	Tangerine - Pillau
Geranium - Swinemunde	Tomato - Oslo Fjord Approaches
Gorse - Quiberon	Trefoils - Texal (South)
Greengage - Cherbourg	Turbot - Ostende
Hawthorn - Esbjerg Approaches	**Undergrowth - Kattegat**
Hollyhock - Travemunde	**Verbena - Copenhagen Approaches**
Hyacinth - St. Malo	Vine Leaves - Dieppe
Jasmine - Travemunde	**Wallflowers - Kiel Bay**
Jellyfish - Brest	Welks - Zuider Zee
Juniper - Antwerp	**Willows - Arcona to River Dievenow**
Krauts – Lim Fjord	Xeranthemums - River Jade
Lettuces - Kiel Canal	**Yams - Heligoland Approaches**
Limpets - Den Helder	**Yewtree – Kattegat** (ud for Frederikshavn)
	Zinneas - River Jade

Areas in Danish Waters and the Western Baltic in bold.
27 of 63 mined areas in Western Europe were located in Danish waters and the Western Baltic Sea.

Appendix II

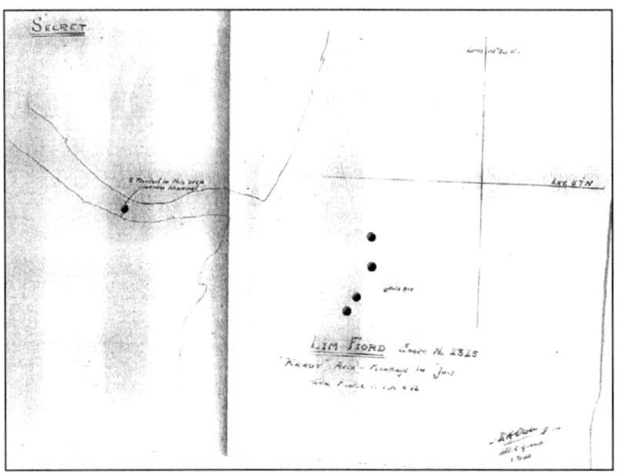

Mines in the 'Kraut' area east of the mouth of the Limfjord, including 5 mines inside the fjord mouth to the left and the rest at Hals Barre.

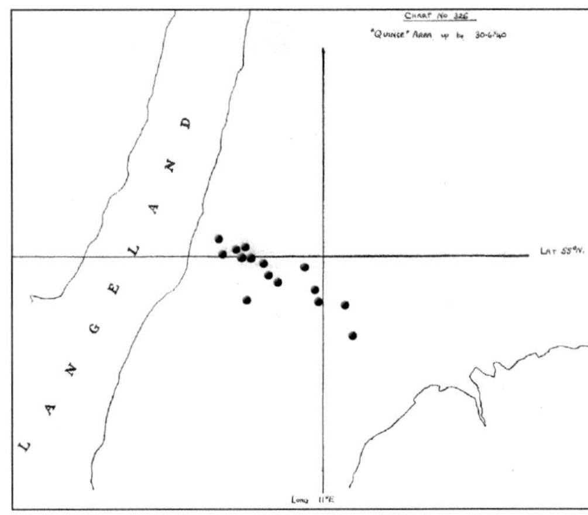

Mining in 'Quince' between Langeland and Lolland.

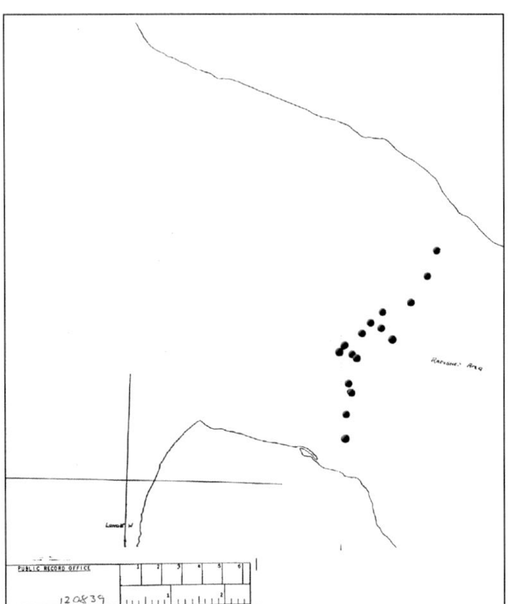

Mines in 'Radishes' on the Rødby-Putgarden ferry route.

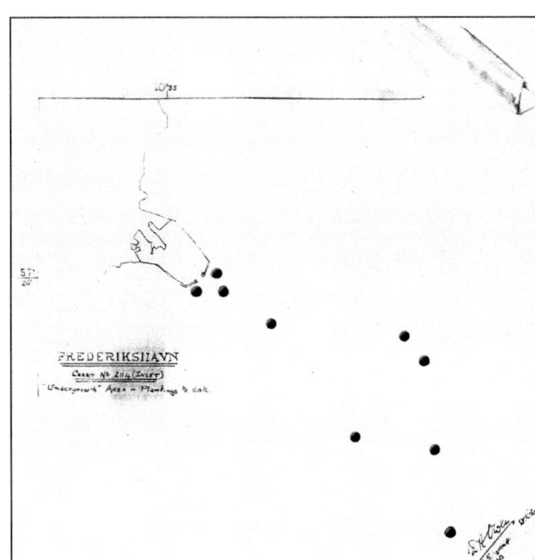

Mines off Frederikshavn in the 'Undergrowth' mining area.

Appendix III

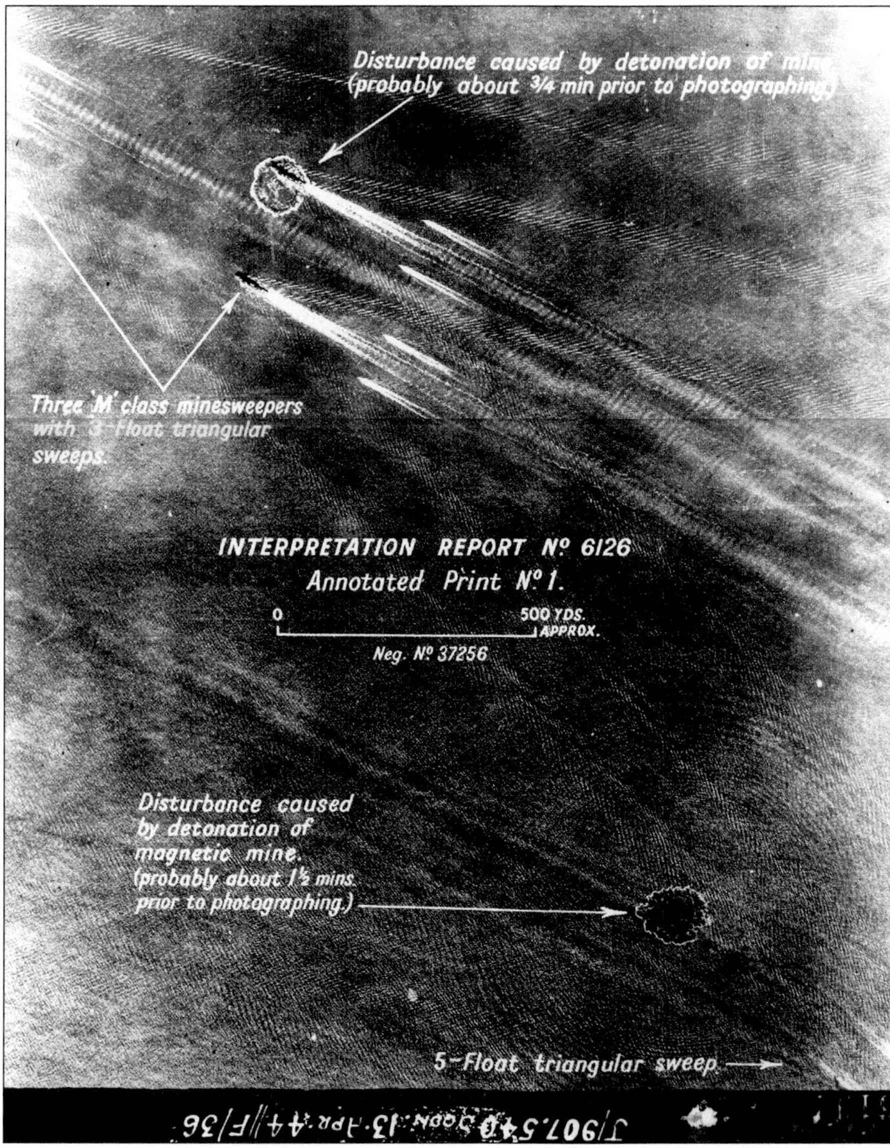

Arial Photo J/907 taken by a/c from 540 Squadron on 13 April 1944.

Bibliography

Primary sources

The starting point for this book has been the Royal Air Force archives held at the National Archives, Kew, London. As part of my master's thesis and other later research projects, I have used archival material from these archives several times between 1983 and 2014.

The archive is systematically organised according to the structure of the RAF:

Air Ministry

↓

Commands: Bomber-, Coastal- and Fighter Command

↓

Groups consisting of several Wings

↓

Wings – operative unit of 3-4Squadrons

↓

Squadrons – operative units typically divided in two Flights

↓

Stations – Airfields with several Wings located

The structure of the RAF, archives of the National Archives, Kew, London.

When an aircraft from a given squadron returned home from a mission, the aircrew was debriefed by an intelligence officer assigned to the airfield where the aircraft was stationed. The information from this debriefing was recorded in the given squadron's war diary, called the Operations Record Book (ORB). Based on each aircrew's report, ORBs were passed up through the operational hierarchy:

At the airfield where the squadron in question was stationed, a 'Station ORB' was kept, in the Group to which the squadron in question was assigned, a 'Group ORB' was kept, and in the Command to which the group in question was assigned, a 'Command ORB' was kept. Here you move from the detailed frog perspective to the bird's eye view. The Command ORB briefly notes that the Group(s) stationed at the Station(s) carried out the mission(s) and why.

The Group ORB is limited to noting that the squadron(s) from that Group made the mission(s) and why – and so on. These operational levels are divided into fixed source groups, so-called Airs:

Air 24	ORB Command
Air 25	Group ORB
Air 26	Wing ORB
Air 27	Squadron ORB
Air 28	ORB Station

At the top of the RAF hierarchy, the Air Ministry, which was the political and military leadership of the RAF, were a large number of political and military functions in the form of staffs, directorates, committees and so on. This work, as well as the staff work from the individual Command and Group headquarters, is catalogued in the other 70 Airs that make up the archive. These Airs contain everything from general political and military considerations to memoranda on the effectiveness and cadence of a given machine gun. Here, all package titles have been reviewed and relevant packages have been selected for inspection. As the list of sources would suggest, the titles rarely indicate anything specific to Denmark, so the search for sources must be based primarily on knowledge and intuition. All of these files have been indispensable, as I have seen it as my primary task not only to describe the mining operations in Danish waters, but also to place them in a larger political and military context.

In principle, a systematic search in Air 24 should be able to retrieve the raids that were carried out over Denmark, as well as information about Squadron, Group and Station, which is the key to a selective search and more detailed information in Air 25, Air 27 and Air 28. Air 26 is a less interesting source group except for the very last phase of the war. This systematic and time-consuming review of Air 24, i.e. of all RAF operations, provides a good chronological overview, but it is very summarised. If you want more detail about the individual missions, you have to search at the lower operational levels and thus engage in more time-consuming work. If you are lucky, you will find the information you need at Group level, otherwise you will have to start with the many squadrons that operated on that particular night or day.

This is typically the case with mine laying missions, which were often carried out in a relatively routine manner and therefore, at both Command ORB and Group level, it was simply stated that so and so many aircraft were 'Gardening in Danish Waters' or 'The Baltic'.

Command ORB and Group ORB have additional packages – often several for each ORB volume. These are also catalogued in Air 24 and Air 25, but have separate reference numbers. The appendix volumes contain typical files that can put the individual operations into military and political perspective, for example in the form of operation orders and smaller memoranda. At the operational level, there is another Air, Air 50. It contains so-called combat reports. If a crew had enemy contact during a mission, they had to submit such a combat report to the base intelligence officer. These very detailed reports are stored in Air 50, which is rather incomplete.

As the mining operations largely involved the British Admiralty, the Admiralty's archives have also been analysed and relevant packages have been selected for perusal. The same applies to the Foreign Office and War Office archives and, to a lesser extent, Cabinet papers. All of these are also held in the National Archives in London.

With regard to British photo documentation, the National Archives photo archive (also catalogued in Airs) has been reviewed, and the Imperial War Museum's photo archive has been searched for relevant material, as far as the somewhat inadequate cataloguing allowed. Finally, I have twice visited an archive of all British air reconnaissance photos, which at the time was located at the University of Keele at Stoke-on-Trent. For Denmark, there are thousands of photos, and only in a few cases where a photo was of particular documentary interest did I use this rich archive.

The other source base in this study is the German Navy's Recent Archive and the Civil Defence Agency's archive, both of which are located in the Danish National Archives in Copenhagen. In the former, I have particularly used and enjoyed *Admiral Dänemark* (Adm. Dän.) KTB and Admiral Skagerrak KTB (*Kriegstagebuch*) and the local war diaries. A grant from the Danish Council for Humanities Research made it possible to acquire a microfilm copy of the relevant material, which I have now handed over to the Bunker Museum in Hanstholm. The German archive material mentions overflights, mine and bomb drops, and these files reflect German thoughts and actions in connection with these. Unfortunately, the KTB is illegible in several cases, and in some periods it is completely missing, for example in the last few months of the war. In the archives of the Danish Civil Defence Agency, I have exclusively used Statens Civile Luftværn (SCL), Meldinger og Rapporter 1940–45. This source group contains instant messages between command centres and reporting posts, the National Reporting Centre's summarising daily reports and finally Fluko (Flugabwehrkommando Dänemark) reports to the National Reporting Centre. Here, all air defence events were meticulously recorded. Thus, there are examples of reports relating to events taking up several thick archive packs in one day. The major shortcoming of this otherwise rich archive is that attacks on German military territory are rarely recorded here, as the *Statens Civile Luftværn* was rarely given access to record reports. However, special mention should be made of two publications based on the records of the *Statens Civile Luftværn*: Luftværnsmæssige begivenheder under krigen, 1940–45 (here called 'Luftbogen') and *Statens Civile Luftværn*, 1938–45 Bd. I-III (referred to as SCL I-III). Both have the character of official, retrospective reports.

I have also used the German Air Force Archive, i.e. the relatively few fragments in the National Archives' Danica collection. The National Archives' collection of *Luftwaffe* files has not been systematic or comprehensive. On the other hand, the RAF archives have contained detailed knowledge about the *Luftwaffe*'s strategies, strengths and measures in Denmark. Through various intelligence methods and sources, the RAF gained a detailed insight into the *Luftwaffe*'s changing dispositions in Denmark. One of the sources turned out to be the Danish illegal intelligence service in Stockholm, where Ebbe Munck's Supplementary Archive, also located in the Danish National Archives, shows a clear connection between the activities of the Danish military intelligence service and the knowledge the RAF possessed, primarily through its own intelligence department, Air Intelligence. There was a dedicated SOE department in Air Intelligence, so there is at least a possible distribution channel for the probably highly selective intelligence that was passed on to the RAF.

Archives

Command Operations Record Books

200	BC ORB 1940
203	BC ORB 1941
204	BC ORB 1942
205	BC ORB 1943
206	BC ORB 1944 Jan-Jun
207	BC ORB 1944 Jul-Dec
209	BC ORB 1945
215	BC App to 1940
216	BC. App. 1940 Apr-May
217	BC. App. 1940 May
218	BC. App. 1940 Apr-May
219	BC. App. 1940 Apr-May
220	BC. App. 1940 Jun-Aug
221	BC. App. 1940 Sep-Dec
222	BC. App. 1940 Jul-Aug
223	BC. App. 1940 Sep-Oct
224	BC. App. 1940 Nov-Dec
225	BC. App. 1940 Jun-Aug
226	BC. App. 1940 Sep-Dec
227	BC. App. 1941 Jan
228	BC. App. 1941 Feb
229	BC. App. 1941 Mar
230	BC. App. 1941 Apr
231	BC. App. 1941 May
232	BC. App. 1941 Jun
233	BC. App. 1941 Jul
234	BC. App. 1941 Aug
235	BC. App. 1941 Sep
236	BC. App. 1941 Oct
237	BC. App. 1941 No
238	BC. App. 1941 Dec
240	BC. App. 1942 Feb
243	BC. App. 1942 May
245	BC. App. 1942 Jul
247	BC. App. 1942 Sep
251	BC. App. 1943 Jan
252	BC. App. 1943 Feb
273/276	BC. App. 1944 May
277/283	BC. App. 1944 June
284/287	BC. App. 1944 July
292/294	BC. App. 1944 Sep
315/318	BC. App. 1945 Apr

Air 2 Air Ministry Correspondence

2940 1939–44. Bombing Committee: Minutes of meetings
5101 1940. Invasion of Denmark and Norway
7757 Enemy occupied countries. Consolidated bombing instructions
7974 Mining of inland waterways in enemy occupied countries
8654 1940–41. Inter-service committee on the analysis of bombing
8655 1940–44. Bombing Committee

Air 8 Chief of the Air Staff, Papers

1127 German air disarmament

Air 14 Bomber Command

146 1939 May–1941 Apr. War orders: policy regarding action of bomber squadrons in war
194 1939–1940. Air Bombardment: Air Ministry policy regarding various plans
213 1940 Apr-June. Reports on Operations for inclusion in Bomber Command daily bulletins
223 Plan W.A.6 – Vulnerability of oil plants and priority list of targets.
350 1937–39, Preparation of bomb target maps in potential enemy countries
1937–40
Dec. War orders. general policy
377 1939 Oct–1941 May. Direction finding policy and memorandum
426 1940 Apr–1943 March. B bombing: reports and general information
531 1940 Feb–1942 Aug, No 5 Bomber group – summary of events
634 1940 Aug–1941 Aug. Enemy night tactics against bombers, vol. I
669 Bomber Command operations during the Norwegian Campaign. Draft dispatch by Air Marshal Portal
673 1940 July–1941 Jan. Bomber operations: reports
676 1940 June-Sept. Bomber operations: reports
700 Feb-Jun 1940. M-mine. Plan WA15 for operations against enemy Shipping
701 Jun-Nov 1940. Gardens mined June-August 1940
702 Nov 1940-Nov 1941
704 Nov 40-Nov 43 App
705 Dec 43-Aug 45 App
709 1940 Feb–1942 March. Coordinated operations: Bomber and Coastal Command
728 July 42-July 44. Mining Operation orders and instructions.
746 Directives No. 2 Group
747 Directives No. 2 Group
748 Directives No. 2 Group
749 Directives No. 2 Group
753 1940 Nov–1945 May. No. 5 group, directives
754 1942–44 July. No 5 group, directives
762 1940 March-May. Night recon. tasks
775 Air Ministry directives
776 Air Ministry directives

777 Air Ministry directives
778 Air Ministry directives
779 Air Ministry directives
780 Air Ministry directives
782 Air Ministry directives
796 1940 Apr–1942 Aug. Gardening operations
797 1941 May–1942 Aug. Gardening operations
800 1940 Sept–1942 July. Bomber attacks on targets in enemy occupied territory: reports
824 1940 Mar-Apr. operation against Hornum seaplane base
1091 1940 Apr.-May. 'X' force for Scandinavia
1199 1940 June–1945 June. German AA defences
1213 Security – code names.
1213 1940 Sep–1946 Jan. Security: Codenames
1215 1943 July–1945 March. Enemy batteries: Coastal illustrations
1217 1940 July–1944 Aug. defences: enemy night fighters
1395 1942 July–46 Apr. operational photography: policy
1552 Feb.-May 44. Bomber Offensive: Minelaying
1557 Jan. 41-July 44. Sea-mining operations results
1561 1944 Jan.-Sept. diversionary operations
1775 1942 Feb–1945 Jan. British intruder activity: Analysis
1889 Enemy decoys: investigations
1890 Enemy decoys: investigations
1891 Enemy decoys: maps + photographs
1925 1940 Apr–1941 Dec. A.O.C. in C. Bomber Command correspondence with Parliamentary and Permanent Under Secretary of State
1929 1940 Apr–1941 Dec. A.O.C. in C. Bomber Command correspondence with Vice Chief of the Air Staff
1934 1940 Jan–1942 Feb. A.O.C. in C. Bomber Command correspondence with Director of Bomber operations
1936 1940 Nov–1941 Sept. A.O.C. No. 2 group Correspondence with A.O.C. in C
2005 1940 Apr–1942 Nov. Bombing operations: general plans
2064 1940 Mar–1943 Dec. Operation 'Gardening'
2068 1942 May–1945 May. Targets: special briefing data
2080 1944 June–1945 July. Raid reports
2086 Raid Reports Apr 1945
2141 1940–1945. intelligence watch diary No. 5 Group
2142 1940–1945. intelligence watch diary No. 5 Group
2427 1943 May–1945 July. intelligence reports.
2484 1944–45. No. 139 Sqdn: use of planned position target indication – photographs
2478 1943 Dec.–1945 Dec. Exceptional and interesting sorties
2489 RAF Waddington. Operations Diary
2490 RAF Waddington. Operations Diary
2491 RAF Waddington. Operations Diary

2494	RAF Waddington. Operations Diary
2595	1940 Apr-May. Operations by Bomber Command from invasion Norway to withdrawal of main British force, 3 May
2651	German airfield photos
2664	1939 Sept.–1940 Apr. Night bomb raid sheets vol. I
2665	1940 May–June. Night bomb raid sheets
2685	1940 Jan.-May. Form 'K' operations reports
2713	1943 Feb.–1945 Apr. operational research reports.
2782	1940 Jan–1941 Jan. Operation reports 1940
2804	June-July 1944. No. 100 Group: Operations logbook
2805	June-July 1944. No. 100 Group: Operations logbook
2822	1939 Aug–1940 Sept. Bomber Command operational instructions
2823	1940 Apr–1941 Sept. Bomber Command operational instructions
2824	1941 Dec. Bomber Command operational instructions
2826	1939–1941 Jan. Bomber Command operation orders and administrative plan
2876	June 1944. No. 100 group: operations logbook
2877	June-July 1944. No. 100 group: operations logbook
2903	1941 July–1944 May. Interpretation reports on W/T targets in France and Denmark
2904	1942 June–1943 Nov. Interpretation reports on W/T targets in France and Denmark
2909	1942 Sept–1944 July. Knickebein radio navigational stations: interpretation reports
2913	1944 July–1945 June. German night fighters
2914	1943 July–1945 May. German night fighters
2982	1940 Jan-Dec. No. 5 group operation orders
2983	1939 Sept–1940 Aug. No. 5 group operation orders
3331	1945 June-Aug. POST MORTEM Exercises
3337	May 42-Mar 45. Analysis of minelaying operations, research
3412	Operational Research Section: final reports on operations, night raids, 1944 June–1945 May
3413	1939 Sept.–1940 July. Intelligence summaries
3414	1940 Aug-Oct. intelligence summaries
3415	Intelligence summaries, Nov-Mar. 41
3416	Intelligence summaries, Apr-Jul. 41
3417	Intelligence summaries, Jul-Dec. 41
3418	Intelligence summaries, Jun-Feb. 43
3510	1942 May. Air Officer Commander-in-Chief correspondence with Ministry of Economic Warfare
3647	Night photographs of operational results
3648	Night photographs of operational results
3649	Night photographs of operational results
3653	Night photographs of operational results
3654	Night photographs of operational results
3666	War album

3667 War album
3668 War album
3669 War album
3670 War album
3671 Goods album
3672 War album
3673 War album
3674 Goods album
3675 War album
3677 War album
3678 War album
3679 War album
3680 War album
3681 War album
3707 1939 Dec.–1941 Dec. A.O.C. in C. Photographs, vol. II ports and shipping
3720 1941 Sept.–1944 Apr. target illustrations: airfields and miscellaneous targets

Air 15 Coastal Command
10 Sweeps into the Skagerak
223 1940 Sept–1942 Feb. No. 1 PRU: reports
245 Jan 40-Dec. Minelaying areas. Weekly intelligence Digest Nov 41-May 43
258 Jan 45-June. Weekly Intelligence reports
267 Oct 42-Dec 44. Minelaying areas
269 Weekly Intelligence Digest Nov 41-May 43
269 Nov 1941-May 43. Weekly intelligence reports
387 May-Jun 42. Operations against *Prinz Eugen*
391 Oct 1944-Apr 45. Operations against enemy shipping in eastern Skagerak and Kattegat.
474 Feb 1944-Jul 45. North Germany and Denmark – survey of damaged shipping.
491 Dec 1940-Aug 43. Norway and Denmark. Operations against naval, military and industrial targets.
29 Jan 41-Jan. 43. Minelaying by Aircraft.
530 Apr 1940-Feb 1945. Minelaying in Norwegian and Danish Waters
539 Apr 1941-May 1945. Attacks on enemy shipping
541 Apr 1942-Apr 1945. No. 16 group: Attacks on enemy shipping off Danish and Dutch coasts
544 Nov 1941-Apr Target Committee
643 July 1940-May 1945. Compilations of sqdn record books form 540 and 541
644 Feb-July 1945
650 Dec 1942-Nov 44. Air Combat reports
666 Oct 1939-May 43. No. 16 Group tactical instructions
744 Bombing Committee papers
745 Bombing Committee papers
772 Apr 40-Jul 41. Sea-mining sheets, no 1–200, vol. 1

Air 16 Fighter Command

542 Dec 41-Jul 43. Intruder: Use of Mosquito A/C
554 Jul 42-Aug 43. Intruder operations room
556 Aug. 42-Dec. 44. Long-range fighter operations
665 Jun.-Aug 1944. Bombing policy in occ. terr.
740 May 41-Nov 43. German Radar System
745 May 1940-Nov 1942. Offensive operations over enemy occupied territory
804 1944 Sept. Offensive operations: use of force
1053 June 1945. Exercise 'Post Mortem'
1054 June 1945. Exercise 'Post Mortem'

Air 20 Air Ministry Unregistered papers

781 1944 Jan-Nov. Attacks on targets in enemy occupied countries
1157 1941 Oct–1943 Dec. Target Committee reports
1638 Feb 1944. German Coastal radar locations
1639 Apr-Jun. 1944. German Coastal radar locations
1640 Feb-Jun. 1944. G.C.I. Station, Control and plotting
1676 July 1942. German Coast watching: R.D.F. Stations
2299 1940 March. Scandinavian and Baltic States: Air station map
2331 Feb 1942-Apr 1945. German anti-aircraft: Intelligence summaries
2781 1940 May-Oct. War Cabinet: Correspondence
2782 1940 Aug War Cabinet: Correspondence
1942 Oct War Cabinet: Correspondence
2783 1943 Jan-Dec War Cabinet: Correspondence
2784 1944 Jan. War Cabinet: Correspondence
1946 July. War Cabinet: Correspondence
2787 June 1940-Dec 1942. War Office, Correspondence
2788 Jan 1943-Aug 1945
4057 1941 Aug. Operations of 2 Group. BC
1943 May. Operations of 2 Group. BC
4272 1940 Apr-July. Scandinavia: Operational reports

Air 22 Air Ministry Periodical returns, summaries and bulletins

8 War room daily summaries Apr 1940
9 War room daily summaries May 1940
12 War room daily summaries Apr-June 1940
16 War room daily summaries Oct 1940
27 War room daily summaries Dec 1941
29 War room daily summaries May-Oct 1942
30 War room daily summaries Nov 42-Jan 43
51 Daily resumes of air operations Jan-June 40
52 Daily resumes of air operations Jan-Dec 40
71 Weekly intelligence summaries Apr-June 40 (Air Ministry)
72 Weekly intelligence summaries July-Sept 40 (Air Ministry)
77 Weekly intelligence summaries Sept 42-Mar 43 (Air Ministry)

207 Confidential reports on air operations 1939–1945, vols I-IV
210 Confidential reports on air operations 1939–1945, vols I-IV
336 War room monthly summary. Bomber Command (1940–42)
363 Daily resumes of air operations Jul-Dec 42
364 Daily resumes of air operations Jan-June 42
366 Daily resumes of air operations July-Dec 42
402 Apr-Dec 1944. Bomber Command and USAAF Bomber Command: Summaries of operations
447 1940 Mon-June. Air Ministry W/T Intel Service
477 Air Ministry W/T intelligence service daily summaries. Mar-Jun 1940
478 Air Ministry W/T intelligence service daily summaries. Jun-Aug 1940
483 Air Ministry W/T intelligence service daily summaries. Jan-May, 1942
502 Air Ministry W/T intelligence service daily summaries. Sep-Dec 1944
503 Air Ministry W IT intelligence service daily summaries. Jan-May 1945

Air 24 Air Historical Branch

Air 37 Directorate of Intelligence Papers
232 Operations Air Intelligence, May 1942, special targets in occupied countries: Copenhagen Etc.
243 P.R.U. 1941–42. Enemy aerodromes camouflage – album of photographs
253 Air Intelligence, April 1943. Attack on German Air Force: Possibilities of concerted attack and selection of targets
347 Assistant Director of Intelligence (Photographic) July 1941-May 1943. Aerial photographs of docks, naval bases, industrial targets, communications et cetera in Germany and German-occupied territory
1139 Chains of Command in the German Air Force, 1939–1945
1159 Air Intelligence 3 (E). June 39-Jan 45. German waterways: locations and size of traffic et cetera
1161 Air Intelligence 3 (E), June 39-Jan 45. German Air Force Erganzungs-gruppen: reports and extracts
1185 Jan 44-Feb 45. Combined strategic targets. Committee working. Committee papers: German Air Force
1211 July 1941. Air Intelligence. Denmark: List of German Air Force bases
1235 Air Intelligence. July 1941-May 1945. Denmark: List of Airfields, landings grounds and seaplane bases and amendments
1247 Sept 1941-May 1945. Air Intelligence
1324 Air Intelligence 3 (E), Apr 45. German Air Force – order of battle of reserve training units and list of training schools
1343 Air Intelligence, Apr 1944-Feb 1945. Beacon Bible: German visual and radio beacons, codenames and locations
1514 Directorate of bomber operations. Oct. 1944-May 1945. Combined strategic target committee: signals to and from Air Ministry
1585 Air Intelligence (Air liaison) Nov 1941-June 1994. Denmark: miscellaneous
1722 Air Intelligence 3 (B), May 40-July. Data for the study of the Norwegian Campaign.

1819 Directorate of Air Tactics, Jan-Apr 1944 Attacks on radar systems
2098 Air Intelligence 3, Apr 45-May. German Air Force in Germany and German-occupied territory, estimated strength and serviceability of aircraft
2156 Directorate of Intelligence. Target list. (Industry, Radar et cetera)
2157 Assistant Directorate of Intelligence (Photographic), Feb-Nov 1942. Coastal Command section. Operations Record Book

Air 40
1181 Captured documents lists no. 70/1945, 70/71. Book: *KTB der Seenotbezirkstelle Aalborg, Jan-Dec 1942*

Air 41
43 RAF in the Maritime War, Sep 39 – Jun 41
47 RAF in the Maritime War, Jul 41 – Feb 43
48 RAF in the Maritime War, Feb 43 – May 44
74 RAF in the Maritime War, Jun 44 – May 45
79 RAF in the Maritime War, Statistics: RAF in the Maritime War, Air Historical Branch (1) Air Ministry

Foreign Office
FO371
47325 Minesweeping in Danish waters, 1945
56142 Minesweeping in Danish waters, 1946
71387 Expenses of German minesweeping in Danish waters, 1948

War Cabinet
CAB 101
324 Air offensive against enemy shipping and Bomber Command's minelaying operations, 1 Sept 44 to 5 May 45

CAB 106
1159 1939–40. Summary of War Cabinet, conclusion on Scandinavia, 20 December 1939–11 May 1940
1174 Comment and reflections on the campaign, Apr 1940-Jun 1940

War Office
WO 208
3117 Apr 1945, German Order of Battle in Denmark
3117 Radar, DF and Radio installations. Apr 1945

WO 220
657 Denmark – Policy and directives

WO 252
65 Aarhus harbour

66 The port of Copenhagen
67 Denmark West Coast
68 Denmark the Skaw, port and Sønderborg (harbour)

Foreign Office
F0371
32760 1942. Situation in Denmark
36787 1943. Situation in Denmark
36788 1943. Situation in Denmark
36789 1943. Situation in Denmark
36790 1943. Situation in Denmark
36791 1943. Situation in Denmark
36792 1943. Situation in Denmark
36799 1943. Policy towards Demark
43151 1944. Report by Ebbe Munck

The Admiralty
ADM 1 Admiralty and Secretariat Papers
10788 Orders and conditions for attacks on shipping by submarines and aircraft in the North Sea, Skagerrak and off Norwegian, Danish, Swedish and German coasts
11308 1941. Minelaying by naval aircraft. Memo on experience
11320 1941. Minelaying by aircraft in German … shipping routes
12735 1943. Organisation for the conduct of mine warfare
13375 1943. Offensive minelaying policy
15412 1942. British minelaying. RAF cooperation
15466 Review of offensive minelaying in … the Baltic 1943–44
17490 1945 Coastal Command RAF memo on the conduct of anti-shipping operations
18630 Royal Navy mining policy in the Baltic, 1945
188858 Use of Speerbrechers for minesweeping in Denmark. 1939–40

ADM 116 Admiralty and secretariat cases
4471 Scandinavian and Baltic States. Tactical and strategic policy to be adopted, 1939–40

ADM 189
196 German minesweeping operations: Photographs, diagrams and their interpretation, 1940–44
197 German minesweeping operations: Photographs, 1941–43
198 German minesweeping operations: Photographs, 1943–44
199 German minesweeping operations: Photographs, 1944
200 German minesweeping operations: Photographs, 1944

ADM 199
153 Minelaying and minesweeping records, 1939–1945
154 Minelaying and minesweeping records, 1939–1945

155	Minelaying and minesweeping records, 1939–1945
156	Minelaying and minesweeping records, 1939–1945
187	Naval operations in the Baltic, North Sea, Engl Chan and Pacific, 1943–45 [Op. Moonshine]
188	Naval operations in the Baltic, North Sea, Engl Chan and Pacific, 1944–45. [Operation Cleaver 45]
535	Minelaying and minesweeping: Reports, 1939–43
539	Minelaying and minesweeping: Reports, 1939–40
544	Minelaying and minesweeping: Reports, 1942–44
550	Minelaying and minesweeping: Reports, 1939–45
551	Minelaying and minesweeping: Reports, 1939–45
843	Naval and air operations: Reports, 1941–45
847	RAF and FAA operations, 1940–47
1171	Enemy mining activity and minesweeping: Summaries, 1939–40
1172	Enemy mining activity and minesweeping: Summaries, 1939–45
1368	Danish, Swedish and Swiss neutrality: Infringements

ADM 213

256	Adm. mining establishment. Report on effectiveness of sweep against British a/c laid mines: VES Speerbrecher, German Technical Translation
852	Technical and operational history of German minesweeping, vol. 1
853	Technical and operational history of German minesweeping, vol. 2
854	Technical and operational history of German minesweeping, vol. 3
855	Technical and operational history of German minesweeping, vol. 4
856	Technical and operational history of German minesweeping, vol. 5

ADM 223 Admiralty intelligence papers

3	Numbered section of the Baltic swept ways 1941. Changes in U-boat exercising areas in the Baltic. 1941. German naval grid. German fleet exercises in the Baltic 23–25/10–1941 New German W/T communications in Denmark, 1942 Notes on German transport movements by sea to Oslo, 1942. Routes used by German warships between Germany and Norway 1942. Western Baltic, numbered ways 1942
4	Record of enemy traffic across Skagerrak to and from Kristiansand South, 10/7-10/8 1943
6	Western Baltic swept channels. 1944–45
43	Special Intelligence. Reports and summaries regarding … and tonnage of Danish troop convoys to South Norway, 27/11-44
64	Operational Intelligence Centre. Enemy reports. 1/1-30/6-44
82	Operational Intelligence. Daily reports. Apr-June 1940
107	Photocopies of papers cited in history of intelligence 1939–45, vol. 2, chap 19

ADM 234

91	Naval Intelligence Division: Denmark 1944
218	British minelaying campaign, Sept 39 – May 1945. 1945–1970
457	Handbook of aircraft mines. Pamphlets nos 1–4, 1943–1954

ADM

Admiralty mine design dept. and Adm. mining establishment: Reports

494 Safe depths of minesweeps against British magnetic mines. 1944

675 German aircraft mine dropped at Shoeburyness, 22/11 1939

Den tyske marines nyere arkiv 1922-1945. (RA)

Oberbefehlshaber der Kriegsmarine

pakke/læg Emne

7/141 D.9/3 1940-4/2 1941: Besprechungspunkte fur Vortråge beim Führer,

81151 D. 1811-27/6 1944: Besprechungspunkte fur Vortråge beim Führer,

38/466 D. 1/7 1944-30/1 1945: Ob. d.M. beim Führer. Niederschriften.

38/467 D. 15/2-18/4: Od. d.M. beim Fuhrer. Niederschriften.

Grossadmiral Raeder - Sammlungen Personlich

2/27 D. 8/3 1939-11/6 1940: Kriegsfragen.

38/463 D. 7/9 1939-22/4 1940: Niederschriften der Besprechungen des Ob. d.M. beim Führer

12/199 D. 17/9 1939-14/6 1940: Personliche Briefe u. Aufzeichnungen.

38/464 D. 2211-17/61942: Niederschriften der Besprechungen des Ob. d.M. beim Führer

Oberkommando der Kriegsmarine

2/34 D. 25/9-14/12 1941: Weisungen PKW (Führer). Weserübung

37/447 D. 9/4-10/4 1940: Lagebericht. Luftwaffenführungsstab.

30/309 1940 udateret: Auszug aus dem Erfarungsbericht der 69. Inf. Div. Norwegen Operation.

Stab des Oberkommandos der Kriegsmarine

30/318 D.23/3 1940-29/5 1941: Akte l, Teil 1.

Marineattachegruppe

30/322 D.9/11 1939-19/51941: Dänemark Etappe.

Archiv der Marine

Tryksager

1/9 1940-1941: Die Kriegsmarine bei der Besetzung Norwegen und Dänemark durch die deutsche Wehrmacht im April1940.

1/1 1942: SB-Plan Dänemark.

1./Seekriegsleitung (Operationsabteilung)

Pakke/læg Emne

Teil A. Kriegstagebücher

3/42 KTB d. 1/4-30/4 1940.

3/45	KTB d. 4/7-27/7 1940.
3/46	KTB d. 1/8-30/8 1940.
3/49	KTB d. 12/11 1940.
3/51	KTB d. 3/2-27/2 1941.
3/52	KTB d. 1/3-26/3 1941.
3/54	KTB d. 12/5-31/5 1941.
3/55	KTB d. 7/6-26/6 1941.
3/56	KTB d. 18/7 1941.
3/58	KTB d. 13/11 1941.
3/61	KTB d. 2/3 1942.
3/62	KTB d. 17/4 1942.
3/63	KTB d. 5/5-27/5 1942.
3/64	KTB d. 2/6-25/6 1942.
3/65	KTB d. 28/8-29/8 1942.
3/66	KTB d. 10/9-30/9 1942.
3/67	KTB d. 2/10-30/10 1942.
3/68	KTB d. 2/11-20/11 1942.
3/71	KTB d. 2/2-25/2 1943.
3/72	KTB d. 2/3-27/3 1943.
3/73	KTB d. 6/4-29/41943.
3/74	KTB d. 6/5-23/5 1943.
3/79	KTB d. 3/10-30/10 1943.
4/80	KTB d. 1/11-20/11 1943.
4/81	KTB d. 2/12-31/121943.
4/82	KTB d. 2/1-21/1 1944.
4/83	KTB d. 212-29/2 1944.
4/84	KTB d. 2/3-29/3 1944.
4/85	KTB d. 1/4-28/41944.
4/86	KTB d. 3/5-27/5 1944.
4/87	KTB d. 1/6-30/6 1944.
4/88	KTB d. 1/7-27/7 1944.
4/89	KTB d. 15/8-31/8 1944.
4/90	KTB d. 3/9-30/9 1944.
4/91	KTB d. 1/10-28/10 1944.
4/92	KTB d. 1/11-30/11 1944.
4/93	KTB d. 1/12-31/12 1944.
12/200	KTB d. 1/2-28/2 1944.
1/17	KTB d. 1/4-20/41944.

Teil B-D

7/133	D. 1/9 1939-20/4 1940: Teil D. Ostsee.
4/97	D. 6/9 1939-10/4 1945: Teil B. III. Lageubersicht Ostsee.
5/105	D. 13/9 1939-8112 1940: Teil B. VIII. Völkerrecht. Propaganda und Politik.
5/109	D. 21/9 1939-30/10 1942: Teil C. III. Ostsee.
5/104	D. 41101939-30/41940: Teil B. VII. Handelsschiffahrt.

6/123 D. 311-12/51940: Teil C. VII. Niederschriften des Chefs der SkI.

6/119 D. 17/6 1942: Überlegungen des Chefs der SkI. und Niederschriften über Vorträge und Besprechungen beim Führer.

6/127 D.20/3 1943-30/101944: Teil C. X. Küsten-und Flakverteidigung.

6/114 D. 20110 1943-10/1 1945: Teil C. III. Ostsee.

5/102 D. 9/11-13/11 1943: Teil B. V Anlagen allgemeines Inhalts.

7/145 D. 13/11-16/6 1943: 1 B. Anlage zum Teil C. II. a. Handakte: Feindliche Großhandlungen.

4/96 D. 1/1-30/4 1944: Teil B. II. a. Lageübersicht Marine-Oberkommando Nordsee für die Monate Januar, Februar, 1944.

6/112 D. 911-27/5 1944: Teil C. III. Ostsee.

5/103 D. 2411-31/5 1944: Teil B. Heft V Anlagen verschiedenen Inhalts, Bd. 9.

1/18 D. 30/6-1/7 1944: Teil C. VIL Niederschriften über die Besprechungen des Ob. d.M. mit dem Führer.

6/113 D. 8/7-16110 1944: Teil C. III. Ostsee.

Lagezimmer

45/523 D. 23/2 1940-30/3 1941: Attache Meldungen L Teil.

45/524 D. 23/2 1940-30/3 1941: Attache Meldungen II. Teil.

37/445 D. 9/4 1940: Angelegenheiten Gruppe Ost.

Minensicherung, Ostsee

10/177 D. 30/6-26/10 1939: Minensicherung in der Ostsee.

10/178 D. 6/11 1939-21/5 1940: Minensicherung in der Ostsee.

Handelskrieg

10/183 D. 11/4-25/4 1940: Norwegenfahrt, Bd.5.

7/136 D. 23/5 1940: Seekrieg. Weisungen der SkI. für die Führung des Seekrieges.

Akter om Danmark

10/184 D. 2/6 1942-16111 1943: 1.C. 1. 1. Kriegsführung durch Deutschland.

12 Dänemark-Norwegen-Unternehmen. B. Dänemark, Bd. 3 u. 4.

11/192 D. 7/10 1943-24111 1944: 1C. 1. B. 4 Dänemark. Die Kriegsgerät und Kriegsschiffe.

11/189 D. 31112 1943-311 1945: 1.C., 1. Bd. 4. Dänemark. A. Allgemeines.

Akten 1o/1 Op Weserübung

9/161 D. 6/3-7/41940: Weserübung, Bd. 8 ,9, 12 u. 13.

9/169 D. 15/4-18/4 1940: Weserübung. Fernschreiben- und Funkspruch-sammlung.

101171 D. 25/4-30/4 1940: Weserübung. Fernschreiben- und Funkspruch-sammlung.

1943-1945

1/8 D. 24/8-31/81943: Fernschreiben- und Funkspruchsammlung.

1/20 D.29/3 1944-15/4 1945: Weisungen OKW (Führer).

39/475 A-BD. 19/3-7/5 1945: Führerbefehle 1945.

2/28 D. 24/4-30/4 1945: Lage Ostsee am 24.4.1945.

38/468 D. 8/5-30/6 1945: Akte I, 4. Bd. 1.

Forskelligt

7/137 D. 26/9-14/81941: Weisungen und Berichte der Marinegruppe Ost.
7/140 D. 24/2-28/2 1940: Unternehmen »Schleswig«.
8/152 D. 12/4 1940-17111 1941: Versorgung Dänemark-Norwegen I.G. 10-2, Beiheft 17.
7/142 D.26/3 1941-10/11 1943: Küstenverteidigung VI. 2. Bd. 1 und 2.
7/144 D. -/7 1941-/4 1943: Akte Nordsee- Norwegen VIII.3. Ostsee.
71143 D. 5112 1943-2/3 1944: Schriftwechsel mit Marineverbindungsoffizier Heeresgruppe B. VI 4. Bd. 1.

2./Seekriegsleitung (Zentralabt. und Nachrichten)

1/6 D. 18/6-19/6 1940: KTB. Anlagen. Nachrichtenubermittelungsdienst bei der Besetzung von Norwegen und Dänemark.

Flottenkommando

12/202 D. 3/6-16/9 1940: Nachschub, Versorgung und Stützpunkte in den besetzen Gebiete.

Marinegruppenkommando West

14/225 D. 4/3-26/41940: Weserübung. Allgemeine Fernschreiben. Akte Chef 17. VIII. Bd. 1.
13/217 D. 6/3-23/3 1940: Weserübung. Befehle und Weisungen des Marinengruppenkommandos Ost. Akt Chef 17.111. Bd. l.
13/214 D. 10/3-4/41940: Weseriibung I. D. 10/3-8/4 1940: Weseriibung. Marinegruppenkommando Ost. Akte Chef 17 .III. Bd. 2.
14/223 D. 27/3-10/4 1940: Weseriibung. Küstenbefestigungen. Operationsbefehle Reer. Akte Chef 17 /VI.
14/220 D. 30/3-14/4 1940: Weserübung. Operationsbefehle. Akte Chef 17.IV. Bd. 2.

Seebefehlshaber West

12/205 D. 1/4-8/5 1940: KTB des Seebefehlshaber West.

Marinenstation der Nordsee

12/206 D. 9/4-17/4 1940: KTB.

Befehlshaber der Sicherung der Nordsee

12/208 D. 114-15/41940: Anlage 2. KTB.

Marinegruppenkommando Ost, Marineoberkommando Ost

15/230 D. 16/12 1939-16/4 1940: KTB des Adm. Carls.
15/231 KTB d. 16/12 1939-30/4 1940.
16/232 KTB d. 115 1939-31/7 1940.
16/237 KTB d. 1/9-31/12 1943.
16/238 KTB d. 8/5-19/8 1944.
17/241 KTB d. 2/11-31/12 1944.

Marinestation der Ostsee. Ostsee-station. Marine Oberkommando Ostsee. Kommandierender Admiral der Marinestation der Ostsee.

17/247 D. 7/3-7/4 1940: Akte Weserübung. Grundsätze. Anordnungen.
16/235 D. 9/4-13/6 1940: KTB des kommandierenden Admirals der Marinestation der Ostsee.
1/11 D. 18/4-30/5 1940: Geheimer Ostsee-Stationstagesbefehle.

Befehlshaber der Sicherung der Ostsee

17/245 KTB BSO d. 2/9 1939-2115 1940.
2/29 D. 10110 1939-26/3 1940: Allgemeines SkI.
15/231 KTB d. 16/12 1939-30/4 1940.

Führer der Seeluftstreitkräfte

33/370 KTB des F.d. Luft West d. 8/4-9/4 1940.
33/369 KTB des F.d. Luft Ost d. 9/4 1940.

General der Luftwaffe bei dem Oberbefehlshaber der Kriegsmarine Oberquartiermeister

33/372 KTB d. 114-30/4 1940.
8/153 1940 udateret: Kriegsakte. Anfragen, Ersuchen, Weisungen und Befehle.

Befehlshaber der Unterseeboote, Karl Donitz

38/473 KTB des F.d. U. West d. 1119 1939-10/5 1940.
38/474 KTB d. 9/2-1114 1940.

Enkelte krigsskibe

35/421 KTB das Minenschiff Hansestadt Danzig, d. 113-10/4 1940.

Küstenbefehlshaber westlicher Ostsee

39/477 D. 2711-15111 1943: KTB und Erfahrungsberichten Küstenbefehlshabers Westlicher Ostsee.

Kommandant im Abschnitt Sylt

12/210 KTB d. 9/4 1940.

Marinebefehlshaber Dänemark. bzw. Admiral Dänemark, bzw. Admiral Skagerrak

17/248 KTB d. 6/4-30/12 1940.
18/249 KTB d. 1/1-30/6 1941.
18/250 KTB d. 1/7-20/9 1941
19/251 KTB d. 1/10-31/12 1942.
19/252 KTB d. 1/1-31/3 1942.
19/253 KTB d. 1/4-30/6 1942.
20/254 KTB d. 1/7-30/9 1942.
20/255 KTB d. 1/10-31/12 1942.
20/256 KTB d. 1/1-23/3 1943
20/257 KTB d. 1/4-30/6 1943.

20/258 KTB d. 1/7-30/9 1943.
21/259 KTB d. 1/10 1943-31/3 1944.
27/277 1943 udateret: Verzeichnis der Dienststellen des Adm. Dänemarks.
21/260 KTB d. 1/4-30/9 1944
21/261 KTB d. 1/10-31/121944
22/262 KTB d. 1/1-28/2 1945.

Kommandant im Abschnitt Nordjütland, bzw. Seekommandant Nordjütland
23/264 A-BKTB 30/41940-30/9 1942.
25/268 KTB d. 1/10 1942-15/21945

Kommandant im Abschnitt West-Dänemark, bzw dänische Westüste, bzw Abschnitt Südjütland, bzw. Seekommandant Südjütland,
22/263 A-BKTB D. 9/4 1940 1511 1943.
28/288 D. 26/4 1940-22/5 1941: Hafenangelegenheiten.
28/278 D. 28/4-8/8 1940: O. Kommandosache 1
28/280 D. 25/6 1940-1/7 1942: Offizier Angelegenheiten.
28/284 D. 30/12-14/4 1940: Nachrichten.
28/289 D. 17/121942-8/51943: Hafenangelegenheiten.
24/266 A-BKTB D. 16/1 1943-15/21945.
28/279 D. 9/3-24/91943: G.I. Allgemeines Bd. 7.
29/292 D. 31/3-4/6 1943: Geheime Kommandosache. Akten.
28/282 D. 26/4-2/11 1943: G. Vc.
29/300 D.12/51943-11/61944: Geheime Kommandosache. Akten 14-15.
28/290 D. 16/5-20/11 1943: Hafenangelegenheiten.
29/293 D. 1/6-31/7 1943: Geheime Kommandosache. Akten I.
29/299 D. 1/6 1943-20/6 1944: Geheime Kommandosache. Akten 15.
29/303 D. 21/6 1943: Geheime Kommandosache. Akten.
29/296 D. 26/6-13/9 1943: Geheime Kommandosache. Akten.
29/303 D. 6/8 1943-3/6 1944: Geheime Kommandosache. Akten 4 u. 15.
29/294 D.24/8 1943-24/3 1944: Geheime Kommandosache. Akten II.
29/295 D. 24/8-13/10 1943: Geheime Kommandosache. Akten Bd. I.
29/297 D. 25/8 1943-23/1 1944: Geheime Kommandosache. Akten 14.
28/291 D. 8/10-11/12 1943: Hafenanlegenheiten.
29/301 D. 26/2-11/5 1944: Geheime Kommandosache.

Kommandant im Abschnitt Südjütland und dänische Inseln, bzw im Abschnitt dänische Inseln, bzw. Seekommandant dänische Inseln, bzw Kommandant der Seeverteidigung dänische Inseln.
23/265A KTB d. 1/41943-31/121944.

8. Sicherungsdivision.
34/405 KTB d. 15/4-30/4 1944.
34/406 KTB d. 1/5-15/5 1944.
34/407 KTB d. 16/5-31/5 1944

34/408 KTB d. 1/6-15/61944.
34/409 KTB d. 16/6-30/6 1944.
34/410 KTB d. 1/7-15/7 1944.
34/411 KTB d. 16/7-31/7 1944.
34/412 KTB d.1/8-15/81944.
34/413 KTB d. 16/8-31/8 1944.
34/414 KTB d. 119-15/9 1944.
34/415 KTB d. 16/9-30/9 1944.
34/416 KTB d. 1/10-15/10 1944.
34/417 KTB d. 16/10-31/101944.
35/418 KTB d. 1/11-15/11 1944.
35/419 KTB d. 16/11-30/11 1944.
35/420 KTB d. 1/12 1944 -15/2 1945.

4. Sicherungsflotille
32/362 KTB d. 1110 1943-28/2 1945.

5. Sicherungsflotille
32/363 KTB d. 31/10 1943-28/2 1945.

8 Sicherungsflotille
32/364 KTB d. 16/9 1943-1/8 1944.
32/365 KTB d. 1/8 1944-15/2 1945.

Kriegsmarinedienstelle Stettin, Zweigstelle Kopenhagen, bzw. des Seetransportchefs Skagerrak, Kopenhagen
27/274 KTB d. 14/61940-31/1 1945.

Kriegsmarinedienstelle Stettin, Zweigstelle Aalborg, bzw. des Kriegsmarinedienststelle Kopenhagen. Zweigstelle Aalborg, bzw. Seetransportstelle Aalborg.
24/267 KTB d. 116 1941-30/9 1942.
25/269 KTB d. 1110 1942-28/2 1945.

Kriegsmarinedienstelle Kopenhagen. Zweigstelle Aarhus, bzw Seetransportstelle Aarhus.
26/270 KTB d. 7/10 1942-28/2 1945.

Hafenkommandant Aarhus
27/273 KTB d. 16/11-30/11 1944.

Hafenschutzflotille Esbjerg
27/272 KTB d. 16/4-15/5 1944.

Transportkommandantur Kopenhagen, Marine- Bahnhofs Kommandantur II Gjedser.
27/276 KTB d. 111-30/6 1943.

Quellensammlung Bidlingmaier
38/470 D. 19/4 1940: Stand und Eignung der Seeluftstreitkrafte West.

Det tyske Luftvåbens arkiv 1940-1945. (RA)
Oberkommando der Luftwaffe
47/570 KTB d. 3/4-18/4 1945.

Luftwaffe Führungsstab
46/536 D. 6/3-28/3 1940: Vorbereitung Weserübung.
46/537 D. 10/3-3/4 1940: Weserübung. Befehle des X. Fliegerkorps. KTB.
46/535 D. 1/4-4/4 1940: Unternehmen Dänemark-Norwegen.
46/539 D.4/4 1940: Nachgang zu Bezugsverfugung.
46/538 1940: Kvadrerede kort over operationsområde for Weserübung.
47/568 D. -/4 1944: Übersichtsliste der Flugplätze.
46/532 D. 261101944-15/3 1945: Änderungen Bezugsverfugung.
46/533-34 D.22/2 1944-30/3 1945: Drohende Gefahr Nord.
46/544 D. 12/5-14/5 1945: Räumung Dänemarks durch die Luftwaffe.
46/531 KTB d. 7/2 1945.

Reichsluftfahrtsministerium: Kriegswissenschaftliche Abteilung
47/562 D. 5/3-8/5 1940: Auswertegruppe Norwegen. Weserübung.
46/546 1940: Weserübung. Luftflotte 5
46/550 KTB d. 16110-22110 1943. Anlageband III.

Lufttransportführer, Weserübung
47/565 D. 1/3-30/4 1940: Anlagen zum Bericht über das Luftlandeunternehmen Dänemark-Norwegen.

Kommando Flughafenbereich 1/XI
47/563 Band D zum KTB d. 22/7 1940-3/8 1942.
46/549 Anlage zum KTB 8, d. 18/4-27/8 1942.
47/558 Anlage zum KTB Nr. 8 Luftlage, d. 16/5-17/7 1942.
45/559 Anlage 2 zum KTB 8, d. 17/5-20/8 1942.
46/552 Anlage a zum KTB 8, d. 1/8-4/9 1942.
47/560 Anlage zum KTB 9. Akte III. Luftlageskizzen, d. 1611-11/3 1943.

Seenotzentrale (L) Westlicher Ostsee
46/548 KTN Nr. 4, d. 24/8-28110 1941.

Reserve Flak-Abteilung 607
47/555 KTB Nr. 2, d. 18/12 1940-17/1 1941.

Archive of the Civil Defence Agency (RA)
Danish Civil Air Defence, messages and reports, 1940–1945 (SCL)
Contains:

Anti-aircraft messages between command centres and reporting posts
The National Reporting Centre's summary daily reports
Fluko messages to the national alarm centre

In addition, the Civil Defence Agency's archive has provided material for the following:
'Statens Civile Luftværn, 1938–45', vol. I–III. Kbh. 1949.
Contains:

Vol. 1. Historical overview, organisation, economy and relation to the Occupation
Vol. 2. The Services, the CBU Corps and Self-Protection
Vol. 3. Evacuation, technical security measures, training and exercises, the volunteer effort and the air raids (in selection)

Printed Sources, Books

Åhlund, Bertil, *Svensk marin säkerhetspolitik 1939–1945* (Stockholm: 1994)
Ahrens, Adolf, *Die Siegesfahrt der 'Bremen'* (Berlin: 1940)
Air Ministry. Air Historical Branch, *The RAF in Maritime War*, vol. 5 *Atlantic & Home Waters – The Victorious Phase May 1944-May 1945* (London: Air Historical Branch, 2012)
Andersen, Bent, *En dråbe I havet* (Rudkøbing: 1994)
Anonymous, *Dokumente über die alleinschuld Englands am Bombenkrieg gegen die Zivilbevolkerung* (Berlin: Zentralverl. d. NSDAP, 1943)
Anonymous, *'Englands fremstød i Norge': Udvalg af den 6. Officielle tyske Hvidbog: Udgivet paa Foranledming af det tyske Udenrigsministerium* (Berlin: Foreign Ministry, 1940)
Anonymous, *Fortegnelse over krigsforliste og krigshavererede danske skibe 1939–1949* (Copenhagen: Ministeriet for handel, industri og søfart, 1950)
Arndt, Peter, *Deutsche Sperrbrecher, 1914–1945* (Stuttgart: 1979)
Assmann, Kurt, *Deutsche Seestrategie in zwei Weltkriegen* (Heidelberg: 1957)
Bang, Kaj Nolsøe, *Styrmænd til Orlogs I: Optakten til 9. April* (Viborg: 1976)
Bang, Kaj Nolsøe, *Styrmænd til Orlogs, II: Marinen under krigen,* (Viborg 1977)
Barfod, Halfdan, *Sømagt og dens indflydelse på Danmarks historie* (Copenhagen: 1936)
Bashow, David L., *None but the Brave: The Essential Contributions of RAF Bomber Command to Allied Victory during the Second World War* (Kingston, Ontario: Canadian Defence Academy Press, 2009)
Beaver, Paul, *E-Boats and Coastal Craft* (Cambridge: Patrick Stephens Ltd, 1980)
Beaver, Paul, *German Capital Ships* (Cambridge: Patrick Stephens Ltd, 1980)
Beaver, Paul, *German Destroyers and Escorts* (Cambridge: Patrick Stephens Ltd, 1980)
Beaver, Paul, *U-Boats in the Atlantic* (Cambridge: Patrick Stephens Ltd, 1979)
Bech, Poul, *Søkrig i danske farvande under Anden Verdenskrig 1939–1942* (Schønberg: 2008)
Bech, Poul, *Søkrig i danske farvande under Anden Verdenskrig 1943–1945* (Schønberg: 2009)
Bennett, Ralph, *Behind the Battle: Intelligence in the War with Germany, 1939–1945* (London: Pimlico, 1999)
Bensel, Rolf, *Die Deutsche Flottenpolitik von 1933 bis 1939* (Berlin: 1958)
Bjerg, Hans Chr, *Dansk Marinehistorisk Bibliografi 1500*–1975 (Kbh, 1975)

Bjørnvad, Anders, *De fandt en vej* (Odense: 1970)
Bjørnvad, Anders, *Faldne allierede flyvere 1939–1945* (Odense: 1978)
Bjørnvad, Anders, *Natten der varede otte dage* (Copenhagen: 1967)
Boelck, Detlef, *Kiel im Luftkrieg 1939–1945* (Kiel: 1980)
Boheman, Erik, *På vakt* (Stockholm: 1964)
Bowyer, Chaz, *Hampden Special* (Shepperton: Ian Allan, 1976)
Bowyer, Chaz, *Royal Air Force Handbook, 1939–1945* (Worthing: Littlehampton Book Services, 1984)
Bowyer, M. J. F., *Action Stations: Wartime Military Airfields of East Anglia* (Cambridge: Paytrick Stephens Ltd, 1979)
Branner, Hans, *Den 9. April – et politisk lærestykke?* (Copenhagen: 1987)
Branner, Hans, *Småstat mellem stormagter* (Copenhagen: 1972)
Brennecke, Jochen, *Das Grosse Abenteuer Deutsche Hilfskreuzer, 1939–45* (Berlin: 1958)
Brütting, Georg, *Das waren die Deutschen Stuka-Asse, 1939–45* (Stuttgart: 1976)
Burrough, H. M., *The Final Stages of Naval War in NW Europe* (London: HMSO, Supplement to *The London Gazette*, 1948)
Churchill, Winston S., *Den Anden Verdenskrig*, 6 volumes (Copenhagen: 1948 on)
Churchill, Winston S., *Krigskorrespondance mellem Churchill og Stalin* (Kbh: 1965)
Cole, Howard N., *Heraldry in War* (Aldershot: Gale & Polden, The Wellington Press, 1946)
Cowie, J. S., *Mines, Minelayers and Minelaying* (Oxford: OUP, 1949)
Craven, Wesley Frank, *The Army Air Forces in World War II*, vols 1–7, (Chicago: University of Chicago Press, 1948–1958)
Creveld, Martin van, *Krig og krigsteori* (Gyldendal: 2003)
Dahl, Niels Uffe, Tysk udenrigs – og kolonipolitik, 1871–1914 (Viborg: 1976)
Dahl, P. Chr, *Strandinger og trandingsgods*, Vols 1–2 (Esbjerg: 1974)
Delve, Ken, *Bomber Command 1936–1968 An Operational & Historical Record* (Barnsley: Pen and Sword, 2005)
Derry, T. K., *The Campaign in Norway* (London: HMSO, 1952)
Dierich, Wolfgang, *Die Verbände der Luftwaffe, 1935–1945* (Stuttgart: 1976)
Dinklage, Ludwig et al, *Die Deutsche Handelsflotte, 1939–1945*, vols 1–2 (Stuttgart: 2001)
Ejgenbroth, N. Aug., *Vor vej til 5. maj." Nordjylland gennem fem krigsaar i billeder og tekst* (Aalborg: Aalborg amtstidendes forlag, 1946)
Elliott, Peter, *Allied Minesweeping in World War 2* (Annapolis: US Naval Institute, 1979)
Espersen, Mogens, *Østersøen – balance og sikkerhed* (Copenhagen: 1979)
Fink, Troels, *Spillet om dansk neutralitet, 1905–09* (Aarhus: 1970)
Forshell, Hans, *Minan i Sjökriget* (Karlskrona: 1959)
Forsvarskommandoen, *Danmarks strategiske betydning* (Copenhagen: 1984)
Frick, Lennart W, *Bakom hemligstämpeln: hemlig verksamhet i Sverige i vår tid* (Lund: Historiska Media, 2004)
Garde, Poul, *Forudsætninger for dansk søminekrigsførelse*, (Copenhagen: Søe-Lieutenant-Selskabet, 1976)
Gee, John, Wingspan. *The Recollections of a Bomber Pilot* (Worcester: Privately Published, 1988)
Gemzell, Carl Axel, *Raeder, Hitler und Skandinavien* (Lund: 1965)
Gibson, Guy, *Mål i sigte* (Haderslev: 1963)

Giverholt, Helge, *Maktspillet omkring Østersjøen* (Bergen: 1952)

Goulter, Christina J. M., *A Forgotten Offensive: Royal Air Force Coastal Command's Anti-Shipping Campaign 1940–1945* (London: Routledge, 1995)

Grehan, John & Mace, Martin, *'Bomber Harris': Sir Arthur Harris' Despatch on War Operations 1942–1945* (Barnsley: Pen and Sword, 2014)

Greiner, Helmth, *Kriegstagebuch des Oberkommandos der Wehrmacht*, 7 volumes (Frankfurt am Main: 1961–1965)

Groos, Otto, *Grænserne for den britiske sømagt* (Lübeck: 1940)

Graa, Poul, *Hundrede år på havene. D.F.D.S. 1866–1966* (Copenhagen: 1966)

Gyllenhaal, Lars, *Tyskar och allierade i Sverige: svensk krigshistoria i nytt ljus* (Stockholm: 2011)

Görnandt, W., *Luftmeldetjeneste i 40 år' Fra Høretragt til EDB* (Odense: 1974)

Haagerup, Niels Jørgen, *Danmarks sikkerhedspolitik* (Copenhagen: Forsvarskommandoen, 1996, 6th edition)

Halley, James J., *The Squadrons of the Royal Air Force* (Tonbridge: Air Britain Historians Ltd, 1980)

Hansen, Volmer, *Vordingborg under 5 aars mørklægning* (Vordingborg: 1947)

Harris, Arthur T. (Sebastian Cox Ed.), *Despatch on War Operations: 23rd February 1942 to 8th May 1945*(London: Routledge, 1995)

Hartmann, Gregory K, *Weapons that Wait* (Annapolis: Naval Institute Press,1979)

Hastings, Max, *Bomber Command* (London: Pan Books, 1st edition 1979, 2nd edition 1982)

Henningsen, Sven, *Det tyvende århundrede*, vol. 2 *1930–1945* (Odense: University of Copenhagen 1972)

Hering, P. G., *Customs and Traditions of the Royal Air Force* (Aldershot: Gale & Polden, 1961)

Hildebrand, Hans H., *Die Deutschen Kriegsschiffe. Biographien - ein Spiegel der Marinegeschichte von 1815 bis zur Gegenwart*, vols 1–7 (Herford: Koehlers, 1982)

Hinsley, F. H., *British Intelligence in The Second World War* (Cambridge: Cambridge University Press, 1979)

Holm, N, *Vakt till sjöss* (Stockholm: 1946)

Holck, Jørgen et al, *Frit hav. Dansk skibsfart i 100 år* (Copenhagen: 1984)

Hornby, Ove, *Ved rettidig Omhu … Skibsreder A.P. Møller* (Copenhagen 1988)

Hubatsch, Walther, *Die Deutsche Besetzung von Dänemark und Norwegen 1940* (Göttingen: 1952)

Hubatsch, Walther, *Kriegswende 1943* (Darmstadt: 1966)

Hugemark, Bo (ed.), *I orkanens öga. 1941 - osäker neutralitet* (Probus: 1992)

Hugemark, Bo (ed.): *Neutralitet och försvar. Perspektiver på svensk säkerhetspolitik 1809–1985* (Stockholm: Militärhistoriska Förlaget, 1986)

Hägglöf, Gunnar, *Svensk krigshandelspolitik under Andra Världskriget* (Stockholm: 1958)

Jackson, Bill, *Three Stripes and Four Brownings* (Battleford: Turner-Warwick Publications, 1990)

Jagd, Palle Bolten, *Danske forsvarsanlæg i 5.000 år*, Part III: *Efter 1932* (Rødovre: 1984)

Jensen, Ole Helmer, *Anden Verdenskrig. Hvornår-skete-det* (Copenhagen: 1968)

Johns, John A., *The History of 135 Squadron, Oct '44-Sept '45, Bomber Command, RAF* (Salisbury: J.A. Johns, 1998)

Johnsen, N .C. D., *Over Storebælt med DSB* (Copenhagen: 1965)

Johnson, Brian, *The Secret War* (Barnsley: Pen & Sword, 2004)
Jones, Geoffry P., *Night Flight. Halifax Squadrons at War* (London: Harper Collins, 1981)
Juel, Axel, *'Himmel og hav.' Marinedigte* (Copenhagen: 1922)
Jung, Dieter, *Tanker und Versorger der deutschen Flotte, 1900–1980* (Stuttgart: 1981)
Jungersen, Kay, *På togt med eskadren* (Copenhagen: 1945)
Jørgensen, A.R., *Spionage mod Danmark* (Gylling: 1987)
Kaarsted, Tage, *Flåden under Første Verdenskrig* (Odense: 1976)
Kaarsted, Tage, *Storbritannien og Danmark, 1914–1920* (Odense: 1974)
Kemp, P. K., *Victory at Sea, 1939–1945* (London: White Lion, 1958)
Kirchhoff, Hans, *Kamp eller tilpasning* (Gyldenda: 1987)
Kludas, Arnold, *Die grossen Passagierschiffe der Welt* (Hamburg: 1971)
Kurowski, Franz, *Seekrieg aus der luft* (Herfords: 1979)
Lagvall, Bertil, *Flottans neutralitetsvakt 1939–1945* (Stockholm: 1967)
Lammers, Karl Chr, *Danmarks historie*. Gyldendal, vol. 7 *Udenrigspol. 1918–33* (Aarhus: 1988)
Lebech, Mogens, *Bæltoverfart i tusind år* (Copenhagen: 1965)
Ledebur, Gerhard Frhr. v., *Die Seemine* (Munich: 1977)
Levie, Howard S., *Mine Warfare at Sea* (Leiden: Brill, 1992)
Lewin, Ronald, *ULTRA Goes to War: The Secret Story* (London: Hutchinson, 1978)
Lidegaard, Bo, *Kampen om Danmark 1933–1945* (Gyldendal: 2006)
Lidegaard, Bo, *Overleveren, 1914–1945* (Nørhaven: Nørhaven Book, 2006)
Lohmann, Walther & Hildebrand, H. H., *Die Deutsche Kriegsmarine 1939–1945*, 3 volumes (Bad Nauheim: 1956–1964)
Lohmann, Walther, Kamaraden aus see zwischen Minen und Torpedos (Berlin: 1943)
Lomholt-Thomsen, Johs., *Problemer i dansk politik 1901–1946* (Copenhagen: 1948)
Lott, Arnold S., *Most Dangerous Sea* (London: Ballantyne, 1959)
Lund, Paul et al, *Out Sweeps! The Story of The Minesweepers in World War II* (London: New English Library, 1978)
Lundberg, Lennart, *Handelsflottan under andra världskriget* (Stockholm: 2007)
Madsen, Finn, *Danmarks sikkerhedspolitiske situation i 1980'erne* (Copenhagen: Udenrigsministeriet, 1984)
Mæsel, Knut, *Luftkriegen over Sörlandet* (Kristiansand: 1982)
Mallmann-Showell, J. P., *Das Buch der deutschen Kriegsmarine, 1935–1945* (Stuttgart: 1989, 5th ed.)
Martienssen, Anthony, *Hitler and his Admirals: A History of the German Navy in World War Two* (Ilkley: Sapere Books, 1948)
Matlok, Siegfried, *Danmark i Hitlers hånd* (Viborg: 1989)
Menger, Manfred, et al, *Expansionsrichtung Nordeuropa* (Berlin: 1987)
Merrick, K. A., Halifax : An Illustrated History of a Classic World War Two Bomber (London: Ian Allan, 1980)
Michaelis, Herbert, *Ursachen und Folgen* (Berlin: 1958–1979)
Middlebrook, Martin & Everitt, Chris, *The Bomber Command War Diaries: An Operational Reference Book 1939–1945* (Bungay: Viking, 1985)
Mitchel, Alan W., *New Zealanders in the Air War* (London: Harrap, 1945)
Moyes, Philip J. R., *Bomber Squadrons of the R.A.F. and Their Aircraft* (London: MacDonald, 1964)

Moyle, Harry, *The Hampden File* (Tonbridge: Air Britain, 1989)
Munson, Kenneth, Wood, John W. et al, *Fighters and Bombers of World War II* (Littlehampton: Littlehampton Books, 1969)
Myhre, Aslak Sira (ed.), *Østersøen igår – idag – imorgen* (Copenhagen: 1982)
Neave, Airey, *Saturday at M.I.9: The Classic Account of the WW2 Allied Escape* (London: Hodder & Stoughton, 1969)
Nielsen, Bo, *Tyskerne på Anholt* (Copenhagen: Nordiske landes bogforlag, 1985)
Nielsen, S. A., *30 år i Orlogsværftets Elektroafdeling 1940–1970 – uddrag af oplevelser, hændelser og episoder* (2003), unpaginated
Nissen, Henrik S., *Danmarks historie*, Gyldendal, vol. 7, *1914–45* (Aarhus: 1988)
Nowarra, Heintz, *Minensuchgruppe Mausi. Mit der Tante Ju im Kampfeinsatz* (Illertissen: Flugzeug Publikations GmbH, 1995)
Olesen, Mogens Nørgaard, *Danske jernbane-dampfærger* (Copenhagen: 1987)
Olesen, Mogens Nørgaard, *Færgerne på Kattegat* (Copenhagen: 1986)
Østrup, J. (Ed.), *Illustreret Verdenshistorie*, vol. 6, Our time (Copenhagen: 1927)
Ousager, Steen, *På sporet 1847–1997*, vol. 2 (Odense: 1997)
Outze, Børge, *Danmark under den anden verdenskrig*, volumes I – IV (Copenhagen:1962–1968)
Pawle, Gerald, *Churchill i krig* (Gentofte, 1964)
Perkins, Kenneth J. (ed.), *Weapons and Warfare* (London: Brasseys, 1987)
Petersen, Carsten, *Luftkrig over Danmark*, vol. IV (Ringkøbing: 1989)
Petersen, Carsten, *Luftkrig over Danmark*, vol. V (Ringkøbing: 1990)
Petersen, Jørgen, *Mit liv i Søværnet, 1934–80* (Odense: 1985)
Poulsen, Henning, *Hitlers krig, 1939–1941* (Den 2. Verdenskrig, I) (Aalborg: 1989)
Philpott, Bryan, *History of the German Air Force* (New York: Gallery Books/Simon & Schuster, 1986)
Philpott, Bryan, *RAF Bomber Units, September 1939–June 1942* (Oxford: Osprey, 1977) Airwar Series no.5
Philpott, Bryan, *RAF Bomber Units, July 1942–1945* (Oxford: Osprey, 1978) Airwar Series no.19
Preston, Adrian, *General Staffs and Diplomacy before the Second World War* (London: Routledge, 1978)
Price, Dr Alfred, *Aircraft versus Submarine* (London: Harper Collins, 1973)
Raeder, Erich, *My Life* (Annapolis: Naval Institute Press, 1960)
Rasmussen, Alan Hjort, *Havet – en vej til frihed* (Hirtshals: 1985)
Refslund, Chr. (ed.), *Fem aar. Indtryk og oplevelser* (Copenhagen: 1945)
Rerup, Lorenz, *Danmarks historie*. Gyldendal, vol. 6, *1864–1914* (Copenhagen: 1989)
Reuter, Frank, *Funkmess – Die entwicklung und das einsatz des Radarverfahrens in Deutschland bis zum ende des Zweiten Weltkrieges* (Wiesbaden: W.D. Verlag, 1971)
Richards, Denis & Saunders, Hilary St George, *Royal Air Force, 1939–1945*, vols 1–3 (London: HMSO, 1953–1954)
Ries, K. & Obermaier, E., *Erfolgsmarkierungen der Deutschen Luftwaffe, 1936–45* (Mainz: 1970)
Robertson, Bruce, *Beaufort Special* (Shepperton: Ian Allan, 1976)
Robertson, Bruce, *Lancaster: The Story of a Famous Bomber* (Letchworth: Harleyford Publications, 1967)

Rockberger, Nicolaus, *Göteborgstrafiken : svensk lejdtrafik under andra världskriget* (Stockholm: 1973)
Roskill, Stephen W., *The Navy at War 1939–1945* (London: HMSO, 1960)
Roskill, Stephen W., *The War at Sea 1939–45*, vols 1–3 (London: HMSO, 1954–1962)
Roslyng-Jensen, Palle, *Værnenes politik – politikernes værn* (Gyldendal: 1980)
Ruge, Friedrich, *Im Küstenvorfeld* (Munich: 1974)
Ruge, Friedrich, *Torpedo und Minenkrieg* (Berlin: 1940)
Røjel, Jørgen, *Kæft, trit og retning. En sabotørs erindringer* (Copenhagen: 1973)
Saabye, E. J., *I medvind. En søofficers erindringer* (Copenhagen: 1981)
Salewski, Michael, *Die Deutsche Seekriegsleitung 1935–1945*, bund 1 & 2 (Frankfurt am Main: 1970 & 1975)
Saward, Dudley, *'Bomber' Harris': The Story of the Marshal of the Royal Air Force Sir Arthur Harris Bt Gcb Obe Afc Lld Air Officer Commanding-In-Chief Bomber Command* (London: Cassell Ltd, 1984)
Scavenius, Erik, *Forhandlingspolitikken under Besættelsen* (Spektrum 1995, 2nd edition)
Schmalenbach, Paul, *Die Deutschen Hilfskreuzer 1895–1945* (Oldenburg: 1977)
Schmalenbach, Paul, *Kreuzer Prinz Eugen. Under 3 Flags* (Herford: 1978)
Schramm, Percy Ernst, *Hitler som feltherre* (Copenhagen 1964)
Schurholz, Peter, *Das Schicksal der Deutschen U-Boote, 1939–45* (Heidenh. U.A., 1946)
Sharp, C. Martin and Michael J. F. Bowyer, *Mosquito* (London: Faber & Faber, 1967)
Showell, Jak P. Mallmann, *Fuehrer Conferences on Naval Affairs, 1939–1945* (Barnsley: Chatham Publishing, 2005)
Showell, Jak P. Mallmann, *The German Navy in World War 2. A Reference Guide to the Kriegsmarine, 1935–45* (Annapolis: US Naval Institute, 1979)
Sipols, Vilnis, *Forhistorien til den tysk-sovjetiske ikke-angrebspagt* (?: Sputnik: 1984)
Smith, Michael, *The Secrets of Station X: How the Bletchley Park Codebreakers Helped Win The War* (Hull: Biteback Publishing, 2011)
Studt, Johannes W., *Als Matrose auf einem Minensucher, 1940–1945* (Hamburg: 2004)
Tagert, Carl, *Der freiheitskampf zur see, 1939–40* (Berlin: 1940)
Taylor, J. C., *German Warships of World War II* (London: Ian Allan, 1966)
Thorburn, Thomas, *Sveriges inrikes sjofart 1818–1949* (Stockholm: 1958)
Tortzen, Christian, *Søfolk og skibe, 1939–1945*, vols 1–4 (Tønder: 1981–85)
Trommer, Aage, *Myte og sandhed i besættelseshistorien* (Copenhagen: 1974)
Trommer, Aage, *Politik og Strategi – 2. Verdenskrig* (Copenhagen: 1982)
Vallerö, Rolf, *Svenska handelsflottans krigsförluster under det andra världskriget* (Stockholm: 1963)
Wagner, Gerhard, *Lagevorträge des Oberbefehlshabers der Kriegsmarine 1939–1945* (Munich: 1972)
Wark, Wesley K., *The Ultimate Enemy. British Intelligence and Nazi Germany 1933–1939* (Oxford: OUP, 1985)
Watson, Bruce W. (Ed.), *The Soviet Naval Threat to Europe* (London: Routledge, 1989)
Weber, Frank et al, *Bomber over Denmark* (Nyt Nordisk Forlag, 2012)
Weber, Frank et al, *Vestallierede luftangreb i Danmark under 2. Verdenskrig* vols 1–2 (Viborg: Aarhus Universitetsforlag, 1988)
Wendt, Herbert, *The Battle for the Baltic Sea* (Berlin: 1943)

Webster, Charles & Frankland, Noble, *The Strategic Air Offensive Against Germany, 1939–1945*, 4 volumes (London: HMSO, 1961)
Werlich, Robert, *Orders and Decorations of All Nations* (Washington: The Quaker Press, 1974)
Werner, Max, *The Military Strength of The Powers* (London: Victor Gollancz, 1939)
Wilson, Michael& Robinson, A. S. L., *Coastal Command Leads the Invasion* (London: Jarrolds, 1946)
Winton, John, *Air Power at Sea, 1939–1945* (London: Sidgwick & Jackson, 1976)
Wirsing, Giselher, *The War 1939/41 in Maps* (Munich: 1942)
Wright, Peter, *Spycatcher* (Harrisonburg: Stoddart, 1987)

Journals/Journal articles

Magazines

Aktuellt och historiskt, Meddelanden från Försvarsstabens krigshistoriska avdel-ning
Dansk Luftværns Blad
Dansk Skibsfart (published by *Danmarks Rederiforening*), Copenhagen
Europäische Wehrkunde. Zeitschrift für alle Wehrfragen Munich
Finest Hour. The Journal of Winston Churchill, no. 157, Winter 2012-2013
Historie/Jyske Samlinger, Viborg.
Historisk Aarbog for Thy, Mors og Vester Han Herred, Thisted
Is – og besejlingsforholdene i danske farvande, 1939–1945
Jahrbuch der Deutschen Kriegsmarine, Leipzig
Janes all the Worlds Aircraft, 1942
Jyske Historiker
Marinerundschau, Zeitschrift für Seewesen, Frankfurt A/M
Maritim Kontakt, Copenhagen
NATO's Sixteen Nations. Independent review of economic, political and military power, Brussels
Tidskrift i Sjöväsendet, Karlskrona
Tidsskrift for Søvæsen, Copenhagen
Udenrigsministeriets Tidsskrift, Copenhagen 1941–42
Underretninger for søfarende, Copenhagen
Vårt Försvar. Allmänna Försvarsföreningens tidsskrift, Stockholm.
Østjysk Hjemstavn, 1984

Articles & Book Chapters

Branner, Hans , 'Østersøen og de danske stræder i engelsk krigsplanlægning 1904–14' in *Historie, Jyske Samlinger*, ny rk. IX, 1972, nr. 4, p.493ff
Cowie, J. S., 'The British Sea-Mining Campaign, 1939–1945' in *Royal United Services Institution. Journal*, volume 93 (1948), pp.22–39
Cox, Sebastian, 'Sir Arthur Harris and some Myths and Controversies of the Bomber Offensive' in *RAF Historical Society Journal*, no. 47 (Witney 2010)
Ekman, P. O., 'Minor för Barbarossa' in *Tidskrift i Sjöväsendet*, 1976, pp.196–216

Fogelberg, Gunnar, 'Sjökriget i Östersjöbäckenet' in *Tidskrift i Sjöväsendet*, 1941, pp.748–752
Garde, H., 'Utmaningar blir inte obesvarade' in *Vårt Försvar*, nr. 8, 1989, pp.8–11
Garde, Poul, 'Forudsætninger for dansk søminekrigsførelse,' *Tidsskr.f.Søvæsen*, 1976, pp.169–206.
Gregersen, Jens J. K., 'Et svensk ekspeditionskorps til Sjælland?' in *Historisk tidsskrift*, volume 15 (1991)
Harris, Daniel G., 'Den danske Flåde 1940–43' in *Marinehistorisk Tidsskrift*, 1989, nr.2
Jones, R. V., 'Navigation and War' in *The Journal of Navigation*, vol. 28, 1975, no. 1
Lundberg, L., 'Översikt av krigshändelserna inom Östersjöområdet åren 1944-1945' in *Tidskrift i Sjöväsendet*, 1946, pp.84–96
Olow, J.E. , 'Om det sovjetiska ubåtskriget i Östersjön 1939–45' in *Aktuellt och historiskt*, 1958, pp.7–123.
Poulsen, Henning et al, 'Krig og samfund' in *Den Jyske Historiker*, 1985
Pushkin, A. , 'Den sovjetiske Østersøflådes kampindsats i krigens slutfase 1944–45.' *Tidsskr.f.Søvæsen*, 1985, nr. 4, pp.191–219
Rasmussen, Erik, 'Velfærdsstaten på vej, 1913–1939' in *Danmarks Historie* vol. 13, (Copenhagen: Politikens forlag, 1965)
Rohwer, Jürgen , 'Sovjetisk ubåtsverksamhet i Östersjön 1939–1945' in *Tidskrift i Sjöväsendet*,1957, pp.817–837
Shevchenko, V., 'Den sovjetiske Østersøflåde ved starten af den Store Fædrelandskrig' in *Tidsskr.f.Søvæsen*, 1987, nr. 3, s.99-114.
Sterling, Christopher H.:'Memories Of The Royal Air Force – Marriage of Convenience, Churchill and 'Bomber' Harris' Finest Hour' in *The Journal of Winston Churchill*, no. 157, Winter 2012–2013, pp.38–40
Tribuc, V. F., 'Die U-Bootoffensive der Baltischen Rotbannerflotte in der Ostsee 1942.' in *Marinerundschau*, 1963/64, pp.81–107
Weber, Frank, 'Bomber Command Minelaying in Danish waters' in *Flying M, The Society of friends of The Royal Air Force Museum*, vol. 13, no. 3, (Hendon, RAF, 1985), pp.21–25
Weber, Frank, 'Danmarks søstrategiske placering i stormagtsspillet 1900–1939' in *Tidsskrift for Søvæsen*, no. 2, 162 (Årg., 1991)
Westermann, C. A. S., 'Flaaden fra 9. April til 29. August' in *Denmark under the Occupation* (Copenhagen: 1946)

Electronic Resources

Anonymous, *Handbook for the Navy 1956* http://www.marinehist.dk/hfs/1956-HfS.pdf
Jeffs, Philip, 'Stirling W7531' www.philipjeffs.dsl.pipex.com/mrr/W7531.htm
Nielsen, John, 'De danske farvande i fred og krig' M/S Museet for Søfarts årbog, 5 https://tidsskrift.dk/mfs_aarbog/article/view/96004

Unpublished

The Ministry of Foreign Affairs' confidential messages to the editors, (unpublished Statsbiblioteket i Aarhus)

Source of Illustrations

1 https://www.keymilitary.com/article/bomber-commands
2 vignette by Frank Weber
3 Søværnets Operative Kommando
4 CH 12687 – Air Ministry Second World War Official Collection
5 https://en.wikipedia.org/wiki/Naval_mine#/media/File:Bushnell_mines.jpg
6 www.gkn-la.com/images/photo_images/Hague%20Convention%201907.jpg
7 S. W. Roskill, The War at Sea, Chapter VI, Map 1 p.96
8 'Marine områder' Faglig rapport fra DMU nr. 254, Miljø- og Energiministeriet, 1998, p.17
9 https://www.navalhistory.dk/Danish/Historien/1914_1918/Mineudlaegning_StoreBaelt_PopUp.htm
10 www.navalhistory.dk/Danish/Historien/1914_1918/Mineudlaegning_Sundet_PopUp.htm
11 http://thedanishscheme.co.uk/
12 www.youtube.com/watch?v=IuneVc41YNA&ab_channel=EXPOLPEDAGOGIKA
13 http://maritime.org/doc/minedisposal/index.htm#part3
14 http://www.navweaps.com/Weapons/WAMGER_Mines.htm
15 https://www.festungswerke-cuxhaven.de/en-gb/seeminen
16 https://healthcare-in-europe.com/en/news/sonic-boom-with-bubbles.html
17 Air Historical Branch 'A survey of damaged shipping' June 1945
18 Minensuchgruppe Mausi. Mit der Tante Ju im Kampfeinsatz, 1995, p.21
19 http://ww2today.com/the-british-dismantle-their-first-magnetic-mine
20 ADM 218/302 - Report on German magnetic mine recovered at Shoeburyness, Nov. 1939
21 http://www.mcdoa.org.uk/news_archive_33.htm
22 https://bombercommandmuseumarchives.ca/gardening.html
23 Based on National Archives, Air 15/245 'Minutes of a meeting held at Air Ministry on Monday 8 April, to discuss plan W.A.15.
24 Map by Frank Weber
25 Keesing's Comtemporary Archives, 1940-43, p.4013 + kortet p.4012
26 The Milwaukee Journal, 15 April 1940

27 https://timelessmoon.getarchive.net/media/raf-bomber-command-1940-hu104630-fdae3a
28 https://www.iwm.org.uk/collections/item/object/205126975
29 Fotos: Axel Sommerby. Kilde: www.airmen.dk/p083axs5.htm
30 Fotos: Axel Sommerby. Kilde: www.airmen.dk/p083axs5.htm
31 J. S. Cowie, The British Sea-Mining Campaign, pp.28–29
32 © Frank Weber
33 Map based on AIR 24/ 728 July 42–July 44, 'Mining: Operation orders and instructions.' © Frank Weber
34 https://d1vzi28wh99zvq.cloudfront.net/pdf_previews/301643-sample.pdf
35 evp.dk/index.php?page=farger-og-skibe—diverse
36 https://wallyswar.wordpress.com/operational-flight/
37 Frank Weber: Gode miner til slet spil 'Operation Gardening' RAF´s minelægninger i de danske farvande 1940-45, p.137
38 Foto fra Orlogsmuseets arkiv http://www.navalhistory.dk
39 Schematic overview based on Avisårbogen 1940, Adm. Dan. 18/2491940 and 'Udenrigsministeriets fortrolige meddelelser til redaktionerne' upublished Statsbiblioteket i Aarhus. © Frank Weber
40 John Nielsen, De danske farvande i fred og krig, p.121
41 http://steensiebken.dk/
42 CH 12677, Air Ministry Second World War Official Collection
43 © Frank Weber
44 © Frank Weber
45 CH 13020, Air Ministry Second World War Official Collection
46 Ralph Bennett, Behind the Battle, 1999 p.178
47 No. 1 PRU RAF, photograph C 5627, the Imperial War Museum
48 © Frank Weber
49 © Frank Weber
50 Imperial War Museum HU 1026
51 https://www.worldwarphotos.info/wp-content/gallery/uk/raf/short- stirling/Ground_crews_loading_mines_on_to_a_Stirling.jpg
52 https://www.kbismarck.com/photo096.html
53 www.navalhistory.dk/Danish/Historien/1939_1945/29august.htm
54 S. W. Roskill, The War at Sea, Chapter VI, Coastal Warfare 1942 - Tables 12, 14, 18 & 20
55 www.lexikon-der-wehrmacht.deWaffenBilderseitenJu52-R.htm
56 http.www.luftarchiv.de/index.htmbordgeratems.htm
57 http.www.luftarchiv.de/index.htmbordgeratems.htm
58 © Frank Weber
59 http://www.626-squadron.co.uk/willem361.jpg

60	© Frank Weber
61	CH 21145, Air Ministry Second World War Official Collection
62	https://www.wikiwand.com/en/articles/No._309_Polish_Fighter-Reconnaissance_Squadron#/media/No._309_Polish_Fighter-Reconnaissance_Squadron|File:Samoloty_Mustang_Mk._III_dywizjonu_309.jpg
63	Carsten Petersen, Luftkrig over Danmark, vol. IV Ringkøbing 1989, p.46
64	Walther Lohmann Die Deutsche Kriegsmarine 1939-1945, vol. 1, ch. 3, p.1
65	https://www.vragguiden.dk/wreck.asp?wreckid=380
66	https://www.flensted.eu.com/1944148.shtml
67	AIR 25/12 - No. 1 (Bomber) Group, Appendices 1944 Apr–June
68	http://www.flensted.eu.com/1944068.shtml
69	http://www.flensted.eu.com/1944068.shtml
70	http://www.flensted.eu.com/1944068.shtml
71	© Frank Weber
72	https://commons.wikimedia.org/wiki/File:Mar-del-Plata-ship_CMB.jpg
73	https://www.worldwarphotos.info/wp-content/gallery/uk/raf/mosquito2/Mosquito_XVI_ML963_8K-K_571_Sqn_4.jpg
74a/b	Air 14/2484
75	© Frank Weber
76	No 1 group mining cartoon 1944 - Air 25-14 TC191874.jpg
77	Arkiv.dk: Hotel Royal in Nyborg. Wurmbach
78	© Frank Weber
79	© Frank Weber
80	https://itoldya420.getarchive.net/amp/media/efterkrigsminsvepning484c37
81	https://www.keymilitary.com/article/beaufighter-attack
82	http://crivensjingsandhelpmaboab.blogspot.dk/2010/04/153-sqn-4th-april-1945.html
83	© Frank Weber
84	http://www.snesejler.dk/holmnakskov.jpg
85	© Frank Weber
86	© Frank Weber
87	© Frank Weber
88	© Frank Weber
89	© Frank Weber
90	© Frank Weber
91	© Frank Weber
92	http://www.teunispats.nl/jack-edward-gibbs.htm
93	http://uamf.org.uk/viewtopic.php?t=1111
94	© Frank Weber
95	© Frank Weber

96 https://218squadron.wordpress.com/report-no-136-bomber-command-report/
97 https://218squadron.wordpress.com/sweet-pea-april-28th29th-1943-black-day-for-218-squadron
98 © Frank Weber
99 © Frank Weber
100 © Frank Weber
101 © Frank Weber
102 © Frank Weber
103 www.flickr.com/photos/dirk_bruin_vlieland/2134275668
104 http://mfs.dk/wp-content/uploads/2016/06/1960lysenetaendes igen, p.133
105 www.ehrenzeichen-orden.de/zweiter-weltkrieg/minensucher-kriegsabzeichen.html
106 © Frank Weber
107 'Flåden i Korsør', 1998, nr. 3, p.8
108 © Frank Weber
109 © Frank Weber
110 https://www.basti.dk/en-GB/inventories/4335
111 http://forsvaret.dk/2ESK/Nyt.//Minerydningsenhederbortspringerminer.asp
112 http://forsvaret.dk/2ESK/Nyt.//Minerydningsenhederbortspringerminer.asp
113 20-04-2010 Forsvaret dk
114 © Frank Weber
115 Air 14/701 Bomber Command June-November 1940: Gardens mined June-August 1940
116 Air 14/701 Bomber Command June-November 1940: Gardens mined June-August 1940
117 Air 14/701 Bomber Command June-November 1940: Gardens mined June-August 1940
118 Air 14/701 Bomber Command June-November 1940: Gardens mined June-August 1940
119 © Frank Weber
120 National Archives ADM 189/199-200 German minesweeing operations: Photographs 1944